A Casebook on GULLIVER
AMONG THE HOUYHNHNMS

A Casebook on Gulliver among the Houyhnhnms

Edited by MILTON P. FOSTER

EASTERN MICHIGAN UNIVERSITY

THOMAS Y. CROWELL COMPANY

New York   Established 1834

ACKNOWLEDGMENTS

The editor wishes to thank the authors, editors, and publishers who kindly gave him permission to reprint materials in this book. He also makes grateful acknowledgment to Catherine Foster and Ethel Ackerman, who assisted him in preparing the manuscript, and to William Van O'Connor and John T. Hawes for valuable advice and encouragement.

Contents

Appendices

Introduction

Anger and playfulness strive together as strange but effective allies in the war that Jonathan Swift fought against evil. Intending to vex the world rather than to divert it, Swift nevertheless succeeded in doing both. He does this most clearly in *Gulliver's Travels*. Here his vexatious anger incites him to strike savage blows at the corruption in society and the basic weaknesses in human nature. Yet playfulness also abounds in *Gulliver's Travels*. For over two centuries children and adults have been diverted by the comic adventures that Gulliver has with the tiny people, the giants, the bungling scientists, and the rational horses. By combining wit, fantasy, and corrosive satire Swift makes us laugh while he lashes us.

In Part IV of *Gulliver's Travels*, "A Voyage to the Country of the Houyhnhnms," Swift reaches his greatest satirical success. His theme is more universal than in the earlier books, his anger becomes more intense, and his comedy becomes more subtle. The theme is human nature, a subject that was an obsession with the great writers of the eighteenth century. Most of them accepted Alexander Pope's dictum that "The proper study of mankind is man." We of the twentieth century see evidence constantly in the major events of our day or in our personal problems that we too need to understand human nature. Gulliver's last voyage is an exploration into the world of the self. It is one of the most penetrating analyses of the subject written in any age. It is as alive, as disturbing, as relevant to the lives of all men today as it was in the eighteenth century. The tormented genius who created this masterpiece wove into it his furious and profound estimation of man's frailties and man's potentialities.

Because Swift confronts such difficult human problems in Part IV as man's attempt to be a rational animal, the temptation of pride, and the search for self-knowledge; and because he writes with irony and ambiguity, this voyage is a complex one. One modern critic refers to Part IV as a dark forest; another predicts that unanimous agreement will never be reached concerning Swift's intention here; and a third points out that the central problem of Swift criticism lies in understanding this section. A vigorous controversy, therefore, has taken shape over the years about the worth and meaning of "A Voyage to the Country of the Houyhnhnms."

Controversy about its worth began before the middle of the eighteenth century. Parts I and II, in which Gulliver visits the Lilliputians and Brobdingnagians, won general admiration, but Part III was considered to be inferior, and Part IV was denounced by many critics for its allegedly complete misanthropy. Samuel Johnson proclaimed that the story of the Houyhnhnms is the part of *Gulliver's Travels* that gives most disgust. Well-known critics in the nineteenth century, such as Sir Walter Scott, Thomas De Quincey, and William Makepeace Thackeray, reacted even more violently, attacking Part IV as obscene, debased, blasphemous, and filthy.

Twentieth-century critics have reversed this opinion and now place Gulliver's "A Voyage to the Country of the Houyhnhnms" near or at the top of Swift's creative achievements. In spite of their general agreement about the excellence of Part IV, modern critics have disagreed about the meaning of this voyage. Numerous articles and books written since 1916 have presented varying interpretations. Some of these writings, which might be classed as traditional interpretations, make the basic assumption that Swift intended the Yahoos to represent man as he is—a filthy beast—and the Houyhnhnms to represent man as he should be—an orderly and rational being. Another group of these writings presents the more recent interpretation that sees the Yahoos as symbolic of the bestiality in man, the Houyhnhnms as symbolic of the intellectuality of man, and Gulliver as symbolic of human nature, which is both bestial and capable of reason. Besides the traditional and newer interpretations there are writings that lean toward one or the other of these two views, but emphasize other aspects of the work. Some of these emphasize Swift's skill with irony and satire, the role of Gulliver in Part IV, Swift's attitude toward the deists, the degree of misanthropy in Part IV, Swift's mental health, the virtues and faults of the

Houyhnhnms, the Yahoos as Christian symbols of man's depravity, or Swift's development of the theme of self-knowledge.

This casebook includes a summary of the first three voyages of Gulliver, a complete reprinting of Gulliver's fourth voyage, and several works from the eighteenth, nineteenth, and twentieth centuries that attempt to evaluate or interpret it. In addition a bibliography for further pursuit of the subject will be found as well as suggestions for research topics. The summary of Parts I through III is included to refresh the student's memory concerning those parts of *Gulliver's Travels* that lead up to the fourth part; the student can then concentrate his efforts on Part IV and the research problems it presents.

This volume is designed for use in college composition and literature courses. In composition courses it can be the basis for controlled research projects of various lengths. The topics listed at the end of the book are for short research exercises to introduce the student to research, for medium-length papers based mainly on material found in this book, and for long papers that require not only the use of this book but also extensive library work. Since satire, irony, and argumentative writing are usually a part of college composition courses, another use of this book could be to study "A Voyage to the Country of the Houyhnhnms" as an illustration of satire and irony and to analyze some of the critical works as examples of argumentation. Both introductory and advanced literature courses often include *Gulliver's Travels*. In such courses this casebook could be used as a stimulus and guide for term papers or as supplementary reading.

A careful study of the controversy over Gulliver among the Houyhnhnms will prove rewarding. It offers the student an introduction to the techniques of literary scholarship and criticism. More importantly, by following this debate of the experts, the student can gain insights that will enable him to better understand the artistry of Jonathan Swift, a writer of great genius. He may become aware of unsuspected levels of meaning in this complex allegorical satire on human nature. With the aid of Swift and his interpreters, the student may even learn more about himself.

MILTON P. FOSTER

April, 1961

PART IV OF
GULLIVER'S TRAVELS
by Jonathan Swift

A Voyage to the Country
of the Houyhnhnms

CHAPTER I

*The Author sets out as Captain of a Ship. His Men conspire against him,
confine him a long Time to his Cabbin, set him on Shore in an unknown
Land. He travels up into the Country. The Yahoos, a strange Sort of
Animal, described. The Author meets two* Houyhnhnms.

I continued at home with my Wife and Children about five Months
in a very happy Condition, if I could have learned the Lesson of
knowing when I was well. I left my poor Wife big with Child, and
accepted an advantageous Offer made me to be Captain of the
Adventure, a stout Merchant-man of 350 Tuns: For I understood
Navigation well, and being grown weary of a Surgeon's Employment at Sea, which however I could exercise upon Occasion, I took
a skilful young Man of that Calling, one *Robert Purefoy*, into my
Ship. We set sail from *Portsmouth* upon the 7th Day of *September*,
1710; on the 14th we met with Captain *Pocock* of *Bristol*, at *Tenariff*,
who was going to the Bay of *Campeachy*, to cut Logwood. On
the 16th he was parted from us by a Storm: I heard since my Return, that his Ship foundered, and none escaped, but one Cabbin-
Boy. He was an honest Man, and a good Sailor, but a little too
positive in his own Opinions, which was the Cause of his Destruction, as it hath been of several others. For if he had followed my

The edition of Part IV of *Gulliver's Travels*, "A Voyage to the Country of the
Houyhnhnms," that follows is from Herbert Davis's *The Prose Works of Swift*
(1941), and has been reprinted in Jonathan Swift, *Gulliver's Travels and
Other Writings* (New York: Modern Library College Editions, 1958), pp.
179–243. It is used with the permission of Basil Blackwell, Publisher, Oxford.

3

Advice, he might at this Time have been safe at home with his Family as well as my self.

I had several Men died in my Ship of Calentures, so that I was forced to get Recruits out of *Barbadoes,* and the *Leeward Islands,* where I touched by the Direction of the Merchants, who employed me; which I had soon too much Cause to repent; for I [179] * found afterwards that most of them had been Buccaneers. I had fifty Hands on Board; and my Orders were, that I should trade with the *Indians* in the *South-Sea,* and make what Discoveries I could. These Rogues whom I had picked up, debauched my other Men, and they all formed a Conspiracy to seize the Ship and secure me; which they did one Morning, rushing into my Cabbin, and binding me Hand and Foot, threatening to throw me overboard, if I offered to stir. I told them, I was their Prisoner, and would submit. This they made me swear to do, and then unbound me, only fastening one of my Legs with a Chain near my Bed; and placed a Centry at my Door with his Piece charged, who was commanded to shoot me dead if I attempted my Liberty. They sent me down Victuals and Drink, and took the Government of the Ship to themselves. Their Design was to turn Pirates, and plunder the *Spaniards,* which they could not do, till they got more Men. But first they resolved to sell the Goods in the Ship, and then go to *Madagascar* for Recruits, several among them having died since my Confinement. They sailed many Weeks, and traded with the *Indians;* but I knew not what Course they took, being kept close Prisoner in my Cabbin, and expecting nothing less than to be murdered, as they often threatened me.

Upon the 9th Day of *May,* 1711, one *James Welch* came down to my Cabbin; and said he had Orders from the Captain to set me ashore. I expostulated with him, but in vain; neither would he so much as tell me who their new Captain was. They forced me into the Long-boat, letting me put on my best Suit of Cloaths, which were as good as new, and a small Bundle of Linnen, but no Arms except my Hanger; and they were so civil as not to search my Pockets, into which I conveyed what Money I had, with some other little Necessaries. They rowed about a League; and then set me down down on a Strand. I desired them to tell me what Country it was: They all swore, they knew no more than my self, but said, that the

---

* [Bracketed figures throughout this book indicate the end of the page on which the selection appeared in the cited source. If the page of the original ended with a hyphenated word, the page number here precedes the word.]

Captain (as they called him) was resolved, after they had sold the Lading, to get rid of me in the first Place where they discovered Land. They pushed off immediately, advising me to make haste, for fear of being overtaken by the Tide; and bade me farewell.

In this desolate Condition I advanced forward, and soon got upon firm Ground, where I sat down on a Bank to rest my self, and consider what I had best to do. When I was a little refreshed, I went up into the Country, resolving to deliver my self to the first Savages I should meet; and purchase my Life from them by some Bracelets, Glass Rings, and other Toys, which Sailors [180] usually provide themselves with in those Voyages, and whereof I had some about me: The Land was divided by long Rows of Trees, not regularly planted, but naturally growing; there was great Plenty of Grass, and several Fields of Oats. I walked very circumspectly for fear of being surprised, or suddenly shot with an Arrow from behind, or on either Side. I fell into a beaten Road, where I saw many Tracks of human Feet, and some of Cows, but most of Horses. At last I beheld several Animals in a Field, and one or two of the same Kind sitting in Trees. Their Shape was very singular, and deformed, which a little discomposed me, so that I lay down behind a Thicket to observe them better. Some of them coming forward near the Place where I lay, gave me an Opportunity of distinctly marking their Form. Their Heads and Breasts were covered with a thick Hair, some frizzled and others lank; they had Beards like Goats, and a Long Ridge of Hair down their Backs, and the fore Parts of their Legs and Feet; but the rest of their Bodies were bare, so that I might see their Skins, which were of a brown Buff Colour. They had no Tails, nor any Hair at all on their Buttocks, except about the *Anus;* which, I presume Nature had placed there to defend them as they sat on the Ground; for this Posture they used, as well as lying down, and often stood on their hind Feet. They climbed high Trees, as nimbly as a Squirrel, for they had strong extended Claws before and behind, terminating on sharp Points, hooked. They would often spring, and bound, and leap with prodigious Agility. The Females were not so large as the Males; they had long lank Hair on their Heads, and only a Sort of Down on the rest of their Bodies, except about the *Anus,* and *Pudenda.* Their Dugs hung between their fore Feet, and often reached almost to the Ground as they walked. The Hair of both Sexes was of several Colours, brown, red, black and yellow. Upon the whole, I never beheld in all my Travels so disagreeable an

Animal, or one against which I naturally conceived so strong an Antipathy. So that thinking I had seen enough, full of Contempt and Aversion, I got up and pursued the beaten Road, hoping it might direct me to the Cabbin of some *Indian*. I had not gone far when I met one of these Creatures full in my Way, and coming up directly to me. The ugly Monster, when he saw me, distorted several Ways every Feature of his Visage, and stared as at an Object he had never seen before; then approaching nearer, lifted up his fore Paw, whether out of Curiosity or Mischief, I could not tell: But I drew my Hanger, and gave him a good Blow with the flat Side of it; for I durst not strike him with the Edge, fearing [181] the Inhabitants might be provoked against me, if they should come to know, that I had killed or maimed any of their Cattle. When the Beast felt the Smart, he drew back, and roared so loud, that a Herd of at least forty came flocking about me from the next Field, howling and making odious Faces; but I ran to the Body of a Tree, and leaning my Back against it, kept them off, by waving my Hanger. Several of this cursed Brood getting hold of the Branches behind, leaped up into the Tree, from whence they began to discharge their Excrements on my Head: However, I escaped pretty well, by sticking close to the Stem of the Tree, but was almost stifled with the Filth, which fell about me on every Side.

In the Midst of this Distress, I observed them all to run away on a sudden as fast as they could; at which I ventured to leave the Tree, and pursue the Road, wondering what it was that could put them into this Fright. But looking on my Left-Hand, I saw a Horse walking softly in the Field; which my Persecutors having sooner discovered, was the Cause of their Flight. The Horse started a little when he came near me, but soon recovering himself, looked full in my Face with manifest Tokens of Wonder: He viewed my Hands and Feet, walking round me several times. I would have pursued my Journey, but he placed himself directly in the Way, yet looking with a very mild Aspect, never offering the least Violence. We stood gazing at each other for some time; at last I took the Boldness, to reach my Hand towards his Neck, with a Design to stroak it; using the common Style and Whistle of Jockies when they are going to handle a strange Horse. But, this Animal seeming to receive my Civilities with Disdain, shook his Head, and bent his Brows, softly raising up his Left Fore-Foot to remove my Hand. Then he neighed three or four times, but in so different a Cadence, that I almost began to think he was speaking to himself in some Language of his own.

While He and I were thus employed, another Horse came up; who applying himself to the first in a very formal Manner, they gently struck each others Right Hoof before, neighing several times by Turns, and varying the Sound, which seemed to be almost articulate. They went some Paces off, as if it were to confer together, walking Side by Side, backward and forward, like Persons deliberating upon some Affair of Weight; but often turning their Eyes towards me, as it were to watch that I might not escape. I was amazed to see such Actions and Behaviour in Brute Beasts; and concluded with myself, that if the Inhabitants [182] of this Country were endued with a proportionable Degree of Reason, they must needs be the wisest People upon Earth. This Thought gave me so much Comfort, that I resolved to go forward until I could discover some House or Village, or meet with any of the Natives; leaving the two Horses to discourse together as they pleased. But the first, who was a Dapple-Grey, observing me to steal off, neighed after me in so expressive a Tone, that I fancied myself to understand what he meant; whereupon I turned back, and came near him, to expect his farther Commands; but concealing my Fear as much as I could; for I began to be in some Pain, how this Adventure might terminate; and the Reader will easily believe I did not much like my present Situation.

The two Horses came up close to me, looking with great Earnestness upon my Face and Hands. The grey Steed rubbed my Hat all round with his Right Fore-hoof, and discomposed it so much, that I was forced to adjust it better, by taking it off, and settling it again; whereat both he and his Companion (who was a brown Bay) appeared to be much surprized; the latter felt the Lappet of my Coat, and finding it to hang loose about me, they both looked with new Signs of Wonder. He stroaked my Right Hand, seeming to admire the Softness, and Colour; but he squeezed it so hard between his Hoof and his Pastern, that I was forced to roar; after which they both touched me with all possible Tenderness. They were under great Perplexity about my Shoes and Stockings, which they felt very often, neighing to each other, and using various Gestures, not unlike those of a Philosopher, when he would attempt to solve some new and difficult Phænomenon.

Upon the whole, the Behaviour of these Animals was so orderly and rational, so acute and judicious, that I at last concluded, they must needs be Magicians, who had thus metamorphosed themselves upon some Design; and seeing a Stranger in the Way, were resolved to divert themselves with him; or perhaps were really amazed at the Sight of a Man so very different in Habit, Feature and Complexion from those who might probably live in so remote a Climate. Upon the Strength of this Reasoning, I ventured to address them in the following Manner: Gentlemen, if you be Conjurers, as I have good Cause to believe, you can understand any Language; therefore I make bold to let your Worships know, that I am a poor distressed *Englishman,* driven by his Misfortunes upon your Coast; and I entreat one of you, to let me ride upon his Back, as if he were a real Horse, to some House or Village, where I can be relieved. In return of which [183] Favour, I will make you a Present of this Knife and Bracelet, (taking them out of my Pocket.) The two Creatures stood silent while I spoke, seeming to listen with great Attention; and when I had ended, they neighed frequently towards each other, as if they were engaged in serious Conversation. I plainly observed, that their Language expressed the Passions very well, and the Words might with little Pains be resolved into an Alphabet more easily than the *Chinese.*

I could frequently distinguish the Word *Yahoo,* which was repeated by each of them several times; and although it were impossible for me to conjecture what it meant, yet while the two Horses were busy in Conversation, I endeavoured to practice this Word upon my Tongue; and as soon as they were silent, I boldly pronounced *Yahoo* in a loud Voice, imitating, at the same time, as near as I could, the Neighing of a Horse; at which they were both visibly surprized, and the Grey repeated the same Word twice, as if he meant to teach me the right Accent, wherein I spoke after him as well as I could, and found myself perceivably to improve every time, although very far from any Degree of Perfection. Then the Bay tried me with a second Word, much harder to be pronounced; but reducing it to the *English Orthography,* may be spelt thus, *Houyhnhnm.* I did not succeed in this so well as the former, but after two or three farther Trials, I had better Fortune; and they both appeared amazed at my Capacity.

After some farther Discourse, which I then conjectured might relate to me, the two Friends took their Leaves, with the same Compliment of striking each other's Hoof; and the Grey made me Signs that I should walk before him; wherein I thought it prudent to comply, till I could find a better Director. When I offered to slacken my Pace, he would cry *Hhuun, Hhuun;* I guessed his Meaning, and gave him to understand, as well as I could, that I was weary, and not able to walk faster; upon which, he would stand a while to let me rest. [184]

CHAPTER II

The Author conducted by a Houyhnhnm *to his House. The House described. The Author's Reception. The Food of the* Houyhnhnms. *The Author in Distress for want of Meat, is at last relieved. His Manner of feeding in that Country.*

Having travelled about three Miles, we came to a long Kind of Building, made of Timber, stuck in the Ground, and wattled a-cross; the Roof was low, and covered with Straw. I now began to be a little comforted; and took out some Toys, which Travellers usually carry for Presents to the Savage *Indians* of *America* and other Parts, in hopes the People of the House would be thereby encouraged to receive me kindly. The Horse made me a Sign to go in first; it was a large Room with a smooth Clay Floor, and a Rack and Manger extending the whole Length on one Side. There were three Nags, and two Mares, not eating, but some of them sitting down upon their Hams, which I very much wondered at; but wondered more to see the rest employed in domestick Business: The last seemed but ordinary Cattle; however this confirmed my first Opinion, that a People who could so far civilize brute Animals, must needs excel in Wisdom all the Nations of the World. The Grey came in just after, and thereby prevented any ill Treatment, which the others might have given me. He neighed to them several times in a Style of Authority, and received Answers.

Beyond this Room there were three others, reaching the Length of the House, to which you passed through three Doors, opposite to each other, in the Manner of a Vista: We went through the second Room towards the third; here the Grey walked in first, beckoning me to attend: I waited in the second Room, and got ready my Presents, for the Master and Mistress of the House: They were two Knives, three Bracelets of false Pearl, a small Looking Glass and a Bead Necklace. The Horse neighed three or four Times, and I waited to hear some Answers in a human Voice, but I heard no other Returns than in the same Dialect, only one or two a little shriller than his. I began to think that this House must belong to some Person of great Note among them, because there appeared so much ceremony before I could gain Admittance. But, that a Man of Quality should be [185] served all by Horses, was beyond my Comprehension. I feared my Brain was disturbed by my Sufferings and Misfortunes: I roused my self, and looked about me in the Room where I was left alone; this was furnished as the first, only after a more elegant Manner. I rubbed mine Eyes often, but the same Objects still occurred. I pinched my Arms and Sides, to awake my self, hoping I might be in a Dream. I then absolutely concluded, that all these Appearances could be nothing else but Necromancy and Magick. But I had no Time to pursue these Reflections; for the Grey Horse came to the Door, and made me a Sign to follow him into the third Room; where I saw a very comely Mare, together with a Colt and Fole, sitting on their Haunches, upon Mats of Straw, not unartfully made, and perfectly neat and clean.

The Mare soon after my Entrance, rose from her Mat, and coming up close, after having nicely observed my Hands and Face, gave me a most contemptuous Look; then turning to the Horse, I heard the Word *Yahoo* often repeated betwixt them; the meaning of which Word I could not then comprehend, although it were the first I had learned to pronounce; but I was soon better informed, to my everlasting Mortification: For the Horse beckoning to me with his Head, and repeating the Word *Hhuun, Hhuun,* as he did upon the Road, which I understood was to attend him, led me out into a kind of Court, where was another Building at some Distance from the House. Here we entered, and I saw three of those detestable Creatures, which I first met after my landing, feeding upon Roots, and the Flesh of some Animals, which I afterwards found to be that of Asses and Dogs, and now and then a Cow dead by Accident or Disease. They were all tied by the Neck with strong Wyths, fastened to a Beam; they held their Food between the Claws of their fore Feet, and tore it with their Teeth.

The Master Horse ordered a Sorrel Nag, one of his Servants, to untie the largest of these Animals, and take him into a Yard. The Beast and I were brought close together; and our Countenances diligently compared, both by Master and Servant, who thereupon repeated several Times the Word *Yahoo.* My Horror and Astonishment are not to be described, when I observed, in this abominable

Animal, a perfect human Figure; the Face of it indeed was flat and broad, the Nose depressed, the Lips large, and the Mouth wide: But these Differences are common to all savage Nations, where the Lineaments of the Countenance are distorted by the Natives suffering their Infants to lie grovelling on the Earth, or by carrying them on their Backs, nuzzling with [186] their Face against the Mother's Shoulders. The Fore-feet of the *Yahoo* differed from my Hands in nothing else, but the Length of the Nails, the Coarseness and Brownness of the Palms, and the Hairiness on the Backs. There was the same Resemblance between our Feet, with the same Differences, which I knew very well, although the Horses did not, because of my Shoes and Stockings; the same in every Part of our Bodies, except as to Hairiness and Colour, which I have already described.

The great Difficulty that seemed to stick with the two Horses, was, to see the rest of my Body so very different from that of a *Yahoo*, for which I was obliged to my Cloaths, whereof they had no Conception: The Sorrel Nag offered me a Root, which he held (after their Manner, as we shall describe in its proper Place) between his Hoof and Pastern; I took it in my Hand, and having smelt it, returned it to him again as civilly as I could. He brought out of the *Yahoo's* Kennel a Piece of Ass's Flesh, but it smelt so offensively that I turned from it with loathing; he then threw it to the *Yahoo*, by whom it was greedily devoured. He afterwards shewed me a Whisp of Hay, and a Fetlock full of Oats; but I shook my Head, to signify, that neither of these were Food for me. And indeed, I now apprehended, that I must absolutely starve, if I did not get to some of my own Species: For as to those filthy *Yahoos*, although there were few greater Lovers of Mankind, at that time, than myself; yet I confess I never saw any sensitive Being so detestable on all Accounts; and the more I came near them, the more hateful they grew, while I stayed in that Country. This the Master Horse observed by my Behaviour, and therefore sent the *Yahoo* back to his Kennel. He then put his Forehoof to his Mouth, at which I was much surprized, although he did it with Ease, and with a Motion that appear'd perfectly natural; and made other Signs to know what I would eat; but I could not return him such an Answer as he was able to apprehend; and if he had understood me, I did not see how it was possible to contrive any way for finding myself Nourishment. While we were thus engaged, I observed a Cow passing by; whereupon I pointed to her, and expressed a Desire to let me go and milk her. This had

its Effect; for he led me back into the House, and ordered a Mareservant to open a Room, where a good Store of Milk lay in Earthen
and Wooden Vessels, after a very orderly and cleanly Manner. She
gave me a large Bowl full, of which I drank very heartily, and found
myself well refreshed.

About Noon I saw coming towards the House a Kind of Vehicle,
drawn like a Sledge by four *Yahoos*. There was in it an [187] old
Steed, who seemed to be of Quality; he alighted with his Hind-feet
forward, having by Accident got a Hurt in his Left Fore-foot. He
came to dine with our Horse, who received him with great Civility.
They dined in the best Room, and had Oats boiled in Milk for the
second Course, which the old Horse eat warm, but the rest cold.
Their Mangers were placed circular in the Middle of the Room, and
divided into several Partitions, round which they sat on their
Haunches upon Bosses of Straw. In the Middle was a large Rack
with Angles answering to every Partition of the Manger. So that
each Horse and Mare eat their own Hay, and their own Mash of
Oats and Milk, with much Decency and Regularity. The Behaviour
of the young Colt and Fole appeared very modest; and that of the
Master and Mistress extremely chearful and complaisant to their
Guest. The Grey ordered me to stand by him; and much Discourse
passed between him and his Friend concerning me, as I found by
the Stranger's often looking on me, and the frequent Repetition of
the Word *Yahoo*.

I happened to wear my Gloves; which the Master Grey observing,
seemed perplexed; discovering Signs of Wonder what I had done to
my Fore-feet; he put his Hoof three or four times to them, as if he
would signify, that I should reduce them to their former Shape,
which I presently did, pulling off both my Gloves, and putting them
into my Pocket. This occasioned farther Talk, and I saw the Company was pleased with my Behaviour, whereof I soon found the
good Effects. I was ordered to speak the few Words I understood;
and while they were at Dinner, the Master taught me the Names
for Oats, Milk, Fire, Water, and some others; which I could readily
pronounce after him; having from my Youth a great Facility in learning Languages.

When Dinner was done, the Master Horse took me aside, and by
Signs and Words made me understand the Concern he was in, that
I had nothing to eat. Oats in their Tongue are called *Hlunnh*. This
Word I pronounced two or three times; for although I had refused

them at first, yet upon second Thoughts, I considered that I could contrive to make of them a Kind of Bread, which might be sufficient with Milk to keep me alive, till I could make my Escape to some other Country, and to Creatures of my own Species. The Horse immediately ordered a white Mareservant of his Family to bring me a good Quantity of Oats in a Sort of wooden Tray. These I heated before the Fire as well as I could, and rubbed them till the Husks came off, which I made a shift to winnow from the Grain; I ground and beat them [188] between two Stones, then took Water, and made them into a Paste or Cake, which I toasted at the Fire, and eat warm with Milk. It was at first a very insipid Diet, although common enough in many Parts of *Europe,* but grew tolerable by Time; and having been often reduced to hard Fare in my Life, this was not the first Experiment I had made how easily Nature is satisfied. And I cannot but observe, that I never had one Hour's Sickness, while I staid in this Island. It is true, I sometimes made a shift to catch a Rabbet, or Bird, by Springes made of *Yahoos* Hairs; and I often gathered wholesome Herbs, which I boiled, or eat as Salades with my Bread; and now and then, for a Rarity, I made a little Butter, and drank the Whey. I was at first at a great Loss for Salt; but Custom soon reconciled the Want of it; and I am confident that the frequent Use of Salt among us is an Effect of Luxury, and was first introduced only as a Provocative to Drink; except where it is necessary for preserving of Flesh in long Voyages, or in Places remote from great Markets. For we observe no Animal to be fond of it but Man: And as to myself, when I left this Country, it was a great while before I could endure the Taste of it in any thing that I eat.

This is enough to say upon the Subject of my Dyet, wherewith other Travellers fill their Books, as if the Readers were personally concerned, whether we fare well or ill. However, it was necessary to mention this Matter, lest the World should think it impossible that I could find Sustenance for three Years in such a Country, and among such Inhabitants.

When it grew towards Evening, the Master Horse ordered a Place for me to lodge in; it was but Six Yards from the House, and separated from the Stable of the *Yahoos.* Here I got some Straw, and covering myself with my own Cloaths, slept very sound. But I was in a short time better accommodated, as the Reader shall know hereafter, when I come to treat more particularly about my Way of living. [189]

CHAPTER III

The Author studious to learn the Language, the Houyhnhnm *his Master assists in teaching him. The Language described. Several* Houyhnhnms *of Quality come out of Curiosity to see the Author. He gives his Master a short Account of his Voyage.*

My principal Endeavour was to learn the Language, which my Master (for so I shall henceforth call him) and his Children, and every Servant of his House were desirous to teach me. For they looked upon it as a Prodigy, that a brute Animal should discover such Marks of a rational Creature. I pointed to every thing, and enquired the Name of it, which I wrote down in my *Journal Book* when I was alone, and corrected my bad Accent, by desiring those of the Family to pronounce it often. In this Employment, a Sorrel Nag, one of the under Servants, was very ready to assist me.

In speaking, they pronounce through the Nose and Throat, and their Language approaches nearest to the *High Dutch or German,* of any I know in *Europe;* but is much more graceful and significant. The Emperor *Charles* V. made almost the same Observation when he said, That if he were to speak to his Horse, it should be in *High Dutch.*

The Curiosity and Impatience of my Master were so great, that he spent many Hours of his Leisure to instruct me. He was convinced (as he afterwards told me) that I must be a *Yahoo,* but my Teachableness, Civility and Cleanliness astonished him; which were Qualities altogether so opposite to those Animals. He was most perplexed about my Cloaths, reasoning sometimes with himself, whether they were a Part of my Body; for I never pulled them off till the Family were asleep, and got them on before they waked in the Morning. My Master was eager to learn from whence I came; how I acquired those Appearances of Reason, which I discovered in all my Actions; and to know my Story from my own Mouth, which he hoped he should soon do by the great Proficiency I made in learning and pronouncing their Words and Sentences. To help my Memory, I formed all I learned into the *English* Alphabet, and writ the Words down with the Translations. This last, after some time, I ventured to do in my Master's Presence. It cost me much Trouble to explain to him what I was [190] doing; for the Inhabitants have not the least Idea of Books or Literature.

In about ten Weeks time I was able to understand most of his Questions; and in three Months could give him some tolerable Answers. He was extremely curious to know from what Part of the Country I came, and how I was taught to imitate a rational Creature; because the *Yahoos*, (whom he saw I exactly resembled in my Head, Hands and Face, that were only visible,) with some Appearance of Cunning, and the strongest Disposition to Mischief, were observed to be the most unteachable of all Brutes. I answered; that I came over the Sea, from a far Place, with many others of my own Kind, in a great hollow Vessel made of the Bodies of Trees: That, my Companions forced me to land on this Coast, and then left me to shift for myself. It was with some Difficulty, and by the Help of many Signs, that I brought him to understand me. He replied, That I must needs be mistaken, or that I *said the thing which was not.* (For they have no Word in their Language to express Lying or Falshood.) He knew it was impossible that there could be a Country beyond the Sea, or that a Parcel of Brutes could move a wooden Vessel whither they pleased upon Water. He was sure no *Houyhnhnm* alive could make such a Vessel, or would trust *Yahoos* to manage it.

The Word *Houyhnhnm*, in their Tongue, signifies a *Horse;* and in its Etymology, *the Perfection of Nature.* I told my Master, that I was at a Loss for Expression, but would improve as fast as I could; and hoped in a short time I should be able to tell him Wonders: He was pleased to direct his own Mare, his Colt and Fole, and the Servants of the Family to take all Opportunities of instructing me; and every Day for two or three Hours, he was at the same Pains himself: Several Horses and Mares of Quality in the neighbourhood came often to our House, upon the Report spread of a wonderful *Yahoo,* that could speak like a *Houyhnhnm,* and seemed in his Words and Actions to discover some Glimmerings of Reason. These delighted to converse with me; they put many Questions, and received such Answers, as I was able to return. By all which Advantages, I made so great a Progress, that in five Months from my Arrival, I understood whatever was spoke, and could express myself tolerably well.

The *Houyhnhnms* who came to visit my Master, out of a Design of seeing and talking with me, could hardly believe me to be a right *Yahoo,* because my Body had a different Covering from others of my Kind. They were astonished to observe me without the usual Hair or Skin, except on my Head, Face and Hands: [191] But I discovered that Secret to my Master, upon an Accident, which happened about a Fortnight before.

I have already told the Reader, that every Night when the Family were gone to Bed, it was my Custom to strip and cover myself with my Cloaths: It happened one Morning early, that my Master sent for me, by the Sorrel Nag, who was his Valet; when he came, I was fast asleep, my Cloaths fallen off on one Side, and my Shirt above my Waste. I awaked at the Noise he made, and observed him to deliver his Message in some Disorder; after which he went to my Master, and in a great Fright gave him a very confused Account of what he had seen: This I presently discovered; for going as soon as I was dressed, to pay my Attendance upon his Honour, he asked me the Meaning of what his Servant had reported; that I was not the same Thing when I slept as I appeared to be at other times; that his Valet assured him, some Part of me was white, some yellow, at least not so white, and some brown.

I had hitherto concealed the Secret of my Dress, in order to distinguish myself as much as possible, from that cursed Race of *Yahoos;* but now I found it in vain to do so any longer. Besides, I considered that my Cloaths and Shoes would soon wear out, which already were in a declining Condition, and must be supplied by some Contrivance from the Hides of *Yahoos,* or other Brutes; whereby the whole Secret would be known. I therefore told my Master, that in the Country from whence I came, those of my Kind always covered their Bodies with the Hairs of certain Animals prepared by Art, as well for Decency, as to avoid Inclemencies of Air both hot and cold; of which, as to my own Person I would give him immediate Conviction, if he pleased to command me; only desiring his Excuse, if I did not expose those Parts that Nature taught us to conceal. He said, my Discourse was all very strange, but especially the last Part; for he could not understand why Nature should teach us to conceal what Nature had given. That neither himself nor Family were ashamed of any Parts of their Bodies; but however I might do as I pleased. Whereupon, I first unbuttoned my Coat, and pulled it off. I did the same with my Wastecoat; I drew off my Shoes, Stockings and Breeches. I let my Shirt down to my Waste, and drew up the Bottom, fastening it like a Girdle about my Middle to hide my Nakedness.

My Master observed the whole Performance with great Signs of Curiosity and Admiration. He took up all my Cloaths in his Pastern, one Piece after another, and examined them diligently; [192] he then stroaked my Body very gently, and looked round me several Times; after which he said, it was plain I must be a perfect *Yahoo;* but that I differed very much from the rest of my Species, in the Whiteness, and Smoothness of my Skin, my want of Hair in several Parts of my Body, the Shape and Shortness of my Claws behind and before, and my Affectation of walking continually on my two hinder Feet. He desired to see no more; and gave me leave to put on my Cloaths again, for I was shuddering with Cold.

I expressed my Uneasiness at his giving me so often the Appellation of *Yahoo,* an odious Animal, for which I had so utter an Hatred and Contempt. I begged he would forbear applying that Word to me, and take the same Order in his Family, and among his Friends whom he suffered to see me. I requested likewise, that the Secret of my having a false Covering to my Body might be known to none but himself, at least as long as my present Cloathing should last: For as to what the Sorrel Nag his Valet had observed, his Honour might command him to conceal it.

All this my Master very graciously consented to; and thus the Secret was kept till my Cloaths began to wear out, which I was forced to supply by several Contrivances, that shall hereafter be mentioned. In the mean Time, he desired I would go on with my utmost Diligence to learn their Language, because he was more astonished at my Capacity for Speech and Reason, than at the Figure of my Body, whether it were covered or no; adding, that he waited with some Impatience to hear the Wonders which I promised to tell him.

From thenceforward he doubled the Pains he had been at to instruct me; he brought me into all Company, and made them treat me with Civility, because, as he told them privately, this would put me into good Humour, and make me more diverting.

Every Day when I waited on him, beside the Trouble he was at in teaching, he would ask me several Questions concerning my self, which I answered as well as I could; and by those Means he had already received some general Ideas, although very imperfect. It would be tedious to relate the several Steps, by which I advanced to a more regular Conversation: But the first Account I gave of my self in any Order and Length, was to this Purpose:

That, I came from a very far Country, as I already had attempted to tell him, with about fifty more of my own Species; that we travelled upon the Seas, in a great hollow Vessel made [193] of Wood, and larger than his Honour's House. I described the Ship to him in the best Terms I could; and explained by the Help of my Handkerchief displayed, how it was driven forward by the Wind. That, upon a Quarrel among us, I was set on Shoar on this Coast, where I walked forward without knowing whither, till he delivered me from the Persecution of those execrable *Yahoos*. He asked me, Who made the Ship, and how it was possible that the *Houyhnhnms* of my Country would leave it to the Management of Brutes? My Answer was, that I durst proceed no farther in my Relation, unless he would give me his Word and Honour that he would not be offended; and then I would tell him the Wonders I had so often promised. He agreed; and I went on by assuring him, that the Ship was made by Creatures like myself, who in all the Countries I had travelled, as well as in my own, were the only governing, rational Animals; and that upon my Arrival hither, I was as much astonished to see the *Houyhnhnms* act like rational Beings, as he or his Friends could be in finding some Marks of Reason in a Creature he was pleased to call a *Yahoo;* to which I owned my Resemblance in every Part, but could not account for their degenerate and brutal Nature. I said farther, That if good Fortune ever restored me to my native Country, to relate my Travels hither, as I resolved to do; every Body would believe that I *said the Thing which was not;* that I invented the Story out of my own Head: And with all possible Respect to Himself, his Family, and Friends, and under his Promise of not being offended, our Countrymen would hardly think it probable, that a *Houyhnhnm* should be the presiding Creature of a Nation, and a *Yahoo* the Brute.

CHAPTER IV

The Houyhnhnms *Notion of Truth and Falshood. The Author's Discourse disapproved by his Master. The Author gives a more particular Account of himself, and the Accidents of his Voyage.*

My Master heard me with great Appearances of Uneasiness in his Countenance; because *Doubting* or *not believing,* are so little known in this Country, that the Inhabitants cannot tell how to behave themselves under such Circumstances. And I remember in frequent Discourses with my [194] Master concerning the Nature of Manhood, in other Parts of the World; having Occasion to talk of *Lying,* and *false Representation,* it was with much Difficulty that he comprehended what I meant; although he had otherwise a most acute Judgment. For he argued thus; That the Use of Speech was to make us understand one another, and to receive Information of Facts; now if any one *said the Thing which was not*, these Ends were defeated; because I cannot properly be said to understand him; and I am so far from receiving Information, that he leaves me worse than in Ignorance; for I am led to believe a Thing *Black* when it is *White*, and *Short* when it is *Long*. And these were all the Notions he had concerning that Faculty of *Lying*, so perfectly well understood, and so universally practised among human Creatures.

To return from this Digression; when I asserted that the *Yahoos* were the only governing Animals in my Country, which my Master said was altogether past his Conception, he desired to know, whether we had *Houyhnhnms* among us, and what was their Employment: I told him, we had great Numbers; that in Summer they grazed in the Fields, and in Winter were kept in Houses, with Hay and Oats, where *Yahoo*-Servants were employed to rub their Skins smooth, comb their Manes, pick their Feet, serve them with Food, and make their Beds. I understand you well, said my Master; it is now very plain from all you have spoken, that whatever Share of Reason the *Yahoos* pretend to, the *Houyhnhnms* are your Masters; I heartily wish our *Yahoos* would be so tractable. I begged his Honour would please to excuse me from proceeding any farther, because I was very certain that the Account he expected from me would be highly displeasing. But he insisted in commanding me to let him know the best and the worst: I told him he should be obeyed. I owned, that the *Houyhnhnms* among us, whom we called *Horses*, were the most generous and comely Animal we had; that they excelled in Strength and Swiftness; and when they belonged to Persons of Quality, employed in Travelling, Racing, and drawing Chariots, they were treated with much Kindness and Care, till they fell into Diseases, or became foundered in the Feet; but then they were sold, and used to all kind of Drudgery till they died; after which their Skins were stripped and sold for what they were worth, and their Bodies left to be devoured by Dogs and Birds of Prey. But the common Race of Horses had not so good Fortune, being kept by Farmers and Carriers, and other mean People, who put them to greater Labour, and feed them worse. I described as well as I could, our Way of Riding; the Shape and [195] Use of a Bridle, a Saddle, a Spur, and a Whip; of Harness and Wheels. I added, that we fastened Plates of a cer-

tain hard Substance called *Iron* at the Bottom of their Feet, to preserve their Hoofs from being broken by the Stony Ways on which
we often travelled.

My Master, after some Expressions of great Indignation, wondered
how we dared to venture upon a *Houyhnhnm's* Back; for he was
sure, that the meanest Servant in his House would be able to shake
off the strongest *Yahoo;* or by lying down, and rouling upon his
Back, squeeze the Brute to Death. I answered, That our Horses were
trained up from three or four Years old to the several Uses we intended them for; That if any of them proved intolerably vicious, they
were employed for Carriages; that they were severely beaten while
they were young for any mischievous Tricks: That the Males, designed for the common Use of Riding or Draught, were generally
castrated about two Years after their Birth, to take down their Spirits,
and make them more tame and gentle: That they were indeed sensible of Rewards and Punishments; but his Honour would please to
consider, that they had not the least Tincture of Reason any more
than the *Yahoos* in this Country.

It put me to the Pains of many Circumlocutions to give my Master
a right Idea of what I spoke; for their Language doth not abound
in Variety of Words, because their Wants and Passions are fewer
than among us. But it is impossible to express his noble Resentment
at our savage Treatment of the *Houyhnhnm* Race; particularly after
I had explained the Manner and Use of *Castrating* Horses among us,
to hinder them from propagating their Kind, and to render them
more servile. He said, if it were possible there could be any Country
where *Yahoos* alone were endued with Reason, they certainly must
be the governing Animal, because Reason will in Time always prevail
against Brutal Strength. But, considering the Frame of our Bodies,
and especially of mine, he thought no Creature of equal Bulk was
so ill-contrived, for employing that Reason in the common Offices of
Life; whereupon he desired to know whether those among whom I
lived, resembled me or the *Yahoos* of his Country. I assured him, that
I was as well shaped as most of my Age; but the younger and the
Females were much more soft and tender, and the Skins of the latter
generally as white as Milk. He said, I differed indeed from other
Yahoos, being much more cleanly, and not altogether so deformed;
but in point of real Advantage, he thought I differed for the worse.
That my Nails were of no [196] Use either to my fore or hinder
Feet: As to my fore Feet, he could not properly call them by that

Name, for he never observed me to walk upon them; that they were too soft to bear the Ground; that I generally went with them uncovered, neither was the Covering I sometimes wore on them, of the same Shape, or so strong as that on my Feet behind. That I could not walk with any Security; for if either of my hinder Feet slipped, I must inevitably fall. He then began to find fault with other Parts of my Body; the Flatness of my Face, the Prominence of my Nose, mine Eyes placed directly in Front, so that I could not look on either Side without turning my Head: That I was not able to feed my self, without lifting one of my fore Feet to my Mouth: And therefore Nature had placed those Joints to answer that Necessity. He knew not what could be the Use of those several Clefts and Divisions in my Feet behind; that these were too soft to bear the Hardness and Sharpness of Stones without a Covering made from the Skin of some other Brute; that my whole Body wanted a Fence against Heat and Cold, which I was forced to put on and off every Day with Tediousness and Trouble. And lastly, that he observed every Animal in this Country naturally to abhor the *Yahoos,* whom the Weaker avoided, and the Stronger drove from them. So that supposing us to have the Gift of Reason, he could not see how it were possible to cure that natural Antipathy which every Creature discovered against us; nor consequently, how we could tame and render them serviceable. However, he would (as he said) debate the Matter no farther, because he was more desirous to know my own Story, the Country, where I was born, and the several Actions and Events of my Life before I came hither.

I assured him, how extreamly desirous I was that he should be satisfied in every Point; but I doubted much, whether it would be possible for me to explain my self on several Subjects whereof his Honour could have no Conception, because I saw nothing in his Country to which I could resemble them. That however, I would do my best, and strive to express my self by Similitudes, humbly desiring his Assistance when I wanted proper Words; which he was pleased to promise me.

I said, my Birth was of honest Parents, in an Island called *England,* which was remote from this Country, as many Days Journey as the strongest of his Honour's Servants could travel in the Annual Course of the Sun. That I was bred a Surgeon, whose Trade is to cure Wounds and Hurts in the Body, got by Accident or Violence. That my Country was governed by a [197] Female Man, whom we called

Queen. That I left it to get Riches, whereby I might maintain my self and Family when I should return. That in my last Voyage, I was Commander of the Ship and had about fifty *Yahoos* under me, many of which died at Sea, and I was forced to supply them by others picked out from several Nations. That our Ship was twice in Danger of being sunk; the first Time by a great Storm, and the second, by striking against a Rock. Here my Master interposed, by asking me, How I could persuade Strangers out of different Countries to venture with me, after the Losses I had sustained, and the Hazards I had run. I said, they were Fellows of desperate Fortunes, forced to fly from the Places of their Birth, on Account of their Poverty or their Crimes. Some were undone by Law-suits; others spent all they had in Drinking, Whoring and Gaming; others fled for Treason; many for Murder, Theft, Poysoning, Robbery, Perjury, Forgery, Coining false Money; for committing Rapes or Sodomy; for flying from their Colours, or deserting to the Enemy; and most of them had broken Prison. None of these durst return to their native Countries for fear of being hanged, or of starving in a Jail; and therefore were under a Necessity of seeking a Livelihood in other Places.

During this Discourse, my Master was pleased often to interrupt me. I had made Use of many Circumlocutions in describing to him the Nature of the several Crimes, for which most of our Crew had been forced to fly their Country. This Labour took up several Days Conversation before he was able to comprehend me. He was wholly at a Loss to know what could be the Use or Necessity of practising those Vices. To clear up which I endeavoured to give him some Ideas of the Desire of Power and Riches; of the terrible Effects of Lust, Intemperance, Malice, and Envy. All this I was forced to define and describe by putting of Cases, and making Suppositions. After which, like one whose Imagination was struck with something never seen or heard of before, he would lift up his Eyes with Amazement and Indignation. Power, Government, War, Law, Punishment, and a Thousand other Things had no Terms, wherein that Language could express them; which made the Difficulty almost insuperable to give my Master any Conception of what I meant: But being of an excellent Understanding, much improved by Contemplation and Converse, he at last arrived at a competent Knowledge of what human Nature in our Parts of the World is capable to perform; and desired I would give him some particular Account of that Land, which we call *Europe,* especially, of my own Country. [198]

CHAPTER V

The Author at his Master's Commands informs him of the State of England. *The Causes of War among the Princes of* Europe. *The Author begins to explain the* English Constitution.

The Reader may please to observe, that the following Extract of many Conversations I had with my Master, contains a Summary of the most material Points, which were discoursed at several times for above two Years; his Honour often desiring fuller Satisfaction as I farther improved in the *Houyhnhnm* Tongue. I laid before him, as well as I could, the whole State of *Europe;* I discoursed of Trade and Manufactures, of Arts and Sciences; and the Answers I gave to all the Questions he made, as they arose upon several Subjects, were a Fund of Conversation not to be exhausted. But I shall here only set down the Substance of what passed between us concerning my own Country, reducing it into Order as well as I can, without any Regard to Time or other Circumstances, while I strictly adhere to Truth. My only Concern is, that I shall hardly be able to do Justice to my Master's Arguments and Expressions, which must needs suffer by my Want of Capacity, as well as by a Translation into our barbarous *English.*

In Obedience therefore to his Honour's Commands, I related to him the *Revolution* under the Prince of *Orange;* the long War with *France* entered into by the said Prince, and renewed by his Successor the present Queen; wherein the greatest Powers of *Christendom* were engaged, and which still continued: I computed at his Request, that about a Million of *Yahoos* might have been killed in the whole Progress of it; and perhaps a Hundred or more Cities taken, and five times as many Ships burnt or sunk.

He asked me what were the usual Causes or Motives that made one Country go to War with another. I answered, they were innumerable; but I should only mention a few of the chief. Sometimes the Ambition of Princes, who never think they have Land or People enough to govern: Sometimes the Corruption of Ministers, who engage their Master in a War in order to stifle or divert the Clamour of the Subjects against their evil Administration. Difference in Opinions hath cost many Millions of Lives: For Instance, whether *Flesh* be *Bread,* or *Bread* be *Flesh:* [199] Whether the Juice of a certain *Berry* be *Blood* or *Wine:* Whether *Whistling* be a Vice or a Virtue:

Whether it be better to *kiss a Post,* or throw it into the Fire: What is the best Colour for a *Coat,* whether *Black, White, Red,* or *Grey;* and whether it should be *long* or *short, narrow* or *wide, dirty* or *clean;* with many more. Neither are any Wars so furious and bloody, or of so long Continuance, as those occasioned by Difference in Opinion, especially if it be in things indifferent.

Sometimes the Quarrel between two Princes is to decide which of them shall dispossess a Third of his Dominions, where neither of them pretend to any Right. Sometimes one Prince quarrelleth with another, for fear the other should quarrel with him. Sometimes a War is entered upon, because the Enemy is too *strong,* and sometimes because he is too *weak.* Sometimes our Neighbours *want* the *Things* which we *have,* or *have* the Things which we want; and we both fight, till they take ours or give us theirs. It is a very justifiable Cause of War to invade a Country after the People have been wasted by Famine, destroyed by Pestilence, or embroiled by Factions amongst themselves. It is justifiable to enter into a War against our nearest Ally, when one of his Towns lies convenient for us, or a Territory of Land, that would render our Dominions round and compact. If a Prince send Forces into a Nation, where the People are poor and ignorant, he may lawfully put half of them to Death, and make Slaves of the rest, in order to civilize and reduce them from their barbarous Way of Living. It is a very kingly, honourable, and frequent Practice, when one Prince desires the Assistance of another to secure him against an Invasion, that the Assistant, when he hath driven out the Invader, should seize on the Dominions himself, and kill, imprison or banish the Prince he came to relieve. Allyance by Blood or Marriage, is a sufficient Cause of War between Princes; and the nearer the Kindred is, the greater is their Disposition to quarrel: *Poor* Nations are *hungry,* and *rich* Nations are *proud;* and Pride and Hunger will ever be at Variance. For these Reasons, the Trade of a *Soldier* is held the most honourable of all others: Because a *Soldier* is a *Yahoo* hired to kill in cold Blood as many of his own Species, who have never offended him, as possibly he can.

There is likewise a Kind of beggarly Princes in *Europe,* not able to make War by themselves, who hire out their Troops to richer Nations for so much a Day to each Man; of which they keep three Fourths to themselves, and it is the best Part of their Maintenance; such are those in many *Northern* Parts of *Europe.* [200]

What you have told me, (said my Master) upon the Subject of War, doth indeed discover most admirably the Effects of that Reason you pretend to: However, it is happy that the *Shame* is greater than the *Danger;* and that Nature hath left you utterly uncapable of doing much Mischief: For your Mouths lying flat with your Faces, you can hardly bite each other to any Purpose, unless by Consent. Then, as to the Claws upon your Feet before and behind, they are so short and tender, that one of our *Yahoos* would drive a Dozen of yours before him. And therefore in recounting the Numbers of those who have been killed in Battle, I cannot but think that you have *said the Thing which is not.*

I could not forbear shaking my Head and smiling a little at his Ignorance. And, being no Stranger to the Art of War, I gave him a Description of Cannons, Culverins, Muskets, Carabines, Pistols, Bullets, Powder, Swords, Bayonets, Sieges, Retreats, Attacks, Undermines, Countermines, Bombardments, Sea-fights; Ships sunk with a Thousand Men; twenty Thousand killed on each Side; dying Groans, Limbs flying in the Air: Smoak, Noise, Confusion, trampling to Death under Horses Feet: Flight, Pursuit, Victory; Fields strewed with Carcases left for Food to Dogs, and Wolves, and Birds of Prey; Plundering, Stripping, Ravishing, Burning and Destroying. And, to set forth the Valour of my own dear Countrymen, I assured him, that I had seen them blow up a Hundred Enemies at once in a Siege, and as many in a Ship; and beheld the dead Bodies drop down in Pieces from the Clouds, to the great Diversion of all the Spectators.

I was going on to more Particulars, when my Master commanded me Silence. He said, whoever understood the Nature of *Yahoos* might easily believe it possible for so vile an Animal, to be capable of every Action I had named, if their Strength and Cunning equalled their Malice. But, as my Discourse had increased his Abhorrence of the whole Species, so he found it gave him a Disturbance in his Mind, to which he was wholly a Stranger before. He thought his Ears being used to such abominable Words, might by Degrees admit them with less Detestation. That, although he hated the *Yahoos* of this Country, yet he no more blamed them for their odious Qualities, than he did a *Gnnayh* (a Bird of Prey) for its Cruelty, or a sharp Stone for cutting his Hoof. But, when a Creature pretending to Reason, could be capable of such Enormities, he dreaded lest the Corruption of that Faculty might be worse than Brutality itself. He seemed therefore confident, that instead of Reason, we were only possessed of some Quality fitted to increase our natural Vices; as the [201] Reflection from a troubled Stream returns the Image of an ill-shapen Body, not only *larger,* but more *distorted.*

He added, That he had heard too much upon the Subject of War, both in this, and some former Discourses. There was another Point which a little perplexed him at present. I had said, that some of our Crew left their Country on Account of being ruined by *Law:* That I had already explained the Meaning of the Word; but he was at a Loss how it should come to pass, that the *Law* which was intended for *every* Man's Preservation, should be any Man's Ruin. Therefore he desired to be farther satisfied what I meant by *Law,* and the Dispensers thereof, according to the present Practice in my own Country: Because he thought, Nature and Reason were sufficient Guides for a reasonable Animal, as we pretended to be, in shewing us what we ought to do, and what to avoid.

I assured his Honour, that *Law* was a Science wherein I had not much conversed, further than by employing Advocates, in vain, upon some Injustices that had been done me. However, I would give him all the Satisfaction I was able.

I said there was a Society of Men among us, bred up from their Youth in the Art of proving by Words multiplied for the Purpose, that *White* is *Black,* and *Black* is *White,* according as they are paid. To this Society all the rest of the People are Slaves.

For example. If my Neighbour hath a mind to my *Cow,* he hires a Lawyer to prove that he ought to have my *Cow* from me. I must then hire another to defend my Right; it being against all Rules of *Law* that any Man should be allowed to speak for himself. Now in this Case, I who am the true Owner lie under two great Disadvantages. First, my Lawyer being practiced almost from his Cradle in defending Falshood; is quite out of his Element when he would be an Advocate for Justice, which as an Office unnatural, he always attempts with great Awkwardness, if not with Ill-will. The second Disadvantage is, that my Lawyer must proceed with great Caution: Or else he will be reprimanded by the Judges, and abhorred by his Brethren, as one who would lessen the Practice of the Law. And therefore I have but two Methods to preserve my *Cow.* The first is, to gain over my Adversary's Lawyer with a double Fee; who will then betray his Client, by insinuating that he hath Justice on his

Side. The second Way is for my Lawyer to make my Cause appear
as unjust as he can; by allowing the *Cow* to belong to my Adversary;
and this if it be skilfully done, will certainly bespeak the Favour of
the Bench. [202]

Now, your Honour is to know, that these Judges are Persons appointed to decide all Controversies of Property, as well as for the
Tryal of Criminals; and picked out from the most dextrous Lawyers
who are grown old or lazy: And having been byassed all their Lives
against Truth and Equity, lie under such a fatal Necessity of favour-
ing Fraud, Perjury and Oppression; that I have known some of them
to have refused a large Bribe from the Side where Justice lay, rather
than injure the *Faculty,* by doing any thing unbecoming their Nature
or their Office.

It is a Maxim among these Lawyers, that whatever hath been done
before, may legally be done again: And therefore they take special
Care to record all the Decisions formerly made against common
Justice and the general Reason of Mankind. These, under the Name
of *Precedents,* they produce as Authorities to justify the most iniqui-
tous Opinions; and the Judges never fail of directing accordingly.

In pleading, they studiously avoid entering into the *Merits* of
the Cause; but are loud, violent and tedious in dwelling upon all
Circumstances which are not to the Purpose. For Instance, in the
Case already mentioned: They never desire to know what Claim
or Title my Adversary hath to my *Cow;* but whether the said *Cow*
were Red or Black; her Horns long or short; whether the Field I
graze her in be round or square; whether she were milked at home
or abroad; what Diseases she is subject to, and the like. After which
they consult *Precedents,* adjourn the Cause, from Time to Time, and
in Ten, Twenty, or Thirty Years come to an Issue.

It is likewise to be observed, that this Society hath a peculiar
Cant and Jargon of their own, that no other Mortal can understand,
and wherein all their Laws are written, which they take special Care
to multiply; whereby they have wholly confounded the very Essence
of Truth and Falshood, of Right and Wrong; so that it will take
Thirty Years to decide whether the Field, left me by my Ancestors
for six Generations, belong to me, or to a Stranger three Hundred
Miles off.

In the Tryal of Persons accused for Crimes against the State, the
Method is much more short and commendable: The Judge first

sends to sound the Disposition of those in Power; after which he can easily hang or save the Criminal, strictly preserving all the Forms of Law.

Here my Master interposing, said it was a Pity, that Creatures endowed with such prodigious Abilities of Mind as these Lawyers, by the Description I gave of them must certainly be, [203] were not rather encouraged to be Instructors of others in Wisdom and Knowledge. In Answer to which, I assured his Honour, that in all Points out of their own Trade, they were usually the most ignorant and stupid Generation among us, the most despicable in common Conversation, avowed Enemies to all Knowledge and Learning; and equally disposed to pervert the general Reason of Mankind, in every other Subject of Discourse, as in that of their own Profession.

CHAPTER VI

A Continuation of the State of England, under Queen Anne. The Character of a first Minister in the Courts of Europe.

My Master was yet wholly at a Loss to understand what Motives could incite this Race of Lawyers to perplex, disquiet, and weary themselves by engaging in a Confederacy of Injustice, merely for the Sake of injuring their Fellow-Animals; neither could he comprehend what I meant in saying they did it for *Hire*. Whereupon I was at much Pains to describe to him the Use of *Money*, the Materials it was made of, and the Value of the Metals: That when a *Yahoo* had got a great Store of this precious Substance, he was able to purchase whatever he had a mind to; the finest Cloathing, the noblest Houses, great Tracts of Land, the most costly Meats and Drinks; and have his Choice of the most beautiful Females. Therefore since *Money* alone, was able to perform all these Feats, our *Yahoos* thought, they could never have enough of it to spend or to save, as they found themselves inclined from their natural Bent either to Profusion or Avarice. That, the rich Man enjoyed the Fruit of the poor Man's Labour, and the latter were a Thousand to One in Proportion to the former. That the Bulk of our People was forced to live miserably, by labouring every Day for small Wages to make a few live plentifully. I enlarged myself much on these and many other Particulars to the same Purpose: But his Honour was still to seek: For he went upon a Supposition that all Animals had a Title to their Share in the Productions of the Earth; and especially those who presided over the rest. Therefore he desired I would let him know, what these costly Meats were, and how any of us happened to want them. Whereupon I enumerated as many Sorts as came into my Head, with the [204] various Methods of dressing them, which could not be done without sending Vessels by Sea to every Part of the World, as well for Liquors to drink, as for Sauces, and innumerable other Conveniences. I assured him, that this whole Globe of Earth must be at least three Times gone round, before one of our better Female *Yahoos* could get her Breakfast, or a Cup to put it in. He said, That must needs be a miserable Country which cannot furnish Food for its own Inhabitants. But what he chiefly wondered at, was how such vast Tracts of Ground as I described, should be wholly without *Fresh water*, and the People put to the Necessity of sending over the Sea for Drink. I replied, that *England* (the dear Place of my Nativity) was computed to produce three Times the Quantity of Food, more than its Inhabitants are able to consume, as well as Liquors extracted from Grain, or pressed out of the Fruit of certain Trees, which made excellent Drink; and the same Proportion in every other Convenience of Life. But, in order to feed the Luxury and Intemperance of the Males, and the Vanity of the Females, we sent away the greatest Part of our necessary Things to other Countries, from whence in Return we brought the Materials of Diseases, Folly, and Vice, to spend among ourselves. Hence it follows of Necessity, that vast Numbers of our People are compelled to seek their Livelihood by Begging, Robbing, Stealing, Cheating, Pimping, Forswearing, Flattering, Suborning, Forging, Gaming, Lying, Fawning, Hectoring, Voting, Scribling, Stargazing, Poysoning, Whoring, Canting, Libelling, Freethinking, and the like Occupations: Every one of which Terms, I was at much Pains to make him understand.

That, *Wine* was not imported among us from foreign Countries, to supply the Want of Water or other Drinks, but because it was a Sort of Liquid which made us merry, by putting us out of our Senses; diverted all melancholy Thoughts, begat wild extravagant Imaginations in the Brain, raised our Hopes, and banished our Fears; suspended every Office of Reason for a Time, and deprived us of the Use of our Limbs, untill we fell into a profound Sleep; although it must be confessed, that we always awaked sick and dispirited; and that the Use of this Liquor filled us with Diseases, which made our Lives uncomfortable and short.

But beside all this, the Bulk of our People supported themselves by furnishing the Necessities or Conveniences of Life to the Rich, and to each other. For Instance, when I am at home and dressed as I ought to be, I carry on my Body the [205] Workmanship of an Hundred Tradesmen; the Building and Furniture of my House employ as many more; and five Times the Number to adorn my Wife.

I was going on to tell him of another Sort of People, who get their Livelihood by attending the Sick; having upon some Occasions informed his Honour that many of my Crew had died of Diseases. But here it was with the utmost Difficulty, that I brought him to apprehend what I meant. He could easily conceive, that a *Houyhnhnm* grew weak and heavy a few Days before his Death; or by some Accident might hurt a Limb. But that Nature, who worketh all things to Perfection, should suffer any Pains to breed in our Bodies, he thought impossible; and desired to know the Reason of so unaccountable an Evil. I told him, we fed on a Thousand Things which operated contrary to each other; that we eat when we were not hungry, and drank without the Provocation of Thirst: That we sat whole Nights drinking strong Liquors without eating a Bit; which disposed us to Sloth, enflamed our Bodies, and precipitated or prevented Digestion. That, prostitute Female *Yahoos* acquired a certain Malady, which bred Rottenness in the Bones of those, who fell into their Embraces: That this and many other Diseases, were propagated from Father to Son; so that great Numbers come into the World with complicated Maladies upon them: That, it would be endless to give him a Catalogue of all Diseases incident to human Bodies; for they could not be fewer than five or six Hundred, spread over every Limb, and Joynt: In short, every Part, external and intestine, having Diseases appropriated to each. To remedy which, there was a Sort of People bred up among us, in the Profession or Pretence of curing the Sick. And because I had some Skill in the Faculty, I would in Gratitude to his Honour, let him know the whole Mystery and Method by which they proceed.

Their Fundamental is, that all Diseases arise from *Repletion;* from whence they conclude, that a great *Evacuation* of the Body is necessary, either through the natural Passage, or upwards at the Mouth. Their next Business is, from Herbs, Minerals, Gums, Oyls, Shells, Salts, Juices, Sea-weed, Excrements, Barks of Trees, Serpents, Toads, Frogs, Spiders, dead Mens Flesh and Bones, Beasts and Fishes, to form a Composition for Smell and Taste the most abominable, nauseous and detestable, that they can possibly contrive, which the Stomach immediately rejects with Loathing: And this they call a *Vomit*. Or else from the same Store-house, with some other poysonous Additions, they [206] command us to take in at the Orifice *above* or *below*, (just as the Physician then happens to be disposed) a Medicine equally annoying and disgustful to the Bowels; which relaxing the Belly, drives down all before it: And this they call a *Purge*, or a *Clyster*. For Nature (as the Physicians alledge) having intended the superior anterior Orifice only for the *Intromission* of Solids and Liquids, and the inferior Posterior for Ejection; these Artists ingeniously considering that in all Diseases Nature is forced out of her Seat; therefore to replace her in it, the Body must be treated in a Manner directly contrary, by interchanging the Use of each Orifice; forcing Solids and Liquids in at the *Anus*, and making Evacuations at the Mouth.

But, besides real Diseases, we are subject to many that are only imaginary, for which the Physicians have invented imaginary Cures; these have their several Names, and so have the Drugs that are proper for them; and with these our Female *Yahoos* are always infested.

One great Excellency in this Tribe is their Skill at *Prognosticks*, wherein they seldom fail; their Predictions in real Diseases, when they rise to any Degree of Malignity, generally portending *Death*, which is always in their Power, when Recovery is not: And therefore, upon any unexpected Signs of Amendment, after they have pronounced their Sentence, rather than be accused as false Prophets, they know how to approve their Sagacity to the World by a seasonable Dose.

They are likewise of special Use to Husbands and Wives, who are grown weary of their Mates; to eldest Sons, to great Ministers of State, and often to Princes.

I had formerly upon Occasion discoursed with my Master upon the Nature of *Government* in general, and particularly of our own *excellent Constitution*, deservedly the Wonder and Envy of the whole World. But having here accidentally mentioned a *Minister of State*; he commanded me some Time after to inform him, what Species of *Yahoo* I particularly meant by that Appellation.

I told him, that a *First* or *Chief Minister of State*, whom I intended to describe, was a Creature wholly exempt from Joy and Grief, Love and Hatred, Pity and Anger; at least makes use of no other Passions but a violent Desire of Wealth, Power, and Titles: That he applies his Words to all Uses, except to the Indication of his Mind; That he never tells a *Truth*, but with an Intent that you should take it for a *Lye*; nor a *Lye*, but with a Design that you should take it for a *Truth*; That those he speaks worst of [207] behind their Backs, are in the surest way to Preferment; and whenever he begins to praise you to others or to your self, you are from that Day forlorn. The worst Mark you can receive is a *Promise*, especially when it is confirmed with an Oath; after which every wise Man retires, and gives over all Hopes.

There are three Methods by which a Man may rise to be Chief Minister: The first is, by knowing how with Prudence to dispose of a Wife, a Daughter, or a Sister: The second, by betraying or undermining his Predecessor: And the third is, by a *furious Zeal* in publick Assemblies against the Corruptions of the Court. But a wise Prince would rather chuse to employ those who practise the last of these Methods; because such Zealots prove always the most obsequious and subservient to the Will and Passions of their Master. That, these *Ministers* having all Employments at their Disposal, preserve themselves in Power by bribing the Majority of a Senate or great Council; and at last by an Expedient called an *Act of Indemnity* (whereof I described the Nature to him) they secure themselves from Afterreckonings, and retire from the Publick, laden with the Spoils of the Nation.

The Palace of a *Chief Minister*, is a Seminary to breed up others in his own Trade: The Pages, Lacquies, and Porter, by imitating their Master, become *Ministers of State* in their several Districts, and learn to excel in the three principal *Ingredients*, of *Insolence*, *Lying*, and *Bribery*. Accordingly, they have a *Subaltern* Court paid to them by Persons of the best Rank; and sometimes by the Force of Dexterity and Impudence, arrive through several Gradations to be Successors to their Lord.

He is usually governed by a decayed Wench, or favourite Footman, who are the Tunnels through which all Graces are conveyed, and may properly be called, *in the last Resort*, the Governors of the Kingdom.

One Day, my Master, having heard me mention the *Nobility* of my Country, was pleased to make me a Compliment which I could not pretend to deserve: That, he was sure, I must have been born of some Noble Family, because I far exceeded in Shape, Colour, and Cleanliness, all the *Yahoos* of his Nation, although I seemed to fail in Strength, and Agility, which must be imputed to my different Way of Living from those other Brutes; and besides, I was not only endowed with the Faculty of Speech, but likewise with some Rudiments of Reason, to a Degree, that with all his Acquaintance I passed for a Prodigy. [208]

He made me observe, that among the *Houyhnhnms,* the *White,* the *Sorrel,* and the *Iron-grey,* were not so exactly shaped as the *Bay,* the *Dapple-grey,* and the *Black;* nor born with equal Talents of Mind, or a Capacity to improve them; and therefore continued always in the Condition of Servants, without ever aspiring to match out of their own Race, which in that Country would be reckoned monstrous and unnatural.

I made his Honour my most humble Acknowledgements for the good Opinion he was pleased to conceive of me; but assured him at the same Time, that my Birth was of the lower Sort, having been born of plain, honest Parents, who were just able to give me a tolerable Education: That, *Nobility* among us was altogether a different Thing from the Idea he had of it; That, our young *Noblemen* are bred from their Childhood in Idleness and Luxury; that, as soon as Years will permit, they consume their Vigour, and contract odious Diseases among lewd Females; and when their Fortunes are almost ruined, they marry some Woman of mean Birth, disagreeable Person, and unsound Constitution, merely for the sake of Money, whom they hate and despise. That, the Productions of such Marriages are generally scrophulous, rickety or deformed Children; by which Means the Family seldom continues above three Generations, unless the Wife take Care to provide a healthy Father among her Neighbours, or Domesticks, in order to improve and continue the Breed. That, a weak diseased Body, a meager Countenance, and sallow Complexion, are the true Marks of *noble Blood;* and a healthy robust Appearance is so disgraceful in a Man of Quality, that the World concludes his real Father to have been a Groom or a Coachman. The Imperfections of his Mind run parallel with those of his Body; being a Composition of Spleen, Dulness, Ignorance, Caprice, Sensuality and Pride.

Without the Consent of this illustrious Body, no Law can be enacted, repealed, or altered: And these Nobles have likewise the Decision of all our Possessions without Appeal. [209]

CHAPTER VII

The Author's great Love of his Native Country. His Master's Observations upon the Constitution and Administration of England, *as described by the Author, with parallel Cases and Comparisons. His Master's Observations upon human Nature.*

The Reader may be disposed to wonder how I could prevail on my self to give so free a Representation of my own Species, among a Race of Mortals who were already too apt to conceive the vilest Opinion of Human Kind, from that entire Congruity betwixt me and their *Yahoos*. But I must freely confess, that the many Virtues of those excellent *Quadrupeds* placed in opposite View to human Corruptions, had so far opened mine Eyes, and enlarged my Understanding, that I began to view the Actions and Passions of Man in a very different Light; and to think the Honour of my own Kind not worth managing; which, besides, it was impossible for me to do before a Person of so acute a Judgment as my Master, who daily convinced me of a thousand Faults in my self, whereof I had not the least Perception before, and which with us would never be numbered even among human Infirmities. I had likewise learned from his Example an utter Detestation of all Falsehood or Disguise; and *Truth* appeared so amiable to me, that I determined upon sacrificing every thing to it.

Let me deal so candidly with the Reader, as to confess, that there was yet a much stronger Motive for the Freedom I took in my Representation of Things. I had not been a Year in this Country, before I contracted such a Love and Veneration for the Inhabitants, that I entered on a firm Resolution never to return to human Kind, but to pass the rest of my Life among these admirable *Houyhnhnms* in the Contemplation and Practice of every Virtue; where I could have no Example or Incitement to Vice. But it was decreed by Fortune, my perpetual Enemy, that so great a Felicity should not fall to my Share. However, it is now some Comfort to reflect, that in what I said of my Countrymen, I *extenuated* their Faults as much as I durst before so strict an Examiner; and upon every Article, gave as *favourable* a Turn as the Matter would bear. For, indeed, who is there alive that [210] will not be swayed by his Byass and Partiality to the Place of his Birth?

I have related the Substance of several Conversations I had with my Master, during the greatest Part of the Time I had the Honour to be in his Service; but have indeed for Brevity sake omitted much more than is here set down.

When I had answered all his Questions, and his Curiosity seemed to be fully satisfied; he sent for me one Morning early, and commanding me to sit down at some Distance, (an Honour which he had never before conferred upon me) He said, he had been very seriously considering my whole Story, as far as it related both to my self and my Country: That, he looked upon us as a Sort of Animals to whose Share, by what Accident he could not conjecture, some small Pittance of *Reason* had fallen, whereof we made no other Use than by its Assistance to aggravate our *natural* Corruptions, and to acquire new ones which Nature had not given us. That, we disarmed our selves of the few Abilities she had bestowed; had been very successful in multiplying our original Wants, and seemed to spend our whole Lives in vain Endeavours to supply them by our own Inventions. That, as to my self, it was manifest I had neither the Strength or Agility of a common *Yahoo;* that I walked infirmly on my hinder Feet; had found out a Contrivance to make my Claws of no Use or Defence, and to remove the Hair from my Chin, which was intended as a Shelter from the Sun and the Weather. Lastly, That I could neither run with Speed, nor climb Trees like my *Brethren* (as he called them) the *Yahoos* in this Country.

That, our Institutions of *Government* and *Law* were plainly owing to our gross Defects in *Reason,* and by consequence, in *Virtue;* because *Reason* alone is sufficient to govern a *Rational* Creature; which was therefore a Character we had no Pretence to challenge, even from the Account I had given of my own People; although he manifestly perceived, that in order to favour them, I had concealed many Particulars, and often *said the Thing which was not.*

He was the more confirmed in this Opinion, because he observed, that as I agreed in every Feature of my Body with other *Yahoos,* except where it was to my real Disadvantage in point of Strength, Speed and Activity, the Shortness of my Claws, and some other Particulars where Nature had no Part; so, from the Representation I had given him of our Lives, our Manners, and our Actions, he found as near a Resemblance in the Disposition of our Minds. He said, the *Yahoos* were known to hate one [211] another more than they did any different Species of Animals; and the Reason usually assigned, was, the Odiousness of their own Shapes, which all could see in the rest, but not in themselves. He had therefore begun to think it not unwise in us to *cover* our Bodies, and by that Invention, conceal many of our Deformities from each other, which would else be hardly supportable. But, he now found he had been mistaken; and that the Dissentions of those Brutes in his Country were owing to the same Cause with ours, as I had described them. For, if (said he) you throw among five *Yahoos* as much Food as would be sufficient for fifty, they will, instead of eating peaceably, fall together by the Ears, each single one impatient to *have all to it self;* and therefore a Servant was usually employed to stand by while they were feeding abroad, and those kept at home were tied at a Distance from each other. That, if a Cow died of Age or Accident, before a *Houyhnhnm* could secure it for his own *Yahoos*, those in the Neighbourhood would come in Herds to seize it, and then would ensue such a Battle as I had described, with terrible Wounds made by their Claws on both Sides, although they seldom were able to kill one another, for want of such convenient Instruments of Death as we had invented. At other Times the like Battles have been fought between the *Yahoos* of several Neighbourhoods without any visible Cause: Those of one District watching all Opportunities to surprise the next before they are prepared. But if they find their Project hath miscarried, they return home, and for want of Enemies, engage in what I call a *Civil War* among themselves.

That, in some Fields of his Country, there are certain *shining Stones* of several Colours, whereof the *Yahoos* are violently fond; and when Part of these *Stones* are fixed in the Earth, as it sometimes happeneth, they will dig with their Claws for whole Days to get them out, and carry them away, and hide them by Heaps in their Kennels; but still looking round with great Caution, for fear their Comrades should find out their Treasure. My Master said, he could never discover the Reason of this unnatural Appetite, or how these *Stones* could be of any Use to a *Yahoo;* but now he believed it might proceed from the same Principle of *Avarice*, which I had ascribed to Mankind. That he had once, by way of Experiment, privately removed a Heap of these *Stones* from the Place where one of his *Yahoos* had buried it: Whereupon, the sordid Animal missing his Treasure, by his loud lamenting brought the whole Herd to the Place, there miserably howled, then fell to biting and tearing the rest; began to pine [212] away, would neither eat nor sleep, nor work, till he ordered a Servant privately to convey the *Stones* into the same Hole, and hide them as before; which when his *Yahoo* had found, he presently recovered his Spirits and good Humour; but took Care to remove them to a better hiding Place; and hath ever since been a very serviceable Brute.

My Master farther assured me, which I also observed my self; That in the Fields where these *shining Stones* abound, the fiercest and most frequent Battles are fought, occasioned by perpetual In-roads of the neighbouring *Yahoos.*

He said, it was common when two *Yahoos* discovered such a *Stone* in a Field, and were contending which of them should be the Pro-prietor, a third would take the Advantage, and carry it away from them both; which my Master would needs contend to have some Resemblance with our *Suits at Law;* wherein I thought it for our Credit not to undeceive him; since the Decision he mentioned was much more equitable than many Decrees among us: Because the Plaintiff and Defendant there lost nothing beside the *Stone* they contended for; whereas our *Courts of Equity,* would never have dismissed the Cause while either of them had any thing left.

My Master continuing his Discourse, said, There was nothing that rendered the *Yahoos* more odious, than their undistinguishing Ap-petite to devour every thing that came in their Way, whether Herbs, Roots, Berries, corrupted Flesh of Animals, or all mingled together: And it was peculiar in their Temper, that they were fonder of what they could get by Rapine or Stealth at a greater Distance, than much better Food provided for them at home. If their Prey held out, they would eat till they were ready to burst, after which Nature had pointed out to them a certain *Root* that gave them a general Evacuation.

There was also another Kind of *Root* very *juicy,* but something rare and difficult to be found, which the *Yahoos* sought for with much Eagerness, and would suck it with great Delight: It produced the same Effects that Wine hath upon us. It would make them some-times hug, and sometimes tear one another; they would howl and grin, and chatter, and roul, and tumble, and then fall asleep in the Mud.

I did indeed observe, that the *Yahoos* were the only Animals in this Country subject to any Diseases; which however, were much fewer than Horses have among us, and contracted not by any ill Treatment they meet with, but by the Nastiness and Greediness of that sordid Brute. Neither has their Language any [213] more than a general Appellation for those Maladies; which is borrowed from the Name of the Beast, and called *Hnea Yahoo,* or the *Yahoo's-Evil;* and the Cure prescribed is a Mixture of *their own Dung* and *Urine,* forcibly put down the *Yahoo's* Throat. This I have since often known to have been taken with Success: And do here freely recommend it to my Countrymen, for the publick Good, as an admirable Specifick against all Diseases produced by Repletion.

As to Learning, Government, Arts, Manufactures, and the like; my Master confessed he could find little or no Resemblance between the *Yahoos* of that Country and those in ours. For, he only meant to observe what Parity there was in our Natures. He had heard indeed some curious *Houyhnhnms* observe, that in most Herds there was a Sort of ruling *Yahoo,* (as among us there is generally some leading or principal Stag in a Park) who was always more *deformed* in Body, and *mischievous in Disposition,* than any of the rest. That, this *Leader* had usually a Favourite as *like himself* as he could get, whose Employment was to *lick his Master's Feet and Posteriors, and drive the Female* Yahoos *to his Kennel;* for which he was now and then rewarded with a Piece of Ass's Flesh. This *Favourite* is hated by the whole Herd; and therefore to protect himself, keeps always *near the Person of his Leader.* He usually continues in Office till a worse can be found; but the very Moment he is discarded, his Successor, at the Head of all the *Yahoos* in that District, Young and Old, Male and Female, come in a Body, and discharge their Excrements upon him from Head to Foot. But how far this might be applicable to our *Courts* and *Favourites,* and *Ministers of State,* my Master said I could best determine.

I durst make no Return to this malicious Insinuation, which debased human Understanding below the Sagacity of a common *Hound,* who hath Judgment enough to distinguish and follow the Cry of the *ablest Dog in the Pack,* without being ever mistaken.

My Master told me, there were some Qualities remarkable in the *Yahoos,* which he had not observed me to mention, or at least very slightly, in the Accounts I had given him of human Kind. He said, those Animals, like other Brutes, had their Females in common; but in this they differed, that the She-*Yahoo* would admit the Male, while she was pregnant; and that the Hees would quarrel and fight with the Females as fiercely as with each other. Both which Practices were such Degrees of infamous Brutality, that no other sensitive Creature ever arrived at. [214]

Another Thing he wondered at in the *Yahoos*, was their strange Disposition to Nastiness and Dirt; whereas there appears to be a natural Love of Cleanliness in all other Animals. As to the two former Accusations, I was glad to let them pass without any Reply, because I had not a Word to offer upon them in Defence of my Species, which otherwise I certainly had done from my own Inclinations. But I could have easily vindicated human Kind from the Imputation of Singularity upon the last Article, if there had been any *Swine* in that Country, (as unluckily for me there were not) which although it may be a *sweeter Quadruped* than a *Yahoo*, cannot I humbly conceive in Justice pretend to more Cleanliness; and so his Honour himself must have owned, if he had seen their filthy Way of feeding, and their Custom of wallowing and sleeping in the Mud.

My Master likewise mentioned another Quality, which his Servants had discovered in several *Yahoos*, and to him was wholly unaccountable. He said, a Fancy would sometimes take a *Yahoo*, to retire into a Corner, to lie down and howl, and groan, and spurn away all that came near him, although he were young and fat, and wanted neither Food nor Water; nor did the Servants imagine what could possibly ail him. And the only Remedy they found was to set him to hard Work, after which he would infallibly come to himself. To this I was silent out of Partiality to my own Kind; yet here I could plainly discover the true Seeds of *Spleen*, which only seizeth on the *Lazy*, the *Luxurous*, and the *Rich;* who, if they were forced to undergo the *same Regimen*, I would undertake for the Cure.

His Honour had farther observed, that a Female *Yahoo* would often stand behind a Bank or a Bush, to gaze on the young Males passing by, and then appear, and hide, using many antick Gestures and Grimaces; at which time it was observed, that she had a most *offensive Smell;* and when any of the Males advanced, would slowly retire, looking often back, and with a counterfeit Shew of Fear, run off into some convenient Place where she knew the Male would follow her.

At other times, if a Female Stranger came among them, three or four of her own Sex would get about her, and stare and chatter, and grin, and smell her all over; and then turn off with Gestures that seemed to express Contempt and Disdain.

Perhaps my Master might refine a little in these Speculations, which he had drawn from what he observed himself, or had been told him by others: However, I could not reflect without some Amazement, and much Sorrow, that the Rudiments of [215] *Lewdness, Coquetry, Censure,* and *Scandal,* should have Place by Instinct in Womankind.

I expected every Moment, that my Master would accuse the *Yahoos* of those unnatural Appetites in both Sexes, so common among us. But Nature it seems hath not been so expert a Schoolmistress; and these politer Pleasures are entirely the Productions of Art and Reason, on our Side of the Globe.

CHAPTER VIII

The Author relateth several Particulars of the Yahoos. *The great Virtues of the* Houyhnhnms. *The Education and Exercise of their Youth. Their general Assembly.*

As I ought to have understood human Nature much better than I suppose it possible for my Master to do, so it was easy to apply the Character he gave of the *Yahoos* to myself and my Countrymen; and I believed I could yet make farther Discoveries from my own Observation. I therefore often begged his Honour to let me go among the Herds of *Yahoos* in the Neighbourhood; to which he always very graciously consented, being perfectly convinced that the Hatred I bore those Brutes would never suffer me to be corrupted by them; and his Honour ordered one of his Servants, a strong Sorrel Nag, very honest and good-natured, to be my Guard; without whose Protection I durst not undertake such Adventures. For I have already told the Reader how much I was pestered by those odious Animals upon my first Arrival. I afterwards failed very narrowly three or four times of falling into their Clutches, when I happened to stray at any Distance without my Hanger. And I have Reason to believe, they had some Imagination that I was of their own Species, which I often assisted myself, by stripping up my Sleeves, and shewing my naked Arms and Breast in their Sight, when my Protector was with me: At which times they would approach as near as they durst, and imitate my Actions after the Manner of Monkeys, but ever with great Signs of Hatred; as a tame *Jack Daw* with Cap and Stockings, is always persecuted by the wild ones, when he happens to be got among them.

They are prodigiously nimble from their Infancy; however, I once caught a young Male of three Years old, and endeavoured [216] by all Marks of Tenderness to make it quiet; but the little Imp fell a squalling, and scratching, and biting with such Violence, that I was forced to let it go; and it was high time, for a whole Troop of old ones came about us at the Noise; but finding the Cub was safe, (for away it ran) and my Sorrel Nag being by, they durst not venture near us. I observed the young Animal's Flesh to smell very rank, and the Stink was somewhat between a *Weasel* and a *Fox*, but much more disagreeable. I forgot another Circumstance, (and perhaps I might have the Reader's Pardon, if it were wholly omitted) that while I held the odious Vermin in my Hands, it voided its filthy Excrements of a yellow liquid Substance, all over my Cloaths; but by good Fortune there was a small Brook hard by, where I washed myself as clean as I could; although I durst not come into my Master's Presence, until I were sufficiently aired.

By what I could discover, the *Yahoos* appear to be the most unteachable of all Animals, their Capacities never reaching higher than to draw or carry Burthens. Yet I am of Opinion, this Defect ariseth chiefly from a perverse, restive Disposition. For they are cunning, malicious, treacherous and revengeful. They are strong and hardy, but of a cowardly Spirit, and by Consequence insolent, abject, and cruel. It is observed, that the *Red-haired* of both Sexes are more libidinous and mischievous than the rest, whom yet they much exceed in Strength and Activity.

The *Houyhnhnms* keep the *Yahoos* for present Use in Huts not far from the House; but the rest are sent abroad to certain Fields, where they dig up Roots, eat several Kinds of Herbs, and search about for Carrion, or sometimes *Weasels* and *Luhimuhs* (a Sort of *wild Rat*) which they greedily devour. Nature hath taught them to dig deep Holes with their Nails on the Side of a rising Ground, wherein they lie by themselves; only the Kennels of the Females are larger, sufficient to hold two or three Cubs.

They swim from their Infancy like Frogs, and are able to continue long under Water, where they often take Fish, which the Females carry home to their Young. And upon this Occasion, I hope the Reader will pardon my relating an odd Adventure.

Being one Day abroad with my Protector the Sorrel Nag, and the Weather exceeding hot, I entreated him to let me bathe in a River that was near. He consented, and I immediately stripped myself stark naked, and went down softly into the Stream. It happened that a young Female *Yahoo* standing behind a Bank, saw the whole Proceeding; and inflamed by Desire, as the Nag [217] and I conjectured, came running with all Speed, and leaped into the Water within five Yards of the Place where I bathed. I was never in my Life so terribly frighted; the Nag was grazing at some Distance, not suspecting any Harm: She embraced me after a most fulsome Manner; I roared as loud as I could, and the Nag came galloping towards me, whereupon she quitted her Grasp, with the utmost Reluctancy, and leaped upon the opposite Bank, where she stood gazing and howling all the time I was putting on my Cloaths.

This was Matter of Diversion to my Master and his Family, as well as of Mortification to my self. For now I could no longer deny, that I was a real *Yahoo*, in every Limb and Feature, since the Females had a natural Propensity to me as one of their own Species: Neither was the Hair of this Brute of a Red Colour, (which might have been some Excuse for an Appetite a little irregular) but black as a Sloe, and her Countenance did not make an Appearance altogether so hideous as the rest of the Kind; for, I think, she could not be above Eleven Years old.

Having already lived three Years in this Country, the Reader I suppose will expect, that I should, like other Travellers, give him some Account of the Manners and Customs of its Inhabitants, which it was indeed my principal Study to learn.

As these noble *Houyhnhnms* are endowed by Nature with a general Disposition to all Virtues, and have no Conceptions or Ideas of what is evil in a rational Creature; so their grand Maxim is, to cultivate *Reason*, and to be wholly governed by it. Neither is *Reason* among them a Point problematical as with us, where Men can argue with Plausibility on both Sides of a Question; but strikes you with immediate Conviction; as it must needs do where it is not mingled, obscured, or discoloured by Passion and Interest. I remember it was with extreme Difficulty that I could bring my Master to understand the Meaning of the Word *Opinion*, or how a Point could be disputable; because *Reason* taught us to affirm or deny only where we are certain; and beyond our Knowledge we cannot do either. So that Controversies, Wranglings, Disputes, and Positiveness in false or dubious Propositions, are Evils unknown among the *Houyhnhnms*. In the like Manner when I used to explain to him our several Systems of *Natural Philosophy*, he would laugh that a Creature pretending to *Reason*, should value itself upon the Knowledge of other Peoples Conjectures, and in Things, where that Knowledge, if it were certain, could be of no Use. Wherein he agreed entirely with the

Sentiments of *Socrates,* as *Plato* delivers them; which I mention as [218] the highest Honour I can do that Prince of Philosophers. I have often since reflected what Destruction such a Doctrine would make in the Libraries of *Europe;* and how many Paths to Fame would be then shut up in the Learned World.

Friendship and *Benevolence* are the two principal Virtues among the *Houyhnhnms;* and these not confined to particular Objects, but universal to the whole Race. For, a Stranger from the remotest Part, is equally treated with the nearest Neighbour, and where-ever he goes, looks upon himself as at home. They preserve *Decency* and *Civility* in the highest Degrees, but are altogether ignorant of *Ceremony.* They have no Fondness for their Colts or Foles; but the Care they take in educating them proceedeth entirely from the Dictates of *Reason.* And, I observed my Master to shew the same Affection to his Neighbour's Issue that he had for his own. They will have it that *Nature* teaches them to love the whole Species, and it is *Reason* only that maketh a Distinction of Persons, where there is a superior Degree of Virtue.

When the Matron *Houyhnhnms* have produced one of each Sex, they no longer accompany with their Consorts, except they lose one of their Issue by some Casualty, which very seldom happens: But in such a Case they meet again; or when the like Accident befalls a Person, whose Wife is past bearing, some other Couple bestows on him one of their own Colts, and then go together a second Time, until the Mother be pregnant. This Caution is necessary to prevent the Country from being overburthened with Numbers. But the Race of inferior *Houyhnhnms* bred up to be Servants is not so strictly limited upon this Article; these are allowed to produce three of each Sex, to be Domesticks in the Noble Families.

In their Marriages they are exactly careful to chuse such Colours as will not make any disagreeable Mixture in the Breed. *Strength* is chiefly valued in the Male, and *Comeliness* in the Female; not upon the Account of *Love,* but to preserve the Race from degenerating: For, where a Female happens to excel in *Strength,* a Consort is chosen with regard to *Comeliness.* Courtship, Love, Presents, Joyntures, Settlements, have no Place in their Thoughts; or Terms whereby to express them in their Language. The young Couple meet and are joined, merely because it is the Determination of their Parents and Friends: It is what they see done every Day; and they look upon it as one of the necessary Actions in a reasonable Being. But the Violation of Marriage, or any other Unchastity, was never heard of: And the [219] married Pair pass their Lives with the same Friendship, and mutual Benevolence that they bear to all others of the same Species, who come in their Way; without Jealousy, Fondness, Quarrelling, or Discontent.

In educating the Youth of both Sexes, their Method is admirable, and highly deserveth our Imitation. These are not suffered to taste a Grain of *Oats,* except upon certain Days, till Eighteen Years old; nor *Milk,* but very rarely; and in Summer they graze two Hours in the Morning, and as many in the Evening, which their Parents likewise observe; but the Servants are not allowed above half that Time; and a great Part of the Grass is brought home, which they eat at the most convenient Hours, when they can be best spared from Work.

Temperance, Industry, Exercise and *Cleanliness,* are the Lessons equally enjoyned to the young ones of both Sexes: And my Master thought it monstrous in us to give the Females a different Kind of Education from the Males, except in some Articles of Domestick Management; whereby, as he truly observed, one Half of our Natives were good for nothing but bringing Children into the World: And to trust the Care of their Children to such useless Animals, he said was yet a greater Instance of Brutality.

But the *Houyhnhnms* train up their Youth to Strength, Speed, and Hardiness, by exercising them in running Races up and down steep Hills, or over hard stony Grounds; and when they are all in a Sweat, they are ordered to leap over Head and Ears into a Pond or a River. Four times a Year the Youth of certain Districts meet to shew the Proficiency in Running, and Leaping, and other Feats of Strength or Agility; where the Victor is rewarded with a Song made in his or her Praise. On this Festival the Servants drive a Heard of *Yahoos* into the Field, laden with Hay, and Oats, and Milk for a Repast to the *Houyhnhnms;* after which, these Brutes are immediately driven back again, for fear of being noisome to the Assembly.

Every fourth Year, at the *Vernal Equinox,* there is a Representative Council of the whole Nation, which meets in a Plain about twenty Miles from our House, and continueth about five or six Days. Here they inquire into the State and Condition of the several Districts; whether they abound or be deficient in Hay or Oats, or Cows or *Yahoos?* And where-ever there is any Want (which is but seldom) it is immediately supplied by unanimous Consent and Contribution. Here likewise the Regulation of Children is settled: As for instance, if a *Houyhnhnm* hath two Males, he changeth one of them with another who hath two Females: [220] And when a Child hath been lost by any Casualty, where the Mother is past Breeding, it is determined what Family shall breed another to supply the Loss.

CHAPTER IX

A grand Debate at the General Assembly of the Houyhnhnms; *and how it was determined. The Learnings of the* Houyhnhnms. *Their Buildings. Their Manner of Burials. The Defectiveness of their Language.*

One of these Grand Assemblies was held in my time, about three Months before my Departure, whither my Master went as the Representative of our District. In this Council was resumed their old Debate, and indeed, the only Debate that ever happened in their Country; whereof my Master after his Return gave me a very particular Account.

The Question to be debated was, Whether the *Yahoos* should be exterminated from the Face of the Earth. One of the *Members* for the Affirmative offered several Arguments of great Strength and Weight; alledging, That, as the *Yahoos* were the most filthy, noisome, and deformed Animal which Nature ever produced, so they were the most restive and indocible, mischievous and malicious: They would privately suck the Teats of the *Houyhnhnms* Cows; kill and devour their Cats, trample down their Oats and Grass, if they were not continually watched; and commit a Thousand other Extravagancies. He took Notice of a general Tradition, that *Yahoos* had not been always in their Country: But, that many Ages ago, two of these Brutes appeared together upon a Mountain; whether produced by the Heat of the Sun upon corrupted Mud and Slime, or from the Ooze and Froth of the Sea, was never known. That these *Yahoos* engendered, and their Brood in a short time grew so numerous as to over-run and infest the whole Nation. That the *Houyhnhnms* to get rid of this Evil, made a general Hunting, and at last inclosed the whole Herd; and destroying the Older, every *Houyhnhnm* kept two young Ones in a Kennel, and brought them to such a Degree of Tameness, as an Animal so savage by Nature can be capable of acquiring; using them for Draught and Carriage. That, there seemed to be much Truth in this Tradition, and that those Creatures could not be *Ylnhniamshy* (or *Aborigines* of the Land) [221] because of the violent Hatred the *Houyhnhnms* as well as all other Animals, bore them; which although their evil Disposition sufficiently deserved, could never have arrived at so high a Degree, if they had been *Aborigines*, or else they would have long since been rooted out. That, the Inhabitants taking a Fancy to use the Service of the *Yahoos*, had very imprudently neglected to cultivate the Breed of *Asses*, which were a comely Animal, easily kept, more tame and orderly, without any offensive Smell, strong enough for Labour, although they yield to the other in Agility of Body; and if their Braying be no agreeable Sound, it is far preferable to the horrible Howlings of the *Yahoos*.

Several others declared their Sentiments to the same Purpose; when my Master proposed an Expedient to the Assembly, whereof he had indeed borrowed the Hint from me. He approved of the Tradition, mentioned by the *Honourable Member*, who spoke before; and affirmed, that the two *Yahoos* said to be first seen among them, had been driven thither over the Sea; that coming to Land, and being forsaken by their Companions, they retired to the Mountains, and degenerating by Degrees, became in Process of Time, much more savage than those of their own Species in the Country from whence these two Originals came. The Reason of his Assertion was, that he had now in his Possession, a certain wonderful *Yahoo*, (meaning myself) which most of them had heard of, and many of them had seen. He then related to them, how he first found me; that, my Body was all covered with an artificial Composure of the Skins and Hairs of other Animals: That, I spoke in a Language of my own, and had thoroughly learned theirs: That, I had related to him the Accidents which brought me thither: That, when he saw me without my Covering, I was an exact *Yahoo* in every Part, only of a whiter Colour, less hairy, and with shorter Claws. He added, how I had endeavoured to persuade him, that in my own and other Countries the *Yahoos* acted as the governing, rational Animal, and held the *Houyhnhnms* in Servitude: That, he observed in me all the Qualities of a *Yahoo*, only a little more civilized by some Tincture of Reason; which however was in a Degree as far inferior to the *Houyhnhnm* Race, as the *Yahoos* of their Country were to me: That, among other things, I mentioned a Custom we had of *castrating Houyhnhnms* when they were young, in order to render them tame; that the Operation was easy and safe; that it was no Shame to learn Wisdom from Brutes, as Industry is taught by the Ant, and Building by the Swallow. (For so I translate the Word *Lyhannh*, although it be a much larger Fowl)

That, [222] this Invention might be practiced upon the younger *Yahoos* here, which, besides rendering them tractable and fitter for Use, would in an Age put an End to the whole Species without destroying Life. That, in the mean time the *Houyhnhnms* should be *exhorted* to cultivate the Breed of Asses, which, as they are in all respects more valuable Brutes; so they have this Advantage, to be fit for Service at five Years old, which the others are not till Twelve.

This was all my Master thought fit to tell me at that Time, of what passed in the Grand Council. But he was pleased to conceal one Particular, which related personally to myself, whereof I soon felt the unhappy Effect, as the Reader will know in its proper Place, and from whence I date all the succeeding Misfortunes of my Life.

The *Houyhnhnms* have no letters, and consequently, their Knowledge is all traditional. But there happening few Events of any Moment among a People so well united, naturally disposed to every Virtue, wholly governed by Reason, and cut off from all Commerce with other Nations; the historical Part is easily preserved without burthening their Memories. I have already observed, that they are subject to no Diseases, and therefore can have no Need of Physicians. However, they have excellent Medicines composed of Herbs, to cure accidental Bruises and Cuts in the Pastern or Frog of the Foot by sharp Stones, as well as other Maims and Hurts in the several Parts of the Body.

They calculate the Year by the Revolution of the Sun and the Moon, but use no Subdivisions into Weeks. They are well enough acquainted with the Motions of those two Luminaries, and understand the Nature of *Eclipses;* and this is the utmost Progress of their *Astronomy.*

In *Poetry* they must be allowed to excel all other Mortals; wherein the Justness of their Similes, and the Minuteness, as well as Exactness of their Descriptions, are indeed inimitable. Their Verses abound very much in both of these; and usually contain either some exalted Notions of Friendship and Benevolence, or the Praises of those who were Victors in Races, and other bodily Exercises. Their Buildings, although very rude and simple, are not inconvenient, but well contrived to defend them from all Injuries of Cold and Heat. They have a Kind of Tree, which at Forty Years old loosens in the Root, and falls with the first Storm; it grows very strait, and being pointed like Stakes with a sharp Stone, (for the *Houyhnhnms* know not the Use of Iron) they stick them erect in the Ground about ten Inches asunder, and then weave in Oat-straw, or sometimes Wattles [223] betwixt them. The Roof is made after the same Manner, and so are the Doors.

The *Houyhnhnms* use the hollow Part between the Pastern and the Hoof of their Fore-feet, as we do our Hands, and this with greater Dexterity, than I could at first imagine. I have seen a white Mare of our Family thread a Needle (which I lent her on Purpose) with that Joynt. They milk their Cows, reap their Oats, and do all the Work which requires Hands, in the same Manner. They have a Kind of hard Flints, which by grinding against other Stones, they form into Instruments, that serve instead of Wedges, Axes, and Hammers. With Tools made of these Flints, they likewise cut their Hay, and reap their Oats, which there groweth naturally in several Fields: The *Yahoos* draw home the Sheaves in Carriages, and the Servants tread them in certain covered Hutts, to get out the Grain, which is kept in Stores. They make a rude Kind of earthen and wooden Vessels, and bake the former in the Sun.

If they can avoid Casualties, they die only of old Age, and are buried in the obscurest Places that can be found, their Friends and Relations expressing neither Joy nor Grief at their Departure; nor does the dying Person discover the least Regret that he is leaving the World, any more than if he were upon returning home from a Visit to one of his Neighbours: I remember, my Master having once made an Appointment with a Friend and his Family to come to his House upon some Affair of Importance; on the Day fixed, the Mistress and her two Children came very late; she made two Excuses, first for her Husband, who, as she said, happened that very Morning to *Lhnuwnh.* The Word is strongly expressive in their Language, but not easily rendered into *English;* it signifies, *to retire to his first Mother.* Her Excuse for not coming sooner, was, that her Husband dying late in the Morning, she was a good while consulting her Servants about a convenient Place where his Body should be laid; and I observed she behaved herself at our House, as chearfully as the rest: She died about three Months after.

They live generally to Seventy or Seventy-five Years, very seldom to Fourscore: Some Weeks before their Death they feel a gradual Decay, but without Pain. During this time they are much visited by their Friends, because they cannot go abroad with their usual Ease and Satisfaction. However, about ten Days before their Death, which they seldom fail in computing, they return the Visits that have been made them by those who are nearest in the Neighbourhood, being carried in a convenient [224] Sledge drawn by *Yahoos;* which Vehicle they use, not only upon this Occasion, but when they grow old, upon long Journeys, or when they are lamed by any Accident. And therefore when the dying *Houyhnhnms* return those Visits, they take a solemn Leave of their Friends, as if they were going to some remote Part of the Country, where they designed to pass the rest of their Lives.

I know not whether it may be worth observing, that the *Houyhnhnms* have no Word in their Language to express any thing that is *evil*, except what they borrow from the Deformities or ill Qualities of the *Yahoos*. Thus they denote the Folly of a Servant, an Omission of a Child, a Stone that cuts their Feet, a Continuance of foul or unseasonable Weather, and the like, by adding to each the Epithet of *Yahoo*. For Instance, *Hhnm Yahoo, Whnaholm Yahoo, Ynlhmnawihlma Yahoo*, and an ill contrived House, *Ynholmhnmrohlnw Yahoo*.

I could with great Pleasure enlarge farther upon the Manners and Virtues of this excellent People; but intending in a short time to publish a Volume by itself expressly upon that Subject, I refer the Reader thither. And in the mean time, proceed to relate my own sad Catastrophe.

CHAPTER X

The Author's Oeconomy and happy Life among the Houyhnhnms. *His great Improvement in Virtue, by conversing with them. Their Conversations. The Author hath Notice given him by his Master that he must depart from the Country. He falls into a Swoon for Grief, but submits. He contrives and finishes a Canoo, by the Help of a Fellow-Servant, and puts to Sea at a Venture.*

I had settled my little Oeconomy to my own Heart's Content. My Master had ordered a Room to be made for me after their Manner, about six Yards from the House; the Sides and Floors of which I plaistered with Clay, and covered with Rush-mats of my own contriving: I had beaten Hemp, which there grows wild, and made of it a Sort of Ticking: This I filled with the Feathers of several Birds I had taken with Springes made of *Yahoos* Hairs; and were excellent Food. I had worked two Chairs with my Knife, the Sorrel Nag helping me in the grosser and more laborious Part. When my Cloaths were [225] worn to Rags, I made my self others with the Skins of

Rabbets, and of a certain beautiful Animal about the same Size, called *Nnuhnoh*, the Skin of which is covered with a fine Down. Of these I likewise made very tolerable Stockings. I soaled my Shoes with Wood which I cut from a Tree, and fitted to the upper Leather, and when this was worn out, I supplied it with the Skins of *Yahoos*, dried in the Sun. I often got Honey out of hollow Trees, which I mingled with Water, or eat it with my Bread. No Man could more verify the Truth of these two Maxims, *That, Nature is very easily satisfied;* and, *That, Necessity is the Mother of Invention.* I enjoyed perfect Health of Body, and Tranquility of Mind; I did not feel the Treachery or Inconstancy of a Friend, nor the Injuries of a secret or open Enemy. I had no Occasion of bribing, flattering or pimping, to procure the Favour of any great Man, or his Minion. I wanted no Fence against Fraud or Oppression: Here was neither Physician to destroy my Body, nor Lawyer to ruin my Fortune: No Informer to watch my Words and Actions, or forge Accusations against me for Hire: Here were no Gibers, Censurers, Backbiters, Pickpockets, Highwaymen, House-breakers, Attorneys, Bawds, Buffoons, Gamesters, Politicians, Wits, Spleneticks, tedious Talkers, Controvertists, Ravishers, Murderers, Robbers, Virtuoso's; no Leaders or Followers of Party and Faction; no Encouragers to Vice, by Seducement or Examples: No Dungeon, Axes, Gibbets, Whipping-posts, or Pillories; No cheating Shopkeepers or Mechanicks: No Pride, Vanity or Affectation: No Fops, Bullies, Drunkards, strolling Whores, or Poxes: No ranting, lewd, expensive Wives: No stupid, proud Pedants: No importunate, over-bearing, quarrelsome, noisy, roaring, empty, conceited, swearing Companions: No Scoundrels raised from the Dust upon the Merit of their Vices; or Nobility thrown into it on account of their Virtues: No Lords, Fidlers, Judges or Dancing-masters.

I had the Favour of being admitted to several *Houyhnhnms*, who came to visit or dine with my Master; where his Honour graciously suffered me to wait in the Room, and listen to their Discourse. Both he and his Company would often descend to ask me Questions, and receive my Answers. I had also sometimes the Honour of attending my Master in his Visits to others. I never presumed to speak, except in answer to a Question; and then I did it with inward Regret, because it was a Loss of so much Time for improving my self: But I was infinitely delighted with the Station of an humble Auditor in such Conversations, where nothing passed but what was useful, expressed in the fewest and [226] most significant Words: Where (as I have already said) the greatest *Decency* was observed, without the least Degree of Ceremony; where no Person spoke without being pleased himself, and pleasing his Companions: Where there was no Interruption, Tediousness, Heat, or Difference of Sentiments. They have a Notion, That when People are met together, a short Silence doth much improve Conversation: This I found to be true; for during those little Intermissions of Talk, new Ideas would arise in their Minds, which very much enlivened the Discourse. Their Subjects are generally on Friendship and Benevolence; on Order and Oeconomy; sometimes upon the visible Operations of Nature, or ancient Traditions; upon the Bounds and Limits of Virtue; upon the unerring Rules of Reason; or upon some Determinations, to be taken at the next great Assembly; and often upon the various Excellencies of *Poetry.* I may add, without Vanity, that my Presence often gave them sufficient Matter for Discourse, because it afforded my Master an Occasion of letting his Friends into the History of me and my Country, upon which they were all pleased to discant in a Manner not very advantageous to human Kind; and for that Reason I shall not repeat what they said: Only I may be allowed to observe, That his Honour, to my great Admiration, appeared to understand the Nature of *Yahoos* much better than my self. He went through all our Vices and Follies, and discovered many which I had never mentioned to him; by only supposing what Qualities a *Yahoo* of their Country, with a small Proportion of Reason, might be capable of exerting: And concluded, with too much Probability, how vile as well as miserable such a Creature must be.

I freely confess, that all the little Knowledge I have of any Value, was acquired by the Lectures I received from my Master, and from hearing the Discourses of him and his Friends; to which I should be prouder to listen, than to dictate to the greatest and wisest Assembly in *Europe.* I admired the Strength, Comeliness and Speed of the Inhabitants; and such a Constellation of Virtues in such amiable Persons produced in me the highest Veneration. At first, indeed, I did not feel that natural Awe which the *Yahoos* and all other Animals bear towards them; but it grew upon me by Degrees, much sooner than I imagined, and was mingled with a respectful Love and Gratitude, that they would condescend to distinguish me from the rest of my Species.

When I thought of my Family, my Friends, my Countrymen, or human Race in general, I considered them as they really were, *Yahoos* in Shape and Disposition, perhaps a little more civilized, [227] and qualified with the Gift of Speech; but making no other Use of Reason, than to improve and multiply those Vices, whereof their Brethren in this Country had only the Share that Nature allotted them. When I happened to behold the Reflection of my own Form in a Lake or Fountain, I turned away my Face in Horror and detestation of my self; and could better endure the Sight of a common *Yahoo*, than of my own Person. By conversing with the *Houyhnhnms*, and looking upon them with Delight, I fell to imitate their Gait and Gesture, which is now grown into a Habit; and my Friends often tell me in a blunt Way, that I *trot like a Horse;* which, however, I take for a great Compliment: Neither shall I disown, that in speaking I am apt to fall into the Voice and manner of the *Houyhnhnms*, and hear my self ridiculed on that Account without the least Mortification.

In the Midst of this Happiness, when I looked upon my self to be fully settled for Life, my Master sent for me one Morning a little earlier than his usual Hour. I observed by his Countenance that he was in some Perplexity, and at a Loss how to begin what he had to speak. After a short Silence, he told me, he did not know how I would take what he was going to say: That, in the last general Assembly, when the Affair of the *Yahoos* was entered upon, the Representatives had taken Offence at his keeping a *Yahoo* (meaning my self) in his Family more like a *Houyhnhnm* than a Brute Animal. That, he was known frequently to converse with me, as if he could receive some Advantage or Pleasure in my Company: That, such a Practice was not agreeable to Reason or Nature, or a thing ever heard of before among them. The Assembly did therefore *exhort* him, either to employ me like the rest of my Species, or command me to swim back to the Place from whence I came. That, the first of these Expedients was utterly rejected by all the *Houyhnhnms*, who had ever seen me at his House or their own: For, they alledged, That because I had some Rudiments of Reason, added to the natural Pravity of those Animals, it was to be feared, I might be able to seduce them into the woody and mountainous Parts of the Country, and bring them in Troops by Night to destroy the *Houyhnhnms* Cattle, as being naturally of the ravenous Kind, and averse from Labour.

My Master added, That he was daily pressed by the *Houyhnhnms* of the Neighbourhood to have the Assembly's *Exhortation* executed, which he could not put off much longer. He doubted, it would be impossible for me to swim to another Country; and therefore wished I would contrive some Sort of Vehicle [228] resembling those I had described to him, that might carry me on the Sea; in which Work I should have the Assistance of his own Servants, as well as those of his Neighbours. He concluded, that for his own Part he could have been content to keep me in his Service as long as I lived; because he found I had cured myself of some bad Habits and Dispositions, by endeavouring, as far as my inferior Nature was capable, to imitate the *Houyhnhnms.*

I should here observe to the Reader, that a Decree of the general Assembly in this Country, is expressed by the Word *Hnhloayn,* which signifies an *Exhortation;* as near as I can render it: For they have no Conception how a rational Creature can be *compelled,* but only advised, or *exhorted;* because no Person can disobey Reason, without giving up his Claim to be a rational Creature.

I was struck with the utmost Grief and Despair at my Master's Discourse; and being unable to support the Agonies I was under, I fell into a Swoon at his Feet: When I came to myself, he told me, that he concluded I had been dead. (For these People are subject to no such Imbecillities of Nature) I answered, in a faint Voice, that Death would have been too great an Happiness; that although I could not blame the Assembly's *Exhortation,* or the Urgency of his Friends; yet in my weak and corrupt Judgment, I thought it might consist with Reason to have been less rigorous. That, I could not swim a League, and probably the nearest Land to theirs might be distant about an Hundred: That, many Materials, necessary for making a small Vessel to carry me off, were wholly wanting in this Country, which however, I would attempt in Obedience and Gratitude to his Honour, although I concluded the thing to be impossible, and therefore looked on myself as already devoted to Destruction. That, the certain Prospect of an unnatural Death, was the least of my Evils: For, supposing I should escape with Life by some strange Adventure, how could I think with Temper, of passing my Days among *Yahoos,* and relapsing into my old Corruptions, for want of Examples to lead and keep me within the Paths of Virtue. That, I knew too well upon what solid Reasons all the Determinations of the wise *Houyhnhnms* were founded, not to be shaken by Arguments of mine, a miserable *Yahoo;* and therefore after presenting him with my humble Thanks for the Offer of his Servants Assistance in making a Vessel, and desiring a reasonable Time for so difficult a Work, I told him, I would endeavour to preserve a wretched Being; and, if ever I returned [229] to England, was not without Hopes of being useful to my own Species, by celebrating the Praises of the renowned Houyhnhnms, and proposing their Virtues to the Imitation of Mankind.

My Master in a few Words made me a very gracious Reply, allowed me the Space of two Months to finish my Boat; and ordered the Sorrel Nag, my Fellow-Servant, (for so at this Distance I may presume to call him) to follow my Instructions, because I told my Master, that his Help would be sufficient, and I knew he had a Tenderness for me.

In his Company my first Business was to go to that Part of the Coast, where my rebellious Crew had ordered me to be set on Shore. I got upon a Height, and looking on every Side into the Sea, fancied I saw a small Island, towards the North-East: I took out my Pocket-glass, and could then clearly distinguish it about five Leagues off, as I computed; but it appeared to the Sorrel Nag to be only a blue Cloud: For, as he had no Conception of any Country beside his own, so he could not be as expert in distinguishing remote Objects at Sea, as we who so much converse in that Element.

After I had discovered this Island, I considered no farther; but resolved, it should, if possible, be the first Place of my Banishment, leaving the Consequence to Fortune.

I returned home, and consulting with the Sorrel Nag, we went into a Copse at some Distance, where I with my Knife, and he with a sharp Flint fastened very artificially, after their Manner, to a wooden Handle, cut down several Oak Wattles about the Thickness of a Walking-staff, and some larger Pieces. But I shall not trouble the Reader with a particular Description of my own Mechanicks: Let it suffice to say, that in six Weeks time, with the Help of the Sorrel Nag, who performed the Parts that required most Labour, I finished a Sort of Indian Canoo, but much larger, covering it with the Skins of Yahoos, well stitched together, with hempen Threads of my own making. My Sail was likewise composed of the Skins of the same Animal; but I made use of the youngest I could get, the older being too tough and thick; and I likewise provided myself with four Paddles. I laid in a Stock of boiled Flesh, of Rabbets and Fowls; and took with me two Vessels, one filled with Milk, and the other with Water.

I tried my Canoo in a large Pond near my Master's House, and then corrected in it what was amiss; stopping all the Chinks with *Yahoos* Tallow, till I found it stanch, and able to bear me, and my Freight. And when it was as compleat as I could possibly make it, I had it drawn on a Carriage very gently by *Yahoos*, to [230] the Sea-side, under the Conduct of the Sorrel Nag, and another Servant.

When all was ready, and the Day came for my Departure, I took Leave of my Master and Lady, and the whole Family, mine Eyes flowing with Tears, and my Heart quite sunk with Grief. But his Honour, out of Curiosity, and perhaps (if I may speak it without Vanity) partly out of Kindness, was determined to see me in my Canoo; and got several of his neighbouring Friends to accompany him. I was forced to wait above an Hour for the Tide, and then observing the Wind very fortunately bearing towards the Island, to which I intended to steer my Course, I took a second Leave of my Master: But as I was going to prostrate myself to kiss his Hoof, he did me the Honour to raise it gently to my Mouth. I am not ignorant how much I have been censured for mentioning this last Particular. Detractors are pleased to think it improbable, that so illustrious a Person should descend to give so great a Mark of Distinction to a Creature so inferior as I. Neither have I forgot, how apt some Travellers are to boast of extraordinary Favours they have received. But, if these Censurers were better acquainted with the noble and courteous Disposition of the *Houyhnhnms,* they would soon change their Opinion.

I paid my Respects to the rest of the *Houyhnhnms* in his Honour's Company; then getting into my Canoo, I pushed off from Shore.

CHAPTER XI

The Author's dangerous Voyage. He arrives at New-Holland, *hoping to settle there. Is wounded with an Arrow by one of the Natives. Is seized and carried by Force into a* Portugueze *Ship. The great Civilities of the Captain. The Author arrives at* England.

I began this desperate Voyage on *February* 15, 171–, at 9 o'Clock in the Morning. The Wind was very favourable; however, I made use at first only of my Paddles; but considering I should soon be weary, and that the Wind might probably chop about, I ventured to set up my little Sail; and thus, with the Help of the Tide, I went at the Rate of a League and a [231] Half an Hour, as near as I could guess.

My Master and his Friends continued on the Shoar, till I was almost out of Sight; and I often heard the Sorrel Nag (who always loved me) crying out, *Hnuy illa nyha maiah Yahoo,* Take Care of thy self, gentle *Yahoo.*

My Design was, if possible, to discover some small Island uninhabited, yet sufficient by my Labour to furnish me with Necessaries of Life, which I would have thought a greater Happiness than to be first Minister in the politest Court of *Europe;* so horrible was the Idea I conceived of returning to live in the Society and under the Government of *Yahoos.* For in such a Solitude as I desired, I could at least enjoy my own Thoughts, and reflect with Delight on the Virtues of those inimitable *Houyhnhnms,* without any Opportunity of degenerating into the Vices and Corruptions of my own Species.

The Reader may remember what I related when my Crew conspired against me, and confined me to my Cabbin. How I continued there several Weeks, without knowing what Course we took; and when I was put ashore in the Long-boat, how the Sailors told me with Oaths, whether true or false, that they knew not in what Part of the World we were. However, I did then believe us to be about ten Degrees *Southward* of the *Cape of Good Hope,* or about 45 Degrees *Southern* Latitude, as I gathered from some general Words I overheard among them, being I supposed to the *South-East* in their intended Voyage to *Madagascar.* And although this were but little better than Conjecture, yet I resolved to steer my Course *Eastward,* hoping to reach the *South-West* Coast of *New-Holland,* and perhaps some such Island as I desired, lying *Westward* of it. The Wind was full *West,* and by six in the Evening I computed I had gone *Eastward* at least eighteen Leagues; when I spied a very small Island about half a League off, which I soon reached. It was nothing but a Rock with one Creek, naturally arched by the Force of Tempests. Here I put in my Canoo, and climbing a Part of the Rock, I could plainly discover Land to the *East,* extending from *South* to *North.* I lay all Night in my Canoo; and repeating my Voyage early in the Morning, I arrived in seven Hours to the *South-East* Point of *New-Holland.* This confirmed me in the Opinion I have long entertained, that the *Maps* and *Charts* place this Country at least three Degrees more to the *East* than it really is; which Thought I communicated many Years ago to my worthy Friend Mr. *Herman Moll,* and gave him my Reasons for it, although he hath rather chosen to follow other Authors. [232]

I saw no Inhabitants in the Place where I landed; and being un-armed, I was afraid of venturing far into the Country. I found some Shell-Fish on the Shore, and eat them raw, not daring to kindle a Fire, for fear of being discovered by the Natives. I continued three Days feeding on Oysters and Limpits, to save my own Provisions; and I fortunately found a Brook of excellent Water, which gave me great Relief.

On the fourth Day, venturing out early a little too far, I saw twenty or thirty Natives upon a Height, not above five hundred Yards from me. They were stark naked, Men, Women and Children round a Fire, as I could discover by the Smoke. One of them spied me, and gave Notice to the rest; five of them advanced towards me, leaving the Women and Children at the Fire. I made what haste I could to the Shore, and getting into my Canoo, shoved off: The Savages ob-serving me retreat, ran after me; and before I could get far enough into the Sea, discharged an Arrow, which wounded me deeply on the Inside of my left Knee (I shall carry the Mark to my Grave.) I apprehended the Arrow might be poisoned; and paddling out of the Reach of their Darts (being a calm Day) I made a shift to suck the Wound, and dress it as well as I could.

I was at a Loss what to do, for I durst not return to the same Land-ing-place, but stood to the *North,* and was forced to paddle; for the Wind, although very gentle, was against me, blowing *North-West.* As I was looking about for a secure Landing-place, I saw a Sail to the *North North-East,* which appearing every Minute more visible, I was in some Doubt, whether I should wait for them or no; but at last my Detestation of the *Yahoo* Race prevailed; and turning my Canoo, I sailed and paddled together to the *South,* and got into the same Creek from whence I set out in the Morning; choosing rather to trust my self among these *Barbarians,* than live with *European Yahoos.* I drew up my Canoo as close as I could to the Shore, and hid my self behind a Stone by the little Brook, which, as I have al-ready said, was excellent Water.

The Ship came within half a League of this Creek, and sent out her Long-Boat with Vessels to take in fresh Water (for the Place it seems was very well known) but I did not observe it until the Boat was almost on Shore; and it was too late to seek another Hiding-Place. The Seamen at their landing observed my Canoo, and rum-maging it all over, easily conjectured that the Owner could not be far off. Four of them well armed searched every Cranny and Lurking-hole, till at last they found me flat on [233] my Face behind the Stone. They gazed a while in Admiration at my strange uncouth Dress; my Coat made of Skins, my wooden-soaled Shoes, and my furred Stockings; from whence, however, they concluded I was not a Native of the Place, who all go naked. One of the Seamen in *Portugueze* bid me rise, and asked who I was. I understood that Language very well, and getting upon my Feet, said, I was a poor *Yahoo*, banished from the *Houyhnhnms,* and desired they would please to let me depart. They admired to hear me answer them in their own Tongue, and saw by my Complection I must be an *European;* but were at a Loss to know what I meant by *Yahoos* and *Houyhnhnms,* and at the same Time fell a laughing at my strange Tone in speaking, which resembled the Neighing of a Horse. I trembled all the while betwixt Fear and Hatred: I again desired Leave to depart, and was gently moving to my Canoo; but they laid hold on me, desiring to know what Country I was of? whence I came? with many other Questions. I told them, I was born in *England,* from whence I came about five Years ago, and then their Country and ours were at Peace. I therefore hoped they would not treat me as an Enemy, since I meant them no Harm, but was a poor *Yahoo,* seeking some desolate Place where to pass the Remainder of his unfortunate Life.

When they began to talk, I thought I never heard or saw any thing so unnatural; for it appeared to me as monstrous as if a Dog or a Cow should speak in *England,* or a *Yahoo* in *Houyhnhnm-Land.* The honest *Portuguese* were equally amazed at my strange Dress, and the odd Manner of delivering my Words, which however they understood very well. They spoke to me with great Humanity, and said they were sure their Captain would carry me *gratis* to *Lisbon,* from whence I might return to my own Country; that two of the Seamen would go back to the Ship, to inform the Captain of what they had seen, and receive his Orders; in the mean Time, unless I would give my solemn Oath not to fly, they would secure me by Force. I thought it best to comply with their Proposal. They were very curious to know my Story, but I gave them very little Satisfaction; and they all conjectured, that my Mixfortunes had impaired my Reason. In two Hours the Boat, which went loaden with Vessels of Water, returned with the Captain's Commands to fetch me on Board. I fell on my Knees to preserve my Liberty; but all was in vain, and the Men having tied me with Cords, heaved me into the Boat, from whence I was taken into the Ship, and from thence into the Captain's Cabbin. [234]

His Name was *Pedro de Mendez;* he was a very courteous and generous Person; he entreated me to give some Account of my self, and desired to know what I would eat or drink; said, I should be used as well as himself, and spoke so many obliging Things, that I wondered to find such Civilities from a *Yahoo.* However, I remained silent and sullen; I was ready to faint at the very Smell of him and his Men. At last I desired something to eat out of my own Canoo; but he ordered me a Chicken and some excellent Wine, and then directed that I should be put to Bed in a very clean Cabbin. I would not undress my self, but lay on the Bed-cloaths; and in half an Hour stole out, when I thought the Crew was at Dinner; and getting to the Side of the Ship, was going to leap into the Sea, and swim for my Life, rather than continue among *Yahoos.* But one of the Seamen prevented me, and having informed the Captain, I was chained to my Cabbin.

After Dinner *Don Pedro* came to me, and desired to know my Reason for so desperate an Attempt; assured me he only meant to do me all the Service he was able; and spoke so very movingly, that at last I descended to treat him like an Animal which had some little Portion of Reason. I gave him a very short Relation of my Voyage; of the Conspiracy against me by my own Men; of the Country where they set me on Shore, and of my five Years Residence there. All which he looked upon as if it were a Dream or a Vision; whereat I took great Offence: For I had quite forgot the Faculty of Lying, so peculiar to *Yahoos* in all Countries where they preside, and consequently the Disposition of suspecting Truth in others of their own Species. I asked him, Whether it were the Custom of his Country to *say the Thing that was not?* I assured him I had almost forgot what he meant by Falshood; and if I had lived a thousand Years in *Houyhnhnmland,* I should never have heard a Lie from the meanest Servant. That I was altogether indifferent whether he believed me or no; but however, in return for his Favours, I would give so much Allowance to the Corruption of his Nature, as to answer any Objection he would please to make; and he might easily discover the Truth.

The Captain, a wise Man, after many Endeavors to catch me tripping in some Part of my Story, at last began to have a better Opinion of my Veracity. But he added, that since I professed so inviolable an Attachment to Truth, I must give him my Word of Honour to bear him Company in this Voyage without attempting any thing against my Life; or else he would continue me a Prisoner till we arrived at

Lisbon. I gave him the Promise [235] he required; but at the same
time protested that I would suffer the greatest Hardships rather than
return to live among *Yahoos.*

Our Voyage passed without any considerable Accident. In Gratitude to the Captain I sometimes sate with him at his earnest Request,
and strove to conceal my Antipathy against human Kind, although
it often broke out; which he suffered to pass without Observation.
But the greatest Part of the Day, I confined myself to my Cabbin,
to avoid seeing any of the Crew. The Captain had often intreated me
to strip myself of my savage Dress, and offered to lend me the best
Suit of Cloaths he had. This I would not be prevailed on to accept,
abhorring to cover myself with any thing that had been on the Back
of a *Yahoo.* I only desired he would lend me two clean Shirts, which
having been washed since he wore them, I believed would not so
much defile me. These I changed every second Day, and washed them
myself.

We arrived at *Lisbon, Nov.* 5, 1715. At our landing, the Captain
forced me to cover myself with his Cloak, to prevent the Rabble
from crouding about me. I was conveyed to his own House; and at
my earnest Request, he led me up to the highest Room backwards.
I conjured him to conceal from all Persons what I had told him of
the *Houyhnhnms;* because the least Hint of a Story would not only
draw Numbers of People to see me, but probably put me in Danger
of being imprisoned, or burnt by the *Inquisition.* The Captain persuaded me to accept a Suit of Cloaths newly made; but I would not
suffer the Taylor to take my Measure; however, Don *Pedro* being
almost of my Size, they fitted me well enough. He accoutred me with
other Necessaries all new, which I aired for Twenty-four Hours before I would use them.

The Captain had no Wife, nor above three Servants, none of which
were suffered to attend at Meals; and his whole Deportment was so
obliging, added to very good *human* Understanding, that I really
began to tolerate his Company. He gained so far upon me, that I
ventured to look out of the back Window. By Degrees I was brought
into another Room, from whence I peeped into the Street, but drew
my Head back in a Fright. In a Week's Time he seduced me down
to the Door. I found my Terror gradually lessened, but my Hatred
and Contempt seemed to increase. I was at last bold enough to walk
the Street in his Company, but kept my Nose well stopped with Rue,
or sometimes with Tobacco.

In ten Days, Don *Pedro*, to whom I had given some Account of my domestick Affairs, put it upon me as a Point of Honour [236] and Conscience, that I ought to return to my native Country, and live at home with my Wife and Children. He told me, there was an *English* Ship in the Port just ready to sail, and he would furnish me with all things necessary. It would be tedious to repeat his Arguments, and my Contradictions. He said, it was altogether impossible to find such a solitary Island as I had desired to live in; but I might command in my own House, and pass my time in a Manner as recluse as I pleased.

I complied at last, finding I could not do better. I left *Lisbon* the 24th Day of *November*, in an *English* Merchant-man, but who was the Master I never inquired. Don *Pedro* accompanied me to the Ship, and lent me Twenty Pounds. He took kind Leave of me, and embraced me at parting; which I bore as well as I could. During this last Voyage I had no Commerce with the Master, or any of his Men; but pretending I was sick kept close in my Cabbin. On the Fifth of *December*, 1715, we cast Anchor in the *Downs* about Nine in the Morning, and at Three in the Afternoon I got safe to my House at *Redriff*.

My Wife and Family received me with great Surprize and Joy, because they concluded me certainly dead; but I must freely confess, the Sight of them filled me only with Hatred, Disgust and Contempt; and the more, by reflecting on the near Alliance I had to them. For, although since my unfortunate Exile from the *Houyhnhnm* Country, I had compelled myself to tolerate the Sight of *Yahoos*, and to converse with Don *Pedro de Mendez*; yet my Memory and Imaginations were perpetually filled with the Virtues and Ideas of those exalted *Houyhnhnms*. And when I began to consider, that by copulating with one of the *Yahoo*-Species, I had become a Parent of more; it struck me with the utmost Shame, Confusion and Horror.

As soon as I entered the House, my Wife took me in her Arms, and kissed me; at which, having not been used to the Touch of that odious Animal for so many Years, I fell in a Swoon for almost an Hour. At the Time I am writing, it is five Years since my last Return to *England*: During the first Year I could not endure my Wife or Children in my Presence, the very Smell of them was intolerable; much less could I suffer them to eat in the same Room. To this Hour they dare not presume to touch my Bread, or drink out of the same Cup; neither was I ever able to let one of them take me by the Hand. The first

Money I laid out was to buy two young Stone-Horses, which I keep in a good Stable, and next to them the Groom is my greatest Favourite; for I feel my Spirits revived by the Smell he contracts in the [237] Stable. My Horses understand me tolerably well; I converse with them at least four Hours every Day. They are Strangers to Bridle or Saddle; they live in great Amity with me, and Friendship to each other.

CHAPTER XII

The Author's Veracity. His Design in publishing this Work. His Censure of those Travellers who swerve from the Truth. The Author clears himself from any sinister Ends in writing. An Objection answered. The Method of planting Colonies. His Native Country commended. The Right of the Crown to those Countries described by the Author, is justified. The Difficulty of conquering them. The Author takes his last Leave of the Reader; proposeth his Manner of Living for the future; gives good Advice, and concludeth.

Thus, gentle Reader, I have given thee a faithful History of my Travels for Sixteen Years, and above Seven Months; wherein I have not been so studious of Ornament as of Truth. I could perhaps like others have astonished thee with strange improbable Tales; but I rather chose to relate plain Matter of Fact in the simplest Manner and Style; because my principal Design was to inform, and not to amuse thee.

It is easy for us who travel into remote Countries, which are seldom visited by *Englishmen* or other *Europeans*, to form Descriptions of wonderful Animals both at Sea and Land. Whereas, a Traveller's chief Aim should be to make Men wiser and better, and to improve their Minds by the bad, as well as good Example of what they deliver concerning foreign Places.

I could heartily wish a Law were enacted, that every Traveller, before he were permitted to publish his Voyages, should be obliged to make Oath before the *Lord High Chancellor*, that all he intended to print was absolutely true to the best of his Knowledge; for then the World would no longer be deceived as it usually is, while some Writers, to make their Works pass the better upon the Publick, impose the grossest Falsities on the unwary Reader. I have perused several Books of Travels with great Delight in my younger Days; but, having since gone over most Parts of the Globe, and been able to contradict many fabulous Accounts from my own Observation; it hath given me a great [238] Disgust against this Part of Reading, and some Indignation to see the Credulity of Mankind so impudently abused. Therefore since my Acquaintance were pleased to think my poor Endeavours might not be unacceptable to my Country; I imposed on myself as a Maxim, never to be swerved from, that I would *strictly adhere to Truth;* neither indeed can I be ever under the least Temptation to vary from it, while I retain in my Mind the Lectures and Examples of my noble Master, and the other illustrious *Houyhnhnms,* of whom I had so long the Honour to be an humble Hearer.

      ——*Nec si miserum Fortuna Sinonem*
    Finxit, vanum etiam, mendacemque improba finget.

I know very well, how little Reputation is to be got by Writings which require neither Genius nor Learning, nor indeed any other Talent, except a good Memory, or an exact *Journal.* I know likewise, that Writers of Travels, like *Dictionary*-Makers, are sunk into Oblivion by the Weight and Bulk of those who come last, and therefore lie uppermost. And it is highly probable, that such Travellers who shall hereafter visit the Countries described in this Work of mine, may by detecting my Errors, (if there be any) and adding many new Discoveries of their own, jostle me out of Vogue, and stand in my Place; making the World forget that ever I was an Author. This indeed would be too great a Mortification if I wrote for Fame: But, as my sole Intention was the PUBLICK GOOD, I cannot be altogether disappointed. For, who can read of the Virtues I have mentioned in the glorious *Houyhnhnms,* without being ashamed of his own Vices, when he considers himself as the reasoning, governing Animal of his Country? I shall say nothing of those remote Nations where *Yahoos* preside; amongst which the least corrupted are the *Brobdingnagians,* whose wise Maxims in Morality and Government, it would be our Happiness to observe. But I forbear descanting further, and rather leave the judicious Reader to his own Remarks and Applications.

I am not a little pleased that this Work of mine can possibly meet with no Censurers: For what Objections can be made against a Writer who relates only plain Facts that happened in such distant Countries, where we have not the least Interest with respect either to Trade or Negotiations? I have carefully avoided every Fault with which common Writers of Travels are often too justly charged. Besides, I meddle not the least with any *Party,* but write without

Passion, Prejudice, or Ill-will against [239] any Man or Number of Men whatsoever. I write for the noblest End, to inform and instruct Mankind, over whom I may, without Breach of Modesty, pretend to some Superiority, from the Advantages I received by conversing so long among the most accomplished *Houyhnhnms.* I write without any View towards Profit or Praise. I never suffer a Word to pass that may look like Reflection, or possibly give the least Offence even to those who are most ready to take it. So that, I hope, I may with Justice pronounce myself an Author perfectly blameless; against whom the Tribes of Answerers, Considerers, Observers, Reflecters, Detecters, Remarkers, will never be able to find Matter for exercising their Talents.

I confess, it was whispered to me, that I was bound in Duty as a Subject of *England,* to have given in a Memorial to a Secretary of State, at my first coming over; because, whatever Lands are discovered by a Subject, belong to the Crown. But I doubt, whether our Conquests in the Countries I treat of, would be as easy as those of *Ferdinando Cortez* over the naked *Americans.* The *Lilliputians* I think, are hardly worth the Charge of a Fleet and Army to reduce them; and I question whether it might be prudent or safe to attempt the *Brobdingnagians:* Or, whether an *English* Army would be much at their Ease with the Flying Island over their Heads. The *Houyhnhnms,* indeed, appear not to be so well prepared for War, a Science to which they are perfect Strangers, and especially against missive Weapons. However, supposing myself to be a Minister of State, I could never give my Advice for invading them. Their Prudence, Unanimity, Unacquaintedness with Fear, and their Love of their Country would amply supply all Defects in the military Art. Imagine twenty Thousand of them breaking into the Midst of an *European* Army, confounding the Ranks, overturning the Carriages, battering the Warriors Faces into Mummy, by terrible Yerks from their hinder Hoofs: For they would well deserve the Character given to *Augustus; Recalcitrat undique tutus.* But instead of Proposals for conquering that magnanimous Nation, I rather wish they were in a Capacity or Disposition to send a sufficient Number of their Inhabitants for civilizing *Europe;* by teaching us the first Principles of Honour, Justice, Truth, Temperance, publick Spirit, Fortitude, Chastity, Friendship, Benevolence, and Fidelity. The *Names* of all which Virtues are still retained among us in most Languages, and are to be met with in modern as well as ancient Authors; which I am able to assert from my own small Reading. [240]

But, I had another Reason which made me less forward to enlarge his Majesty's Dominions by my Discoveries: To say the Truth, I had conceived a few Scruples with relation to the distributive Justice of Princes upon those Occasions. For Instance, A Crew of Pyrates are driven by a Storm they know not whither; at length a Boy discovers Land from the Top-mast; they go on Shore to rob and plunder; they see an harmless People, are entertained with Kindness, they give the Country a new Name, they take formal Possession of it for the King, they set up a rotten Plank or a Stone for a Memorial, they murder two or three Dozen of the Natives, bring away a Couple more by Force for a Sample, return home, and get their Pardon. Here commences a new Dominion acquired with a Title by *Divine Right*. Ships are sent with the first Opportunity; the Natives driven out or destroyed, their Princes tortured to discover their Gold; a free Licence given to all Acts of Inhumanity and Lust; the Earth reeking with the Blood of its Inhabitants: And this execrable Crew of Butchers employed in so pious an Expedition, is a *modern Colony* sent to convert and civilize an idolatrous and barbarous People.

But this Description, I confess, doth by no means affect the *British* Nation, who may be an Example to the whole World for their Wisdom, Care, and Justice in planting Colonies; their Liberal Endowments for the Advancement of Religion and Learning; their Choice of devout and able Pastors to propagate *Christianity;* their Caution in stocking their Provinces with People of sober Lives and Conversations from this the Mother Kingdom; their strict Regard to the Distribution of Justice, in supplying the Civil Administration through all their Colonies with Officers of the greatest Abilities, utter Strangers to Corruption: And to crown all, by sending the most vigilant and virtuous Governors, who have no other Views than the Happiness of the People over whom they preside, and the Honour of the King their Master.

But, as those Countries which I have described do not appear to have a Desire of being conquered, and enslaved, murdered or driven out by Colonies; nor abound either in Gold, Silver, Sugar or Tobacco; I did humbly conceive they were by no Means proper Objects of our Zeal, our Valour, or our Interest. However, if those whom it may concern, think fit to be of another Opinion, I am ready to depose, when I shall be lawfully called, That no *European* did ever visit these Countries before me. I mean, if the Inhabitants ought to be believed. [241]

But, as to the Formality of taking Possession in my Sovereign's Name, it never came once into my Thoughts; and if it had, yet as my Affairs then stood, I should perhaps in point of Prudence and Self-Preservation, have put it off to a better Opportunity.

Having thus answered the *only* Objection that can be raised against me as a Traveller; I here take a final Leave of my Courteous Readers, and return to enjoy my own Speculations in my little Garden at *Redriff;* to apply those excellent Lessons of Virtue which I learned among the *Houyhnhnms;* to instruct the *Yahoos* of my own Family as far as I shall find them docible Animals; to behold my Figure often in a Glass, and thus if possible habituate my self by Time to tolerate the Sight of a human Creature: To lament the Brutality of *Houyhnhnms* in my own Country, but always treat their Persons with Respect, for the Sake of my noble Master, his Family, his Friends, and the whole *Houyhnhnm* Race, whom these of ours have the Honour to resemble in all their Lineaments, however their Intellectuals came to degenerate.

I began last Week to permit my Wife to sit at Dinner with me, at the farthest End of a long Table; and to answer (but with the utmost Brevity) the few Questions I asked her. Yet the Smell of a *Yahoo* continuing very offensive, I always keep my Nose well stopt with Rue, Lavender, or Tobacco-Leaves. And although it be hard for a Man late in Life to remove old Habits; I am not altogether out of Hopes in some Time to suffer a Neighbour *Yahoo* in my Company, without the Apprehensions I am yet under of his Teeth or his Claws.

My Reconcilement to the *Yahoo*-kind in general might not be so difficult, if they would be content with those Vices and Follies only which Nature hath entitled them to. I am not in the least provoked at the Sight of a Lawyer, a Pick-pocket, a Colonel, a Fool, a Lord, a Gamester, a Politician, a Whoremunger, a Physician, an Evidence, a Suborner, an Attorney, a Traytor, or the like: This is all according to the due Course of Things: But, when I behold a Lump of Deformity, and Diseases both in Body and Mind, smitten with *Pride*, it immediately breaks all the Measures of my Patience; neither shall I be ever able to comprehend how such an Animal and such a Vice could tally together. The wise and virtuous *Houyhnhnms*, who abound in all Excellencies that can adorn a rational Creature, have no Name for this Vice in their Language, which hath no Terms to express any thing that is evil, except those whereby they describe the [242] detestable Qualities of their *Yahoos;* among which they were not able to distinguish this of Pride, for want of thoroughly understanding Human Nature, as it sheweth it self in other Countries, where that Animal presides. But I, who had more Experience, could plainly observe some Rudiments of it among the wild *Yahoos.*

But the *Houyhnhnms,* who live under the Government of Reason, are no more proud of the good Qualities they possess, than I should be for not wanting a Leg or an Arm, which no Man in his Wits would boast of, although he must be miserable without them. I dwell the longer upon this Subject from the Desire I have to make the Society of an *English Yahoo* by any Means not insupportable; and therefore I here intreat those who have any Tincture of this absurd Vice, that they will not presume to appear in my Sight. [243]

FINIS.

EVALUATIONS AND
INTERPRETATIONS

from *Remarks on the Life and Writings of Dr. Jonathan Swift*

JOHN BOYLE, fifth Earl of Orrery

It is with great reluctance, I shall make some remarks on Gulliver's voyage to the Houyhnhnms. In this last part of his imaginary travels, Swift has indulged a misanthropy that is intolerable. The representation which he has given us of human nature, must terrify, and even debase the mind of the reader who views it. His sallies of wit and humour lose all their force, nothing remaining but a melancholy, and disagreeable impression: and, as I have said to you, on other parts of his works, we are disgusted, not entertained; we are shocked, not instructed by the fable. I should therefore chuse to take no notice of his Yahoos, did I not think it necessary to assert the vindication of human nature, and thereby, in some measure, to pay my duty to the great author of [184] our species, who has created us in a very fearful, and a very wonderful manner.

We are composed of a mind, and of a body, intimately united, and mutually affecting each other. Their operations indeed are entirely different. Whether the immortal spirit, that enlivens this fine machine, is originally of a superior nature in various bodies (which, I own, seems most consistent and agreeable to the scale and order of beings) or, whether the difference depends on a symmetry, or peculiar structure of the organs combined with it, is beyond my reach to determine. It is evidently certain, that the body is curiously formed with

From *Remarks on the Life and Writings of Dr. Jonathan Swift, Dean of St. Patrick's, Dublin, in a Series of Letters from John, Earl of Orrery, to his Son, the Honourable Hamilton Boyle* (London, 1752), Letter XV, pp. 184–191.

proper organs to delight, and such as are adapted to all the necessary uses of life. The spirit animates the whole; it guides the natural appetites, and confines them within just limits. But, the natural force of this spirit is often immersed in matter; and the mind becomes subservient to passions, which it [185] ought to govern and direct. Your friend Horace, although of the Epicurean doctrine, acknowledges this truth, where he says, *Atque affigit humo divinae particulam aurae.*

It is no less evident, that this immortal spirit has an independent power of acting, and, when cultivated in a proper manner, seemingly quits the corporeal frame within which it is imprisoned, and soars into higher, and more spacious regions; where, with an energy, which I had almost said was divine, it ranges among those heavenly bodies, that, in this lower world, are scarce visible to our eyes; and we can at once explain the distance, magnitude, and velocity of the planets, and can foretell, even to a degree of minuteness, the particular time when a comet will return, and when the sun will be eclipsed in the next century. These powers certainly [186] evince the dignity of human nature, and the surprising effects of the immaterial spirit within us, which, in so confined a state, can thus disengage itself from the fetters of matter. It is from this pre-eminence of the soul over the body, that we are enabled to view the exact order, and curious variety of different beings; to consider, and cultivate the natural productions of the earth; and to admire, and imitate the wise benevolence which reigns throughout the whole system of the universe. It is from hence, that we form moral laws for our conduct. From hence, we delight in copying that great original, who, in his essence, is utterly incomprehensible, but, in his influence, is powerfully apparent to every degree of his creation. From hence too, we perceive a real beauty in virtue, and a distinction between good and evil. Virtue acts with the utmost generosity, and with no view to her own advantage: while vice, like a glutton, feeds herself [187] enormously, and then is willing to disgorge the nauseous offals of her feast. But I shall wander too far, especially as I flatter myself, that your mind is so good, and so unprejudiced, that you will more easily feel, than I can illustrate, the truth of these assertions.

Swift deduces his observations from wrong principles; for, in his land of Houyhnhnms, he considers the soul and body in their most degenerate, and uncultivated state; the former as a slave to the appetites of the latter. He seems insensible of the surprising mechanism, and beauty of every part of the human composition. He forgets the fine description which Ovid gives of mankind: *Os homini sublime dedit, coelumque tueri Jussit, et erectos ad fidera tollere vultus.*

In painting Yahoos he becomes one himself. Nor is the picture, which he draws of the Houyhnhnms, inviting or [188] amusing. It wants both light and shade to adorn it. It is cold and insipid. We there view the pure instincts of brutes, unassisted by any knowledge of letters, acting within their own narrow sphere, merely for their immediate preservation. They are incapable of doing wrong, therefore they act right. It is surely a very low character given to creatures, in whom the author would insinuate some degree of reason, that they act inoffensively, when they have neither the motive nor the power to act otherwise. Their virtuous qualities are only negative. Swift himself, amidst all his irony, must have confessed, that to moderate our passions, to extend our munificence to others, to enlarge our understanding, and to raise our idea of the Almighty by contemplating his works, is not only the business, but often the practice, and the study of the human mind. It is too certain, that no one individual has ever possessed every [189] qualification and excellence: however such an assemblage of different virtues, may still be collected from different persons, as are sufficient to place the dignity of human nature in an amiable, and exalted station. We must lament indeed the many instances of those who degenerate, or go astray from the end and intention of their being. The true source of this depravity is often owing to the want of education, to the false indulgence of parents, or to some other bad causes, which are constantly prevalent in every nation. Many of these errors are finely ridiculed in the foregoing parts of this romance: but the voyage to the Houyhnhnms is a real insult upon mankind.

I am heartily tired of this last part of Gulliver's travels, and am glad, that, having exhausted all my observations on this disagreeable subject, I may finish my letter; especially as the conclusion of it naturally turns my thoughts from Yahoos, to one of the dearest pledges I have [190] upon earth, yourself: to whom I am a most

Affectionate Father,

Orrery [191]

from *An Essay upon the Life, Writings, and Character of Dr. Jonathan Swift*

DEANE SWIFT

I have been told that some others, beside the grand remarker [John Boyle, fifth Earl of Orrery] upon the works of Dr. Swift, have thought proper to censure Gulliver's voyage to the Houyhnhnms. But whether indeed their animadversions [218] proceeded from the infirmity of their judgment, or from some Yahoo depravity in their own nature, I shall not vouchsafe to enquire; as the daily occurrences of this wretched world prove, illustrate, and confirm all the sarcasms of the Doctor. Shall we praise the excellent moralist, the humorous Hogarth, for exposing midnight revels, debaucheries, and a thousand other vices and follies of humankind, in a series of hieroglyphicks, suited to the improvement and the correction of the wild, the gay, the frolick, and the extravagant? And shall we condemn a preacher of righteousness, for exposing under the character of a nasty unteachable Yahoo the deformity, the blackness, the filthiness, and corruption of those hellish, abominable vices, which inflame the wrath of God against the children of disobedience; and subject them without repentance, that is, without a thorough change of life and practice, to everlasting perdition? Ought a preacher of righteousness; ought a watchman of the Christian faith, (who is accountable for his talents,

From *An Essay upon the Life, Writings, and Character of Dr. Jonathan Swift* by Deane Swift (London, 1755), pp. 218–221.

and obliged to warn the innocent, as well as terrify the wicked and the prophane) to hold his peace, like a dumb dog that cannot bark when avarice, fraud, cheating, violence, rapine, extortion, cruelty, oppression, tyranny, rancour, envy, malice, detraction, hatred, revenge, murder, [219] whoredom, adultery, lasciviousness, bribery, corruption, pimping, lying, perjury, subornation, treachery, ingratitude, gaming, flattery, drunkenness, gluttony, luxury, vanity, effeminacy, cowardice, pride, impudence, hypocrisy, infidelity, blasphemy, idolatry, sodomy, and innumerable other vices are as epidemical as the pox, and many of them the notorius characteristicks of the bulk of humankind? I would ask these mighty softeners; these kind pretenders to benevolence; these hollow charity-mongers; what is their real opinion of the Old Serpent, which, like a roaring lion, traverseth the globe, seeking whom he may devour? Was he not created by the Almighty pure, faultless, intelligent? But is there now throughout the whole system of created existences, any Beast, any Yahoo, any Tyrant so vile, so base, so corrupted: And whence originally proceeded the change? Was it not from the abuse of that freedom, without which no created Intelligence can be reputed faithful, wise, brave, or virtuous, in the eyes of his Creator? And surely, if this once great, once glorious spirit hath been reduced for many thousands of ages, for aught we know to the contrary, below all the several gradations of created beings, whether intelligent, animal, or insensible; and exposed to the fury of that avenging, although merciful God, who is the fountain [220] of all wisdom, goodness, and virtue; are we not to conclude by an exact parity of reason, that every moral agent is equally accountable to God for that degree of intelligence and perfection, which determine the nature of his existence? And upon this very principle, which cannot be denied without running into the last of absurdities; and which in fact is the reasoning of St. Peter throughout his whole second chapter of his second epistle; that creature man, that glorious creature man, is deservedly more contemptible than a brute beast, when he flies in the face of his Creator by enlisting under the banner of the enemy; and perverts that reason, which was designed to have been the glory of his nature, even the directing spirit of his life and demeanour, to the vilest, the most execrable, the most hellish purposes. And this manifestly appears to be the groundwork of the whole satyre contained in the voyage to the Houyhnhnms. [221]

from *The Life of the Rev. Dr. Jonathan Swift*

THOMAS SHERIDAN

The last charge, as before mentioned, against Swift, and which has gained most general credit, is that of perfect misanthropy; and this is chiefly founded upon his supposed satyr on human nature, in the picture he has drawn of the Yahoos. This opinion has been so universally adopted by almost all who have read *Gulliver's Travels,* that to controvert it would be supposed to act in opposition to the common sense and reason of mankind. And yet I will undertake to overthrow it, by appealing to that very reason and common sense, upon which they suppose it to be founded. I shall only beg of my reader that he would lay aside for a while any prepossession he may have entertained of that kind, and candidly examine what I shall advance in support of the opposite side of the question; and if he finds the arguments there laid down unanswerable, that he will not obstinately persist in error, by whatever numbers it may be supported, but ingenuously yield to conviction. The position I mean to prove is, that the whole apologue of the Houyhnhnms and [432] Yahoos, far from being intended as a debasement of human nature, if rightly understood, is evidently designed to shew in what the true dignity and perfection of man's nature consists, and to point out the way by which it may be attained.

In order to do this, let us first see with what design the fourth book of the Travels was written. In the first three books he has given

From *The Life of the Rev. Dr. Jonathan Swift, Dean of St. Patrick's, Dublin* by Thomas Sheridan (London, 1787), Second Edition, pp. 432–437.

various views of the different vices, follies, and absurdities of mankind, not without some mixture of good qualities, of virtue and wisdom, though in a small proportion to the others, as they are to be found in life. In his last book, he meant to exhibit two new portraits; one, of pure unmixed vice; the other, of perfect unadulterated virtue. In order that the native deformity of the one, might excite in us a deeper abhorrence of evil; and the resplendent charms of the other, allure us to what is good. To represent these to us in sensible forms, he cloaths the one with the body of a man; the other, with that of a horse. Between these two he divides the qualities of the human mind, taking away the rational soul from the Yahoo, and transferring it to the Houyhnhnm. To the Yahoo he leaves all the passions and evil propensities of man's nature, to be exerted without check or controul, as in the case of all other animals. The rational soul in the Houyhnhnm, acts unerringly as by instinct; it intuitively perceives what is right, and necessarily acts up to the dictates of reason. The Yahoo, as here described, is a creature of fancy, the product of the author's brain, which never had any thing similar to it upon earth. It has no resemblance to man, but in the make of its body, and the vicious propensities of its nature. It differs from him wholly in all the characteristical marks which distinguish man from the rest of the animal world. It has not a ray of reason, it has no speech, and it goes, like other quadrupedes, upon all [433] four. Now, as reason, speech, and walking upright on two legs, are the universal properties of the human race, even in the most savage nations, which peculiarly mark their superiority over brutes, how, in the name of Heaven, has it come to pass, that by almost all who have read Gulliver, the Yahoos have been considered as beings of the human species, and the odious picture drawn of them, as intended to vilify and debase our nature? But it is evident from the whole account given of this creature of his fancy, that the author intended it should be considered as mere beast, of a new species; for he has not only deprived it of all the characteristical distinctions of man before recited, but has superadded some material differences even in his bodily organs and powers, sufficient to distinguish it from the human race. He says,— "They climbed high trees as nimbly as a squirrel, for they had strong extended claws before and behind, terminating in sharp points, and hooked." Now it is well known, that the human nails, when suffered to grow to any considerable length, never assume that shape, and unless pared, disable the hands from discharging their office. He says in another place,—"They are prodigiously nimble from their infancy." This is directly opposite to the nature of the children of men, who are the most helpless in infancy, and the slowest in arriving at any degree of strength or agility, of all living creatures. Indeed it was necessary to the author's end, that of shewing the vicious qualities of man's nature in their pure unmixed state, that the creature in whom they were placed should be a mere brute, governed as all others are by an irresistible instinct, without any controul from a superior faculty; and [434] accordingly he seems to have thrown in these additional circumstances to distinguish it from any thing human. At the same time it was also necessary to give this creature the human form, in order to bring the lesson home to man, by having the vicious part of his nature reflected back to him from one in his own shape; for in the form of any other creature, he would not think himself at all concerned in it. Yet it is on account of its bodily form only, represented as it is in so hideous a light, that the pride of man was alarmed, and made him blind to the author's design, so as to charge him with an intention of degrading and vilifying the whole of human nature below that of brutes. I have already shewn that the whole of human nature has no concern in what is related of this creature, as he is entirely deprived of all the characteristic properties of man which distinguish him from, and elevate him above all other animals. I have also shewn, that even his body, however resembling in outward form, is not the body of a man, but of a beast. In the first place it is prone, like all other beasts, which never was the case in any human creature, *Os homini sublime dedit, coelumque tuert Jussit*. In the next, he has long hooked claws, which enable him to climb the highest trees with the nimbleness of a squirrel, and to dig holes in the earth for his habitation. Their faces too, as in some other tribes of animals, were all alike, being thus described: "The face of this animal indeed was flat and broad, the nose depressed, the lips large, and the mouth wide." When we consider too, that these features were never enlivened by the rational soul, nor the countenance lighted up by the benevolent sensations in man, which constitute the chief beauty of [435] the human face, but on the contrary were continually distorted by a variety of malevolent passions, we must conclude with Gulliver, that such a man-beast must be the most odious animal that ever crawled upon the face of the earth; and that his description of it, disgusting as it is, is not in the least exaggerated. At first sight they had so little resemblance to any thing human, that Gulliver mistook them for some new species of cattle belonging to the inhabitants. After having given a description of them as they appeared to him when he first saw a number of them near him, where he lay concealed behind a thicket, in order to mark their form more distinctly, he says, "So that thinking I had seen enough, full of contempt and aversion, I got up and pursued the beaten road, hoping it might direct me to the cabbin of some Indian. I had not got far, when I met one of these creatures, full in my way, and coming up directly to me. The ugly monster, when he saw me, distorted several ways every feature of his visage, and started as at an object he had never seen before; then approaching nearer, *lifted up his fore-paw,* whether out of curiosity or mischief, I could not tell: but I drew my hanger, and gave him a good blow with the flat side of it, for I durst not strike with the edge, fearing the inhabitants might be provoked against me, if they should come to know that I had killed or maimed any of *their cattle.*" And it was not till afterwards, when he had an opportunity of examining one of them more closely in his kennel, that he perceived its resemblance to the human figure. But it may be asked, to what end has such an odious animal been produced to view? The answer is obvious. The design of the author, in the whole of this apologue, is, to place before the eyes of man a picture of the two different parts of his frame, detached from each other, in order that he may the better estimate the true value of [436] each, and see the necessity there is that the one should have an absolute command over the other. In your merely animal capacity, says he to man, without reason to guide you, and actuated only by a blind instinct, I will shew you that you would be degraded below the beasts of the field. That very form, that very body, you are now so proud of, as giving you such a superiority over all other animals, I will shew you owe all their beauty, and all their greatest powers, to their being actuated by a rational soul. Let that be withdrawn, let the body be inhabited by the mind of a brute, let it be prone as theirs are, and suffered like theirs to take its natural course, without any assistance from art, you would in that case be the most deformed, as to your external appearance, the most detestable of all creatures. And with regard to your internal frame, filled with all the evil dispositions, and malignant passions of mankind, you would be the most miserable of beings, living in a continued state of internal vexation, and of hatred and warfare with each other.

On the other hand, I will shew another picture of an animal endowed with a rational soul, and acting uniformly up to the dictates of right reason. Here you may see collected all the virtues, all the great qualities, which dignify man's nature, and constitute the happiness of his life. What is the natural inference to be drawn from these two different representations? Is it not evidently a lesson to mankind, warning them not to suffer the animal part to be predominant in them, lest they resemble the vile Yahoo, and fall into vice and misery; but to emulate the noble and generous Houyhnhnm, by cultivating the rational faculty to the utmost; which will lead them to a life of virtue and happiness. [437]

from the Introduction to *Gulliver's Travels* in *The Works of Jonathan Swift*

SIR WALTER SCOTT

The Voyage to the Land of Houyhnhnms, is, beyond contest, the basest and most unworthy part of the work. It holds mankind forth in a light too degrading for contemplation, and which, if admitted, would justify or palliate the worst vices, by exhibiting them as natural attributes, and rendering reformation from a state of such base depravity a task too desperate to be attempted. As no good could possibly be attained by the exhibition of so loathsome a picture of humanity, as it may even tend to great evil, by removing every motive for philanthropy, the publication has been justly considered as a stain upon the character of the ingenious author. Allowance, however, is to be made for the soured and disgusted state of Swift's mind, which doubtless was even then influenced by the first impressions of that incipient mental disease which, in his case, was marked by universal misanthropy, as in [10] many others by particular and individual antipathy. Even when he was plunged into total idiocy, Swift's temper continued irritable in the highest degree, however ineffectual his indignation; but while he retained mind to conceive, and ability to express, the fervour of his angry passions, their explosion was as powerful as violent. We are accordingly, frequently

From *The Works of Jonathan Swift*, edited by Sir Walter Scott (London, 1883), Second Edition, Vol. XI, pp. 10–11. The first edition was published in 1816.

compelled to admire the force of his talents, even while thus un-
worthily employed, in exposing the worst parts of our nature with
the art of an anatomist dissecting a mangled and half-putrid carcase.
As the previous departments of the satire were levelled against the
court of George I, against statesmen, and against philosophers, the
wider sweep of this last division comprehends human nature in every
stage and variety, and, with an industry as malicious as the author's
knowledge of life is extensive, holds it up to execration in all.

It is some consolation to remark, that the fiction on which this
libel on human nature rests, is, in every respect, gross and improbable,
and, far from being entitled to the praise due to the management of
the two first parts, is inferior in plan even to the third. The Voyage
to Laputa, if we except the flying island, which has often been regarded as an unnecessary violation of the laws of nature, the picture
of the Struldbruggs, and the powers of the governor of Balnibarbi,
(from both of which an excellent moral is extracted,) falls within
the rank of such ideal communities as the republic of Plato, and the
Utopia of Sir Thomas More. But the state of the Houyhnhnms is
not only morally but physically impossible, and, as Dr. Beattie has
remarked, self-contradictory, also, since these animals are represented
with attributes inconsistent with their natural structure. We may
grant to the framer of an apologue that beasts may be endued with
reason, but we can hardly conceive a horse riding in a carriage, and
much less milking cows, building houses, and performing other functions of the same kind, to which its limbs are not adapted. This circumstance is sufficient of itself to refute the reflections thrown upon
the conformation of the human body, since the meanest and most
simple of the works which our configuration enables us to execute,
cannot, without the grossest violation of probability, be imputed to
almost any species of the inferior creation. [11]

from *A History of Eighteenth Century Literature*

EDMUND GOSSE

But in all these miscellaneous excursions there is little or nothing which displays to us the darker side of Swift's genius. That side is, however, exemplified to excess in the final part, the Voyage to the Country of the Houyhnhnms. It is difficult not to believe that this was written during the last illness of Stella, when Swift was aware that his best companion was certainly leaving him, and when that remorse which he could not but feel for his conduct to the woman who had so long loved him was turning what milk remained in his nature to gall. In the summer of 1726 the loss of Stella's conversation made him, he tells us, weary of life, and he fled from Ireland in a horror lest he should be a witness of her end. Delany tells us that from the time of her death, and probably from a few months earlier, Swift's character and temper underwent a change. His vertigo became chronic, and so did his misanthropy, and it seems probable that the first literary expression of his rage and despair was the awful satire of the Yahoos. It was with the horrible satisfaction of disease that Swift formed a story which could enable him to describe men as being, though "with some appearance of cunning, and the strongest disposition to mischief, yet the most unteachable of all brutes," and there is something which suggests a brain not wholly under control in the very machinery of this part of the romance. In Lilliput and in Brobdingnag we are struck by the ingenious harmony of

From *A History of Eighteenth Century Literature* by Edmund Gosse (New York: The Macmillan Company, 1889), pp. 161–162.

the whole design, there being no detail which is not readily credible if we admit the possibility of the scheme; but among the Houyhnhnms probability is ruthlessly sacrificed to the wild pleasure the author takes in trampling human pride in the mire of his sarcasm. Of the horrible foulness of this [161] satire on the Yahoos enough will have been said when it is admitted that it banishes from decent households a fourth part of one of the most brilliant and delightful of English books. [162]

from *English Humourists*
of the Eighteenth Century

WILLIAM MAKEPEACE THACKERAY

But the best stroke of humour, if there be a best in that abounding book, is that where Gulliver, in the unpronounceable country describes his parting from his master the horse. "I took," he says, "a second leave of my master, [34] but as I was going to prostrate myself to kiss his hoof, he did me the honour to raise it gently to my mouth. I am [35] not ignorant how much I have been censured for mentioning this last particular. Detractors are pleased to think it improbable that so illustrious a person should descend to give so great a mark of distinction to a creature so inferior as I. Neither am I ignorant how apt some travellers are to boast of extraordinary favours they have received. But if these censurers were better acquainted with the noble and courteous disposition of the Houyhnhnms they would soon change their opinion."

The surprise here, the audacity of circumstantial [36] evidence, the astounding gravity of the speaker, who is not ignorant how much he has been censured, the nature of the favour conferred, and the respectful exultation at the receipt of it, are surely complete; it is truth topsy-turvy, entirely logical and absurd.

As for the humour and conduct of this famous fable, I suppose there is no person who reads but must admire; as for the moral, I think it horrible, shameful, unmanly, blasphemous; and giant and great as this Dean is, I say we should hoot him. Some of this audience may

From *English Humourists of the Eighteenth Century* by William Makepeace Thackeray (New York, 1853), pp. 34–38.

not have read the last part of Gulliver, and to such I would recall the advice of the venerable Mr. Punch to persons about to marry, and say "Don't." When Gulliver first lands among the Yahoos, the naked howling wretches clamber up trees and assault him, and he describes himself as "almost stifled with the filth which fell about him." The reader of the fourth part of Gulliver's Travels is like the hero himself in this instance. It is Yahoo language; a monster gibbering shrieks and gnashing imprecations against mankind,—tearing down all shreds of modesty, past all sense of manliness and shame; filthy in word, filthy in thought, furious, raging, obscene.

And dreadful it is to think that Swift knew the tendency of his creed—the fatal rocks towards which his logic desperately drifted. That last part of Gulliver is only a consequence of what has gone before; and the worthlessness of all mankind, the pettiness, cruelty, pride, imbecility, the general vanity, the foolish pretension, the mock greatness, the pompous dullness, the mean aims, the base successes —all these were present to him; it was with the din of these curses of the world, blasphemies against Heaven, shrieking [37] in his ears, that he began to write his dreadful allegory—of which the meaning is that man is utterly wicked, desperate, and imbecile, and his passions are so monstrous, and his boasted powers so mean, that he is and deserves to be the slave of brutes, and ignorance is better than his vaunted reason. What had this man done? What secret remorse was rankling at his heart, what fever was boiling in him, that he should see all the world blood-shot? We view the world with our own eyes, each of us; and we make from within us the world we see. A weary heart gets no gladness out of sunshine; a selfish man is sceptical about friendship, as a man with no ear does not care for music. A frightful self-consciousness it must have been, which looked on mankind so darkly through those eyes of Swift. [38]

from On the Philosophical
Background of *Gulliver's Travels*

T. O. WEDEL

In the world of political thought, the clash between old and new is
perhaps nowhere so concretely exhibited as in the contrasting theories
regarding the state of nature. For not in *Gulliver* only are Yahoos
set over against Houyhnhnms. In fact it looks like too simple a discovery to point out that in the last voyage of the *Travels* we have,
designedly or not, Hobbes contrasted with Locke. And yet the parallel holds good suprisingly well. Men in Hobbes' state of nature, like
Swift's Yahoos, are "in that condition which is called war; and such
a war, as is of every man against every [442] man . . . with no arts,
no letters, no society, and, which is worst of all, continual fear of
violent danger; and the life of man, solitary, poor, nasty, brutish,
and short." [31] And while Hobbes' brevity of description with regard
to his state of war prevents elaboration of the parallel, the corresponding similarity between Locke and Swift is certainly tempting.
Men in Locke's state of nature, like the Houyhnhnms, are rational
creatures, "living together according to reason, without a common
superior,"—in a state of liberty without license, every one admin-
istering the laws of nature for himself, laws of temperance and
mutual benevolence. [32] The relation of Swift to Hobbes and to Locke
is a subject for separate investigation. On the whole, I think (and

Reprinted from *Studies in Philology*, XXIII (October 1926), 442–450. By
permission.
[31] Hobbes, *Leviathan*, Part I, chap. 13.
[32] Locke, *Two Treatises on Government*, Book II, Chaps. 2, 3.

Swift's political writings would furnish evidence in abundance), he stands nearer to Hobbes. In *Gulliver's Travels*, however, Swift is clearly neither Hobbes nor Locke. Gulliver is neither Yahoo nor Houyhnhnm. He cannot attain to the rational felicity of the Houyhnhnms. Neither has he sunk to the level of the Yahoos, though this is a doubtful advantage. He lacks the strength of a healthy animal, and his glimmering of reason has unhappily burdened him with responsibility of conscience.

Indeed, if Swift's own hints regarding the meaning of his book are heeded, it is in the contrast between Yahoo and Houyhnhnm that his main thesis lies hid. Gulliver, occupying a position between the two, part beast, part reason, is Swift's allegorical picture of the dual nature of man. He is not Houyhnhnm, *animal rationale*, nor is he Yahoo. He is *rationis capax:* One could apply to *Gulliver's Travels* a passage of Cicero, quoted with approval by both St. Augustine and Bayle: "Nature has been to man not a mother, but a step-mother— sending him into the world naked, frail, and infirm, toiling under a burden of care, fearful, slothful, and given over to lust, but not without a spark of divine reason." [33]

Animal rationale—animal rationis capax! Swift's somewhat [443] scholastic distinction turns out, in the light of seventeenth century thought, to be by no means scholastic. It symbolizes, in fact, the chief intellectual battle of the age. Swift seems to have seen clearly enough that in assaulting man's pride in reason, he was attacking the new optimism at its very root. His enmity to rationalistic dogmatising was the one enduring intellectual passion of his life. It animates his orthodoxy in his sermon on the Trinity; it prompts the dangerous laughter of *The Tale of a Tub;* it explains his merciless satire of the Deists.

The phrase *animal rationale* can be traced at least as far back as Seneca [34] and ancient Stoicism. This fact alone explains much. For it is precisely the circle of ideas represented by Stoicism, however changed in form through centuries of filtration, which the seventeenth century, like the fifth, was still finding it difficult to assimilate. Stoicism has ever been associated with optimism. It is the Stoic who

[33] "Homo non ut a matre, sed ut a noverca natura editus est in vitam, corpore nudo, et fragili, et infirmo, animo autem anxio ad molestias, humili ad timores, molli ad labores, prono ad libidines, in quo tamen in esset tamquam obrutus quidam divinus ignis ingenii et mentis." See Bayle, *Dictionnaire*, article "Ovid," Remark E.

[34] Seneca, *Epist.*, 41, 8.

worships pride. And despite the noble appeal of its ethical heroism, —or perhaps one had better say because of it—Stoicism has constituted one of Christianity's gravest dangers. *Corruptio optimi pessima est.* No Christian in the Augustinian sense could have said with Epictetus: "I was never hindered in my will or compelled against my wish. . . . Who can hinder me against my own judgments, or put compulsion on me? I am as safe as Zeus." [35] The Stoic faith in a beneficent deity and a rational world robbed the universe of evil. To follow nature was to obey God and reason. The wise man, to be sure, had to conquer his passions; but the passions themselves were merely wrong opinion. The Stoic was still master of his fate.

It was Stoicism in the form of the Pelagian heresy against which St. Augustine threw the whole weight of his eloquence in the last great doctrinal war of his career. Man for Pelagius, too, was not by nature evil. "For they think," so St. Augustine defines the belief of his enemies, "that, by the strength of their own will, they will fulfill the commands of the law; and wrapped up in their pride, they are not converted to assisting grace." [36] Conceive [444] of God as goodness and benevolence, of nature as His creation, include man in nature, let the myth of the Fall imply, as it did for Locke, merely a legal death penalty laid upon otherwise innocent descendants of Adam, who are rational beings, free to choose good and evil, and you have the Pelagian heresy.[37]

Of the popularity of Stoicism in this period there can be no doubt. According to Strowski,[38] the author oftenest reprinted in the first half of the seventeenth century was Du Vair, whose *Philosophie Morale des Stoïques* was one of the chief Stoic texts, together with a similar compendium of Justus Lipsius. Coming to the fore by way of translation and paraphrase, Stoicism, as I shall try to show a little later, soon suffered a sea-change, and was destined in its new form, to conquer the world. For the moment, however, its victory was delayed, though the warfare against it was confused, and though many

[35] Epictetus, *Discourses*, IV, 1. 12.

[36] Augustine, *Anti-Pelagian Writings* (*Nicene and Post-Nicene Fathers*, ed. Schaff, New York, 1902), p. 412.

[37] The history of Stoicism in the seventeenth and eighteenth centuries has never been written. I am inclined to think that the best guide is still Sainte-Beuve's *Port Royal*. See also Strowski, *Pascal et son Temps*, Paris, 1907; Lanson's article on Descartes in *Rev. de Mét. et Morale*, 1896, pp. 517 ff.; Busson, *Les Sources du Rationalisme dans la Renaissance* (Paris, 1922); Zanta, *La Renaissance du Stoicisme au Seizième Siècle*, Paris, 1914.

[38] Strowski, *Pascal et son Temps*, I, 106.

a skirmish was fought on secondary issues. The passions, for one thing, found defenders against the Stoic attitude of disdain. Positivistic observers of man simply denied that man was ruled by reason. Balzac [39] ridicules the Stoics as "that inhuman sect which, in cutting off from man his passions and his feelings, desires to rob him of half of himself. In place of having created a wise man, the Stoics have merely created a statue." Or as Swift himself puts it in one of his maxims: "The Stoical scheme of supplying our wants by lopping off our desires is like cutting off our feet, when we want shoes." [40] La Rochefoucauld, man of the world, sees human nature as merely the dupe of the ruling passion of self-love. As the century advances, optimism itself takes to throwing stones at the Stoics, actually defending the passions as good in themselves. Sénault writes a treatise [41] proving the Stoic [445] wise man a fiction and the passions useful in the moral life. A similar defense is found in the *Enchiridion Ethicum* of the Cambridge Platonist, Henry More. The Augustinian tradition, of course, is against the Stoics. Jansen's *Augustinus* is an attack upon them; so is Arnauld's *Fréquente Communion*.[42] And Pascal, dualist always, accepts neither the man of the world's cynical acceptance of man as a creature of the passions, nor the Stoic's pride in having conquered them. It is he who expresses the conviction of the mystic: "The heart has its reasons, which the reason knows not of." [43] Machiavellians, Epicureans, and Christians are at one in laughing at the Stoic's vain pretensions that the passions can be conquered, and that the will is free.

Combatants of divergent loyalties again united in attacking Stoic rationalism itself—Montaigne, Bayle, Pascal: Epicurean, sceptic, and Christian. Montaigne indeed may be said to be all three in one. And to understand Swift's own position, Montaigne is of particular importance. The best commentary on *Gulliver's Travels* is the great *Apologie de Raymond Sébonde*. According to Busson's recent study of rationalism in the Renaissance, Montaigne sums up in popular form the scepticism of the preceding centuries of enlightenment. Now the rationalism of the Renaissance differed from that of the eighteenth century precisely in that it was a sceptical balancing of

[39] Strowski, *op. cit.*, I, 104.
[40] Swift, *Thoughts on Various Subjects* (*Prose Works*, I, 277).
[41] Sénault, *De l'Usage des Passions*, Paris, 1641.
[42] Strowski, *op. cit.*, I, 124.
[43] Pascal, *Thoughts* (Temple Classics), No. 277.

reason against faith, including reason itself among the objects of doubt. *Que sais je?* asks Montaigne. What do I know? Montaigne's *Apologie,* like *Gulliver's Travels* is a scathing attack upon Stoic pride. Man is placed on a level almost lower than that of the dog and the horse. In fact Montaigne's primitivism, imitated by Swift—his disgust with the pompous boasts of civilization—is a good deal softened in *Gulliver's Travels*.[44] [446] Montaigne mistrusts dogmatic theology on the one hand, man's reason on the other. Hence, like Bayle a century later, he falls back on faith.[45] It is absurd for man, so Montaigne closes his *Apologie,* to attempt to raise himself above humanity. "For to make the handful bigger than the hand, and the armful larger than the arm, and to hope to stride farther than our legs can reach, is impossible and monstrous; or that man should rise above himself and humanity; for he cannot see but with his own eyes, nor seize but with his power. He shall rise if God will extraordinarily lend him His hand; he shall rise by abandoning and renouncing his own proper means, and by suffering himself to be raised and elevated by means purely celestial. It belongs to our Christian faith, and not to his stoical virtue, to pretend to that divine and miraculous metamorphosis." And however mystifying Montaigne's philosophy may be when viewed as a whole, it is, I think, a gross misunderstanding of the role which scepticism has played in religion to accuse either Montaigne or Bayle of entire bad faith. Upon the twin pillars of scepticism and the corruption of human nature Pascal built his own *apologie,* as did Newman in more recent times his defense of the Catholic church. Newman merely echoes Montaigne when he says: "Quarry the granite rock with razors, or moor the vessel with a thread

[44] The problem of Swift's primitivism—his admiration for the simple government of Brobdingnag and the rational Utopia of the Houyhnhnms—is not easy of solution. In fact, the primitivistic tradition in the seventeenth century invites further investigation. Swift's position could be compared with a passage in Aristotle's *Politics* (Book 1, chap. 2): "Man, when perfected, is the best of animals, but when separated from law and justice, he is the worst of all; since armed injustice is the more dangerous, and he is equipped at birth with the arms of intelligence and with moral qualities which he may use for the worst ends. Wherefore, if he have not virtue, he is the most unruly and the most savage of animals, and the most full of lust and gluttony."

[45] See Busson, *Les Sources du Rationalisme dans la Renaissance,* Paris, 1922, p. 439: "Il [Montaigne] a seulement parcouru, à la suite des padouans, le cercle dangereux qui n'éloigne le philosophie de la foi que pour l'y ramener, le conduisant de la foi au fidéisme, du fidéisme au scepticisme, du scepticisme à la nouvelle académie, de la nouvelle académie au pyrrhonisme, et, par une brusque volteface, du pyrrhonisme à la foi."

of silk; then you may hope with such keen and delicate instruments as human knowledge and human reason to contend against those giants, the passion and the pride of man." [46]

But by the time that Swift wrote his own treatise to vex the world, scepticism and the belief in the corruption of human nature had given way to rationalism and an optimistic faith in man. The Stoic creed had suffered its sea-change. Sceptic, Epicurean, dualistic Christian had surrendered. [447]

And the founder of the new faith was no other than the father of modern philosophy, Descartes himself. To the layman, burrowing his way into the history of ideas in the seventeenth century, it is almost disconcerting to discover how all roads lead to the author of the *Discourse on Method*. Let any one, after reading Montaigne's *Apologie*, turn to Descartes' treatise on the passions and a new planet swims into his ken. For the first assumption of Descartes is precisely the Stoic faith in a beneficent God and an uncorrupted nature. A good God cannot deceive us, and our reason is from God; hence our reason is to be trusted. And while the Stoicism of Epictetus still left within man a dualism of reason and passion, this, too, is obliterated by Descartes. The passions become good. *Elles sont toutes bonnes.* Vicious and evil instincts are denied the name of passions—ingratitude, impudence, effrontery. Reversing the method of La Rochefoucauld, Descartes dissolves a bad passion into that good one which nearly resembles it. Envy, for example, becomes a praiseworthy love of distributive justice. Pride is good, except when wrongly applied. Humility is scored as evil when it persuades us that we are feeble or unable to exercise our free will. [47] Descartes' treatise on the passions does not, of course, yet picture the man of sentiment of Vauvenargues, or Rousseau; man is still decidedly *animal rationale,* master over himself like the heroes of Corneille:

> Je suis, maître du moi, comme de l'univers;
> Je le suis, je veux l'être.

[46] Newman, *Idea of a University,* Discourse V (Longman's edition, New York, 1912), p. 121.

[47] See on Descartes and Stoicism, besides Lanson's article mentioned above, Brunetière, *Jansénistes et Cartésiens* (*Études Critiques,* fourth series); Faguet, *Dix-septième Siècle.* In the *Passions de l'Âme,* one may refer particularly to such passages as article 50: "Qu' il n'y a point d'âme si faible qu'elle ne puisse, étant bien conduite, acquérir un pouvoir absolu sur ses passions," art. 62, on Envy; art. 159, on "bad" humility; art. 182, 194, 207, on ingratitude, etc., not being passions. Cf. also a letter of Descartes to Chanut, cited in Bouillier's *Hist. de la Phil. Cartésienne* (3d ed., 1868), i, 126.

But one may perhaps already see the eighteenth century in the offing—Deism, Shaftesbury, even the new anti-rationalism of Rousseau.

Though Cartesianism, as we have seen, found plentiful enemies in the seventeenth century, its ultimate victory was a foregone [448] conclusion. It became for a time the ally of orthodoxy itself. Deceived by the first-fruits of the Cartesian method, resulting as it did in a dogmatic faith in God and immortality, the Church, fifty years later, discovered that she had fallen victim to seduction. The Deism of Toland, for example, is almost pure Descartes. Eighteenth century orthodoxy, itself turned rationalist and optimist, found no weapons adequate to fight the Deists. Swift was one of few bold enough to oppose them squarely with an appeal to the weakness of human reason. Bossuet [48] still saw the danger, as did the light-hearted Bayle.[49] And Pascal rested his dualism precisely on the necessity of reconciling Montaigne and Descartes. Nowhere, perhaps, is the issue fought out in the seventeenth century more clearly expressed than in Pascal's little dialogue between himself and M. de Saci, in which Montaigne is set over against Epictetus—Montaigne, for whom man was on a level with the beasts; Epictetus (Descartes), for whom man was a god.

Clearly Swift belongs with Montaigne, La Rochefoucauld, and Bayle, among those who see man without illusion. But can he also be said to be a disciple of Pascal, the Christian? I do not think so. He did not, like Montaigne, achieve Epicurean tranquillity. He was decidedly not at ease in his inn. Neither could he feel kinship with the saints as could Pascal. Swift was not a mystic. One might apply to *Gulliver's Travels* Pascal's words: "It is dangerous to make man see too clearly his equality with the brutes, without showing him his greatness." [50] Even Swift's Utopia is the Utopia of Locke, not Plato's philosopher's kingdom, nor St. Augustine's City of God. He was a rationalist with no faith in reason. Against the language of the heart he harbored an almost Freudian complex. [449] Wesley, we

---

[48] One of the most interesting comments by a contemporary on the course of ideas in the seventeenth century is a letter of Bossuet to a disciple of Malebranche (May 21, 1687, *Works*, Paris, 1888, IX, 59): "Je vois," says Bossuet, criticizing the Cartesian philosophy from many sides, "non-seulement en ce point de la nature et de la grace, mais encore en beaucoup d'autres articles trés-importants de la religion, un grand combat se préparer contre l'Église sous le nom de la philosophie Cartésienne. . . . Car j'y trouve à la fois les inconvenients de toutes les sectes, et en particulier ceux du pélagianisme."

[49] Bayle, *Dictionnaire*, article "Hobbes," Remark E.

[50] Pascal, *Thoughts* (Temple Classics), No. 418.

may be sure, would have found him strange company. Sceptic and misanthrope, Swift fell back upon *saeva indignatio* and the established religion of his country.

Yet Swift's view of man, as Wesley perceived, and as Professor Bernbaum [51] has pointed out in our own time, is essentially the view of the classical and Christian tradition. Almost any fair definition of that tradition would absolve *Gulliver's Travels* from the charge of being an isolated example of misanthropy. I can, in truth, find no better closing comment on *Gulliver's Travels* than a passage from Sainte-Beuve's *Port Royal*.[52] It is a definition of Christianity, written by one who was not himself a Christian, who throughout his sympathetic study of seventeenth century mysticism preserved the calm detachment of the critic.

"One of the most direct ways to conceive the essence of Christianity is to accept the view of human nature as a fallen human nature, exactly as do Hobbes, La Rochefoucauld, and Machiavelli [and Sainte Beuve might surely have added Swift], those great positive observers of life. The more such a view arouses a feeling of sadness, either in a soul not too hardened, or in a soul which, in spite of being hardened, is capable of compassion and which yearns for happiness, the more it disposes and provokes such a soul to accept the extreme remedy, the remedy of hope. Such a soul will ask itself if this is the true and final view of life, and will seek a way of escape beyond this earth and this state of misery, even in the vastnesses of heaven, in the awful infinite silences. This entering by the narrow gate, this unhoped-for way of escape to safety, this is Christianity. And I speak of that which is verifiable." [450]

---

[51] *Gulliver's Travels*, ed. Bernbaum, New York, 1920, pp. x-xii.
[52] Sainte-Beuve, *Port-Royal*, Paris, 1878, III, 238.

The Rôle of Gulliver

JOHN B. MOORE

In Swift's *Gulliver's Travels,* who is Gulliver; what is he? It is easy to give two wrong answers in a breath: he is Swift in disguise; or he is, as William A. Eddy puts it, "the allegorical representative of man, as truly as Christian is in *Pilgrim's Progress.*" [1] Since Gulliver is the one figure absolutely vital to the scheme of Swift's most complicated and effective book, this figure may well be worth all the analysis anyone is able to give it, as it doubtless embodies all that Swift was capable of in artistic creation of character.

That Gulliver is not Swift himself in either intellect or disposition is abundantly certain. The Swift of 1726–27 (the period of *Gulliver's Travels*) was in his intellectual perceptions, witness his achievements up to that time in politics [2] and in literature, [3] almost as keen as any recorded human being. With Gulliver, it is a very different matter: a good sound fellow enough, but slow to seize upon even an obvious new idea; far from brilliant. And Gulliver's disposition is equally remote from Swift's. Gulliver possesses an easy good nature. He is ready of his sympathy and affection. He has a just sense of his own mediocrity (at least to begin with, he has!) and appears almost

Reprinted from *Modern Philology,* XXV (May 1928), 469–480. By permission of The University of Chicago Press. Copyright 1928 by the University of Chicago. Footnotes have been renumbered for this reprinting.

[1] William A. Eddy, *Gulliver's Travels, a Critical Study,* p. 100.

[2] From 1710 to 1713, it would be difficult to maintain that any man in England wielded greater political weapons than Swift. Ten years later (1724), Swift showed his political pre-eminence in Ireland.

[3] Before 1726, Swift had published, among many lesser things, *The Tale of a Tub,* 1704; *Battle between the Ancient and Modern Books,* 1704; *The Drapier Letters,* 1724.

humbly unobtrusive in his ways. But in Gulliver lies that most precious capacity for acquiring knowledge: slowly, surely, he learns. Swift seems, on the other hand, to be afire with impatience that comes from too clear insight. While he was undoubtedly sympathetic, his sympathy was frequently obscured to the world by his so-called arrogance. (Can a man so genuinely superior as Swift was to his associates, in many ways, be justly called arrogant for realizing his superiority?) Swift was capable of devotion to individuals such as we look for in vain in Gulliver. Swift was profoundly humorous, while Gulliver, though he may be the cause that wit sparkles in other men, is hardly witty in himself. Scorn and rage at iniquity constitute the very [469] temper of Swift. In Gulliver, these things are induced gradually, against the grain. Only that passion in readers for assuming the autobiographic can account for any confusion of Gulliver with Swift.

No more is Gulliver "the allegorical representative of man." He is not everyman, by any means, but as much an individual, almost, as Parson Adams or Squire Western (figures, both of them, somewhat typical and somewhat special). In certain ways, he surpasses the average man and, in certain other ways, he is peculiar or just different from the average without being superior or inferior. He is, to be sure, an example of a man getting knowledge or wisdom. But Swift is able for his purposes to create a human being much more perfectly appropriate and more real than a mere average or representative figure. So quietly natural is the process of creation in Swift's hands that it has scarcely been appreciated as a marvel of artistry. Gulliver is an entirely credible and probable person at the same time that he is precisely the person to enforce Swift's demonstration. Swift, obviously enough, desires to communicate his own thoughts and passions regarding human beings to the readers of his book. That is, in a general sense, one of the reasons for all efforts of an artistic sort. To infect others with his own ardent misanthropy,[4] Swift could not have chosen a more effective human instrument than Lemuel Gulliver, it would seem.

Gulliver's individual traits stand forth sufficiently for anyone who seeks, in the two earlier voyages—that to Lilliput and that to Brobdingnag. Here we have the "given quantity" (but how far from a stiff

[4] Yet note upon this point Ernest Bernbaum in his Introduction to *Gulliver's Travels* (1920).

symbol is Gulliver) upon which the demonstration is to be performed. It is, consequently, very important to comprehend the man
as "given" in these two voyages before he has been perceptibly modi-
fied by his astonishing experiences.

The very first hints about Gulliver himself are unobtrusively but
meticulously conveyed through the prefatory letter from Richard
Sympson, publisher, to the reader, and through a second letter from
Captain Gulliver (as it were, after the fact of publication) to his
cousin Sympson.[5] In the former letter, Sympson apologizes for the
travels as "a little too circumstantial"; while he excuses the [470]
tediousness, in some measure, on the ground that "the author was so
distinguished for his veracity, that it became a sort of proverb among
his neighbors at Redriff, when any one affirmed a thing, to say it was
as true as if Mr. Gulliver had spoke it." The letter from Gulliver to
Sympson, in so far as it exhibits Gulliver, must be considered in
any study of his rôle last rather than first, for it was supposed to have
been written some time subsequent to the voyage to the Houyhnhnms. The quiet exposition of Gulliver's capacities and inclinations during his sojourn in Lilliput gives ample materal for a reader's
information; the man's intellectual caliber and emotional caliber are
rather more than suggested though not altogether unfolded. He
studied "physic," mathematics, and navigation (these three more
than other things) for three years at Cambridge and for two years
and seven months at Leyden. He must have had a share of brains,
one would deduce. It was not all theory with him, either. After Leyden, he was three years ship's surgeon on voyages to the Levant. He
then married and attempted to practice medicine in London, but
without success. Six more years as ship's surgeon followed; three
consecutive years on land again; poor fortune brought him as usual to
the sea. Thus comes the voyage to Lilliput.[6] His province was evidently "marine" surgery and he worked with uniform success in his
own province. Yet Gulliver was exceptional among marine surgeons,
for he tells us:

> My hours of leisure I spent in reading the best authors, ancient and
> modern, being always provided with a good number of books; and when

---

[5] In all unabridged editions of *Gulliver's Travels* these two letters immediately precede "A Voyage to Lilliput."

[6] "Lilliput," chap. i. . . . The biographical material surveyed up to this
point is all to be found in the early pages of the chapter indicated.

I was ashore in observing the manners and dispositions of the people, as well as learning their language, wherein I had a great facility by the strength of my memory.[7]

Besides having sufficiently good brains for a considerable period of study, he had a remarkably agile and accurate memory.

Among the Lilliputians, Gulliver's character, both intellectual and moral, is thrown into relief. His natural inclinations emerge in spite of the astonishing circumstances, partly because of them. As always (or nearly always) he shows himself resourceful in ordinary and extraordinary physical emergencies. His bellowing and struggling very soon subside into meek-enough compliance and trust. "I thought it the [471] most prudent method to lie still. . . . ."[8] Gulliver soon finds ways of getting along tolerably, be the people big, little, or equine. He is adaptable in the restricted sense of being able to endure all sorts of uncouth occurrences equably. This does not imply much plasticity on his part. Intellectually he is deliberate if not actually slow; for he fails to realize the implications for mankind in the absurdities of Lilliputian politics, wars, religion, education. It is only at the close of the conversations with the King of Brobdingnag [9] that he gets an inkling of the significance to himself, to any Englishman, to any human being, of these adventures among the pygmies and the giants. He comes near to being a stolid Englishman. Not only is he intellectually deliberate; he is unsophisticated in many ways and capable only with considerable pains of sophistication. The whole book (all four voyages) might, not altogether inappropriately, be entitled *The Sophistication of Lemuel Gulliver*.

He is, congruously enough, decidedly good natured. He likes people—from six-inchers to sixty-footers. The Lilliputians who amused themselves by wantonly discharging arrows at Gulliver were treated by him with great gentleness.[10] He is compact of various loyalties.

---

[7] "Lilliput," chap. i.

[8] *Ibid.* And a little later in the same chapter we find: "I confess I was often tempted while they were passing backwards and forwards on my body, to seize forty or fifty of the first that came in my reach, and dash them against the ground. But the remembrance of what I had felt . . . . and the promise of honour I made them, for so I interpreted my submissive behavior, soon drove out these imaginations."

[9] "Brobdingnag," chap. vi.

[10] "Lilliput," chap. ii: ". . . . As to the sixth, I made a countenance as if I would eat him alive. The poor man squalled terribly . . . . but I soon put him out of fear: for, looking mildly, and immediately cutting the strings he was bound with, I set him gently on the ground, and away he ran."

Who is more enthusiastic about his "dear native land" than Gulliver? In his protracted account of England,[11] her people and institutions, to the King of Brobdingnag, Gulliver is positively chauvinistic.

> For I have always borne that laudable partiality to my own country which Dionysius Halicarnassensis with so much justice recommends to an historian: I would hide the frailties and deformities of my political mother, and place her virtues and beauties in the most advantageous light. This was my sincere endeavour in those many discourses I had with that mighty monarch, although it unfortunately failed of success.[12] [472]

And for all the harsh criticism leveled at English institutions by the attentive King,[13] Gulliver never admits that his own faith in her is at all seriously shaken. He is intellectually and temperamentally disinclined to alter his outlook upon human affairs and human beings; but we may probably assume that such downright condemnation of those beings and affairs as issued from the admired monarch's lips found subconscious lodgment in Gulliver's heart or brain. So his acquisition of wisdom may be supposed to have begun definitely in Brobdingnag; whereas his mature intellectual and temperamental stiffness had been proof against, what seems to most readers, the rather obvious exposure of the falseness of human affairs and human beings in Lilliput. It is clear that Gulliver is a loyal defender of human beings as such (as well as of Englishmen) from such passages as the following, addressed to the King of Brobdingnag:

> I one day took the freedom to tell his majesty, that the contempt he discovered towards Europe, and the rest of the world, did not seem answerable to those excellent qualities of the mind he was master of. That reason did not extend itself with the bulk of the body: but on the contrary, we observed in our country, that the tallest persons were usually least provided with it. . . . . And that, as inconsiderable as he took me to be, I hoped I might live to do his majesty some signal service.[14]

Here Gulliver undoubtedly conceives himself as a sort of defender of the essential excellence of the human species.

---

[11] "Brobdingnag," chaps. vi, vii.

[12] *Ibid.*, chap. vii. Cf. in chap. vi: "Imagine with thyself, courteous reader, how often I then wished for the tongue of Demosthenes or Cicero, that might have enabled me to celebrate the praise of my own dear native country in a style equal to its merits and felicity."

[13] Note particularly the concluding paragraph of "Brobdingnag," chap. vi.

[14] "Brobdingnag," chap. vi.

Perhaps the honest optimism and good nature of the man emerge more distinctly in his relations with individuals in Lilliput and Brobdingnag. It is not in him to be mean or resentful either to creatures one-twelfth his size or to those twelve times his size. In spite of the frightful plots [15] contrived against him at the instance of Skyresh Bolgolam and Flimnap, Gulliver flees without any impulse to vengeance. His good nature after such imminent perils is touched only to the point of resolving ". . . . never more to put confidence in princes or ministers, where I could possibly avoid it; . . . ." [16] Nowhere does Gulliver's good will to human beings shine clearer than in his sojourn at Brobdingnag; witness his forgiveness of the nearly fatal pranks [473] played upon him by the farmer's boy [17] and the Queen's dwarf,[18] and, more positively, witness his genuine (though not passionate) affection for Glumdalclitch.[19] Not yet disillusioned by his experiences in Lilliput, he readily gives his unaffected admiration and friendship to the King and Queen of Brobdingnag (who happen to deserve what he bestows!).[20] This Gulliver is truly reluctant to be taught wisdom by experience.

As one voyage succeeds another, the student of the character of Lemuel Gulliver must carefully examine the framework of each adventure—what might be called the departures and the landfalls. There are two points to note: his attitude as husband and father and his professional experiences. He is presented to us as a loving and attentive husband up to the time of his return from Houyhnhnmland.[21] His business has always been one that necessitates long absences from wife and children. To be sure, he has an "insatiable desire of seeing foreign countries," but that implies no "disaffection" for his family; it was not a case of taking one and rejecting the other.

---

[15] "Lilliput," chap. vii.

[16] *Ibid.*, chap. viii. In this connection, note *ibid.*, chap. vii: "I had been hitherto all my life a stranger to courts, for which I was unqualified by the meanness of my condition."

[17] "Brobdingnag," chap. i.   [18] *Ibid.*, chap. iii.

[19] e.g., "Brobdingnag," chaps. ii, viii.

[20] See *ibid.*, chap. vii; and chap. v (for the Queen's virtues).

[21] After his return from Lilliput, Gulliver remains with his family two months. Then the desire "of seeing foreign countries would suffer me to continue no longer." That does not mean any discontent with his family, however; for he takes the greatest pains to provide them with "a good house" and "fifteen hundred pounds" and "an estate in land of about thirty pounds a year," etc. See "Lilliput," chap. viii, final paragraph.

He had tried business at home and failed at it.[22] How naturally he chronicles his leave-taking for the voyage that led him to Brobdingnag.

My son Johnny, named so after his uncle, was at the Grammar School, and a towardly child. My daughter Betty (who is now well married, and has children) was then at her needle-work. I took leave of my wife, and boy and girl, with tears on both sides, and went on board the Adventure, a merchantship. . . . .[23]

Gulliver is not a uxorious family-man, obviously; yet is a normal, kindly father and husband.

The second point to note in these bits of preface and conclusion is that Gulliver is getting ahead professionally. He may suffer many shipwrecks, but he keeps advancing; so it is impossible to maintain [474] that lack of worldly success or recognition was souring his nature. The first voyage ". . . . I accepted an advantageous offer from Captain William Pritchard, master of the Antelope, who was making a voyage to the South-Sea." [24] The second voyage, he merely records that he "took shipping" in a certain ship with a certain commander. But with the third voyage he achieves a better position.

. . . . At last he [a captain] plainly invited me, though with some apologies, to be surgeon of the ship; that I should have another surgeon under me besides our two mates; that my salary should be double to the usual pay; and that having experienced my knowledge in sea-affairs to be at least equal to his, he would enter into any engagement to follow my advice, as much as if I had share in the command.[25]

Gulliver is now a man of solid professional repute, capable of large responsibility, still retaining his cheerful appetite for travel, "the thirst I had of seeing the world." The fourth voyage represents further professional advancement, the positive measure of success.

I continued at home with my wife and children about five months in a very happy condition, if I could have learned the lesson of knowing

[22] See *ibid.*, chap. i, the second and third paragraphs. And another attempt at setting down is chronicled in the fourth paragraph! See also the concluding lines of "Brobdingnag," chap. viii.

[23] "Lilliput," chap. viii, last paragraph: On his return from Laputa via Luggnagg and Japan, Gulliver "went straight to Redriff . . . . and found my wife and family in good health" ("Laputa," chap. xi, last paragraph).

[24] "Lilliput," chap. i.   [25] "Laputa," chap. i.

when I was well. I left my poor wife big with child, and accepted an advantageous offer made me to be Captain of the Adventurer, a stout merchantman of 350 tons: for I understood navigation well, and being grown weary of a surgeon's employment at sea, ... I took a skilful young man of that calling. . . . .[26]

Gulliver, our given quantity, turns out then, briefly, to be not an extraordinarily keen man in any way, not blessed (or cursed) with flashing and piercing insight. At the same time he is extraordinarily (though far from uniquely) endowed with a zest for experience, a curiosity to see and to know. He is, here, well above the average. In temperament, Gulliver is, again, not a mere typical man but a noticeably kindly, friendly, patriotic, perhaps even optimistic man. Sufficiently happy both in his family and in his profession, Gulliver is of a nature almost immune to meanness, selfishness, hatred, morbidity of any sort. If native land, wife, children, human race become dark and sinister and vile in his eyes, it will be (we must all admit) only for very potent, indubitable causes. His every predisposition is against misanthropy. But he has the capacity slowly and honestly to think. The human race may be conceived as individually pinning their faith to [475] Gulliver, and reflecting, the while, "If Gulliver ever becomes a man-hater that will be the perfect demonstration (for such of us as can think) that the race is hateful. Experiences that transform the good Gulliver into a misanthropist would much more surely transform us others should we pass through them." At least, Swift seems to calculate some such effect of Gulliver upon readers of the book.

Gulliver's Travels is in some sort the education of this man—his higher education, that is—and we see his so-to-speak Freshman and Sophomore experiences in Lilliput and Brobdingnag, bewildering experiences to him, with little seemingly vital result, but nevertheless an indispensable first tilling of the intellectual soil from which no genuine fruits are to be expected until later. This "later" means in Laputa and in Houyhnhnms-land. His final years may now be viewed, leading as they do to a sort of degree of ultimate understanding or sophistication. The goal of the book is not reached until the last page. To deal with it otherwise than as an organic unit is altogether to mutilate it.

In "Laputa" there are signs that the middle-aged, good-natured

---

[26] "Houyhnhnms," chap. i. Note the tone of tenderness at the beginning of this quotation. Gulliver has not yet attained by any means to true wisdom.

Gulliver is no longer impervious to the terrible suggestions and implications for him (and for any man!) of present events. He begins to apply what he observes to the case of human beings as such, wherever. Having been told of the way in which the wife of a prime minister in Laputa has twice deserted her indulgent but preoccupied husband to take up her abode with "an old deformed footman, who beat her every day," having heard this, Gulliver promptly remarks:

This may perhaps pass with the reader rather for an European or English story, than for one of a country so remote. But he may please to consider, that the caprices of womankind are not limited by any climate or nation, and that they are much more uniform than can be easily imagined.[27]

That his disillusionment is well under way is indicated by certain reflections that we would never have heard upon the lips of that Gulliver who dealt so naïvely with the King and ministers of Lilliput.

These unhappy people were proposing schemes for persuading monarchs to choose favourites upon the score of their wisdom, capacity, and virtue; of teaching ministers to consult the public good; of rewarding merit, great abilities, eminent services; of instructing princes to know their true interest by placing it on the same foundation with that of their people; of choosing for employments persons qualified to exercise them; with many other wild impossible chimaeras. . . . .[28] [476]

In many instances, in the third voyage, it would not be difficult to maintain that, for the time, Swift speaks through the lips of Gulliver. That does not mean, of course, that Gulliver is a disguise for Swift but merely that Gulliver is attaining wisdom.

There is a late flare-up of Gulliver's native good nature, philanthropy, and idealism in his experience at Luggnagg, apropos of the Struldbrugs or the people who never die. Certain persons of quality in Luggnagg volunteer to expound and exhibit the Struldbrugs to Gulliver. The mere prospect moves him more profoundly than any danger or any marvel previously encountered in the travels.

I freely own myself to have been struck with inexpressible delight upon hearing this account: [the account was very vague up to this point]. . . . . I could not forbear breaking out into expressions perhaps a little too extravagant. I cried out as in a rapture; Happy nation where every child hath at least a chance for being immortal! Happy people who enjoy

[27] "Laputa," chap. ii.   [28] *Ibid.,* chap. vi.

so many living examples of ancient virtue, and have masters ready to instruct them in the wisdom of all former ages! but, happiest beyond all
comparison are those excellent Struldbrugs, who being born exempt from
that universal calamity of human nature, have their minds free and dis-
engaged, without the weight and depression of spirits caused by the
continual apprehension of death.[29]

Not content with this exhortation, Gulliver proceeds (for the last
time in his life, we may be sure) to pour forth his most cherished as-
pirations, which are characteristically marked by great good will to
man. It impresses as the final struggle of Gulliver's buoyant soul
against the inevitable, imminent wisdom of misanthropy.

. . . . If it had been my good fortune to come into the world a
Struldbrug, as soon as I could discover my own happiness by understanding the difference between life and death, I would first resolve by all
arts and methods whatsoever to procure myself riches. . . . . In the
second place, I would from my earliest youth apply myself to the study
of arts and sciences, by which I should arrive in time to excell all others
in learning. Lastly, I would carefully record every action and event of
consequence that happened in the public, ... with my own observations on every point. . . . . By all which acquirements, I should be a
living treasury of knowledge and wisdom, and certainly become the oracle
of the nation. . . . . I would entertain myself in forming and directing
the minds of hopeful young men. . . . . But my choice and constant
companions should be a set of my own immortal brotherhood. . . . .
Where any of these wanted fortunes, I would provide them with convenient lodges round my own estate. . . . . [477]
    These struldbrugs and I would mutually communicate our observations
and memorials through the course of time, remark the several gradations
by which corruption steals into the world, and oppose it in every step,
by giving perpetual warning and instruction to mankind; which, added
to the strong influence of our own example, would probably prevent that
continual degeneracy of human nature so justly complained of in all
ages.[30]

Such words and ideas could flow only from a temperament sufficiently sanguine, a generous disposition. No sooner has Gulliver's
nature thus expressed itself than he receives a chilling lesson. The
inhabitants of Luggnagg are diverted at his ingenuousness. They inform him that an immortal (struldbrug) becomes, *ipso facto*, a prey
to "not only all the follies and infirmities of other old men, but many

[29] *Ibid.*, chap. x.   [30] "Laputa," chap. x.

more which arose from the dreadful prospect of never dying." [31] Furthermore, typical struldbrugs are exhibited to Gulliver. The point for a student of Gulliver's character and rôle to note here is the remarkable docility with which he learns the lesson in all its implications. He has surmounted that dulness which prevented him from appreciating the suggestions for human nature and human affairs at Lilliput and Brobdingnag. The seed of the idea sprouts promptly in the brain so long apparently sluggish or impenetrable. He admits a great loss of "appetite for perpetuity of life," and even entertains the project of transporting "a couple of struldbrugs to my own country, to arm our people against the fear of death." [32] Disillusioned as he is in many respects, Gulliver still is concerned to benefit people. His education is not finished; his pilgrimage as yet uncompleted.

In the light of the first three books of the *Travels*, it is not only necessary but natural to expect the fourth. The reader has been lured in the steps and into the thoughts of Gulliver by an unobtrusive and unwavering art not immeasurably less masterly though perhaps less lovely than the art of Milton in tracing the degeneration of Satan or that of Shakespeare in patiently following the gradual ruin of King Lear's body and mind.

Gulliver, after dwelling for a period among the admirable Houyhnhnms and observing with horror their filthy but thoroughly human slaves, the Yahoos, shows himself such an adept at receiving unfamiliar and uncongenial ideas that he may be pronounced educated or sophisticated more utterly than any other recorded man! For a [478] measure of his growth in comprehension of things,[33] it is convenient to contrast his account to his master, the Dapple Gray Houyhnhnm,[34] of mankind (particularly Englishmen) with his account of the same species to the King of Brobdingnag.[35] Every item in the account to the Dapple Gray is presented in a disgraceful light where each had been set forth with bellicose patriotism and philanthropism in the account at Brobdingnag. Our long and intimate acquaintance with Lemuel Gulliver in the earlier voyages has led us almost imperceptibly to cherish a not inconsiderable liking for him and (more significantly) to feel a measure of confidence in his good nature and his

---

[31] *Ibid.*   [32] *Ibid.*, last two paragraphs.

[33] A comprehension of things means to Swift (beyond doubt) a conviction of the vileness of men as such—of their absolutely incurable vileness. So the views of Gulliver and of Swift finally coincide, though they show no identity of intellect or disposition.

[34] "Houyhnhnms," chaps. v and vi.   [35] "Brobdingnag," chaps. vi and vii.

general capacity. The result is that we find ourselves inclined to accept his views. Shocking and ferocious as the attack on man may be in the "Voyage to the Houghnhnms," we are conducted with singular gentleness, everything considered, by our friend Gulliver through all the desolation of humanity. We tend to believe him until the tale is done and we have had a chance to appreciate the indictment. Then comes the ferocious shock rather than in the reading.

Gulliver explains innocently his reason for the new attitude toward mankind:

> I must confess, the many virtues of those excellent quadrupeds [i.e., the Houyhnhnms] placed in opposite view to human corruptions, had so far opened my eyes and enlarged my understanding, that I began to view the actions and passions of man in a very different light, and to think the honor of my own kind not worth managing [i.e., manipulating]; . . . .[36]

It is hard not to credit the words of a friend who evidences a yearning for ideal virtue.

> I had not been a year in this country, before I contracted such a love and veneration for the inhabitants, that I entered on a firm resolution never to return to human kind, but to pass the rest of my life among these admirable Houyhnhnms in the contemplation and practice of every virtue; . . . .[37]

Gulliver's education is coming not only to flower but to fruit. He no longer considers ways of benefiting man as he had even so recently as during his visit to the struldbrugs. The final revelation of wisdom has [479] been apparently to refrain from human contact—a revelation convincing enough to transform a philanthropic Gulliver.

The full force of Gulliver's attainment of knowledge is not felt until he is forced back among men—an indubitable Yahoo. He is constrained to admit his Yahoo-nature humbly; to admit, also, that as a Yahoo he must depart the land of virtue forever.[38] It is only when he finally reaches England and his wife and children that the realization comes of his utter disillusion, his complete wisdom! ". . . . The sight of them filled me only with hatred, disgust and contempt. . . . ."[39] We know from our long intimacy with Gulliver

---

[36] "Houyhnhnms," chap. vii.   [37] Ibid.

[38] When Gulliver hears his doom he confesses "that I knew too well upon what solid reasons all the determinations of the wise Houyhnhnms were founded, not to be shaken by arguments of mine, a miserable Yahoo."

[39] "Houyhnhnms," chap. xi.

that he is incapable of cruelty, hard-heartedness. We know he is not morbid or easily bored. He must have attained to whatever is the final attainment, extraordinary as the results of it may seem. From this new point of vantage (if we may so call it), Lemuel Gulliver writes to his publisher and cousin Richard Sympson that letter which forms an essential Preface to *Gulliver's Travels*—he writes condemning his own general attitude toward men in his earlier days. He protests: "I should never have attempted so absurd a project as that of reforming the Yahoo race in this kingdom; but I have now done with all such visionary schemes for ever." [40] These are the ultimate words from the pen of Lemuel Gulliver. He has played out his rôle to perfection. Or possibly we might say that he has gone another pilgrim's progress, this time not to the Celestial City, but to a place equally difficult of human attainment if we may believe Swift—to Misanthropolis. And the pilgrimage is real to us in the reading (if not in the after-thought) because Gulliver is in disposition and in intellect so credible, probable, recognizable, and trustworthy. [41] [480]

[40] "A Letter from Captain Gulliver to His Cousin Sympson," printed just before "A Voyage to Lilliput" in *Gulliver's Travels*.

[41] In calling attention to the fact that Gulliver should not be viewed merely as the representative of Swift himself or simply as the representative of mankind, I have not considered a possible view of Gulliver as a regular, undistinguished, eighteenth-century traveler. At first thought, what more plausible than that he is the conventional figure upon whom strange adventures may be hung like hats upon a hat-tree! Now no man of the period has made use of such figures more frequently than Defoe, and from his narratives we can gather just how little care had been bestowed upon travelers to make them recognizable human beings. Captain Singleton is surely a typical traveler of the time—an empty image. To compare Singleton with Gulliver is to feel the latter's individuality.

from Jonathan Swift: Some Observations

D. NICHOL SMITH

Gulliver's Travels is sometimes spoken of as if it were the bitter fruit of [Swift's] disappointment, but his satire never varied in kind. Writing to Pope when the *Travels* were finished but not published, he said, "I desire you and all my friends will take a special care that my disaffection to the world may not be imputed to my age, for I have credible witnesses ready to depose that it has never varied from the twenty-first to the fifty-eighth year of my life." The witnesses whom we have to call are his writings. We could easily make a selection of passages which it would not be possible to date, or even to place in chronological order, by the test of substance or purpose. Take this passage on political parties:

> Man is so apt to *imitate*, so much of the Nature of *Sheep* (*Imitatores, servum pecus*) that whoever is so bold to give the first *great Leap over the Heads of those about him* (tho' he be the worst of the Flock), shall be quickly followed by the rest. Besides, when Parties are once formed, the Stragglers look so ridiculous, and become so insignificant, that they have no other way but to run into the Herd, which at least will hide and protect them; and where to be much considered, requires only to be very violent.

From *Essays by Divers Hands, Being the Transactions of the Royal Society of Literature of the United Kingdom* (London: Oxford University Press, 1935), XIV, 41–48. By permission of D. Nichol Smith. A few minor changes have been made by Professor Nichol Smith in this reprinting of the article.

In the same pamphlet he calls the parliamentary recess the "lucid interval." It was his first pamphlet, published three years before the *Tale of a* [41] *Tub*. But many years before that he had proclaimed—

> My hate, whose lash just Heaven has long decreed
> Shall on a day make sin and folly bleed;

and he had spoken of—

> What oft I vainly strive to hide,
> That scorn of fools, by fools mistook for pride.

Later, in his great London days, he says, "I never expect sincerity from any man, and am no more angry at the breach of it than at the colour of his hair." The *Tale* caused a stir in his own time, but now his great offence seems to be the Yahoos. I sometimes wonder what we should have heard about Swift's misanthropy had he not written that fourth book.

There is some evidence that Swift liked that book best, and there are some readers—shall I say a select few?—who like it best. I cannot think that the critics who hold, in the words of one of them, that "the Yahoo is the embodiment of the bestial element in man, and Swift in his wrath takes the bestial for the predominating element" —I cannot think that they have tried to see the book as Swift saw it. In Lilliput we are in a land where the inhabitants are twelve times smaller than we are, in Brobdingnag twelve times greater, and we engage in what a later poet called a willing suspension of disbelief; but the suspension appears to be less willingly granted when we are taken to a land where the relation of man to [42] one of the so-called lower animals is not as we know it. All four books are based on an abnormal experience. Most satirists deal with things directly. Pope is direct enough. Jane Austen, in her kinder way, is direct enough. If there is an allegory, as in "Absalom and Achitophel," still the persons play their part in an ordinary human drama. But Swift asks us to look at ourselves under strange conditions, on the chance that we shall see some things in ourselves a little more clearly.

He asks us to imagine a land where the horse is in power. Not to put too great a strain on our imagination he chooses the animal which we agree in calling the noblest. He does not choose the dog, or the fox, or the sheep, or the worm; he chooses the horse. Our complacency may be insulted by our dethronement from the lordship of creation; but so much the better. Is not the horse in some respects our superior? He does not commit murder, or cheat, or wage war, or lord it over his neighbours. Does he not lead a moral life? Does he not lead a better life, by all standards of morality, than many professing Christians?

Let me remind you how Sir Philip Sidney began his "Apologie for Poetrie." He tells us that when in Italy he was instructed in riding by a teacher who grew lyrical about the horse:

Then would he add certain praises by telling what a peerless beast a horse was; the only serviceable courtier without flattery, the beast of most beauty, faithfulness, courage, and such more, that if I had not been a piece of a logician before I came to him, I think he would have persuaded me to have wished myself a horse. [43]

Now Swift never wished himself a horse, such as he knew in either England or Ireland. All the horses that he ever knew—and he knew many, for he was a great rider—were degenerate Houyhnhnms. When Gulliver returns to England, he proceeds to apply those excellent lessons of virtue which he had learned among the Houyhnhnms, and—

to lament the Brutality of *Houyhnhnms* in my own Country, but always treat their Persons with Respect, for the Sake of my noble Master, his Family, his Friends, and the whole *Houyhnhnm* Race, whom these of ours have the Honour to resemble in all their Lineaments, however their Intellectuals came to degenerate.

The Houynhnms were not horses as we know them. Similarly the Yahoos who were their slaves were not men such as we are. Gulliver was taken by the Houyhnhnms to be a superior kind of Yahoo, "a perfect Yahoo," and as such he surprised them. They had never seen an animal quite like him.

We may be led to think of a prehistoric time before the mastery of man or of the horse had been established. Swift says nothing about that; but he certainly asks us to assume that in the course of years animal life, and particularly the intellectual and moral life, has passed on to what Keats calls "a fresh perfection," or has receded. He asks us to imagine a land where the horse has been at liberty to develop his virtues, and man, living in a state of subjection, has ceased to develop and has degenerated. The idea ought not to be difficult to us. The doctrine of evolution may be a commonplace [44] now, but something of it is implicit in the fourth book of *Gulliver's Travels*.

Gulliver is a Yahoo; the Brobdingnagians, the great people whose cultured and beneficent king thought that the natives of Gulliver's country must be "the most pernicious race of little odious vermin that nature ever suffered to crawl upon the surface of the earth"— they were Yahoos. They were the "least corrupted" of Yahoos, but they were Yahoos none the less. All this we are too apt to forget. In ordinary usage nowadays the word has a much narrower meaning than Swift gave it.

Grant the simple fiction, and the rest follows. Swift never gave himself a better opportunity for exhibiting the sin, and the folly, and the unpleasantness of man. His attack is levelled above all at pride, the deadliest of the seven deadly sins—pride intellectual, moral, political, personal, physical. Towards the conclusion he says so in so many words:

When I behold a Lump of Deformity, and Diseases both in Body and Mind, smitten with *Pride*, it immediately breaks all the Measures of my Patience; neither shall I be ever able to comprehend how such an Animal and such a Vice could tally together.

There are no signs of impatience in the writing of the book, which is all of a piece, all directed to the same end and unflinching. If he wrote in his wrath, as has been said, his wrath was wonderfully well controlled. This book was his greatest sermon on humility.

When the four books were finished he said to the friend with whom he corresponded most intimately, in a letter which has only recently been published: [45]

I have finished my Travells, and I am now transcribing them; they are admirable Things, and will wonderfully mend the World.

These words sound the top note of exaltation in all his writings. Had he suspected that the letter was to be printed, he would have been ironically grave. But for this once we catch him unawares and are given a glimpse of his conviction that *Gulliver's Travels*, these "admirable things," would shake man into seeing what a knave or a fool he generally is, and so put him on the fair way to mend. The book was written to "mend the world." His satire was—

with a moral view designed
To cure the vices of mankind.

"I wrote for their amendment, and not their approbation."

I believe—and I give this only as an impression, though if it is wrong I do not know how to account for the persistent quality of his satire—I believe (and here I revert) that Swift was a definitely religious man with an overmastering sense of the weakness of human nature. His admiration of his friends, such as Arbuthnot, served only to strengthen his aversion from what he despised. With hyprocrisy and selfishness and knavery in any form he would not come to terms, and he bludgeoned them. Who will say that he bludgeoned them from the mere joy of destruction? If I find misanthropy in *Gulliver's Travels*, it is a misanthropy that is bent on defeating itself. But to find hopelessness is to make the book incomprehensible.

I have said nothing about Stella. To-day is her [46] birthday, March 13th. Latterly, and perhaps from an earlier year than we know, Swift celebrated it with a poem. I should like to quote from the last of the series. Her health had long been declining, and he knew what was at hand:

> This Day, whate'er the Fates decree,
> Shall still be kept with Joy by me:
> This Day then, let us not be told,
> That you are sick, and I grown old,
> Nor think on our approaching Ills,
> And talk of Spectacles and Pills;
> Tomorrow will be Time enough
> To hear such mortifying Stuff.

Hitherto he had been playful in his birthday verses, but on this occasion he says—

> From not the gravest of Divines,
> Accept for once some serious Lines.

He argues, simply, that just as our bodies are built up by food, so past actions, which we may have forgotten, have contributed to make our minds what they are; and thus he comes to this conclusion:

> Believe me *Stella*, when you show
> That true Contempt for Things below,
> Nor prize your Life for other Ends
> Than merely to oblige your Friends,
> Your former Actions claim their Part,
> And join to fortify your Heart.
> For Virtue in her daily Race,
> Like *Janus*, bears a double Face;
> Looks back with Joy where she has gone,
> And therefore goes with Courage on.

She at your sickly Couch will wait,
And guide you to a better State. [47]
    O then, whatever Heav'n intends,
Take Pity on your pitying Friends;
Nor let your Ills affect your Mind,
To fancy they can be unkind.
Me, surely me, you ought to spare,
Who gladly would your Suff'rings share;
Or give my Scrap of Life to you,
And think it far beneath your Due;
You, to whose Care so oft I owe,
That I'm alive to tell you so.

In this poem, which was intended only for the eyes of Stella, Swift speaks from the heart, and reveals a side of his character which he was at pains to disguise in his prose for the public. It was written a few months after the appearance of *Gulliver's Travels*, and is the next piece, with the exception of some letters, to which we can give a definite date. A strange epilogue to that bitter satire, you may think; but there is no contradiction. Swift wore a mask in print; and what he said in print we understand the better by knowing what he said intimately to his friends. [48]

from *The Mind and Art of Jonathan Swift*

RICARDO QUINTANA

The great Voyage which brings *Gulliver's Travels* to an end was written directly after the second Voyage, the first draft being finished by January 1724. What above all distinguishes part iv from the three preceding parts is its rigorous artistic unity, which produces a cumulative effect of the greatest power. Fantastic realism is again employed,—indeed, it is the satirical mode of the entire Voyage,—but behind it is a terrible logic to be found nowhere in the first Voyage and only fleetingly in the second. The satiric intention presiding over A Voyage to the Houyhnhnms can be summed up in a single phrase: an assault upon man's Pride by way of *le mythe animal.* Unless this is borne in mind [319] the dominant tone of the piece will not be caught nor will the minor and sometimes contrasting tones. Thus, the total effect of the last Voyage is anything but a humorous one, and yet there are many passages in which humour is the principal ingredient. Take, for instance, the lecture delivered by Gulliver's master on man's physical inferiority: man's nails are of no use either to his fore or hinder feet; his fore feet are not feet at all, since he never walks on them; going only on his hinder feet, if these slip he must invariably fall;

From *The Mind and Art of Jonathan Swift* by Ricardo Quintana (London: Oxford University Press, 1936), pp. 319–326. By permission. *Swift: An Introduction* by Ricardo Quintana (London: Oxford University Press, 1955) should also be consulted for further development of Professor Quintana's views on *Gulliver's Travels.*

He then began to find fault with other parts of my Body; the Flatness of my Face, the Prominence of my Nose, my Eyes placed directly in Front, so that I could not look on either Side without turning my Head: That I was not able to feed my self, without lifting one of my fore Feet to my Mouth: And therefore Nature had placed those Joints to answer that Necessity. He knew not what could be the Use of those several Clefts and Divisions in my Feet behind; that these were too soft to bear the Hardness and Sharpness of Stones without a Covering made from the Skin of some other Brute; that my whole Body wanted a Fence against Heat and Cold, which I was forced to put on and off every Day with Tediousness and Trouble. (Chap. iv.)

Certain critics have declared this to be an unforgivable libel on the Human Form Divine, but the modern reader has no right to laugh so long as he himself reads the passage as downright satire. There are few flagitious aspects of man's nature which are not dwelt upon at some point or other in this Voyage, and at the end Pride has been left without a single prop, yet in the course of his grim demonstrations the satirist sometimes winks at us.

A Voyage to the Honyhnhnms is a series of skilfully interwoven variations on two themes, one proclaiming the bestiality of man while under the control of the irrational, the other descriptive of the life of reason. There can be no doubt as to which of these is the more effectively developed. Through the Yahoos, a perfect symbol for the communication of disgust, moral degradation is made emotionally repulsive. The life of reason, on the other hand, is given merely an intellectual statement, for though we understand the admirable Houyhnhnms we are not moved by them, and [320] this not because horses are an inappropriate symbol but because ideal civilization as conceived by Swift is an emotionless thing. That the two themes are not treated with equal artistic success is shown by the fact that part iv has so often been taken to mean one thing only —namely, that man is all Yahoo. The bestiality of man must of course be heavily underscored if the attack on Pride is to find its mark, but it was not Swift's intention to allow this negative theme to smother the positive one descriptive of the life of reason.

The equivalence between irrational man and the Yahoo is established with great skill. Gulliver has scarcely been put ashore by his mutinous crew and has not yet met with any of the noble Houyhnhnms when he is set upon by some forty of the most loathsome creatures he has ever seen. Describing them at length, he remarks,

"I never beheld in all my Travels so disagreeable an Animal, or one against which I naturally conceived so strong an Antipathy," but in this first encounter he perceives nothing of their resemblance to himself. It is only after he has been led home by a Houyhnhnm, who takes him into the courtyard and compares him with one of the Yahoos tied up there, that he grasps their similarity to men, observing with horror and astonishment a perfect human figure in this abominable animal. The physical resemblance having been established, the moral similarity is built up by degrees as Gulliver comes to appreciate the impassive virtues of his noble masters and thereby to despise himself and his race. But the physical resemblance and the disgust which it occasions are never allowed to slumber in the reader's consciousnes, incident after incident—one of the most striking being the bathing scene in chapter viii—inciting the emotions afresh.

Back of all this is an indictment of man and society perhaps as comprehensive and detailed as was ever penned by a satirist. It begins in chapter iv with Gulliver's description of his crew—there is no kind of immorality with which they are not familar, drinking, whoring, gaming, treason, murder, theft, poisoning, robbery, perjury, forgery, counterfeiting, rape, sodomy, desertion—and continues through chapter vi. War as it is waged in Europe is described, together with the [321] motives of bellicose princes and ministers and the weapons used at sea and in the field. At this point Gulliver's master can contain himself no longer:

. . . although he hated the *Yahoos* of this Country, yet he no more blamed them for their odious Qualities, than he did a *Gnnayh* (a Bird of Prey) for its Cruelty, or a sharp Stone for cutting his Hoof. But, when a Creature pretending to Reason, could be capable of such Enormities, he dreaded lest the Corruption of that Faculty might be worse than Brutality itself. He seemed therefore confident, that instead of Reason, we were only possessed of some Quality fitted to increase our natural Vices; as the Reflection from a troubled Stream returns the Image of an ill-shapen Body, not only *larger*, but more *distorted*. (Chap. v.)

From war Gulliver passes on to the absurdities and injustices of the law, to the inequalities between rich and poor, to the social and economic evils resulting from luxury and intemperance, to the diseases common in Europe, and ends by glancing at physicians, ministers of state, and the nobility (chap. vi). The anti-rational view of man, upon which this entire indictment rests, is emphasized in chapter vii, where Gulliver's master, now fully informed concerning Europeans, enlarges upon their similarity to the Yahoos; ". . . he looked upon us," Gulliver writes,

as a Sort of Animals to whose Share, by what Accident he could not conjecture, some small Pittance of *Reason* had fallen, whereof we made no other Use than by its Assistance to aggravate our *natural* Corruptions, and to acquire new ones which Nature had not given us. That, we disarmed our selves of the few Abilities she had bestowed; had been very successful in multiplying our original Wants, and seemed to spend our whole Lives in vain Endeavours to supply them by our own Inventions.

Of the five remaining chapters, viii and ix are given over to the development of the second theme, a statement of the principles of rational conduct. It is not, of course, the first appearance of this theme, which is introduced the moment the Houyhnhnms enter the story and from then on is interwoven with the satire on bestiality—the gravity, common sense, cleanliness, and truthfulness of the horses serving as a foil for the loathsomeness of Yahoos and corrupt men. But not until the first theme has been fully and dramatically [322] treated is the ideology of the Houyhnhnms set forth at length and their society portrayed.

The Houyhnhnms "thought, Nature and Reason were sufficient Guides for a reasonable Animal . . . in shewing us what we ought to do, and what to avoid" (chap. v). They are, in this respect, perfect children of the Enlightenment, grounding their intellectual life upon the law of the universality of reason. The question will at once arise whether they always mean by *nature* the same thing as *reason*, or whether at times they think of *nature* as something purer than civilization and standing in opposition to it. Once or twice, indeed, they speak like noble and uncorrupted children of nature, as when they express surprise on discovering the secret of Gulliver's clothes, declaring that they are unable to understand "why Nature should teach us to conceal what Nature had given" since they themselves are not ashamed of any parts of their bodies (chap. iii). But at such moments they are off centre. Actually, they are not horrified by European society because it is too civilized but because it is not civilized at all. Their prescription is not that man should revert to a primitive state—which to them suggests the Yahoos—but that he should begin to live by reason. To them life according to nature means this life of reason.

Their grand maxim, "to cultivate *Reason,* and to be wholly governed by it," leads immediately to an intense anti-intellectualism.
They believe, that is, that there are certain truths which strike the
mind with immediate conviction, and that beyond these truths nothing can be known with certainty. Thus they fix rigorous limits to
every kind of speculation, which must become vain and useless the
moment it begins to deal with matters other than those presented by
the general sense. ". . . Controversies, Wranglings, Disputes, and
Positiveness in false or dubious Propositions," we are told by Gulliver,

are Evils unknown among the *Houyhnhnms.* In the like Manner when
I used to explain to [my master] our several Systems of *Natural Philosophy,* he would laugh that a Creature pretending to *Reason,* should value
itself upon the Knowledge of other [323] Peoples Conjectures, and in
Things, where that Knowledge, if it were certain, could be of no Use.
Wherein he agreed entirely with the Sentiments of *Socrates,* as *Plato*
delivers them. . . . (Chap. viii.)

On the side of behaviour and social conduct their thorough-going
adherence to the dicta of reason—here we have to do with that
"rationalism" out of which Swift's rigid ethical theories arose—ren-
ders them almost passionless creatures. Unperturbed by any violent
emotions, they regard one another with serene good will but never
with what properly can be called affection, even their own offspring
failing to excite in them any different feeling from that which they
have for all colts and foals. They marry in accordance with eugenic
principles and practise birth-control through restraint. Their young
they educate with great care—*"Temperance, Industry, Exercise*
and *Cleanliness,* are the Lessons equally enjoyed to the young ones
of both Sexes: And my Master thought it monstrous in us to give
the Females a different Kind of Education from the Males. . . ."
Every fourth year a representative council of the whole nation is
assembled, which draws up a national plan—regulating, among
other things, the population—for the ensuing quadrennium. (Chap.
viii.)

Since the Houyhnhnms are without letters, their knowledge is
wholly traditional. Subject to no diseases, they have no need of physicians. Of astronomy they know only enough to enable them to
calculate the year by sun and moon. Their poetry is of superlative
excellence by reason of the justness of the similes, the minuteness
and exactness of the descriptions, and the matter—"Their Verses

. . . usually contain either some exalted Notions of Friendship and Benevolence, or the Praises of those who were Victors in Races, and other bodily Exercises." In the presence of death they maintain their habitual composure, facing it themselves with perfect resignation and accepting the loss of friends and relatives without a tinge of grief. (Chap. ix.)

Chapters x, xi, and xii together make up the long and cunningly wrought conclusion of the Voyage. It has already been pointed out that the contrasts experienced by Gulliver [324] on his return to civilization from Lilliput and Brobdingnag are almost solely of the physical order. Not so the contrasts which assail him when, banished by decree from Houyhnhnm-land, he is forced back to human society. Well before his ostracism he has come to a full realization of his own physical and moral repulsiveness; he is a Yahoo, his family, his friends, his countrymen, the entire human race are Yahoos, and when he sees his reflection in water he turns away with horror and detestation. His own desire is to live his life out among the horses, his noble masters.

I enjoyed perfect Health of Body, and Tranquility of Mind; I did not feel the Treachery or Inconstancy of a Friend, nor the Injuries of a secret or open Enemy. I had no Occasion of bribing, flattering or pimping, to procure the Favour of any great Man, or of his Minion. I wanted no Fence against Fraud or Oppression: Here was neither Physician to watch my Body, nor Lawyer to ruin my Fortune: No Informer to destroy my Words and Actions, or forge Accusations against me for Hire: Here were no Gibers, Censurers, Backbiters, Pick-pockets, Highwaymen, House-breakers, Attorneys, Bawds, Buffoons, Gamesters, Politicians, Wits, Spleneticks, tedious Talkers, Controvertists, Ravishers, Murderers, Robbers, Virtuoso's; no Leaders or Followers of Party and Faction; no Encouragers to Vice, by Seducement or Examples: No Dungeon, Axes, Gibbets, Whipping posts, or Pillories; No cheating Shop-keepers or Mechanicks: No Pride, Vanity or Affectation: No Fops, Bullies, Drunkards, strolling Whores, or Poxes: No ranting, lewd, expensive Wives: No stupid, proud Pedants: No importunate, over-bearing, quarrelsome, noisy, roaring, empty, conceited, swearing Companions: No Scoundrels raised from the Dust upon the Merit of their Vices; or Nobility thrown into it on account of their Virtues: No Lords, Fidlers, Judges or Dancing-Masters. (Chap. x.)

When he is told that he may no longer dwell among the Houyhnhnms he has already foreseen the mental tortures which he must endure upon a return to his native land.

From the moment when Gulliver, about to put to sea, prostrates himself before his Master and reverently kisses his hoof, to the end of the story Swift's inventiveness in devising incidents which will convey his hero's disgust for his kind has no parallel in satiric literature, though it is a question whether it does not finally degenerate into sensationalism.

The final chapter (xii) is a kind of coda. First comes a [325] diatribe against those Europeans who sail to new lands, there to plunder and enslave the natives. Montaigne had protested against this cruelty to uncivilized peoples, as had many later writers, so that Swift was here taking a well-established line. The last paragraphs canalize all the satiric energy generated in the preceding pages of the Voyage and direct it against the Pride of man:

My Reconcilement to the *Yahoo*-kind in general might not be so difficult, if they would be content with those Vices and Follies only which Nature hath entitled them to. I am not in the least provoked at the Sight of a Lawyer, a Pick-pocket, a Colonel, a Fool, a Lord, a Gamester, a Politician, a Whoremunger, a Physician, an Evidence, a Suborner, an Attorney, a Traytor, or the like: This is all according to the due Course of Things: But, when I behold a Lump of Deformity, and Diseases both in Body and Mind, smitten with *Pride*, it immediately breaks all the Measures of my Patience; neither shall I be ever able to comprehend how such an Animal and such a Vice could tally together. [326]

The Final Comedy
of Lemuel Gulliver

JOHN F. ROSS

Nominally, everyone regards *Gulliver's Travels* as one of the world's very great satires; the difficult intellectual feat, apparently, is to realize how satiric it is. Critical appraisals of *Gulliver*, at any rate, fall into confusion over the fourth voyage. Confronted by Swift's most unrelenting and severe attack on the Yahoo nature of man, the critic, from some obscure fellow feeling, refuses to read *Gulliver* to the end as complex satire. He thereby misses the final comic absurdity inherent in what is the climax not only of the fourth voyage, but of the satire as a whole. Swift may not be a comic figure, but Gulliver decidedly is.

I

Consider, in this regard, the common evaluation of Gulliver as voiced by Thackeray, Leslie Stephen, and their twentieth-century followers. Whatever their differences, and they have many, they are in substantial agreement on several points. (1) *Gulliver* is one of the world's great satires, and perhaps the most severe. (2) Voyage IV is its climax. And this voyage is plainspoken, terrible, and overwhelming, upsetting in the extreme to our normally optimistic view of man's nature and achievement. (3) The Yahoos are not a true representation of mankind, nor can horses talk and reason. (4) It

Reprinted from *Studies in the Comic, University of California Publications in English*, VIII (1941), 175–196. By permission.

follows from 2 and 3 that the fourth voyage is indecent and shameful, an insult to humanity. (5) Since Swift lost his mind at an advanced age, he was insane when, years before, he wrote the fourth voyage. (6) Therefore (the conclusion is expressed or implicit) it is advisable not to read this particular work of art to its conclusion, but to stop halfway,—that is to say, with the end of the second voyage. [175]

A more logical conclusion for those who hold this attitude is this: great and severe satire should never be written, and if written, should be publicly burned—and the satirist with it. But logic has little enough to do with the matter; the attitude is self-contradictory. It resolves itself really into an acknowledgment of Swift's greatness and an admission of the validity of his satiric attack even in the fourth voyage, coupled with a determined refusal to admit that his attack is valid. The rationalization of the situation is not convincing, even when Swift's insanity is thrown in for good measure.

More thoughtful modern critics have abandoned this attitude, yet they too are troubled by Voyage IV. Severe satire, insults to humanity, and madness appear to worry them little; they have other objections. Something has gone wrong with Swift's craftsmanship. The last voyage is psychologically unconvincing. Even if we accept the Yahoos, we cannot accept the Houyhnhnms; and furthermore, the drab and limited life of the horses is wholly unsatisfactory as a Utopia, as Swift himself should have known. Perhaps it is simply that, carried away by the impetus of his severe attack, Swift has lost control. Of the fourth voyage, W. A. Eddy says in his critical study of *Gulliver*, "someone has blundered, and I fear me it is Swift." Ricardo Quintana, in his careful and penetrating study of Swift, has many doubts concerning the last voyage, and shakes his head over its "sensationalism." This modern type of analysis is on much firmer ground than the older attitude, and is not to be carelessly dismissed. Yet in it an old error persists: by identifying the later Gulliver too completely with Swift, it takes the fourth voyage much too literally as a statement of Swift's final position. For instance, W. A. Eddy writes:

Swift tells us that the Houyhnhnms are more reasonable than Gulliver, but the Houyhnhnms do not bear him out. To me the defect of the fourth voyage is not the brutality of the satire, but the stupidity of the Houyhnhnms, whose judgments of Gulliver prove nothing beyond their own incompetence to judge. Gulliver is quick to recognize the [176] excellent qualities of the horses. How is it then that the Houyhnhnms, who we are assured are so much more sensible, are unable to recognize that the human body is much more suitable than their own for the common needs of life? . . .

Swift was careless of his story; the fires of misanthropy obscured his judgment, and vitiated his argument. Much may be said for Swift's Yahoo conception of man, but much more against his misconception of the ideal Houyhnhnms. Powerfully as he reiterates and supports his postulate that the horse is the better creature, the Houyhnhnms refute it on every page.

Here Swift and Gulliver are completely identified, regarded as of one mind. Actually, all the postulates are Gulliver's postulates. It is Swift who permits Gulliver to reveal in his narrative the horses' "incompetence to judge."

The most recent attempt to deal with the problem of the fourth voyage is an essay in *Perilous Balance,* by W. B. C. Watkins. Here the solution offered is that the fourth voyage leaves the realms of satire for those of tragedy. The essay is admirable in stressing the profound seriousness and significance of Swift's view of the problem of evil; but in holding that this view is essentially tragic the author misses the demonstrable satiric structure and conclusion of the voyage.

Since no one seems to have had difficulty in reading the first two voyages of *Gulliver* as satire, whence arise the difficulties over the last voyage? One chief source of trouble, I have no doubt, lies outside of Swift and his book, in certain assumptions which are so traditional and conventional that the critic may not only not express them, but may even be unaware of them. It s commonplace to distinguish two modes of satire: the genial, laughing, urbane satire of Horace, and the severe, lashing satire of Juvenal. Whatever hostility the first mode may contain, it nevertheless works largely in terms of laughter. For convenience, it may be termed comic satire. The second mode emphasizes a severely satiric attack in which laughter is at a minimum, or perhaps even [177] lacking. This may be termed caustic or corrosive satire. Swift, like Juvenal, holds a commanding position as a satirist in large part because of the corrosive satire of which he was capable. Yet—and any considerable reading in the history and criticism of satire will support the view—most critics are repelled by corrosive satire and prefer rather to deal with comic satire. I share that preference, indeed, and regard comic satire as a richer, more complete treatment of humanity than purely corrosive satire; but if one unconsciously comes to identify good satire with comic satire only, he is almost certain to have trouble with the fourth voyage of *Gulliver*. Unconsciously expecting the smile or the laugh as a partial balm to severe satiric attack, and finding that this balm is scarcely present in the effective first nine chapters of the last voyage, he may decide that he is no longer reading satire, and hence miss Swift's rounding of the whole of *Gulliver* in a superb return of comic satire.

For we should not assume that, if someone has blundered in the last voyage, the blunderer was therefore Swift. That assumption is dangerously close to the idea that we are superior to Swift because we are superior to Lemuel Gulliver. But Swift paid his readers a higher compliment than most readers will pay him. He assumed, as any ironic satirist by the very nature of his work assumes, that he and his readers were on terms of equality in sharing an important secret, which is that there is far more in literal statement then meets the literal eye. It may be granted that for nine chapters the corrosive satire of the last voyage of *Gulliver* is of unparalleled intensity, and that its recurrent waves are overwhelming enough to swamp minds of considerable displacement, as well as cockleshell intellects. Yet Swift offers us the opportunity to ride out the storm with him, and even goes to some trouble to keep us afloat. If we choose to disregard Swift himself and the last part of Voyage IV, and to go down finally for the third time, with Gulliver, it is hardly Swift's blunder. [178]

II

One of my main concerns here is to show that Gulliver in the last voyage is not Swift. That done, we shall be able to see how Swift, though his corrosive satire continues to the last page of the volume, superadds to it a comic satire of great significance. But our understanding of the last voyage will be made easier if we appreciate certain complex effects achieved by Swift in the earlier voyages. Just as a great composer has a variety of single orchestral instruments which he uses to produce complex music, so Swift has a variety of instruments wherewith he produces the complexity which is *Gulliver's Travels*. Ready to his hand he has the modes of straight narrative, of comedy, of comic satire, and of corrosive satire. And he has the double voice of irony.

Though the voyage to Lilliput is commonly held to be the merriest and most diverting of the four voyages, the greater part of it, quantitatively considered, holds our interest chiefly as ingenious narrative. In the first four chapters, besides a few comic and satiric touches, there is one outstanding passage of comic satire, that concerning the High-Heels and Low-Heels, and the Big-Endians and the Little-Endians. The narrative then resumes chief importance until we reach the end of chapter vi, with its comic passage in which Gulliver defends the reputation of the Lilliputian lady whose name had been scandalously linked with his.

In chapter vii occurs the severest satire of the first voyage. Gulliver, who has deserved the highest gratitude from the Lilliputians, is impeached for capital offenses—chiefly, for making water within the precincts of the burning royal palace "under colour of extinguishing the fire," and for traitorously refusing to reduce the empire of Blefuscu to a province and put to death all the Big-Endian exiles. Though the episode is introduced with a trace of comic absurdity in the articles of impeachment, and in their pompous phrasing, the court's debate on how to dispose of [179] Gulliver is corrosive satire, savage and ironic. It is suggested that Gulliver be put to a painful and ignominious death, his house set on fire, and thousands of poisoned arrows shot into his face and hands. His servants are to strew poisonous juices on his shirt, to make him tear his own flesh and die in the "utmost torture." At this point Reldresal proves himself Gulliver's "true friend" by suggesting that blindness would be a sufficient punishment; but Gulliver's enemies argue against this proposal. His Imperial Majesty, gracious and lenient, holds out against the death sentence, but hints that punishments in addition to blindness may be inflicted on Gulliver. Finally, again through the friendship of Reldresal, it is decided to blind Gulliver and to starve him to death.

In this episode, which is the longest satiric passage in the first voyage and the climax of the voyage, the satiric attack is bitter. As Swift shows the refinements of hypocrisy, ingratitude, and cruelty achieved by the Lilliputian court, mirth leaves him, and he is as severe as in any part of Voyage IV.

Yet the general sense that the voyage is a merry one is sound. The one passage of essentially corrosive satire is largely outweighed by incidental comedy, by the famous passage of comic satire, and by the wealth of sheerly narrative detail. By the end of chapter vii the corrosive attack has ceased—Gulliver is in Blefuscu, lying on the ground in order to "kiss his Majesty's and the Empress's hand." In the final chapter he is returned to England, and is in familiar and kindly surroundings, enjoying the company of his "dear pledges" and breeding Lilliputian sheep in the absurd hope of improving the English woolen manufacture. Furthermore, there is the basic comic absurdity which pervades the entire voyage, namely, Gulliver's attitude in reporting his experiences. Constantly before our eyes we have the incredible double scale of size, human and Lilliputian, reported without comment by Gulliver, who accepts the Lilliputian scale as easily as the human. It is the comic incongruity of inadequate [180] reporting, felt as inadequate when we visualize the scenes and episodes described by Gulliver. And Swift permits Gulliver so great a use of specific visual detail, in which the two scales of size are constantly blended, that even the unimaginative reader has no difficulty in seeing the picture. Thus the scandal about Gulliver and the Lilliputian lady is immediately comic to the reader. But as Gulliver goes through his elaborate defense of her reputation (and his), the comedy is immensely heightened by the reader's realization of Gulliver's inadequate sense of the situation; in his long defense he never mentions the one particular that makes the scandal perfectly absurd, the difference in physical scale.

If one is thinking primarily of the writer, Swift, one may see in this aspect of Gulliver only a device for understatement. But Swift is achieving his effects by means of a created character; and we see that it is not deliberate understatement for Gulliver, it is simply a result of his character. It is all he finds worth saying. He has definite limitations of mind, which in spite of his development he never outgrows, even in the last voyage.

The second voyage, like the first, has much interesting descriptive and narrative material that is essentially neither comic nor satiric. But there is an increased proportion of comic episode, and the corrosive satire carries far more weight than in the first voyage.

The increased comic effect is achieved principally at the expense of Gulliver, for in the second voyage he is reduced in status and becomes obviously an object of comic satire. He retains a pride and self-esteem which would be perfectly normal for him among his physical equals, but which is ridiculous under the circumstances, and which results in his being made the comic butt in several episodes. The increased corrosive effect is achieved principally by the long passage wherein Gulliver and the king discuss mankind. To this passage we need to give close attention, for the satiric structure

of Voyage IV (although on a different plane) is in important ways
parallel to it. [181]

Swift permits Gulliver to give the king a favorable statement about
the English system. The king perceives that all is not well with Gulliver's civilization; and being a reasonable, thoughtful monarch, he asks
Gulliver a long series of questions. These questions are direct and
to the point; the answers, which are obviously called for, show defects in Gulliver's world. In the passage thus far, there is little or no
emotional, ironic, or comic effect as the king conducts his grave and
judicial inquiry. Finally, when the king has thought over his audiences with Gulliver, he delivers quite calmly his famous criticism of
the human race. As he concludes it, he courteously hopes that Gulliver may have escaped many vices of his kind—nevertheless the bulk
of humanity is "the most pernicious race of little odious vermin that
nature ever suffered to crawl upon the surface of the earth."

So much for the human race, apparently, as judged by a reasonable being who has heard the best case Gulliver can make out for
his kind. And the quality is corrosive, not comic. Yet it is only a
preliminary to the satire that follows. Gulliver's hope to impress the
king has had the reverse effect, but Gulliver himself has not come
off badly. Swift now proceeds to allow Gulliver to reveal himself as
a typical member of the race, and at the same time drives the satiric
attack deeper. Gulliver expresses his great embarrassment at hearing his "noble and most beloved country" so injuriously treated. At
this point, and for the first time in the long passage, Swift calls into
play the double voice of irony. The squirming Gulliver reveals that
he has given "to every point a more favorable turn by many degrees
than the strictness of truth would allow"; but nevertheless he con-
descendingly suggests that "great allowances should be given to a
King who lives so wholly secluded from the rest of the world" and
hence must have an insufficiency of knowledge and "a certain narrowness of thinking, from which we and the politer countries of
Europe are wholly exempted." [182]

Gulliver's comments here have further worsened his case for mankind, besides revealing the absurdity of his sense of superiority to
the king. Another satirist might pause at this point, but Swift has
still to reach his satiric climax and to reduce Gulliver utterly. Gulliver blunders on: "To confirm what I have now said, and further, to
show the miserable effects of a confined education, I shall here in-

sert a passage which will hardly obtain belief." In a word, Gulliver offers the king the secret of gunpowder, giving a notion of its effectiveness by means of a few graphic and specific details. The king is horrified, regards Gulliver as inhuman in advancing such thoughts, and forbids him to mention the matter again. Gulliver is still blind, and shakes his head over the king's reaction, which seems to him "a strange effect of narrow principles and short views."

This long, satiric passage is relatively simple at first, but it becomes elaborate before it ends. We have, first, Gulliver's theme of the excellence of mankind. Next is added the calm and generalized, but corrosive, satire of the king's queries and final dismissal of mankind —a note which sounds through the rest of the passage. Swift then calls irony, and, when he is ready, adds the emotional impact of his most forceful and graphic prose (specific details concerning the effective use of gunpowder). Gulliver's bland assumption that he is doing the king a favor coexists in the reader's mind with the shocking demonstration of what man's inhumanity is capable of; Gulliver is demolishing himself with the reader as well as the king; and Swift is achieving a bitter yet comic irony in Gulliver's naïve unawareness and continued self-assurance. And underlying the whole satiric structure of the long passage is the substructure of physical absurdity: with all his fine words and superiority, Gulliver can be taken into the king's hand and stroked—he is "little Grildrig."

Even so brief an analysis as the foregoing reveals several points important to our discussion. Swift moves from the simpler to the [183] more complex for his satiric climax; to corrosive satire he adds comic and ironic notes. And it is of particular significance to our view of Voyage IV that in achieving his effects Swift has caused Gulliver, unawares, to make a lamentable spectacle of himself.

As we accompany Gulliver to the end of the second voyage, we are in no danger of confusing him with Swift. Gulliver remains likeable—indeed he remains likeable to the end; but Swift always uses him deliberately, even ruthlessly, to further the Swiftian satiric purpose. And Gulliver's characteristics are admirable for this purpose. He is a man of some education, has traveled, and by the end of the second voyage has had very surprising experiences. But he is and remains a type of ordinary, normal man—even a rather simplified version of the type. He is capable with his hands, and quick to meet physical emergency. He is essentially a man of good will, friendly, honest, and ethical according to his lights. His mental makeup is simple and direct, and it permits almost no complexity. He is not torn by any inner conflict, for his psyche is unwilling to admit the diverse possibilities which make for such conflicts. He can be the Gulliver of the first voyage, a man whose normal humanity seems good in the light of petty and ungrateful Lilliputian policy. He can be the Gulliver of the second voyage, whose normal acceptance of the standards and values of his civilization seems bad in the light of largeness and humaneness of spirit. He is much the same man in these two voyages: Swift has shown first the better side of ordinary values, secondly, the worser side. And Gulliver's mind is not at first closed; new experiences occur and give new directions to his thought, or —as in the fourth voyage—produce a shift in his attitude. But the simplicity and naïveté remain; his mind is a single-track one. It never compasses the complex and the contradictory; it cleaves to the best line it knows, but to that line alone.

That Gulliver's mind is not at first closed, but yet is limited, has important consequences. Thus, while he is open-minded, he can [184] change from one attitude to another under the pressure of what he sees and hears about him. Although always a giant in Lilliput, he adopts easily the prevailing Lilliputian scale. Although he is miniature in Brobdingnag, being completely surrounded by a gigantic environment he comes to take the gigantic scale as normal. That new attitude having become habitual with him, the fact of his own minuteness (though constant to his experience) drops out of his mind and ceases to have any meaning. And his new, oversimplified attitude has a narrowness and rigidity which continues after he leaves the land of the giants, and results in comedy when he returns to a world built to his scale. Back in England, he says, "I was afraid of trampling on every traveller I met, and often called aloud to have them stand out of the way, so that I had like to have gotten one or two broken heads for my impertinence." He behaves so unaccountably toward his family that they conclude he has lost his wits. In effect, his new attitude prevents him from believing the evidence of his own eyes. But his mind is not closed, and gradually the physical realities recall him to a proper sense of scale. On Voyage IV, however, in the simple intellectual and moral environment of the Houyhnhnms, and horrified at the Yahoos, Gulliver has that final intellectual development and illumination which leads to the completely closed mind. It is a situation which permits Swift to develop his corrosive attack, but we ought not be surprised to find that Swift remains superior to his puppet to the end, and reveals an attitude different from Gulliver's.

III

The first two voyages of *Gulliver* are two complementary parts which make up one large unit of satire. The fourth part of the book is not simply an additional voyage, more severely satirical but on the whole to be read like the earlier voyages; it is a voyage different in concept and in treatment, and hence it is not to be judged by the same criteria. [185]

We notice at once that the fourth voyage lacks the picturesque and interesting descriptive and narrative detail so abundantly present in the earlier voyages. There is, for instance, no double physical scale, and there is little narrative action. Swift does, of course, embody the chief elements of his satiric analysis in the concrete symbols of the horse and the Yahoo, and he describes the Yahoo in full and unpleasant detail. Even so, the spirit and scheme of the fourth voyage employ far less narrative richness than is expended on Lilliput and Brobdingnag, since Swift shifts the emphasis of his attack. The satire of the earlier voyages is concerned with the flaws and defects of man's actions. Voyage IV cuts deeper. Actions and doings are symptomatic of man's nature—the corrosive satire of the last voyage is concerned with the springs and causes of action, in other words, with the inner make-up of man. Hence, though there is a narrative thread in Voyage IV, and considerable detail about the Yahoo, the voyage is characterized less by fullness of narrative than by fullness of analysis.

Another difference in the fourth voyage should be noted. Here the reader himself is inescapably an object of satiric attack. In the first voyage he may remain calm in the face of the satire. There is not only a good deal else to divert his attention; there is also the fact that the activities of monarchs and statesmen are the actions of an exceedingly small group of people. The reader's withers are unwrung. He may even remain relatively detached emotionally in reading of Gulliver's offer of gunpowder to the Brobdingnagian king. After all, war has been so far only an intermittent activity of nations, and the reader probably disapproves of it in theory as much as Swift does. But the reader cannot evade the attack in the last voyage: Swift is attacking the Yahoo in each of us.

Furthermore, it has now become Swift's purpose to drive home the satire, insistently and relentlessly. Had he wished to achieve [186] only the diverting and comic satire of Voyages I and II, with occasional touches of the severer sort, he need not have written the last voyage. But he chose to go on, and in the fourth voyage corrosive satire at last comes home deeply and profoundly to his readers. In truth, the constant protests against it are evidence of its effectiveness.

Mere narrative or comic detail concerning either the Yahoos or the Houyhnhnms would inevitably tend to weaken, divert, or block off the intensity of the attack; hence Swift makes little use of such detail. He sharply cuts human nature into two parts. He gives reason and benevolence to the Houyhnhnms. Unrestrained and selfish appetites, and a mere brutish awareness, are left for the Yahoo. Since he is writing satire rather than panegyric, the good qualities are given the nonhuman form of the horse, and the bad qualities the nearly human form of the Yahoo. Consider how much less effective the satire would have been had the Houyhnhnms been merely a superior human race—the reader would naturally evade the satiric attack by identifying himself as a Houyhnhnm. Again, for intensity of attack, Swift dwells with unpleasant particularity on Yahoo form and nature: the emphasis is necessarily on Yahoo form and nature. In this connection, it should be said that the unpleasant physical characteristics of the Yahoos are in themselves hardly as repellent as the disgusting physical details Gulliver has noted among the Brobdingnagians. The microscopic eye among the giants produces perhaps as repulsive a series of physical images as can be found in literature; but, for all that, we are aware of a fantastic enlargement, and this makes for relative unreality. The Yahoos are not giants, they resemble us all too closely in some ways, and their unpleasant physical traits are displayed to us without the variety of relief permitted in Voyage II.

Swift's aim in the last voyage is to spare us nothing. If we could chuckle and laugh at the Yahoos, or be diverted by their [187] activities, by so much would Swift have weakened his corrosive satire. And the same exigency governs his treatment of the Houyhnhnms. To make much of them for comic or narrative effect would impair Swift's chief purpose.

One further point: In the first nine chapters of Voyage IV, Swift further simplifies and concentrates his attack by making almost no use of irony; the attack on Yahoo-man is not only severe, but literal and direct.

Is the misanthropy of the fourth voyage, then, too much to accept? Is Swift's hatred all-consuming? Has it abandoned itself to wanton and animus-ridden insult? Has the sanity of his rich and complex genius been dissipated? Before we agree with the many who have answered "Yes" to such questions, let us contemplate the voyage as a whole. For Swift not only wrote the first nine chapters of Voyage IV; he also wrote the last three. To neglect these final chapters is like ignoring the final couplet in a Shakespearean sonnet, the last part of a tragi-comedy like *The Winter's Tale,* or the last three chapters of *Moby Dick.* It is true that Swift's final attitude may not be obvious to a superficial reader, or to one inhibited (perhaps unconsciously) from reading *Gulliver* as a complete satire. But great and complex artists usually make some demands on their readers, and Swift is no exception. *Gulliver's Travels* is easier to understand than *A Tale of a Tub;* but it by no means follows that Lemuel Gulliver's naïve and simple misanthropy can be equated with the sophisticated satirist who recounted Gulliver's adventures. One should be on guard against simplifying an elaborate ironist.

Swift himself has warned us, if we are at all wary. To say that the first nine chapters of the fourth voyage are almost continuous corrosive satire is not to say that there are not some narrative and comic touches. Swift obviously visualized the Houyhnhnms very definitely as horses. It must have been a temptation to his constructive and comic imagination not to avail himself of the [188] opportunities offered by the horse form. Generally he restrains himself: thus Gulliver remembers once seeing some Houyhnhnms "employed in domestic business," but he does not specify what business. Yet Swift cannot resist an occasional bit of fun at the expense of the Houyhnhnms. They have an absolute self-assurance in the completeness of their knowledge and experience. The etymology of the word Houyhnhnm means "horse," but also "the perfection of nature." Their intellectual limitations and arrogance are divertingly illustrated in the passage wherein the Houyhnhnm criticizes the human form. In every point wherein man and horse differ, the Houyhnhnm automatically and even absurdly assumes that the advantage lies obviously with the horse; for example, that four legs are better than two, or that the human anatomy is defective since Gulliver cannot eat without lifting one of his "fore feet" to his mouth. While Swift, in pursuit of his purpose, is chary of making the horses absurd, there are enough comic touches to guard the attentive reader from assuming that Swift accepts Gulliver's worshipful attitude toward the horses.

Further evidence that Swift was well aware that the Houyhnhnms were, after all, horses, and that they offered more material for comedy than he had permitted himself to use in his text, may be found in a letter he wrote his publisher, Motte, concerning illustrations for a new edition of the *Travels*. Since he tells Motte that a return of his deafness has put him "in an ill way to answer a letter which requires some thinking," and since the letter also indicates that he has not re-read *Gulliver* but is trusting to memory, it may be presumed that his remarks indicate his normal attitude toward the book. The relevant part of his letter reads:

The Country of Horses, I think, would furnish many [occasions for illustration]. Gulliver brought to be compared with the Yahoos; the family at dinner and he waiting; the grand council of horses, assembled, sitting, one of them standing with a hoof extended, as if he were speaking; the she-Yahoo embracing Gulliver in the river, who [189] turns away his head in disgust; the Yahoos got into a tree, to infest him under it; the Yahoos drawing carriages, and driven by a horse with a whip in his hoof. I can think of no more, but Mr. Gay will advise you.

Swift's suggestions for illustrations, added to the few ludicrous suggestions in the first nine chapters of the fourth voyage, indicate that he took as a matter of course that there was a certain amount of comic effect in the rather simple horses visualized in their relationship of superiority to Gulliver and the Yahoos. Since Gulliver's Houyhnhnm worship is a vital element in making the corrosive attack on Yahoo nature effective, it might seem that Swift had bungled his craft in permitting even slight evidences of the limitations of the Houyhnhnms. Actually, without weakening the main attack of the early part of the voyage, these slight hints foreshadow Swift's attitude in the last three chapters. As a composer of music, giving almost complete emphasis to a main theme, may suggest from time to time a new theme before he develops it fully, so Swift, while developing misanthropic and corrosive satire at length, hints from time to time at another theme.

The horses and Gulliver have it all their own way for the first nine chapters of the last voyage. Yahoo-man has been presented in all his horror; Swift has achieved the most blasting and unrelieved satiric attack possible, and at great length. What simple and indignant reason can say against the flaws and defects of human nature has been said, and said exhaustively. Gulliver's revolt against his kind is so complete that Swift is able to give the knife a final twist: mankind is, if anything, worse than the Yahoo, since man is afflicted by pride, and makes use of what mental power he has to achieve perversions and corruptions undreamed of by the Yahoo.

At this point of the satiric attack many readers have ceased really to read the book, and have concluded that this was Swift's final word because it is Gulliver's final word. Swept away by the [190] force of the corrosive attack on Yahoo-man, they conclude that Gulliver is at last Swift. (Such a misconception is facilitated no doubt by Swift's temporary abandonment of irony for straightforward invective.) In the last three chapters, however, Swift shows that Gulliver's word cannot be final.

Swift, satirist and realist, is well aware that there is more of the Yahoo in humanity than there is of benevolence and reason. And he develops his attack as forcibly as he can, by means of corrosive satire, in terms of pessimism and misanthropy. But this is only a part of Swift. He is also perfectly aware that the problem is not so simply solved as it is for the Houyhnhnms and for Gulliver. He knows that there is much to be hated in the animal called man, but he knows also that there are individuals whom he loves. The horses have no room for anything between Houyhnhnm and Yahoo, and Gulliver takes over this too simple attitude. Just as his physical sense of proportion was upset by his voyage to the country of the giants, so here his intellectual sense of proportion is overbalanced. The limited, simplified Houyhnhnm point of view is obviously better to him than the Yahoo state; and he cleaves to it. Swift can keep clear the double physical scale of Gulliver and giant; not so, Gulliver. Swift can differentiate between Yahoo and Gulliver, and does—but Gulliver himself is convinced he is a Yahoo. The attentive reader will realize that Gulliver is the one actual human being present through the first nine blighting chapters of the last voyage. Hence he is not only a constant reminder that horse and Yahoo are symbols, but also a constant demonstration that a human being is not a Yahoo.

Swift has fun with Gulliver in chapter x. Gulliver has finally come to the conclusion that human beings are, if anything, worse than Yahoos. As much as possible he tries to transform himself into a horse:

By conversing with the Houyhnhnms, and looking upon them with delight, I fell to imitate their gait and gesture, which is now grown [191] into a habit, and my friends often tell me in a blunt way, that I trot like a horse; which, however, I take for a great compliment. Neither shall I disown that in speaking I am apt to fall into the voice and manner of the Houyhnhnms. . . .

And in the paragraph immediately following this excerpt, with Gulliver at the height of his enchantment, Swift has the horses, with more ruthlessness than benevolence, order Gulliver to leave the island and swim back to the place whence he came. Gulliver swoons. He is allowed two months to finish a boat, and is granted the assistance of a sorrel nag, who "had a tenderness" for him. It is a diverting picture: Gulliver and the sorrel nag working away together to make a canoe, "covering it with the skins of Yahoos well stitched together" and "stopping all the chinks with Yahoos' tallow." When the moment of parting comes:

His Honor, out of curiosity and perhaps (if I may speak it without vanity) partly out of kindness, was determined to see me in my canoe. . . . I took a second leave of my master; but as I was going to prostrate myself to kiss his hoof, he did me the honor to raise it gently to my mouth. I am not ignorant how much I have been censured for mentioning this last particular. For my detractors are pleased to think it improbable that so illustrious a person should descend to give so great a mark of distinction to a creature so inferior as I. . . .

My master and his friends continued on the shore till I was almost out of sight; and I often heard the sorrel nag (who always loved me) crying out, *Hnuy illa nyha majah Yahoo,* Take care of thyself, gentle Yahoo.

It is heartbreaking for Gulliver; but for Swift and the reader it is not wholly a matter for tears.

Gulliver's design is to make his way to an "uninhabited island," but he is eventually found by the crew of a Portuguese ship. Gulliver's meeting with the crew returns him to the real world; he is no longer the sole representative of humanity, placed between horse and Yahoo. In the earlier voyages, Swift had spent only a few pages on Gulliver's return to the real world; in the last, he gives two chapters to it. Those chapters deserve very careful [192] reading: they are, as the book now stands, the climax of Swift's whole satire as well as the end of the fourth voyage. Gulliver, hating himself and all men as Yahoos, is reintroduced to the world of actual men and women. What happens? If Swift's view is the same as Gulliver's, he ought to go on with his severe satire against mankind, now even deepening it with specific examples of Yahoo nature. He does noth-

ing of the sort. Rather, he shows us very carefully and at some length
the insufficiency of Gulliver's new attitude. Gulliver continues to
"tremble between fear and hatred" when confronted by human beings, while at the same time his own account of affairs shows that
the persons with whom he comes into contact are essentially honest,
kindly, and generous. It is the same limited mentality in Gulliver
which has been noted in previous voyages. He has adopted a final
rigid and oversimplified attitude, which so completely possesses him
that he cannot believe the evidence of his own experience; since he
now sees man only as Yahoo, he cannot even take in contradictory
evidence when faced with it.

The Portuguese crew speak to Gulliver "with great humanity"
when they find him; but he is horrified. Concluding that his misfortunes have "impaired his reason" (as indeed they have), they
deliver him up to the captain.

[The captain's] name was Pedro de Mendez; he was a very courteous
and generous person; he entreated me to give some account of myself,
and desired to know what I would eat and drink; said I should be used as
well as himself, and spoke so many obliging things, that I wondered to
find such civilities in a Yahoo. However, I remained silent and sullen; I
was ready to faint at the very smell of him and his men.

Gulliver finally promises the captain not to attempt anything against
his own life, but at the same time protests that he will "suffer the
greatest hardships rather than return to live among Yahoos." In
the course of the voyage home, out of gratitude to Don Pedro, Gulliver sometimes sits with the captain and tries to [193] conceal his
antipathy to mankind. The captain offers Gulliver the best suit of
clothes he has; Gulliver will accept only two clean shirts, which,
he thinks, will not so much "defile" him. In Lisbon, the captain still
further aids Gulliver, takes him into his house, and persuades him
to accept a newly made suit of clothes. Gulliver finds that his terror
at humanity gradually lessens: the captain's "whole deportment was
so obliging, added to a very good *human* understanding, that I really
began to tolerate his company." But though the terror might lessen,
Gulliver's "hatred and contempt seemed to increase."

Why does Swift give us Don Pedro, the kindly, generous individual? Obviously as a foil to Gulliver's misanthropy, as evidence that
Gulliver has gone off the deep end and cannot recover himself from
the nightmare view of Yahoo-man. Chapter xi is almost wholly a

demonstration that Gulliver is absurd in his blind refusal to abandon his misanthropic convictions. His conduct upon his return home is the ultimate result of his aberration. His family receive him with joy, but the sight of them fills Gulliver with hatred, contempt, and disgust. When his wife kisses him, he falls "into a swoon for almost an hour." His adopted attitude of mind, directed by the too simple Houyhnhnm view, permits him to see only the Yahoo in man or woman. Even after five years he will not permit any member of his family to take him by the hand. But we may allow him to characterize his mode of life himself:

The first money I laid out was to buy two young stone-horses, which I keep in a good stable, and next to them the groom is my greatest favorite, for I feel my spirits revived by the smell he contracts in the stable. My horses understand me tolerably well; I converse with them at least four hours every day.

Gulliver's attitude is not the solution, and Swift knew it. It is too unbalanced and unrealistic for a final attitude, and Swift presents its absurdity—so clearly as to make one wonder how he [194] could have been so misunderstood. Gulliver's attitude is in effect a complete quarrel with man, a final refusal to accept the nature of mankind. To charge Swift with the same final refusal is to ignore the evidence. In this connection a passage from the second voyage, where surely Swift is speaking through Gulliver, is helpful. Gulliver has been reading a Brobdingnagian book, and says:

This writer went through all the usual topics of European moralists, showing how diminutive, contemptible, and helpless was man in his own nature [i.e., the sixty-foot nature of the Brobdingnagians]. . . . The author drew several moral applications useful in the conduct of life, but needless here to repeat. For my own part, I could not avoid reflecting how universally this talent was spread, of drawing lectures in morality, or indeed matter for discontent and repining, from the quarrels we raise with nature.

I do not by any means wish to say that Swift was always superior to drawing matter for discontent and repining from quarrels raised with nature. He was clear-sighted and sensitive; he was an ethical moralist and a satirist. Much in the nature of man was hateful and detestable to him, and he often attacked it and quarreled with it in no uncertain terms. But, though Gulliver's soul was completely discontented, completely repining, Swift could rise to a far higher plane, and did so. Swift was much more than a corrosive satirist only; he had a high sense of the comic, and in the final satiric vision of the concluding chapters of *Gulliver* the Gulliverian discontent is supplemented by, and enclosed in, comic satire, with Gulliver himself as the butt.

In Voyage IV, Swift gives his severest satiric vision full scope, but knows that conclusions growing out of this nightmare vision are inadequate and invalid. He lets Gulliver go the whole horse, and up to the last page the negative, corrosive attack is present. But what else he does in those last chapters is unique in the history of satiric literature: the severe attack with its apparently rational basis and its horrifying conclusions continues to the end in the personal narrative of Swift's puppet. Thus severe satire [195] remains the main theme, but the new theme of Gulliver's absurdity complicates the issue. By rising to a larger and more comprehensive view than he permits to Gulliver, Swift is satirically commenting on the insufficiency of the corrosive attitude. The evils in the world and in man are such that it is no wonder that a simple and ethical nature may be driven to despair and misanthropy. Nevertheless, such an attitude Swift demonstrates to be inadequate and absurd.

Gulliver's attitude, in its simplicity and finality, is a kind of misanthropic solution of the problem of evil. It is a tempting solution for a severe satirist; but Swift found it too limited and too unreal. So far as I can see, Swift offers no answer of his own, no solution. But he does transcend the misanthropic solution. He could see that his own severest satire was the result of a partial and one-sided view, which was therefore properly a subject for mirth.

This seems to me the final comedy of Lemuel Gulliver—that Swift could make an elaborate and subtle joke at the expense of a very important part of himself. We may leave Lemuel in amiable discourse in the stable, inhaling the grateful odor of horse. But Swift is not with him, Swift is above him in the realm of comic satire, still indignant at the Yahoo in man, but at the same time smiling at the absurdity of the view that can see *only* the Yahoo in man. [196]

from The Significance
of *Gulliver's Travels*

ARTHUR E. CASE

The opening paragraph of the last book [of *Gulliver's Travels*] speaks of his [Gulliver's] remaining at home "in a very happy condition" about four months, but this statement is for the purpose of providing a contrast with Gulliver's change of heart during the final voyage—a change of heart more significant and more carefully depicted than any that has gone before.

The changing attitude of Gulliver toward the yahoos and the Houyhnhnms is of the first importance in determining the significance of those two species and, in consequence, of the whole voyage in deed, of the entire *Travels*. At the opening of the voyage Gulliver is a representative European, somewhat better, perhaps, than most of his class, but by no means a paragon, and certainly a man who has adjusted himself to [117] a consciousness of the ordinary and even the extraordinary vices and follies of humanity. In this state he does not recognize that the yahoos have any likeness to man: they are, to him, "ugly Monsters," to be described as a traveler would describe any curious and loathesome beast he encountered in the course of his adventures. It is not until the Houyhnhnms place him beside a yahoo for purposes of comparison that he sees any resemblance between himself and these "abominable Animals," and then he emphasizes those physical aspects which the yahoos have in common with "savage Nations." At the same time he stresses the difference between the behavior of Europeans and that of yahoos, which is apparently something more repulsive than he has encountered in the whole breadth of his travels. For a considerable time he protests against being identified with the yahoos, and even begs his master not to apply the word "yahoo" to him. During the first three chapters he avoids speaking of Europeans as yahoos, calling them "others of my own Kind," "Creatures like myself," or "our Countrymen." Acknowledging the physical resemblance between human beings and yahoos, he protests that he cannot account for the "degenerate and brutal nature" of the latter. Gradually, in the course of the conversations with his master which occupy the fourth, fifth, sixth, and seventh chapters, Gulliver falls into the habit of referring to Europeans as yahoos, partly for convenience and partly because, as the perfection of the Houyhnhnms is borne in upon him and contrasted with the actions and thoughts of his countrymen, he becomes aware, little by little, of the discrepancy between ideal and actual man. This new consciousness is intensified by his contemplation of the Houyhnhnms and their institutions, as they are described in the eighth and ninth chapters. The ultimate state of mind produced in Gulliver by this gradual process of education through contact with a superior race is expressly stated in the tenth chapter.

At first, indeed, I did not feel that natural Awe which the *Yahoos* and all other Animals bear towards them; but it grew upon me by Degrees, much sooner than I imagined, and was mingled with a respectful Love and Gratitude, that they would [118] condescend to distinguish me from the rest of my Species. ([Bk.] 4. [Ch.] 10. [Par.] 3.)

The attitude of the Houyhnhnms toward Gulliver is of particular interest. From the first they distinguish him from the yahoos of the island—partly, it is true, because of his clothes, but also because of his behavior. The master Houyhnhnm at once admits Gulliver to the house, a privilege which he would not have accorded an ordinary yahoo, and is astonished at the "Teachableness, Civility and Cleanliness" of this prodigy. All the Houyhnhnms who meet Gulliver are similarly impressed. The master describes him to the quadrennial assembly as a "wonderful *Yahoo*" with all the qualities of that animal, "only a little more civilized by some Tincture of Reason, which however was in a degree as far inferior to the *Houyhnhnm* Race as the *Yahoos* of their Country were to [Gulliver]." This placing of Gulliver midway between the Houyhnhnms and the yahoos, by a creature possessing absolute accuracy of judgment, is extremely significant. In the end the master dismisses Gulliver with regret and shows no disinclination to his society. In other words, a somewhat-above-average Englishman was not altogether unacceptable company for a perfect being.

The natural result of Gulliver's experiences among the Houyhnhnms, and of his mental development, is to be found in the last two chapters of the *Travels* and in the *Letter to Sympson*. The expressions about humanity which are found here are not those of Gulliver in his normal state of mind. Swift is employing a device which he has used once before, at the conclusion of the second voyage, when his hero returned from the earlier and less nearly perfect Utopia of Brobdingnag. Evidently Swift was fascinated by the idea of the difficulty of readjusting oneself to ordinary existence after a prolonged exposure to extraordinary conditions. In the second voyage the extraordinary conditions have to do with physical dimensions: and Swift, delighting in the play of his imagination, spends nearly half of the last chapter in describing Gulliver's inability to accustom himself to the size of the [119] captain and crew of the ship which rescues him, and his odd behavior on his arrival in England.

As I was on the Road, observing the Littleness of the Houses, the Trees, the Cattle and the People, I began to think my self in *Lilliput*. I was afraid of trampling on every Traveller I met, and often called aloud to have them stand out of the way, so that I had like to have gotten one or two broken Heads for my Impertinence.

When I came to my own House, for which I was forced to enquire, one of the Servants opening the Door, I bent down to go in (like a Goose under a Gate) for fear of striking my Head. My Wife ran out to embrace me, but I stooped lower than her Knees, thinking she could otherwise never be able to reach my Mouth. My Daughter kneeled to ask me Blessing, but I could not see her till she arose, having been so long used to stand with my Head and Eyes erect to above sixty Foot; and then I went to take her up with one Hand, by the Waste. I looked down upon the Servants and one or two Friends who were in the House, as if they had been Pigmies, and I a Giant. I told my Wife she had been too thrifty, for I found she had starved herself and her Daughter to nothing. In short, I behaved my self so unaccountably, that they were all of the Captain's Opinion when he first saw me, and concluded I had lost my Wits. This I mention as an Instance of the great Power of Habit and Prejudice. (2.8.15–16.)

In the same way, but dealing with a far more significant matter—readjustment to mental and spiritual, rather than physical conditions —Swift shows us at the end of the fourth voyage his conception of the effects which would be produced in the mind of an intelligent man who spent a long period in the company of creatures who were perfect in every way. Such a man, Swift believed, would tend to exaggerate his own imperfections and those of the race to which he belonged, and would, in the end, find living with his former associates intolerable. Anything less than perfection would be abhorrent: degrees of imperfection would be imperceptible and irrelevant. The opinions concerning mankind which Gulliver gives vent to are his own, not those of his creator. To emphasize this, Swift provides Gulliver with an unusual [120] rescuer from his last adventure— Captain Pedro de Mendez. The majority of the seamen in the *Travels* are a good sort, but Mendez is a paragon. His generosity, his acute perception of the state of Gulliver's mind, his unfailing kindliness in the face of repeated rebuffs, mark him as the finest of all the European characters in the book. Yet Gulliver, controlled by the exalted conception of virtue he has acquired from living with Houyhnhnms, and by his now fixed belief in the utter worthlessness of all yahoos, with whom he has come to group the human race, is unable to perceive even the most extraordinary goodness when it manifests itself in one of the hated species. The effects of this mental alteration are, of course, more lasting than those which resulted from the journey to Brobdingnag, but they are not permanent: after five years Gulliver is able in retrospect to appreciate the virtues of Mendez (4.11.14), and he gradually becomes more accustomed to his family (4.12.12). *The Letter to Sympson* is a flare-up of the old idealism: it is also Swift's attempt to do the almost impossible—to write a second climax to his book more powerful than the first.

Parallel with the deepening of Gulliver's character run other literary devices which reinforce it. The most interesting of these has to do with the events leading up to his various adventures. In the first case he suffers shipwreck, caused by sheer mischance, or at the most mischance combined with natural human carelessness. On his arrival in Brobdingnag he is deserted by his terrified comrades under circumstances which make their cowardice understandable and perhaps excusable. At the beginning of the third voyage he experiences violence and cruelty from pirates. Finally he is marooned on Houyhnhnmland by the treachery of his own men. So effective a progression can hardly have been the result of accident.

There is plenty of other evidence of the careful planning and equally careful revision of the book before publication. Swift's first reference to the *Travels* in his letters to Ford [34] indicates that the large design was already clear in his mind in April, 1721. Apparently he devoted from fourteen to seventeen months to the draft of the first two voyages,[35] and a [121] year and a half to the fourth [36] (the latter period, near its end, being disturbed by the culmination of the affair of Vanessa). It is interesting to find that he composed the third voyage last, evidently feeling that the main theme was chiefly developed in the others: yet as he embarked upon the third voyage he wrote to Ford in words which show that he had previously conveyed to his friend the plan he intended to follow.[37] The writing of the third voyage (interrupted by the *Drapier's Letters*) took another year and a half,[38] and finally he required more than half a year to correct, augment, and transcribe the whole of the *Travels*.[39] This hardly agrees with the theory that the four voyages show a lack of unified planning, and that their tone and subject matter indicate that they were the product of events which occurred while Swift was writing and of the moods which these events created in the author's mind. Indeed, it is strange that anyone familiar with Swift's political pamphlets of the last four years of Anne's reign, with their masterly adjustment of tone to the audience and to the end desired, should suppose that in his greatest work, over the composition and revision of which he spent far more time and pains than over any other of his books, he should have been the slave of passing moods.

Above all it is necessary to insist upon the fact that Swift never

[34] *The Letters of Jonathan Swift to Charles Ford*, ed. David Nichol Smith, Oxford, 1935, p. 97.

[35] This is on the assumption that Swift began the *Travels* between January and April, 1721 (*vide supra*, pp. 97 and 106–7), and finished the first two voyages about June or July, 1722 (*vide supra*, p. 98).

[36] The fourth voyage was finished by January, 1723–4: see the letter to Ford, *supra*, p. 99.

[37] See the letter to Ford, *supra*, p. 99.

[38] The draft was apparently finished by August, 1725: see the letter to Ford, *supra*, p. 100.

[39] This assumes that Swift did not finish the emendations until shortly before he went to England in the spring of 1726. It is, of course, possible to interpret Swift's statements in his letter to Pope on September 29, 1725 (*supra*, pp. 100–101) to mean that the emendations had been completed by that time.

allowed specific incidents to interfere with his general purpose, though like most good authors he was quick to seize upon them when he could turn them to account. Dante, when he wished to rebuke the vices of his day, often inveighed against them in the persons of unimportant contemporaries. Swift, attacking the ignorance and ingratitude displayed by the public in its treatment of its leaders, drew upon the careers of two of his friends who were of unquestionable importance and who, he felt sincerely, had suffered from these vices of the populace. But Swift was more skillful than Dante at least in this: his readers might apprehend the full meaning of his sermon without bothering their heads about Oxford or Bolingbroke. The parable of the rebellion of Lindalino could carry its message, and can still carry it, to those who care nothing for eighteenth-century Dublin and Wood's brass [122] money. Swift's use of this latter incident in *Gulliver's Travels* is the best example of his subordination of personal and local interests to his greater design. Had he been governed by an egotistic desire to exalt his own importance, what an opportunity this story afforded him! Had he been the Irishman prosecuting a war against England, how much he might have made of a sectional quarrel! But he was here concerned with the larger issue of tyranny over the whole British nation by a despotic king and his court. If there is an "Irish period" in Swift's writings it does not show itself in *Gulliver's Travels*, either here or in his picture of the yahoos, whom some would have to be "the old savage Irish." These miserable, mistreated people could, indeed, have furnished Swift with material for his physical description of the subhuman creatures so deeply detested by the Houyhnhnms, but so could the poorer classes in England, where crime, poverty, dirt, drunkenness and disease had not yet been done away with, as Hogarth's drawings testify. Swift, in his greatest work, had set up a larger canvas: his *atelier* was Ireland, his model England, his portrait that of western civilization. Of his purpose we have his own testimony both before and after the publication of Gulliver. Writing to Ford in 1725 he said his *Travels* were admirable things and would wonderfully mend the world. In the summer of 1727 the Abbé des Fontaines, who had translated the *Travels* into French, wrote to Swift apologizing for the omission of some passages not suitable for France. Swift replied,

If the volumes of Gulliver were designed only for the British Isles, that traveler ought to pass for a very contemptible writer. The same vices and the same follies reign everywhere; at least in the civilized countries of

Europe: and the author who writes only for one city, one province, one kingdom, or even one age, does not deserve to be read, let alone translated.[40]

The two passages just quoted emphasize a fact too often ignored by readers of *Gulliver's Travels*—that Swift conceived himself as a positive moral and social reformer. From his earliest to his latest writings there is plentiful evidence of his conviction that he knew not only what was wrong with the world, but also the means by which the world could be brought [123] nearer to perfection. Living as he did in an age which was habituated to a belief that the world tended to decline, whether from the Golden Age of classical mythology or from the Garden of Eden of Hebrew legend, it is not surprising that he proposed reforms which often (though by no means always) called for a return to a real or an imagined earlier practice that was nearer to perfection. The range and the detailed practicality of his schemes may be studied in his pamphlets, from those which describe the ideal "gothic" form of government to those which recommend the licensing of beggars or the correction of the English language. In the *Travels,* as elsewhere, his advice is expressed sometimes directly, sometimes by inversion. In the sixth chapter of the first voyage, and generally in his description of the Brobdingnagians, he points to practical devices, such as the public reward of virtue among the Lilliputians, which Europe might well adopt. But he is equally clear, and perhaps more effective, when he suggests the way of life he believes in by a satiric attack upon its opposite. Only a dull intellect could fail to understand that a man who rails at filth advocates cleanliness. The Houyhnhnms and the yahoos represent the extremes between which human behavior may range. Swift certainly did not expect humanity to achieve the height or sink to the depth: he did feel that for the moment, at least, man's tendency was downward, and that strenuous efforts were needed if the trend was to be reversed. To this end he bent his efforts with increasing fervor. Occasionally, as at the conclusion of the *Letter to Sympson,* his missionary zeal expressed itself in a jeremiad:

[40] *The Correspondence of Jonathan Swift, D.D.,* ed. F. Elrington Ball (6 vols.), London, 1910, 3.407. In the original French the passage runs: "Si donc les livres du sieur Gulliver ne sont calcules que pour les isles Britanniques, ce voyageur doit passer pour un tres pitoyable ecrivain. Les memes vices et les memes folies regnent partout; du moins, dans tous les pays civilisés de l'Europe: et l'auteur, que n'ecrit que pour une ville, une province, un royaume, ou meme un siecle, merite si peu d'être traduit, qu'il ne merite pas d'etre lû."

I must freely confess, that since my last Return, some Corruptions of my *Yahoo* Nature have revived in me by conversing with a few of your Species, and particularly those of mine own Family, by an unavoidable Necessity; else I should never have attempted so absurd a Project as that of reforming the *Yahoo* Race in this Kingdom; but I have now done with all such visionary Schemes for ever. (Par. 9.)

But some years later, in the *Verses on the Death of Dr. Swift*, he made his defender say of him, [124]

> His Satyr points at no Defect
> But what all Mortals may correct; . . .[41]

What drove Swift to his occasional outbursts of fury was the consciousness of his own helplessness. In his youth his discontent had been due largely to the postponement of his entry into the world of affairs in a position suited to his capacity. During the few short years of the Oxford–Bolingbroke administration he had employed all his energies in attempts to put into effect certain ideas with which he felt his powerful friends were in sympathy. Then had followed the blasting of his hopes by the triumph of the Whigs, and the gradually growing, bitter conviction that never again in his lifetime would he be in a position of political power. It is hardly to be wondered at that he sometimes allowed himself the relief of savage invective.

It is this savage invective that is responsible for the common belief that Swift was a misanthrope. Swift himself lent some color to this legend by his own statement in a letter already quoted.

. . . the chief end I propose to myself in all my labours is to vex the world rather than divert it; and if I could compass that design, without hurting my own person or fortune, I would be the most indefatigable writer you have ever seen, without reading. . . . when you [Pope] think of the world, give it one lash the more at my request. I have ever hated all nations, professions, and communities, and all my love is toward individuals: for instance, I hate the tribe of lawyers, but I love Counsellor Such-a-one, and Judge Such-a-one: so with physicians—I will not speak of my own trade—soldiers, English, Scotch, French, and the rest. But principally I hate and detest that animal called man, although I heartily love John, Peter, Thomas, and so forth. This is the system upon which I have governed myself many years, but do not tell, and so I shall go on till I have done with them. I have got materials toward a treatise, proving the falsity of that definition *animal rationale*, and to show it would be

---

[41] *The Poems of Jonathan Swift* (ed. Harold Williams), 2.571 (ll. 463–4).

only *rationis capax*. Upon this great foundation of misanthropy, though not in Timon's manner, the whole building of my Travels is erected; and I never will have peace of mind till all honest men are of my opinion.[42] [125]

The words of this letter themselves show that Swift's "misanthropy" was something far different from the state of mind usually associated with the term. The actions of men in the mass infuriated Swift by their folly and criminality: for individuals he had boundless affection. If his letter had not thus made clear his real attitude toward mankind his whole biography would have done so. It is impossible to ignore the extent of Swift's practical charities, often contrived at the cost of great personal sacrifice of time and money: the daily round of Dublin beggars, the bequest to the hospital for the insane. It is impossible to forget the interest he displayed in the welfare of these who had been placed in his personal care, either as servants or as parishioners: the daily prayers conducted for his domestic staff so quietly that visitors in the house were often unaware of them; the services in the church, day after day and year after year, however thinly attended, lest a worshiper be turned away unministered to. And above all it is impossible to shut one's eyes to Swift's need for human companionship and sympathy. This need Swift often tried to conceal, perhaps because of pride in a cherished self-sufficiency, but his constant seeking out of friends and his correspondence with those who were beyond his reach betray him. Conscience compelled him, as a self-appointed father to the world, to chasten his children, but he wanted their love as well as their obedience. And sometimes this craving for understanding and affection found expression—never more clearly than in the *Verses on the Death of Dr. Swift*, written some five years after *Gulliver's Travels* had fixed in the minds of many contemporaries the fiction of Swift, the enemy of mankind. It is an appeal that from a lesser man would have been pathetic: coming from a genius of the magnitude of Swift it lays bare a tragedy. [126]

[42] *The Correspondence of Jonathan Swift, D.D.*, ed. F. Elrington Ball (6 vols.), London, 1910, 3.276–7.

The Unity of *Gulliver's Travels*

SAMUEL KLIGER

It is universally agreed that *Gulliver's Travels* is one of the world's irreplaceable masterpieces. Agreement is lacking, however, as to the means which Swift employed to gain the clarity of purpose, clarity of thought, and clarity of expression which, presumably, are the essential characteristics of the literary masterpiece. Historical explanations of one sort or another have been offered as the key to Swift's purpose and thought, without, however, resulting in a noticeable sharing of agreement. Progress has indeed been made, and recently the historical method of analysis has itself been questioned. Seeking to surmount the limitations in the historical approach, Professor Merrell D. Clubb, in a survey of the reception of *Gulliver's Travels* among critics since its publication, has discovered the historical causes operating to defeat the critics.[1] Thus, Clubb points out that eighteenth-century notions of benevolence, and, in the next century, Victorian prudery, were responsible for the critical misunderstanding of the allegory and for the charge of misanthropy leveled at Swift's head. In the novel's own day, according to Clubb, the benevolists "afflicted . . . with an unctuous and sentimental pride . . . became suddenly conscious of a heavenly vocation to vindicate the race" from Swift's supposedly fiendish attack.[2] In the nineteenth century, Victorian prudes, as a result of their "rigidly literalistic attitude

Reprinted from the *Modern Language Quarterly*, VI (December 1945), 401–415. By permission.
[1] Merrell D. Clubb, "The Criticism of Gulliver's 'Voyage to the Houyhnhnms,' 1726–1914," *Stanford Studies in Language and Literature: Fiftieth Anniversary of the Founding of Stanford University*, ed. Hardin Craig (Stanford University Press, 1941), 203–32.
[2] *Ibid.*, p. 212.

toward the allegory," failed to appreciate the subtlety of Swift's irony, and accordingly perpetuated the eighteenth-century tradition that Swift was a misanthrope.[3] In other words, the limitations in the approach of the eighteenth- and nineteenth-century critics arose precisely from the fact that they were able to answer the question whether Swift was a misanthrope only in accordance with the view of human nature they already held. Since each century makes its own assumptions about human nature, the result is that the meaning of the novel never becomes fixed. The true meaning of the novel recedes each time that the critic approaches it in the light of a new *a priori* assumption about human nature. Presumably, the assumptions of the twentieth-century critic, made from the viewpoint of Freudian psychology, let us say, will similarly [401] defeat the aim to comprehend what the novel itself has to say about human nature.

It is questionable whether Clubb's own analysis of the novel avoids the errors of the historical-deductive method which he exposes. Clubb's postulate of a period of gloom in Swift's life during which the book was composed purports to deal with the misanthropy in this particular book. Actually, however, his postulate deals with the misanthropy in such a way that it becomes only a particular illustration of a universal, *a priori* truth concerning the relationship between a novel—any novel, that is—and the state of the author's health, finances, love-life, and so forth, during or immediately preceding the period of a novel's composition.[4] From such historical explanations, in short, we learn more and more about the author but progressively less about the novel itself. The deductive critic discovers only such combinations of universal qualities as he is seeking, but never the particularity of the novel, or poem, or play, itself. The critical attitude towards *Gulliver's Travels* clearly needs to be revised, but there is no gain in casting out an error only to bring it in again under a new guise. The real question is not whether Swift is a misanthrope, but whether Gulliver is a misanthrope; in the latter case, the novel furnishes its own answers to the question. If the novel is self-explanatory, it is pure supererogation to seek explanations from the field of psychiatry.

[3] *Ibid.*, pp. 224–25.
[4] The same assumption has died a hard, lingering death in Shakespearian criticism in explanation of the dramatist's so-called "tragic period"; it is kept alive only in exceptional academic circles. Clubb retains the principle but applies it to *Gulliver.*

The method of the literary artist, as Aristotle's *Poetics* has made abundantly clear, is always an inclusive and organic one: a presentation of a whole. From this viewpoint, it becomes clear at once that *Gulliver's Travels* does not merely contain but organizes ideas. Swift's ideas are plotted, as well as made explicit, in the novel. Critical commentary, therefore, instead of being aimed at discovering special combinations between the novel's ideas and such universal, extrinsic ideas as are derivable from psychiatry and sociology, ought to be aimed at a consistent analysis of the novel itself with a view to discovering the implicative relations between ideas raised in different parts of the novel in different ways. The critical account of the novel will, as a result, illuminate those features of relationship and order interrelating the parts in a coherent scheme of action which alone forms our understanding of the novel. A second strong objection to Clubb's hypothesis of an analogical relationship between a period of personal disillusionment in Swift's life and the bitter treatment of mankind in the novel is that the hypothesis, if true, would constrain Clubb to treat *Gulliver's Travels* not as a unique work but as an undifferentiated part of the corpus of works which [402] Swift wrote (or which he might have written) as he passed through the supposed period of gloom. Furthermore, when any one part of the novel is arbitrarily set off from the remainder as presenting the main critical question, it becomes obvious that the critical commentary is missing the progressive unfolding of the meaning of the novel through the interrelation of all its parts taken together.

The features of relationship and order among the parts of *Gulliver's Travels* stand out boldly. Relationship and order in Swift's allegory are achieved, as this essay purposes to make clear, through balance and contrast. Balance and contrast are the expository devices by means of which Swift expresses his ideas. In this essay, these devices will be dealt with as the internal causes producing the unique effect on the reader of Swift's fictional masterpiece.

I

Structurally (and hence, thematically, if the point of view of this paper is soundly taken) the significance of the balance and contrast in the allegory arises from the fact that Swift first introduces an idea or motif with deliberate casualness in an earlier book; however, when the idea is reintroduced in a later book, Swift's intent is not merely to effect a balance or contrast but always to load the idea upon its recurrence with a heavy freight of satire.

We may begin with balance and contrast in the return motif. Gulliver's return to England from Lilliput necessitates that he make a physical adjustment to English conditions of living. Thus, Gulliver's care in not crushing the tiny Lilliputians as he walked among them has become a habit, and, upon his return, he is still apprehensive lest he crush Englishmen of normal size:

> As I was on the road, observing the littleness of the houses, the trees, the cattle, and the people I began to think myself in Lilliput. I was afraid of trampling on every traveller I met, and often called aloud to have them stand out of the way, . . .[5]

Upon his return from Brobdingnag, Gulliver is similarly compelled to make a physical adjustment, as this time he mistakes Englishmen for giants. When the sailors discover Gulliver inside the box in which the Brobdingnagians set him afloat on the sea, Gulliver asks the sailors to "let one of the crew put his finger into the ring, and take the box out of the sea into the ship." [6] Gulliver had seen, of course, similar feats of physical prowess among the giants, but he soon realizes that he has overestimated the physical strength of his fellow countrymen: [403]

> Some of them upon hearing me talk so wildly thought I was mad; others laughed; for indeed it never came into my head that I was now got among people of my own stature and strength.[7]

Gulliver's association with the giants also induces him unconsciously to bellow at his countrymen since, as he says, "when I spoke in that country, it was like a man talking in the street to another looking out from the top of a steeple." [8]

Gulliver's physical difficulties are, obviously, a part of the account of the marvelous which the reader expects to find in a travel tale. But Swift's allegory runs deeper than mere entertainment. The casual, humorous account of Gulliver's difficulties in making physical adjustments serves the basic satiric theme when the narrative soon reveals that, in reality, Gulliver's difficulty is in making not physical but moral adjustments to Englishmen. After his blissful sojourn

---

[5] Book II, Chapter 8, page 154, of the edition of Arthur E. Case (New York: Thomas Nelson and Sons, 1941). All references are to this edition.
[6] II, 8, p. 148.   [7] II, 8, p. 148.   [8] II, 8, p. 152.

among the kindly Houyhnhnms, Gulliver sadly returns to the world of men, and for a year he cannot endure the presence even of his family. It is precisely at this point that the charge of misanthropy is introduced into discussion of the allegory. But a livelier appreciation of the features of relationship and order in the story will make clear the real meaning of the balance and contrast between Gulliver's necessity to make physical adjustments on the one hand, and his necessity to make moral adjustments on the other. The first compulsion placed upon Gulliver is introduced casually, but the second compulsion bears high satirical voltage when the reader learns the extent of human folly which makes it so very difficult for the returning voyager to make readjustment. Swift dallies with fantasy in his casual account of Gulliver's physical difficulties. But in the end, Swift achieves his fundamental satiric purpose not in spite of the fantasy but precisely because he has managed to hold the reader's interest by means of a superb mastery of the craft of fiction.

The balance and contrast in the management of the return motif draws the reader's attention to the fact that Gulliver, in every instance of his return, is reacting excessively in a way which belies his own nature and the situation itself; sooner or later, Gulliver's good sense appraises the situation, and he makes either the physical or the moral adjustment which the situation calls for. Accordingly, his excessive behavior is symbolic of a contrast which Swift is trying to enforce between an impossible and a possible situation, between the ideal and the actual circumstances which govern life. The novel here is furnishing its own answer to the question whether or not Gulliver is a misanthrope. Gulliver has experienced perfection among the wise and kindly horses, but he is no perfectionist when he judges his fellow men. Consequently, he does not rail, as the misanthrope [404] does, on the imperfections of men. Naturally, Gulliver is destined to experience difficulty in readjusting himself to men. He is simply in the predicament of a traveler who has been away for so long a time and has lived under such totally different conditions that his problem has become simply one of readjustment to his native environment and ordinary circumstances of life. The year's delay upon his return from Houyhnhnm-land in restoring his mental outlook to equilibrium is Swift's way of emphasizing the gravity of the moral situation among men.

Swift, like his great contemporary, Mandeville, appreciated keenly the grave disparity between the strict ethics of orthodox

Christianity and the plain facts of human nature as we find it in the world. This is the true meaning of Swift's famous *apologia pro sua vita:* "I tell you after all, that I do not hate mankind: it is vous autres who hate them, because you would have them reasonable animals and are angry for being disappointed." In this passage Swift brings his anti-perfectionism into accord with his pyrrhonism or skepticism of reason (an accord similarly effected by Mandeville, as Professor F. B. Kaye in his magnificent edition of the *Fable of the Bees* has made clear). But even if this *apologia* had never been made or preserved for posterity, from a careful reading of the novel, with proper attention to the return theme and similar devices, we should learn the same. In Brobdingnag, the farmer is greedy for money, the natives are boors, the maids are lewd, the boy is malicious, the queen's table manners are disgusting. All these are true, but Swift insists that they are relatively unimportant inasmuch as the state affairs are conducted by the principle of common sense. Swift's skepticism of reason is reflected in the same context of discussion from the viewpoint of anti-perfectionism when the king scorns Gulliver's pretense to knowledge of political science gained from a reading of books. In short, Swift is proposing a Utopia based on common sense and attainable within the limits imposed by man's occasional lapses into lewdness, greed, boorishness, and so forth. Swift, like Mandeville, gave over perfection to a millenial kingdom; they both insisted that before men are children of light they are children of the world. But both men have been fated to be libeled as a result of a misunderstanding of the brilliance of their paradoxes.

Swift, like Mandeville, was not encouraging men to be greedy and mischievous; nor was he condoning these faults because socially extended they are capable of producing a social good. Swift was rather pointing out the inconsistency in the position of Christian asceticism which defined virtue as a triumph of sheer reason over the passions, a self-conquest. Actually, however, Swift firmly argues, reason itself produces the deadliest of animosities, as in war between nations or civil strife in politics and religion. Men are foolish in [405] many ways but they are never so foolish, or potentially so dangerous, as in their pride of intellect. This ambivalent judgment on reason is at the heart of Swift's, as well as Mandeville's, paradox. Of the two men, Swift is perhaps more daring in his challenge to orthodoxy, as we shall presently see from his treatment of the "happy beast" in Book IV; Mandeville evidently found satisfaction in a formula which brought his anti-asceticism into an easier accord with his skepticism by pointing to a "rational ambition of doing good," a formula which promises simultaneously self-conquest and social good.[9]

The novel must be regarded as an ordered form. Otherwise we overlook the expository devices of balance and contrast which are peculiar to this novel, and as a result, we fail to appreciate the paradoxical solution which Swift offers to the problem of human folly from his double viewpoint: anti-perfectionism and skepticism of abstract reasoning.[10] What this paper seeks to emphasize is that the novel itself makes clear the double viewpoint through the various balances and contrasts set up in its different parts. Its historical background in the skeptical, anti-rigoristic movement in philosophical discussion of Swift's period does not explain anything about the novel itself; the historical explanation merely prevents the misconception and irrelevant criticism that Swift was a solitary opponent of benevolence in ethics. As such, the historical explanation has some, but a decidedly limited, value.[11]

Through a series of connected episodes, whose separate meanings become clear only when we see the episodes related as parts of the whole, Swift exposes the discrepancy between the demands made on human nature by Christian asceticism and the facts of actual human experience, in the process of making clear the basis upon which Gulliver must make his readjustment to men when the horses decide to banish him. When the Houyhnhnm master informs Gulliver that it is time for him to depart, his grief is so great that he swoons.[12] The horses remain unmoved by Gulliver's pleas to be permitted to remain, and, sadly, he makes preparations to depart. Gulliver's reluctance to return to civilization is so great that he formulates a plan to live elsewhere on a deserted island.[13] He lands on what [406] ap-

---

[9] Mandeville's *Fable of the Bees*, ed. F. B. Kaye, 2 vols. (Oxford, Clarendon, 1924), critical introduction, I, xlvii.

[10] Cf. II, 7, p. 139, a passage satirizing pride of intellect and a predilection for "ideas, entities, abstractions, and transcendentals."

[11] It is not intended in this paper to give an exhaustive account of the formal features of the novel; rather it is the purpose to theorize from a sufficient number of instances. I wish to express, however, my indebtedness to the commentary supplied by Professor Case in his edition of the text. The contrast drawn by Professor Case between the attainable Utopia of Book II and the unattainable Utopia of Book IV first aroused my interest in a Mandevillean analysis of the problem. The conclusions that I draw below, however, are at variance with Professor Case's interpretation of the same contrast.

[12] IV, 10, p. 304.   [13] IV, 11, p. 308.

pears to be an uninhabited spot, but soon he is attacked by wild men
and he flees. While in flight, he spies a European ship, but, instead
of welcoming it, he turns about to the island, choosing rather to
trust the barbarians than the Europeans.[14] The ship overtakes him,
and, in spite of Gulliver's entreaties to be left behind, the sailors
carry him aboard the ship. Gulliver is a sullen captive and he finally
makes an effort to escape by jumping overboard. The captain now
takes the situation in hand, and his kindnesses to Gulliver during the
remainder of the voyage are so numerous that Gulliver gradually
loses his antipathy toward men. All of these episodes clearly belong
to a series, and only on the basis of our understanding of these related
events can we determine what Swift wishes to say about Gulliver's
search for a *modus vivendi* with men. What Gulliver responds to in
the captain are moral qualities of the simplest sort. This is, therefore, Swift's way of expounding his conviction that the question of
perfect behavior among men is irrelevant. On the basis of the simple
virture of charity, men can mitigate their lot in this world, and
Swift adds, with carefully measured hopefulness, that men can even
win for themselves a measure of mutual forbearance.

The novel hews closely to the anti-perfectionist line, but in order
to see how Swift joins his anti-perfectionism with his skepticism, we
must take note of Gulliver's own explanation of the reason why he
has become willing to adjust himself to the captain: "At last I descended to treat him like an animal which had some little portion
of reason." [15]

In order to understand fully what Gulliver means by "some little
portion of reason," we must follow the thread of skepticism as it shut-
tles in and out of the story on its own level of balance and contrast.
Again, the theme is introduced casually at first, later with deliberate
satiric intent. The skeptical theme appears, as we shall see, in connection with the mystification over Gulliver's clothing.

II

The Brobdingnagian farmer who finds Gulliver hiding in the
cornfield is obviously mystified by what he has found: "[he] began
to look upon me as a curiosity. . . ." The farmer is especially mystified by Gulliver's clothing: "[he] therewith lifted up the lappets of

---

[14] IV, 11, p. 310.   [15] IV, 11, p. 312.

my coat; which it seems he thought to be some kind of covering that nature had given me." [16]

We hear of the lappets again under circumstances of mystification in Book IV, but this time the Houyhnhnms do not speculate as idly as the Brobdingnagian farmer. The difference is created by [407] Swift's favorite device of contrast between an idea first introduced casually and later reintroduced with satiric animus. In addition, the reader should recall that, because of the vogue in the eighteenth century of primitivistic discussion, the term "nature" had established itself as symbolic of an antithesis between the "arts" (man-made) and that which was in "nature" (God-made); the antithesis supplied the indication whether civilization was progressing over the primitive state of "nature" because of man's progress in the "arts" and "manufactures" (in this case, clothing), or conversely, whether civilization was on the retrograde precisely because the arts and manufactures represented not improvement, but a perversion of "nature" (in this case, man in his pristine, naked glory). The entire discussion by the Houyhnhnms hinges on this antithesis.

The bewilderment felt by the horses concerning Gulliver's appearance is stressed again and again in a way which makes clear the importance of the theme in the allegory. Upon Gulliver's first meeting with a Houyhnhnm,

the horse started a little when he came near me, but soon recovering himself looked full in my face with manifest tokens of wonder: he viewed my hands and feet, walking round me several times.[17]

As a second horse joins the first, they are evidently mystified by Gulliver's clothing:

The two horses came up close to me, looking with great earnestness upon my face and hands. The grey steed rubbed my hat all round with his right forehoof, and discomposed it so much that I was forced to adjust it better, by taking it off, and settling it again; whereat both he and his companion (who was a brown bay) appeared to be much surprised; the latter felt the lappet of my coat, and finding it to hang loose about me, they both looked with new signs of wonder.[18]

As the story unfolds, the mystification of the horses is discovered to rest on a two-fold basis, depending in the first instance on Gulliver's obvious resemblance to a Yahoo, and in the second instance

---

[16] II, 1, p. 83.   [17] IV, 1, p. 242.   [18] Idem.

on his equally obvious difference from a Yahoo. From the general
contours of Gulliver's body and his limb appendages, the first impression gained by the Houyhnhnms is that Gulliver is a Yahoo:

The master horse ordered a sorrel nag, one of his servants, to untie the
largest of these animals [Yahoos] and take him into the yard. The beast
and I were brought close together, and our countenances diligently
compared, both by master and servant, who thereupon repeated several
times the word 'yahoo.' [19]

To his horror, Gulliver discovers that the comparision is not un-
reasonable: [408]

My horror and astonishment are not to be described, when I observed in
this abominable animal, a perfect human figure. . . . The forefeet of the
Yahoo differed from my hands in nothing else but the length of the nails,
the coarseness and brownness of the palms, and the hairiness on the backs.
There was the same resemblance between our feet, with the same differences, which I knew very well, though the horses did not, because of
my shoes and stockings; the same in every part of our bodies, except as to
hairiness and colour which I have already described.
   The great difficulty that seemed to stick with the two horses, was to
see the rest of my body so very different from that of a Yahoo, for which I
was obliged to my clothes, whereof they had no conception.[20]

Gulliver himself recognizes that but for the mystery of his clothing
(whether it is his skin or an extracutaneous layer) the Houyhnhnms
would be certain that he is a Yahoo. As it is, however, their impression of Gulliver is a mixed one: he is a Yahoo, and yet, somehow, he
is not a Yahoo, since he has a different skin from the loathesomely
hirsute Yahoos. Gulliver's clothing becomes, accordingly, the pivotal
consideration in the ultimate judgment which the allegory places on
human nature. The horror of Gulliver's discovery that but for his
"skin," he might be taken for a Yahoo is, at this point in the narrative,
the reader's horror as well. The satiric shaft has reached its objective,
and it is managed through a calculated balance and contrast between
the earlier casual introduction of the clothing theme and the later
satiric use to which the theme is directed.
   But when the mystification is at last cleared up, we must carefully
observe that the results are disappointing, since they do not lead
to the better judgment on men we are led to expect; the clarification
of the mystery leads, rather, to a severer judgment on mankind.

[19] IV, 2, p. 247.   [20] IV, 2, p. 247.

When Gulliver disrobes in preparation for retiring to sleep, he is accidentally discovered by the horses. The Houyhnhnms deliberate on the matter in council, and the decision which they reach is, as we shall presently see, not only the final statement in building up the mystery, but also the center of the entire allegory towards which the whole interrelated, intricate scheme of action has been directed. The Houyhnhnm master voices the carefully considered judgment of the council in declaring that Gulliver

differed indeed from other Yahoos, being much more cleanly, and not altogether so deformed, but in point of real advantage he thought I differed for the worse.[21]

The horses, that is, grant that Gulliver is superior to the Yahoos, but the full weight of the passage bears not on Gulliver's superiority but on his inferiority to the Yahoos: "in point of real advantage he thought I differed for the worse."

The care which Swift expended in creating the clothing mystery, in order, apparently, to lead the reader to a conclusion directly [409] contrary to the one he is led to expect, would seem to be pure caprice. Actually, however, the unfavorable comparison of men with animals towards which the clothing mystery leads is precisely the conclusion required by Swift's skepticism of reason in its capacity for guiding men to the good life. And once again, some regard for the expository device of balance and contrast in the novel will make clear that the unexpected solution to the clothing mystery is not entirely unprepared for.

Actually, the Brobdingnagian king first draws the unfavorable comparison of men with animals, a move which parallels the effort of the Houyhnhnms to set Gulliver apart by singling out some trait in his nature which would differentiate him from the Yahoos. On his first sight of Gulliver, the Brobdingnagian king is disinclined to see in him anything more than "a piece of clockwork contrived by some ingenious artist." [22] A searching examination is carried out by three great scholars of the realm; in council with the king, they arrive at the decision that Gulliver is indeed human. Aside from the parallel with the similar council called for the same purpose by the horses, it is important to observe that the giants, as well as the horses, find Gulliver's human qualities to be the mark not of his superiority but of his inferiority to animals:

[21] IV, 4, p. 260.   [22] II, 3, p. 100.

[The scholars] all agreed that I could not be produced according to the regular laws of nature, because I was not framed with a capacity of preserving my life, either by swiftness, or climbing of trees, or digging holes in the earth. They observed by my teeth, which they viewed with great exactness, that I was a carnivorous animal; yet most quadrupeds being an overmatch for me, and field mice, with some others, too nimble, they could not imagine how I should be able to support myself, unless I fed upon snails and other insects, which they offered by many learned arguments to evince that I could not possibly do.[23]

The animals, in short, fend for themselves, obtain food more efficiently, preserve themselves from danger, and in general, preserve the species far better than men.

A book which Gulliver finds in Glumdalclitch's bedchamber instructs Gulliver further on the subject of the better life in the animal kingdom. The book points out

how diminutive, contemptible, and helpless an animal was man in his own nature; how unable to defend himself from the inclemencies of the air, or the fury of wild beasts; how much he was excelled by one creature in strength, by another in speed, by a third in foresight, by a fourth in industry.[24]

Swift's device of shuttling his ideas in and out of the narrative with a view towards balancing and contrasting an earlier [410] noncommittal statement with a later satirical statement, has been illustrated in two instances; the recurrence in Book IV of the comparison between the "happy beast" and inept man is not surprising, therefore.[25] The "happy-beast" theme is somewhat exceptional in the novel, however, since the discussion in Book II is by no means devoid of satirical point. The king's scorn of Gulliver's pretense to knowledge derived from books and the common-sense principle which guides political discussion in Book II by bringing to a focus Swift's skepticism of reason leave the clear implication that man is inept in comparison with the beast precisely because man's reason incapacitates him for leading the happy life. What is true, however, is that the discussion of the "happy beast" in Book IV takes place

[23] II, 3, p. 101.   [24] II, 7, pp. 140–41.

[25] The "happy-beast" theme and its relations with the cognate ideas of skepticism and primitivism have been admirably treated by George Boas in a study entitled *The Happy Beast in French Thought of the Seventeenth Century* (Baltimore, 1933); the study contains a valuable introductory essay by Arthur O. Lovejoy, to whom we are indebted for the series of studies on primitivism to which this book belongs.

under altered circumstances which intensify the satire by making the implication explicit. The main differences are two. In the first place, Gulliver is actually placed in juxtaposition with animals, and secondly, the assumptions which are made in Book IV on a basis of primitivistic theory are used to determine the outcome of the argument.

The passage which states that Gulliver "in point of real advantage . . . differed for the worse" continues by contrasting explicitly man's ineptitude with the soundness of animal nature. Thus, the Houyhnhnm master points out that Gulliver's

nails were of no use either to my fore or hinder feet; as to my forefeet, he could not properly call them by that name, for he never observed me to walk upon them; that they were too soft to bear the ground; that I generally went with them uncovered, neither was the covering I sometimes wore on them of the same shape or so strong as that on my feet behind. That I could not walk with any security, for if either of my hinder feet slipped, I must inevitably fall. He then began to find fault with other parts of my body, the flatness of my face, the prominence of my nose, my eyes placed directly in front, so that I could not look on either side without turning my head: that I was not able to feed myself without lifting one of my forefeet to my mouth; and therefore nature had placed those joints to answer that necessity. He knew not what could be the use of those several clefts and divisions in my feet behind; that these were too soft to bear the hardness and sharpness of stones without a covering made from the skin of some other brute; that my whole body wanted a fence against heat and cold, which I was forced to put on and off every day with tediousness and trouble.[26]

The discussion continues, emphasizing constantly the contrast of human ineptitude with the animal's success in instinctive behavior. But the searching investigation to which Gulliver's nature [411] is subjected very soon makes clear why men compare unfavorably with animals; human reason is itself at fault and the latent implications in the contrast between Brobdingnagian common sense and Gulliver's pride of intellect are finally made explicitly clear in an attack from the viewpoint of skepticism on the sin of pride of intellect. The master horse declared:

that he looked upon us as a sort of animal to whose share, by what accident he could not conjecture, some small pittance of *reason* had fallen,

[26] IV, 4, pp. 260–61.

whereof we made no other use than by its assistance to aggravate our *natural* corruptions, and to acquire new ones which Nature had not given us. That we disarmed ourselves of the few abilities she had bestowed, had been very successful in multiplying our original wants, and seemed to spend our whole lives in vain endeavours to supply them by our own inventions. That as to myself, it was manifest I had neither the strength or agility of a common Yahoo, that I walked infirmly on my hinder feet, had found out a contrivance to make my claws of no use or defence, and to remove the hair from my chin, which was intended as a shelter from the sun and weather. Lastly, that I could neither run with speed, nor climb trees like my 'brethren' (as he called them) the Yahoos in this country.[27]

The master horse concluded, reaffirming his original observation,

that I agreed in every feature of my body with other Yahoos, except where *it was to my real disadvantage* in point of strength, speed, and activity, the shortness of my claws. . . .[28]

Although it is quite true that the "happy-beast" theme in Book II is not totally devoid of satiric meaning, the difference created by the active juxtaposition of men with animals in Book IV becomes apparent. The mystification hovering over Gulliver's outward appearance and his clothing in Brobdingnag leads to conclusions about Gulliver's ineptitude as compared with beasts in a way which is in part satirical; but for the greater part, the discussion belongs to the element of the marvelous and the fantastic present in every travel tale, whether fictional or authentic. The bewilderment of the Brobdingnagians is natural in view of the strangeness of Gulliver's size. The comparison of Gulliver with beasts suggests itself to the Brobdingnagians rather as an afterthought or as a partial explanation of what it is that makes Gulliver appear so strange. In fact, the final explanation which the giants reach, unsatisfactory and incomplete though it may be, is that Gulliver is a "lusus naturae," a freak of nature.[29]

The situation in Book IV is different not only because the propinquity of Gulliver to the Yahoos forces on the Houyhnhnms the comparison of men with animals, but also because the hint that Gulliver is a "lusus naturae" is made explicit in a thoroughgoing [412] account of a natural scheme of biological creations, or, in a word, in an account based on genetic assumptions.

[27] IV, 7, p. 280.   [28] IV, 7, p. 281. Italics mine.   [29] II, 3, p. 101.

In the first place, the seriousness of the genetic problem is reflected in the fact that the question of the origin of the Yahoos is the only matter which ever ruffled the equanimity of the Houyhnhnms: "In this council was resumed their old debate, and indeed, the only debate which ever happened in that country." [30] In this unique debate, the genetic line of approach to the problem of coping with the evil Yahoos is evidently of considerable importance. One member of the council

took notice of a general tradition, that Yahoos had not been always in that country; but that many ages ago two of these brutes appeared together upon a mountain, whether produced by the heat of the sun upon corrupted mud and slime, or from the ooze and froth of the sea, was never known.[31]

Gulliver's arrival in the land gives the horses a fresh insight into the problem which clarifies not only the question whence the Yahoos acquired their natures, but Gulliver's status as well. Since the Yahoos are not aborigines, the discussion continues, they evidently had become "in process of time much more savage than those of their own species in the country" [32] of their origin. Gulliver is, therefore, an original Yahoo but "only a little more civilized by some tincture of reason." [33] Thus, the Houyhnhnms account for the Yahoos' retrogression and Gulliver's progression, at the same time. *Pari passu,* their genetic account also makes clear that, while in their origins in a primeval ooze all creatures are undifferentiated, men are differentiated by their quality of reason.

The coincidence of the genetic concept with the "happy-beast" theme thus presents the solution to the problem of human evil. The basic point is that man's distinguishing quality of reason is a distinction which cuts in two directions. Though men may be superior to animals in their "tincture of reason," actually, "in point of real advantage," men are inferior; animal nature and instinctive behavior guide animals better to the good life. On the other hand, the well-known human predilection for war, civil strife, and political corruption, the fatuous schemes of the crackpot inventors in Book III, make it only too clear that men, despite their rationality, are far below the Houyhnhnms in wisdom.

A recognition of the way in which the "happy-beast" theme and the genetic concept are made to coincide and complement one

[30] IV, 9, p. 294.　　　[31] *Idem.*　　　[32] IV, 9, p. 296.　　　[33] *Idem.*

another finally makes clear how Swift's skeptical viewpoint has determined the outcome of the discussions. We have reason, Swift [413] is saying, but neither reason enough to render us really superior to animals, nor reason enough to bring us up to the level of the wise and kindly horses. We have reason enough to create mischief but not enough to prevent it. Gulliver, as he reflects on human destiny, says of men:

I considered them as they really were, Yahoos in shape and disposition, only a little more civilized, and qualified with the gift of speech, *but making no other use of reason than to improve and multiply those vices* whereof their brethren in this country had only the share that nature allotted them.[34]

Perfection among men is, therefore, totally irrelevant, since nature allots certain vices in any case. Reason, on the other hand, cannot cope with the problem of evil, traditional Christian ethics notwithstanding; Swift on this point is in perfect agreement with his famous contemporary, Mandeville. As a matter of self-conquest, reason may be able to control the passions, but reason itself, socially extended, will create far more deleterious results in religious and political warfare, and in fantastic schemes for social reform, such as those perpetrated by the academicians in Book III. Common sense is not only enough for men; it is precisely the only solution held open to men whose natures are so tragically limited by their "pittance of reason." Thus, the solution reached in Book II from the double viewpoint of anti-perfectionism and skepticism of reason presents itself as the only possible solution of the dilemma created by man's middle state in the genetic scheme. Either we revert to sound animal instinct or else we make the desperate effort to gain complete rationality. The dilemma is exactly the one described by Pope:

> Placed on this isthmus of a middle state,
> A being darkly wise and rudely great:
> With too much knowledge for the skeptic side,
> With too much weakness for the stoic's pride,
> He hangs between: in doubt to act, or rest;
> In doubt to deem himself a god, or beast;
> In doubt his mind or body to prefer;
> Born but to die, and reasoning but to err;
> Alike in ignorance his reason such,

[34] IV, 10, p. 303. Italics mine.

> Whether he thinks too little, or too much;
> Chaos of thought and passion, all confused;
> Still by himself abused, or disabused;
> Created half to rise, and half to fall;
> Great lord of all things, yet a prey to all;
> Sole judge of truth, in endless error hurled:
> The glory, jest, and riddle of the world! [35] [414]

III

This investigation of the features of relationship and order in *Gulliver's Travels* has made clear that ideas in a novel take on whatever meaning they have as a result of their appropriateness to the *form* in which they are presented. In the case of the travel tale, the type of novel under consideration, the element of the marvelous, the strange, and the exotic, which the traveler naturally encounters and brings to his travelogue, is made to discharge a satiric function which becomes apparent only when the features of relationship and order as they were worked out in balance and contrast are found to form the coherent scheme of action which gives us our understanding of the novel. Expository devices for clarifying ideas in the travel tale and the ideas themselves become mutually appropriate in this sense of coherence. Presumably, our judgment of this novel as a masterpiece is dependent on our recognition that it is in this sense of mutual appropriateness of ideas to fictional form that the novel has gained the clarity of purpose, thought, and expression which mark it as a masterpiece.

If all the parts of the novel are mutually appropriate and interrelated in a coherent scheme of action, then the novel is self-explanatory and furnishes its own answers to whatever critical questions are raised. Psychiatry and sociology are thus irrelevant to the understanding of the unique features of mutually appropriate parts in *Gulliver's Travels*.

As a final example of such a critical approach to Swift's masterpiece, the question might be raised, as it frequently is: What is the explanation of Swift's undeniable preoccupation with filth and scatology in this book? The subject has provided a field day for psychiatrists with a taste for dabbling in literature and for literary critics

---

[35] Pope, *Essay on Man*, Epistle II, lines 3–18 (ed. Elwin and Courthope, *Works*, II, 375–76).

with a taste for dabbling in psychiatry. Actually, the novel explains itself in that it indicates that the scatology functions artistically in the novel as one of its interrelated parts. The point is simply that since Swift is operating as a satirist for the purpose of exposing man in his egotistical pride, the scatology becomes a legitimate satirical device for pointing out the physical basis upon which the human ego rests. Basically, the situation is not a whit different from the comparison of men with beasts in the "happy-beast" theme; both are integral parts of the narrative. Neither is particularly flattering to men, but that is beside the point, for the novel itself explains the scatology. Other explanations from the field of psychoanalysis are irrelevant and supererogatory. [415]

from Jonathan Swift

LOUIS A. LANDA

It is rare indeed that a commentator appraises any work of Jonathan Swift without reference to biographical fact. If one of Swift's minor efforts is under discussion, as the poem "The Lady's Dressing Room," we may expect the critical judgment to rest upon some such basis as that presented by Sir Walter Scott, who wished the poem to be interpreted in the light of the author's peculiar habits and state of mind. If Part III of *Gulliver's Travels,* where Swift attacks the corruptions of learning, is the object of consideration, the commentator is certain to make an excursion back to Swift's student days at Trinity College, Dublin, to explain that here began his life-long hatred of science and philosophy. And so with the other works, to the point that the criticism of Swift is a sustained endeavor to interpret the writings in the light of the man, although anyone who reads the critics of Swift will be aware too of a simultaneous and converse process—attempts to interpret the man in the light of the works.

With respect to Swift we are often confronted not [20] only with the critical significance of biographical evidence but as well with the biographical significance of critical evidence. It is easy to find commentators who will have it both ways, commentators, for example, who assume a morbid state of mind in Swift as an explanation of his scatalogical verse, then use the scatalogical verse to prove that the author undoubtedly was morbid. Traditionally the criticism of Swift's works is so inextricably mingled with biography

From "Jonathan Swift," *English Institute Essays, 1946* (New York: Columbia University Press, 1947), pp. 20–35. By permission. A few minor changes have been made by Professor Landa in this reprinting of the article.

that one looks almost in vain for critical judgments based upon merely aesthetic assumptions.

The persistent tendency of the commentators has been to assume a direct and fairly simple reflection in the works of the nature and personality of Swift; and such a work as *Gulliver's Travels* has as often as not been viewed as both a strange and puzzling psychological case history and a representation of its author's objective experiences. No one can doubt for a moment the validity and the fruitfulness of the biographical approach to *Gulliver's Travels* in particular or to Swift's works in general. Considering the character of his writings —their personal, intimate, and topical nature—this approach is the natural one. Yet I think that the interpretation of Swift has at times suffered somewhat from this tendency, this unwillingness of the commentator to detach the work from the man. But the overemphasis upon this approach is rather less disturbing than its misapplication or its loose and incautious use. Commentators who would doubtless feel some hesitation in equating Fielding with Tom Jones or Sterne with Tristram Shandy can accept with [21] apparent ease as a premise of their criticism that Swift is Gulliver. In what follows I wish, first of all, to comment on certain recurring biographical considerations which have played a part—a not very happy part—in the criticism of Swift's works for a period of two centuries, and, secondly, to present some instances in which other biographical considerations of value for criticism have not been explored sufficiently.

The problem which has most preoccupied Swift's critics has been the pessimism and misanthropy of *Gulliver's Travels* and the endeavor to explain these qualities in the work by searching for exactly corresponding qualities in Swift himself. Part IV of *Gulliver's Travels,* with its contrasting picture of Yahoo and Houyhnhnm, has been the focal point of the discussions, and ordinarily the commentators have acted on the assumption, though not always consciously, that here in Part IV is the real key to Swift. It is maintained or implied that in Part IV are the possibilities of a final comprehension and the basis of a final judgment. The image of Swift—the rather horrendous image—which has been transmitted from generation to generation is chiefly the image deduced from Part IV, enforced by a careful selection of biographical fact or myth appropriately chosen to stress the severe lineaments of his character. Only occasionally is the image, a monochrome, softened by reference to the playful Swift, to Swift the author of delightful light verse, the punster, the genial companion of Queen Anne's Lord Treasurer and her Secretary of State, or to the Swift who was a charming guest at great houses and [22] who had a genius for friendship among both sexes.

Perhaps for purposes of discussion we may ignore the volume and range of Swift's works and grant the unwarranted assumption that the masterpiece is somehow the man, and that a particular portion of the masterpiece—Part IV of *Gulliver*—is of such fundamental significance as to outweigh various other considerations. If we trace the progress of the criticism of *Gulliver's Travels* from Swift's earliest biographer, the Earl of Orrery, to the twentieth century, we find preponderantly and repetitiously a set of severe judgments passed on Part IV, judgments referable back to Swift the man. In his *Remarks on the Life and Writings of Dr. Jonathan Swift* (1752), Orrery climaxes his comment with the statement that "no man [was] better acquainted [than Swift] with human nature, both in the highest, and in the lowest scenes of life" (p. 338). Yet, contradictorily, in discussing Part IV of *Gulliver* he observes that Swift's misanthropy is "intolerable," adding that "the representation which he has given us of human nature, must terrify, and even debase the mind of the reader who views it" (p. 184). Orrery then proceeds to a lengthy vindication of mankind mingled with violent charges against Swift, among them that in painting the Yahoos Swift became one himself and that the "voyage to the Houyhnhnms is a real insult upon mankind" (p. 190). Orrery is significant because with few exceptions his is the tone and pretty much the method of criticism of the Fourth Voyage for a century and a half. The fundamental points raised are concerned with the motives or the personality of [23] the author who would present this particular conception of human nature; and Orrery's explanation of Part IV in terms of injured pride, personal disappointments, and a soured temper becomes as time goes on the traditional one.

Even an occasional defender of Swift, as his good friend Patrick Delany, who answers Orrery point by point, is unwilling to undertake the defense of the last book of *Gulliver;* and he too lets fall such phrases as "moral deformity" and "defiled imagination." The eighteenth-century commentators, taking a high moral line, maintained that Swift's misanthropy had led him to write, as James Beattie phrased it, "a monstrous fiction." It was variously and characteristically stated: the gloomy and perverse Dean had talents that tended toward the wicked rather than the sublime; he was motivated by a malignant wish to degrade and brutalize the human race; he had written a libel on human nature. Though generally these commentators prefer to denounce the moral aspects of the Voyage to Houyhnhnmland and the degraded nature of the author, they leave no doubt that they think Part IV an artistic failure as well. In their eyes moral culpability and artistic failure have a necessary connection. The premise seems to be that a person of unsound views concerning human nature or of false moral views cannot write an artistically sound work. It is as though a Buddhist should deny literary value to Dante's *Divine Comedy* or Milton's *Paradise Lost* because these works are ethically and religiously unsound.

Yet it ought to be said to the honor of the [24] eighteenth-century commentators that they generally paid the author of *Gulliver* the compliment of believing him a sane man. It remained for certain nineteenth-century critics to take a new tack and to elaborate a less defensible charge. Though they accepted the view that the Fourth Voyage could be explained in terms of a depraved author, they *added* that it might well be explained in terms of a mad author. The charge of madness was usually presented with a certain caution. Two commentators in the middle of the century may be taken as examples of the willingness to accuse Swift of insanity and the unwillingness, at the same time, to come out unreservedly. In the *North British Review* of 1849 a reviewer writes of Swift's work that it is "*more* or *less* symptomatic of mental disease" (italics mine), and in the following year, in the London *Times*, a writer says that Swift was "more or less mad." It is possible that Sir Walter Scott is responsible for this wavering between outright and qualified assertion. In his edition of Swift's *Works* (1814) he writes that we cannot justify, by saying that it has a moral purpose, "the nakedness with which Swift has sketched this horrible outline of mankind degraded to a bestial state" (1883 ed., I, 315). He prefers to explain the misanthropy of *Gulliver* as the result of "the *first* impressions of . . . *incipient* mental disease" (italics mine). There are nineteenth-century commentators who felt that the Fourth Voyage should not be read. Thackeray gave such advice to the audience who listened to his lectures on the English humorists of the eighteenth century in 1851; and, later, Edmund Gosse —using such phrases as [25] "the horrible satisfaction of disease" and a brain "not wholly under control"—declared that the "horrible foulness of this satire on the Yahoo . . . banishes from decent households a fourth part of one of the most brilliant and delightful of English books." It is somewhat more surprising to find W. E. H. Lecky, who usually showed a well-balanced and sympathetic understanding of Swift, falling into the jargon. He can see Swift's misanthropy as a constitutional melancholy "mainly due to a physical malady which had long acted upon his brain." [1] It is not surprising, however, that in the twentieth century the psychoanalysts have seized on so attractive a subject as Swift; and now we find *Gulliver* explained in terms of neuroses and complexes. The following quotation is taken from the *Psychoanalytic Review* of 1942; *Gulliver's Travels* "may be viewed as a neurotic phantasy with coprophilia as its main content." It furnishes

abundant evidence of the neurotic makeup of the author and discloses in him a number of perverse trends indicative of fixation at the anal sadistic stage of libidinal development. Most conspicuous among those perverse trends is that of coprophilia, although the work furnishes evidence of numerous other related neurotic characteristics accompanying the general picture of psychosexual infantilism and emotional immaturity.

By a diligent search this psychoanalyst was able to discover in *Gulliver's Travels* strains of misogyny, misanthropy, mysophilia, mysophobia, voyeurism, exhibitionism, and compensatory potency reactions. If [26] this psychoanalytic approach seems to have in it an element of absurdity, we should recognize that it is only a logical development of the disordered-intellect theory of the nineteenth-century critics, the chief difference being that the terminology has changed and that the psychoanalyst frankly sees *Gulliver's Travels* as case history, whereas the critics were presumably making a literary appraisal. Perhaps these crude and amateur attempts deserve little attention, yet they are a phenomenon that the serious student of Swift can hardly ignore in the light of their recurrence and their effectiveness in perpetuating myths. And they sometimes come with great persuasiveness and literary flavor, as witness Mr. Aldous Huxley's essay in which, by virtue of ignoring nine tenths of Swift's works, he can arrive at an amazingly oversimplified explanation of Swift's greatness: "Swift's greatness," Mr. Huxley writes, "lies in the intensity, the almost insane violence, of that 'hatred of bowels' which is the essence of his misanthropy and which underlies the whole of his work" (*Do What You Will*, 1930, p. 105).

[1] Introduction to the *Prose Works of Jonathan Swift*, ed. T. Scott, 1897, I, lxxxviii.

I suggest that the commentators who have relied on a theory of insanity or disordered intellect to explain Swift's works have weakened their case, if they have not vitiated it entirely, by resorting to ex post facto reasoning. The failure of Swift's mental faculties toward the end of his life—some fifteen or sixteen years after the publication of *Gulliver's Travels*—was seized upon to explain something the critics did not like and frequently did not understand. It seemed to them valid to push his insanity back in time, to look [27] retrospectively at the intolerable fourth book of *Gulliver's Travels,* and to infer that Swift's insanity must have been at least incipient when he wrote it. One recent commentator, rather more zealous than others, hints that the madness can be traced as far back as *A Tale of a Tub.* Commentators who observe manifestations of a disordered intellect in the Fourth Voyage have not thought to question the intellect behind the Third Voyage, yet we know now that the third was composed in point of time after the fourth. And these commentators have nothing but praise for the vigor, the keenness, the sanity, and the humanity of the mind that produced the *Drapier's Letters,* yet we have reasonable assurance that Swift completed the draft of Part IV of *Gulliver* in January of 1724 and was at work on the first of the *Drapier's Letters* in February.

Another procedure which the critics of Swift are fond of deserves to be scanned: the habit of taking an isolated statement or an isolated incident and giving it undue significance to support their prepossessions. In a recent study of Swift, in many respects of more than ordinary perceptiveness, the author considers Part IV of *Gulliver* as an embodiment of the tragic view of life. In so doing he passes from the work to the facts or presumed facts of Swift's life to enforce his interpretation, adducing as evidence the report of Swift's manner, in his later years, of bidding friends good-by: "Good night, I hope I shall never see you again." If Swift really used this remark, if he used it seriously, some weight may be attached to it; but I should want to know to whom he used it and in what tone or spirit. [28] It sounds very much like his usual banter, his manner of friendly insult and quite genial vituperation which so often distinguishes his letters to friends who understood his ironic turn and his liking for the inverted compliment. How can we rely on such casual remarks or possibly know what weight to give them? But such a remark is related to Swift's habit of reading certain parts of the Book of Job to prove that he hated life, and is made to seem of a piece with the Fourth Voyage of *Gulliver's Travels.* This is typical of the commentators who have culled from Swift's letters, from the biographies, and from other documents all the presumed evidence of gloom and misanthropy in order to uncover what they have a strong prepossession to uncover, the essential misery of his existence. This is the way to prove, in support of the interpretation of the Fourth Voyage, that "Swift's life was a long disease, with its disappointments, its self-torture, its morbid recriminations."

But a matter of statistical balance is involved here: the facts listed and weighted heavily have been too much of one complexion. Too much has been made of the last years of Swift's life, when he bothered less to conceal his moods and his irritations—and when he seemed to get a certain satisfaction in talking about his ailments. I should like to see some biographer counter the gloomy approach by emphasizing Swift's zest for life, his vitality, and the playfulness of his mind. There is ample evidence in his letters—and in what we know of his activities—of high spirits, good humor, and daily satisfactions. Such a study might very well, [29] without distortion, evidence an unexpected mathematical balance between happiness and unhappiness.

I should not want to be put into the position of denying Swift a considerable pessimism and a fair share of misanthropy. These qualities, however, were not so raw or so unassimilated or so crudely operative in his daily existence as has been often represented. The manner in which these personal qualities have been used to explain *Gulliver* deserves to be questioned. It has been an overly simple process of equating biographical fact and artistic statement, of viewing the work as a transcription of the author's experiences or as a precise and complete representation of his personal philosophy—or as a final explanation of his personality. There is an obvious danger in seeing an artistic or imaginative construction as mere duplication. *Gulliver's Travels* is a work of mingled fantasy and satire; it is Utopian literature, highly allusive and symbolic, charged with hidden meanings and projected to a level several removes from the real world of its author.

To leaven the biographical approach other questions deserve attention. What are the artistic necessities of a work of this type? What are the aesthetic principles, quite apart from other considerations, that shape the work? To what extent is there a compromise between these principles and the conscious or the undeliberate tendency of the author to reflect his experiences and his personality?

If the biographical approach to Swift has been crudely used or overemphasized in certain respects, [30] there are other respects in which biographical considerations of critical value have been left almost wholly unexplored. The most significant of these seems to me to be Swift's profession as a Christian divine. Is there in this some clue to an explanation of Part IV of *Gulliver?* If a reading of the sermons can be trusted, the eighteenth-century divine relished his duty to expatiate on the evils and corruptions of this world and the inadequacies of this life. He seemed to enjoy measuring the imperfections before him against a higher set of values. Swift, I think, would have held an optimistic divine to be a contradiction in terms; and his own pessimism is quite consonant with the pessimism at the heart of Christianity. One of Swift's sermons begins as follows:

The Holy Scripture is full of expressions to set forth the miserable condition of man during the whole progress of his life; his weakness, pride, and vanity, his unmeasurable desires, and perpetual disappointments; the prevalency of his passions, and the corruptions of his reason, his deluding hopes, and his real, as well as imaginary, fears . . . his cares and anxieties, the diseases of his body, and the diseases of his mind. . . . And the wise men of all ages have made the same reflections.[2]

If Swift had written his own comment on *Gulliver's Travels*, he might very well have used the words of this sermon. *Gulliver's Travels* certainly is full of expressions to set forth the miserable condition of man—his weakness, pride, and vanity, his unmeasurable desires, the prevalency of his passions and the [31] corruptions of his reason—and so on through the catalogue. Indeed, Swift's few sermons and those of other eighteenth-century divines could easily be used to annotate *Gulliver's Travels*. It is difficult for me to believe that a contemporary could fail to see the affinity between the Fourth Voyage—or the whole of *Gulliver*—and many of the conventional sermons on human nature and the evils of this life. Swift's emphasis on depraved human nature and his evaluation of man's behavior are certainly *not* at odds with Christian tradition. There is no need to ascribe such views solely to personal bitterness or frustrations or melancholia. His thinking and status as a divine had an effect much more profound than is generally recognized.

Although *Gulliver's Travels* is secular, an exploration of man's social and moral nature in non-theological terms, a contemporary divine

[2] *On The Poor Man's Contentment.*

in reading it may well have felt that Swift's allegory veiled a quite orthodox view of human nature and society, a view in fact which, by extension, reinforced the doctrine of redemption and man's need of grace.

Only an occasional commentator has recognized and stressed the essentially Christian philosophy of the Fourth Voyage. The first was Swift's relative, Deane Swift, who declared that the Christian conception of the evil nature of man is the "groundwork of the whole satyre contained in the voyage to the Houyhnhnms." Then this cousin of Jonathan Swift, this lesser Swift, delivers himself of a catalogue of vices worthy of his great cousin: [32]

Ought a preacher of righteousness [he asks], ought a watchman of the Christian faith . . . to hold his peace . . . when avarice, fraud, cheating, violence, rapine, extortion, cruelty, oppression, tyranny, rancour, envy, malice, detraction, hatred, revenge, murder, whoredom, adultery, lasciviousness, bribery, corruption, pimping, lying, perjury, subornation, treachery, ingratitude, gaming, flattery, drunkenness, gluttony, luxury, vanity, effeminacy, cowardice, pride, imprudence, hypocrisy, infidelity, blasphemy, idolatry, sodomy, and innumerable other vices are as epidemical as the pox, and many of them the notorious characteristicks of the bulk of mankind? [3]

"Dr. Swift," he adds, "was not the first preacher, whose writings import this kind of philosophy." Surely those clergymen who week after week exposed the deceitfulness of the human heart would have agreed with Deane Swift.

It seems to be true, as T. O. Wedel has pointed out,[4] that Swift's view of human nature was opposed to certain contemporary attitudes in which the passions of men were looked on kindly and in which the dignity of human nature was defended in such a way that the doctrine of original sin lost its efficacy. In his *Reasonableness of Christianity* (1695) John Locke could deny, without raising much serious protest, that the fall of Adam implies the corruption of human nature in Adam's posterity. It is this same current of thought [33] that later in the century disturbed John Wesley, who complains in one of his sermons (No. XXXVIII, "Original Sin") that "not a few persons of

---

[3] *Essay upon the Life, Writings, and Character of Dr. Swift* (1755), pp. 219–20.
[4] For the relationship between Swift and Wesley stated in this paragraph see an article to which I am much indebted, T. O. Wedel, "On the Philosophical Background of *Gulliver's Travels*," *Studies in Philology*, XXIII (1926), 434–50.

strong understanding, as well as extensive learning, have employed
their utmost abilities to show, what they termed, 'the fair side of
human nature in Adam's posterity.' " "So that," Wesley continues,
"it is now quite unfashionable to say anything to the disparagement
of human nature; which is generally allowed, notwithstanding a few
infirmities, to be very innocent, and wise, and virtuous." Is it not
significant, when Wesley comes to write his treatise on *The Doctrine
of Original Sin* (1756), that he should turn to Swift, to Part IV of *Gulliver* for quotations? In this treatise Wesley refers scornfully to those
"who gravely talk of the dignity of our nature," and then quotes
several times from what he calls "a late eminent hand." The "late
eminent hand" is Swift's, whose words from Part IV of *Gulliver*
describing man as "a lump of deformity and disease, both in body
and mind, smitten with pride" Wesley has seized on. Wesley refers
again and again to the "many laboured panegyrics . . . we now
read and hear on the dignity of human nature"; and he raises a
question which is, I think, a clue to Swift. If men are generally
virtuous, what is the need of the doctrine of Redemption? This is
pretty much the point of two sermons by Swift, where he is obviously in reaction to the panegyrics on human nature which came
from Shaftesbury and the benevolists, from the defenders of the
Stoic wise man, and from proponents of the concept of a man of
honor. Swift sensed the [34] danger to orthodox Christianity from
an ethical system or any view of human nature stressing man's goodness or strongly asserting man's capacity for virtue. He had no faith
in the existence of the benevolent man of Shaftesbury and the anti-
Hobbists, the proud, magnanimous man of the Stoics, or the rational
man of the deists; his man is a creature of the passions, of pride and
self-love, a frail and sinful being in need of redemption. The very
simple and wholly unoriginal strain of apologetics in Swift's sermons
is based upon an attitude common in traditional Christian thought;
and to my way of thinking Swift the clergyman is reflected in *Gulliver's Travels*. [35]

from Moral Satire

HERBERT DAVIS

But it is after all the fable of the Fourth book which has most shocked Swift's readers, though it is a simple and traditional moral tale, rather vividly dramatized with the help of animal symbolism. It is perhaps a little mediaeval in its extravagant and sometimes unpleasant burlesque of some of the qualities of man's brute nature, and in the complete separation of his rational qualities as they might conceivably exist in some utopian world. But the real source of our fear of Swift's satire is that we are progressively led on with Gulliver from a comparatively happy condition in which we were in that blessed state of being well deceived—the serene peaceful state of being a fool among knaves—until we have made the painful discovery of the knavery of human life and of the stupidity and malice of mankind. But many moralists and prophets and satirists have made this same discovery and travelled by this same road, and have found the world a wilderness and life a sorry condition, and they [99] have turned to the past or the future or to another world for consolation, and in some way or other have justified the fact of life. But Swift leaves us no escape, no place for dreams or imaginings; he can see no reason for it at all. He has not been able to keep out at any point in his travels this plain dislike of human existence, the protest of the individual against the sum of things,

> a stranger and afraid.
> In a world I never made.

But his protest is put in a quite simple non-romantic way, some development of the theme stated in one of his own Pensées, printed under the title, *Thoughts on Religion.*

Although reason were intended by providence to govern our passions, yet it seems that, in two points of the greatest moment to the being and continuance of the world, God hath intended our passions to prevail over reason. The first is, the propagation of our species, since no wise man ever married from the dictates of reason. The other is, the love of life, which, from the dictates of reason every man would despise, and wish it at an end, or that it never had a beginning.

This colours that passage in the sixth chapter of the Voyage to Lilliput concerning the relations between parents and children: [100]

. . . they will never allow that a Child is under any Obligation to his father for begetting him, or to his mother for bringing him into the world; which considering the miseries of human life, was neither a benefit itself nor intended so by his parents, whose thoughts in their love-encounters were otherwise employed and therefore they conclude that parents are the last of all others to be trusted with the education of their own children.

More dramatically and more memorably he plays with the same theme at the end of the Fourth book, when, returning from his experience of a rational Utopia under the influence of beings who were the perfection of nature, Gulliver freely confesses that the sight of his wife and family filled him "only with Hatred, Disgust and Contempt; and the more, by reflecting on the near Alliance [he] had to them." This is further developed in the following paragraph in a way which one cannot help feeling afforded Swift the keenest satisfaction.

As soon as I entered the House, my Wife took me in her Arms, and kissed me; at which, having not been used to the Touch of that Odious Animal for so many Years, I fell in a Swoon for almost an Hour. At the Time I am writing, it is five years since my last Return to *England:* During the first Year I could not endure my Wife or Children in my Presence, the very Smell of them was intolerable; much less could I suffer them to eat in the [101] same Room. To this Hour they dare not presume to touch my Bread, or drink out of the same Cup; neither was I ever able to let one of them take me by the Hand.

But even this is not such a violent satire upon "love of life" as Swift reserved for the last episode of the third voyage, which may well have been in point of composition the last chapter he wrote. For we know that he wrote the Fourth book mainly in 1723, and did not complete the Third—apart from final revisions—until 1725. It is a chapter entirely complete in itself—a perfect little irony. I cannot understand why it has not been more praised, and used in anthologies, or in books of piety. Swift himself draws particular attention to it, and evidently considered it to be quite original. He says:

I thought this account of the Struldbruggs might be some Entertainment to the Reader, because it seems to be a little out of the common Way; at least, I do not remember to have met the like in any Book of Travels that hath come to my Hands.

Gulliver is asked one day whether he had seen any of their immortals, and after hearing an account of them, indulges in his most endearingly innocent way in extravagant expressions of rapture at the thought of a people so blessed. He is then asked by his amused hosts what he would do if he were an immortal. After enlarging upon many topics [102] "which the natural desire of endless life and sublunary happiness could easily furnish," he is told what the Struldbruggs are really like and finally has an opportunity to see five or six of them, the youngest not above two hundred years old.

They were the most mortifying sight I ever beheld . . . and my keen appetite for perpetuity of life was much abated.

He would have been glad to send a couple home to arm people against the fear of death, but that was forbidden by the laws of the kingdom. Nevertheless, he tells us again with disarming innocence, he was led to believe that if he were to write down a simple and wholly truthful account of his travels, it might possibly do his countrymen some good. He can claim to be above any possible censure, having avoided every fault commonly charged against writers of travels:

I write for the noblest End, to inform and instruct Mankind, over whom I may, without Breach of Modesty, pretend to some Superiority, from the Advantages I received by conversing so long among the most accomplished Houyhnhnms. I write without any View towards Profit or Praise.

Is Gulliver then after all only another moral tale, another rationalist's utopian dream to turn men from the folly of their ways and bring about some [103] improvement in human society? Swift indeed allows Lemuel Gulliver to enter unsuspectingly the company of the eighteenth century philosophers, and to believe for a while, as even the most sceptical of them did, even a Hume or a Voltaire, that humanity could enter into a heavenly city of its own if only it could be released from the bonds of superstition and ignorance. But Swift allowed Gulliver to go thus far only to undeceive him utterly, and take from him his last illusion.

When the book appeared for the first time pretty much as Swift had written it, published under his direction in Dublin in 1735, it had been provided with an epilogue, in the form of a letter from Captain Gulliver to his cousin Richard Sympson, who had been responsible for getting the book printed. In this final statement Swift is careful to separate himself from the other historians and philosophers, and even from the rest of the satirists, turning his satire full upon them and their vain hopes to do something to improve the human species:

I do in the next place complain of my own great Want of Judgment, in being prevailed upon . . . very much against my own Opinion, to suffer my Travels to be published. Pray bring to your Mind how often I desired you to consider, when you insisted on the Motive of *publick Good;* that the Yahoos were a species of animal utterly incapable [104] of Amendment by Precepts or Examples: And so it hath proved; for instead of seeing a full Stop put to all Abuses and Corruptions, at least in this little Island, as I had reason to expect: Behold, after above six Months Warning, I cannot learn that my Book hath produced one single effect according to my Intentions: . . . And, it must be owned, that seven Months were a sufficient Time to correct every Vice and Folly to which Yahoos are subject; if their Natures had been capable of the least Disposition to Virtue or Wisdom.

Swift could not escape from this final irony. He did not wish to prescribe for the sickness of humanity, having no hope of its recovery; but he could not refrain from probing, anatomizing and diagnosing its malady, though convinced that the further he went the more he would find to stir his indignation and his pity. And from his youth he had known it and written it down with a kind of foolish pride, that he was one

> whose lash just Heaven has long decreed
> Shall on a day make sin and folly bleed.

To the end it was his peculiar satisfaction as a moralist and a satirist, in all his various disguises, and employing all the tricks of his trades, to make us see what a world we live in, to make us feel its brutality and its degradation, to disturb all our [105] complacencies and to leave us unreconciled to the "unestimable sum of human pain." [106]

Swift and the Horses: Misanthropy or Comedy?

EDWARD STONE

Some thirteen years ago Ricardo Quintana attempted to raise the siege that criticism has laid to Part IV of *Gulliver's Travels*. He balanced Swift's "misanthropy" with a reminder that Swift "was also bent upon creating a work which should win universal acclaim," [1] and, in attempting to account for the abuse heaped upon the *Travels* since the original acclamation, suggested that "the softening of ethical doctrine and the rise of sentimentalism induced a certain amount of that horror which critics began to feel for *Gulliver's Travels*, particularly part IV." [2]

It is regrettable that the challenge implicit in Professor Quintana's reminder has not been accepted by Swift scholars. Their task would obviously be both difficult and unenviable, to be sure: it would be undertaken in defiance of the long tradition of critical disparagement ranging from Johnson's impersonal reproval to the vituperation of Thackeray, and would necessitate venturing into the illusive field of the aesthetics of an age removed from our own by two hundred years. Nevertheless, it is time that at least a brief attempt be made to question the justice of the over-all verdict that Part IV of the *Travels* was an unprovoked outburst of misanthropy, that its chief merit was the doubtful one of not having succeeded in damaging

Reprinted from *Modern Language Quarterly*, X (September 1949), 367–376. By permission.

[1] *The Mind and Art of Jonathan Swift* (New York, 1936), p. 294.
[2] *Ibid.*, p. 305.

the comic success of Parts I and II. In such an attempt it is to the point to consider: (1) the intent of the author; (2) the significance of the Beast-Fable tradition, and Swift's use of it; (3) the characterization of Gulliver; and (4) what has been recorded concerning the reception of the supposedly offensive Part IV by its first readers.

I

It is impossible to "answer" our first question, but that should not preclude reopening it: what was Swift's intent in writing Part IV? At first glance, misanthropy. Swift himself keynoted the critics' attitude with his famous Vex-the-world-rather-than-divert-it letter, with his injunction to Pope to "give the world one lash the more" at his request. Moreover, Swift's apparently misanthropic intent had already caused his friends some alarm. Bolingbroke (getting his information from Ford) gave thanks that Stella, at least, stood between the Dean and complete misanthropy,[3] and Pope was equally [367] apprehensive.[4] In the face of this evidence, what can be said for Swift?

Inasmuch as he is considered his own accuser, it is only fair to let Swift vindicate himself and explode for us the familiar myth that he was working with the frenzy of a monomaniac to pull the world down upon his own head. Our first surprise is to learn that, so far from being contentedly immured in misanthropy, Swift actually complained to Ford that he lacked proper critics to "censure and correct what I write."[5] And there is a noticeable air of caution in the letter in which he tells Pope that "however I may have been soured by personal ill treatment, or by melancholy prospects for the public, I am too much a politician to expose my own safety by offensive

---

[3] ". . . if she had not fix'd his course . . . he had been att this very instant . . . in that country which he discover'd not long ago, where Horses & mules are the reasonable Creatures, and men the Beasts of burden. But thanks to heaven & Stella, that danger is over. since he loves a woman he will not forget that he is a man." Letter to Ford, December 25, 1723. *Letters of Jonathan Swift to Charles Ford*, ed. David Nichol Smith (Oxford, 1935), p. 238.

[4] "But I find you would rather be employed as an avenging angel of wrath, to break your vial of indignation over the heads of the wretched, pitiful creatures of this world; nay, would make them eat your book, which you have made, I doubt not, as bitter a pill for them as possible." Letter to Swift, October 15, 1725. *Correspondence of Jonathan Swift, D.D.*, ed. F. Elrington Ball (London, 1910–1914), III, 360.

[5] Letter of January 19, 1723/24. *Letters of Swift to Ford*, ed. Smith, p. 101.

words." [6]   Moreover, there is a hidden playfulness in his letters at this time. In September, 1725, he exhorted Pope to "embrace" *Gulliver's* message "and procure that all who deserve my esteem may do so too"—an injunction which the alarmed Pope seems to have interpreted literally. But the tongue-in-cheek is apparent in Swift's writing to Ford that "I have finished my Travells, and I am now transcribing them; they are admirable Things, and will wonderfully mend the World" [7]—a pseudopontifical pose that Swift continued in the "Letter to Sympson." Such a remark, usually interpreted literally, would in truth be significant coming from a fledgling journalist or a messianic Zarathustra; but it is important to recall that Swift was neither. Finally, the playfulness with which Swift referred to the Horses after *Gulliver* appeared was already present in his letter to Ford concerning Bolingbroke's apprehensions about the forthcoming book:

Tis hard that Folks in France will not let us in Ireland be quiet. I would have him [Bolingbroke] and you know that I hate Yahoos of both Sexes, and that Stella and Madame de Villette [Lady Bolingbroke] are onely tolerable at best, for want of Houyhnhnms.[8]

II

But the proof is in the story itself. Consider, first, the Yahoos. That they are repulsive, no one will deny; but this does not mean that Swift's readers found them merely repulsive. As a matter of fact, his audience had good reason for appreciating the cleverness of what may [368] revolt us.[9] As R. W. Frantz and Willard H. Bonner have pointed out,[10] the travel books of the preceding fifty years had had many accounts of Yahoo-like Hottentots, Hodmadods, and Indians, and Swift was thoroughly familiar with them. Like the Yahoos, the

[6] January 10, 1721/22. *Correspondence,* ed. Ball, III, 122–23. He is referring, of course, to *politically* offensive words, but the remark is worth noting.

[7] August 14, 1725. *Letters of Swift to Ford,* ed. Smith, p. 122.

[8] January 19, 1723/24. *Letters of Swift to Ford,* ed. Smith, p. 100.

[9] That even the gentle Joseph Addison was capable of an "offensive" allegory Macaulay pointed out long ago. Cf. his reference (probably to *Tatlers* No. 100 and No. 102) in "The Life and Writings of Addison," *Critical and Historical Essays,* Everyman Edition (1907), II, 493.

[10] R. W. Frantz, *The English Traveller and the Movement of Ideas, 1660–1732,* University Studies (Lincoln, Nebraska, 1934), XXXII–XXXIII; Willard H. Bonner, *Captain William Dampier* (Stanford, 1934), Chap. 9. The surprisingly large number of parallels displayed therein, both in style and subject matter, demonstrates that Swift's satire made capital, step by step, of the contents of travel books which were popular in his day. In this connection, cf. R. W. Frantz, "Swift's Yahoos and the Voyagers," *MP,* XXIX (1932), 49–57.

monkeys and aborigines in Dampier "live nastily, cohabit bestially, and display no glimmer of reason . . . smell foul and eat putrid flesh . . . move . . . chattering in the branches of trees and flinging down their excrement." [11] To have presented his Yahoos as foul-smelling, subhuman natives of a far-off land was to suggest beings familiar at once to Swift's readers: it was the readers' familiarity with such beings, plus the suggestion that the Yahoos were faintly like themselves, that would evoke laughter.[12]

That Swift never meant the Yahoos to be identified closely with humans is evident. They usually walk on all fours and are also amphibious. Moreover, as Gulliver observes, they "appear to be the most unteachable of all animals, their capacities never reaching higher than to draw or carry burthens." How, then, did they come to be associated with humans? As we shall see, the association is effected not by Swift, but by Gulliver himself, who also identifies the Houyhnhnms with actual animals. In so doing, Gulliver betrays his own comic lack of understanding: despite the insistence of the Houyhnhnms, he is not at all like the beastly Yahoos; and the marvelous qualities he attributes—with equally comic consequences—to the Houyhnhnms are the result, we shall see, of (1) his temporary loss of reason, and (2) of Swift's evident intent to satirize the spinners of fantastic travel yarns.

Proportionately, the Yahoos take up only a small section of Part IV. The key to the humor here, accordingly, is the Horses themselves. Professor W. A. Eddy long ago prepared the way for this [369] interpretation:

Swift tells us that the Houyhnhnms are more reasonable than Gulliver, but the Houyhnhnms do not bear him out. To me the defect . . . is not the brutality of the satire, but the stupidity of the Houyhnhnms, whose judgments of Gulliver prove nothing beyond their own incompetence to judge. Gulliver is quick to recognize the excellent qualities of the horses. How is it then that the Houyhnhnms, who we are assured are so much

[11] Bonner, op. cit., p. 177.
[12] As for the often lamented excretory incidents—Augustan Londoners appear to have had nostrils less sensitive than ours. They had laughed not only at Rabelais, but at their own Ned Ward and John Gay. Even the exemplary Martin Martin had included in his popular Description of the Western Islands of Scotland (1703) a long anecdote about defecation. Cf. John Pinkerton, A General Collection of . . . Voyages (Philadelphia, 1811), III, 634. That the English of 1726, therefore, found Gulliver's plight under the tree and that of the discarded Yahoo leader comically distressing is highly probable. (The nasty trick the little imp of a Yahoo plays on Gulliver is, of course, due to Gulliver's own overzealousness, or "enthusiasm.")

more sensible, are unable to realize that the human body is much more suitable than their own for the common needs of life? . . .

Again, the horses themselves are grotesque, inconsistent creatures. . . . Where is the "horse-sense" in a fable that makes horses build houses and lay clay floors, weave mats, excell in pottery, milk cows, build fires, and thread needles? [13]

He concludes that "Swift was careless of his story; the fires of misanthropy obscured his judgment, and vitiated his argument",[14] and yet he has presented us with the weapon with which to defend the contention that the humor of the earlier voyages has carried over into the "terrible logic" of Part IV.

To begin with, there was nothing new (or, therefore, shocking) in Swift's mock-serious device of presenting animals as equal or superior to human beings; it is the near-extinction of the device in the succeeding centuries that has interfered with the interpretation of Part IV. Professor Eddy himself has gone to great lengths to discover precedents for such a situation, and Professor George Boas has furnished still more.[15] The argument of "theriophilism" was a familiar one: the beasts are more prudent, temperate, and chaste than men, and more restrained in their desires; their pleasures are natural ones, they have no useless arts, they are clever at learning, and so on. This theriophilism of Pliny, of Plutarch, or of Montaigne, grotesque as it seems to us, was familiar enough to be generally entertaining to Swift's London. Its essence was *paradox*, "certainly not written for other than conversational purposes." [16] The motive "was simply to wound man's pride, reduce his arrogance, a moral like that of most satirists and no more to be taken as founded on a serious zoology than *Gulliver's Travels*." [17] Not only were these Beast Fables still current in Swift's own time: the type was so fashionable that Addison spoke out against it in *Spectator* No. 209, wherein he deplored satire that "endeavours to shew by some superficial Strokes of Wit, that Brutes are the most excellent Creatures of the two." [18] Or (keeping

[13] W. A. Eddy, *Gulliver's Travels: A Critical Study* (Princeton, 1923), pp. 188–89.

[14] *Ibid.*, p. 189.

[15] *Ibid.*, pp. 172–87; George Boas, *The Happy Beast* (Baltimore, 1933).

[16] Boas, *op. cit.*, p. 10.   [17] *Ibid.*, p. 56.

[18] Addison was referring to the Boileau satire in which an ass, after observing the human comedy for an hour, decides that humans—not he—should pull carts. In *Tatler* No. 108 Addison had reproved those who "endeavour to make no distinction between man and man, or between . . . men and . . . brutes," and had singled out Rochefoucauld.

in mind Gulliver's eccentric conduct when he returns from [370] Houyhnhnm-land) there was the English Gentleman in *Spectator* No. 474, who had retired to the country but had been badgered by visiting hunters:

It is to me an insupportable affliction, to be tormented with the narrations of a set of people, who are warm in their expressions of the quick relish of that pleasure which their dogs and horses have a more delicate taste of. . . . There is in particular a young hound of great expectation, vivacity, and enterprise, that attends my flights wherever he spies me. This creature observes my countenance, and behaves himself accordingly. His mirth, his frolic, and joy upon the sight of me has been observed, and I have been gravely desired not to encourage him so much, for it spoils his parts . . . but I foresee *in a little while he and I must keep company with one another only, for we are fit for no other in these parts.*[19]

Animal, then, as having human rationality, was a playful concept familiar to and popular with Swift's audience. Not that the essential core of truth was unapparent: pursued to the absurd lengths of Part IV, however, the concept naturally broke down into the comic. The "horse-sense," then, that enables the Houyhnhnms to build houses and thread needles, also enables them to put their forehooves to their mouth (at which Gulliver is "much surprised"!) and to discourse on poetry. They belong to the same gifted animal group as Pliny's crabs, which reach the oyster by throwing pebbles between its open shells so that they cannot close,[20] and as Martin Martin's dextrous seals, which "eat no fish till they first take off the skin: they hold the head of the fish between their teeth, and pluck the skin off each side with their sharp pointed nails; this I observed several times",[21] all, of course, are as plausible as the Jubjub or the Jabberwock.

And yet on his return from Brobdingnag Gulliver had rejected the suggestion that he record his experiences, stating that he did not consider them "extraordinary" enough to satisfy a travels-surfeited public. What then has happened to our unfortunate traveler in the meantime?

III

The inherent humor of Gulliver's bewitchment by the Horses and of his final return to civilization seems generally to have been over-

---

[19] Italics mine. [20] Boas, *op. cit.*, p. 28 f.
[21] Pinkerton, *op. cit.*, III, 595.

looked. Critics have interpreted the outcome as unmitigated tragedy and misanthropy, and, substituting Swift for Gulliver, have found in Gulliver's return all the trappings of *Swift's* disgust with mankind. That the effects of Gulliver's final return were perhaps intended as exaggeratedly calamitous (and, therefore, comic) is a conclusion approached, however, by two critics. Professor Arthur Case points out that "the expressions about humanity which are found [in the last two chapters and in the "Letter to Sympson"] are not those of Gulliver in his normal state of mind," [22] and Professor Samuel Kliger believes that [371]

The balance and contrast in the management of the return motif draws the reader's attention to the fact that Gulliver, in every instance of his return, is reacting excessively in a way which belies his own nature and the situation itself. . . .[23]

Now it is just this *excessiveness* of Gulliver's reactions that Swift used as an instrument of humor, not only in Gulliver's final return, but throughout Part IV, and that was meant to be treated as on a level with the excessive nastiness of the Yahoos and the grotesque perfection of the Horses. To see this, it will be advisable to take stock of Gulliver himself.

Need it be reiterated that the narrator is not the Dean, but a middle-class English sea captain? If there is any clue to his identity, it is in his name, which suggests a *hoax*. The protagonist of Swift's "misanthropic" comedy is, if anything, the scornful reader of travel books gone a-traveling himself. The author is, of course, in the wing directing his satire of the travel books, and they have their revenge on Gulliver (as, to be sure, Swift has his laugh at society), not so much by stripping society of the last vestiges of virtue, however, as by depriving Gulliver of his wits.

Granted that he is an average Englishman, he is also a fool, albeit a *reiner Narr*. Actually the misfortunes of which he complains are largely of his own making.[24] After his first voyage he remains at home only two months: "my *insatiable* desire of seeing foreign countries

---

[22] Arthur E. Case, *Four Essays on Gulliver's Travels* (Princeton, 1945), p. 119.

[23] Samuel Kliger, "The Unity of *Gulliver's Travels*," *MLQ*, VI (1945), 404.

[24] Professor J. R. Moore contends that the inaccuracies of Gulliver's navigation are evidence of Swift's desire to ridicule the errors of the map makers, that Swift "set his voyagers afloat at sea in a Flying Dutchman's orgy of adverse winds and incredible geography." "The Geography of *Gulliver's Travels*," *JEGP*, XL (1941), 214–28.

would suffer me to continue no longer." Even after his ordeal in Brobdingnag, he resists the next enticement only briefly, "the *thirst* I had of seeing the world, *notwithstanding my past misfortunes*, continuing as *violent* as ever." [25] After another four months at home he accepts a third offer (advantageous, to be sure) to go to sea; as he admits, he has still not learned the lesson of knowing when he is well off. He laments Captain Pocock's loss at sea, saying that "if he had followed my advice he might have been safe at home with his family, as well as myself." When he is forced to get recruits, then, is it any wonder that the men turn out to be buccaneers? [26]

But the comic lengths to which his gullible nature leads him are most strikingly evident in his experiences in Houyhnhnm-land. He [372] lives there for three years without human company, and during that time changes perceptibly: the gentle sea captain is gradually convinced by the Houyhnhnms that he is a Yahoo! After the bathing incident, neither he nor the Houyhnhnms have any more doubt of his identity. Inasmuch as the Yahoos have mistreated him, and the lordly Houyhnhnms insist on lumping him with these degenerates, Gulliver's only recourse is to repudiate the Yahoos and, encouraged by their kindness, to imitate the Houyhnhnms. His allegiance is a natural one, but with the passing of time it has an almost tragic effect: in short, his mind becomes temporarily deranged.

Thus, when the generous Gulliver, who has always found his wife loving, chaste, and submissive, includes in his endless tirade "ranting, lewd, expensive wives," he is a somewhat befuddled traveler who has made one voyage too many, rather than a person to be taken seriously. Don Quixote goes mad from reading chivalric romances, and makes a laughingstock of himself by finding chivalric situations in the trivialities of everyday life; Gulliver goes mad from three years' isolation and from admiration of the fantastic Horses, and betrays his condition by denouncing mankind in a list of vices that is magnified to absurdity. Years earlier Gulliver had qualified the Brobdingnagian

[25] Italics in this paragraph are my own.
[26] Professor Case notes: "In the first case [Gulliver] suffers shipwreck, caused by sheer mischance. . . . On his arrival in Brobdingnag he is deserted by his terrified comrades under circumstances which make their cowardice understandable and perhaps excusable. At the beginning of the third voyage he experiences violence and cruelty from pirates. Finally he is marooned on Houyhnhnmland by the treachery of his own men. So effective a progression can hardly have been the result of an accident." *Op. cit.*, p. 121. But note that the pirates set him down at sea, whereas his own mutineers put him ashore, with some inconvenience to themselves. Surely this is *variety*, not progression.

monarch's scathing indictment of mankind by reflecting (perhaps with some irony) that "great allowances should be given to a being who lives wholly secluded from the rest of the world." Ironically, it is now Gulliver who has finally reached the point from which he cannot render a rational judgment. Though his ranting against the informers, backbiters, pickpockets, fops, bullies, scoundrels, fiddlers, and dancing masters is incongruous in the mouth of a man who, on his arrival in Houyhnhnm-land, says that "there were few greater lovers of mankind, at that time, than myself," at least it is sufficiently congruous with temporary derangement. And when, not as a solitary Elijah or John the Baptist, but as a middle-class, well-traveled Englishman of the "tranquillity of mind" that was his long before he arrived in Houyhnhnm-land, he reconciles himself to a diet of birds, honey, and bread, and to the companionship of quadrupeds that no imagination other than his own can make real, he is patently a figure used by Swift not only to satirize complacency and primitivism,[27] but also to amuse his audience. Like the pseudo-misanthropic *Spectator* contributor and the Beast-Fabulists, Swift is employing the familar technique of mock-serious satire.

In this disordered state of mind, Gulliver prepares to return home. About to take leave of his "master," he would prostrate himself to kiss the latter's hoof, saying: [373]

I am not ignorant how much I have been censured for mentioning this last particular. For my detractors are pleased to think it improbable, that so illustrious a person could descend to give so great a mark of distinction to a creature so inferior as I. *Neither have I forgot how apt some travellers are to boast of extraordinary favours they have received.*[28]

[27] The attack on complacency and pride is broad enough; what does need remembering are the glowing accounts in some travel books of the superiority of primitive civilizations that are being lampooned here. For Martin Martin's, cf. Pinkerton, *op. cit.*, III, 724–25; also, cf. Frantz, *The English Traveller*. Swift would have seen both as irrational excesses.

[28] *Gulliver's Travels*, ed. Arthur S. Case (New York, 1938), p. 307. Here (particularly in the sentence I have italicized) is Swift's own proof that, so far from conveying his disgust for his kind, he is only mocking the welcome supposedly offered other travelers. Cf. Martin Martin's "One of the natives would needs express his high esteem for my person, by making a turn round about me sun-ways, and at the same time blessing me, and wishing me all happiness; but I bade him let alone that piece of homage . . . but this poor man was . . . disappointed, as were also his neighbours . . . and one of them told me that this was a thing due to my character from them . . . and they could not, nor would not fail to perform it." Pinkerton, *op. cit.*, III, 580–81.

When the crew of the kindly Don Pedro's ship comes upon him, he is flat on his face, hiding behind a stone. At sea he tries to jump overboard. When he gets to Lisbon, he peeps into the street from his window, then withdraws his head in fright; when he does emerge, it is with stuffed nostrils. Is this misanthropy or comedy?

The Gulliver, then, who loses consciousness for almost an hour at the kiss of "that odious animal" who is his faithful and loving wife, who refuses to touch her or his children, and whose spirits are revived only by the smell of the stable where his beloved stallions are kept, is temporarily unbalanced, but is so because of his own folly as much as the world's, and therefore, like Don Quixote, is an object of laughter as much as of pity.

That his readers would laugh as he lectured, Swift must have been sure. In any event, the irony of Gulliver's leave-taking in Chapter XII is inescapable: all *other* travelers are liars, but

it hath given me a great disgust against [travel books], and some indignation to see the credulity of mankind so impudently abused. Therefore . . . I imposed on myself as a maxim, never to be swerved from, that I would *strictly adhere to truth. . . .*

Then, reversing the practical recommendations usually found at the end of travel books, Swift gives his fable the final touch of seriousness:

But instead of proposals for conquering the magnanimous nation [the Houyhnhnms], I rather wish they were in a capacity, or disposition, to send a sufficient number of their inhabitants for civilizing Europe, by teaching us the first principles of honour, justice, truth, temperance, public spirit . . . and fidelity.

Interpretation here calls for the usual grain of salt—an ingredient automatically furnished by Swift's own age in a recipe that has been lost with the passage of the centuries.

The "Letter to Sympson" is the final example of the tongue-in-cheek. As he leaves us, Gulliver is in the position of desisting from lecturing mankind because his becoming a Yahoo again (suspicions of which motivated his lecture) is imminent. In fact, he appears to have become a Yahoo again in the middle of the last sentence of the volume! [374]

IV

The *Travels* took London by storm, as we know, and the tributes of Pope, Gay, Arbuthnot, the duchess dowager of Marlborough, and others are familiar. But it is significant that praise of Part IV was not lacking. The Earl of Peterborough wrote to Swift (with some ironic exaggeration, surely):

. . . I am forced to write to you in the Yahoo language. The new one in fashion is much studied, and great pains taken about the pronunciation. Everybody, since a new turn, approves of it; but the women seem most satisfied, who declare for few words and horse performance. It suffices to let you know, that there is a neighing duetto appointed for the next opera.[29]

Joining in the fun, Pope wrote several poems celebrating the *Travels*, in one of which Gulliver is hailed by an English horse (writing in numbers) as a champion of horses' rights:

> To thee, we wretches of the Houyhnhnm band,
> Condemn'd to labour in a barbarous land,
> Return our thanks. Accept our humble lays,
> And let each grateful Houyhnhnm neigh thy praise. . . .[30]

In another, Pope explored the comic possibilities of the husband-wife relationship on Gulliver's return. In this Epistle the bewildered Mary Gulliver reproaches Lemuel with "those visits to the sorrel mare," watches him reject the dearly purchased fowl and asparagus in favor of oats, and declares:

> . . . would kind Jove my organs so dispose,
> To hymn harmonious Houyhnhnm through the nose,
> I'd call thee Houyhnhnm, that high-sounding name;
> Thy children's noses all should twang the same.
> So might I find thy loving spouse of course
> Endu'd with all the virtues of a horse.

And the fact that, but for Pope's refusal, the printer "would have printed 'em before the second Edition of the Book" [31] indicates that the latter was fully aware of the appeal of Part IV as comedy.

[29] November 29, 1726. *Correspondence*, ed. Ball, III, 370.

[30] With the following extract, taken from Whitwell Elwin and William John Courthope, ed., *Works of Alexander Pope* (London, 1882), IV, 509–13.

[31] Letter from Pope to Swift, February 18, 1727. *Correspondence*, ed. Ball, III, 380.

There were objections too, of course. What that famous suffragette, Lady Mary Wortley Montagu, thought of having horses supplant women in men's affections may be guessed.

. . . great eloquence have they [the authors] employed to prove themselves beasts, and shew such a veneration for horses, that, since the Essex Quaker, nobody has appeared so passionately devoted to that species; and to say truth, they talk of a stable with so much warmth and affection, I cannot help suspecting some very powerful motive at the bottom of it.[32] [375]

But even the sentimental Richardson's Miss Byron admits general approbation of Part IV, even while she scorns it:

Swift . . . for his abominable Yahoo story, has complimented with a knowledge of human nature; but I hope that the character of human nature . . . of creatures made in the image of the Deity, is not to be taken from the overflowings of such dirty imaginations.[33]

The Countess of Suffolk, perceiving the spirit of the book, wrote to Swift on *Gulliver's* appearance:

I cannot conclude without telling you, that our island is in great joy; one of our Yahoos, having been delivered of a creature, half ram and half Yahoo; and another has brought forth four perfect black rabbits. May we not hope . . . that in time our female Yahoos will produce a race of Houyhnhnms![34]

And Swift, who long before 1726 had become fond of his animal creations, was amused at her signature and answered:

I will tell you an odd accident, that this night, while I was caressing one of my Houyhnhnms, he bit my little finger so cruelly that I am hardly able to write; and I impute the cause to some foreknowledge in him, that I was going to write to a Sieve Yahoo, for so you are pleased to call yourself.[35]

Doubtless other encomiums would reward the collector's search, but perhaps the examples cited are indicative of the strong possibility that the reputation of Part IV has undergone an unfortunate de-

[32] Letter to Countess of Mar, November, 1726. *Letters and Works of Lady Mary Wortley Montagu*, ed. Lord Wharncliffe, third edition, with additions and corrections by W. Moy Thomas (London, n.d.), I, 502.
[33] *Sir Charles Grandison* (London, 1754), II, 83.
[34] November 17, 1726. *Correspondence*, ed. Ball, III, 362.
[35] February 1, 1727. *Correspondence*, ed. Ball, III, 375.

terioration. This is, of course, not to infer that Swift conceived of Houyhnhnm-land solely as benevolent comedy, or that his audience received it only as such. Actually, so brief a study as the foregoing is but a preliminary step toward the rediscovery of what Swift was trying to say and of how it was received by his audience. Surely the greatness of the *Travels* makes it a step worth taking. [376]

Gulliver's Voyage
to the Houyhnhnms

KATHLEEN M. WILLIAMS

It has long been recognised that the fourth Voyage of *Gulliver's Travels,* far from being the outburst of a misanthrope who delighted in "degrading human Nature," is the culmination of Swift's lifelong attack on the pride of man, especially the pride which convinces him that he can live by the light of his unaided reason, the pride that Swift himself sums up, in the title of one of his imaginary discourses in *A Tale of A Tub,* as "An Universal Rule of Reason, or Every Man his own Carver." In particular, he is taking up a position opposed to the doctrines of natural goodness which pervade eighteenth century thought and which find systematic expression in the writings of "Toland, Collins, Tindal, and others of the fraternity," who, as Swift remarks, all talk much the same language and whose ideas are dismissed in the *Argument against Abolishing Christianity* as "Trumpery." It is clear, both from the satires and the religious writings, that Swift was hostile to all doctrines of the natural self-sufficiency of man, whether they were expressed in Deistic terms or in the related pride of neo-Stoicism; and the Fourth Voyage of *Gulliver's Travels* embodies that hostility. But while the object of attack is established, it is not immediately clear, from the Voyage itself, whether any positive position is implied in the Houyhnhnms or in the other characters. The Yahoos, clearly, embody the negative intention, and are to be condemned. This is what happens to man when he tries to

Reprinted from *ELH* [*Journal of English Literary History*], XVIII (December 1951), 275–286. By permission of The Johns Hopkins Press.

live by reason and nature; he falls, as has been pointed out,[1] into a "state of nature" nearer to that envisaged by Hobbes than that of Locke's *Two Treatises of Government*. It is significant that, according to one Houyhnhnm theory, the Yahoos were descended from a pair of human beings, driven to the country by sea: "coming to Land and being forsaken by their Companions, they retired to the Mountains, and degenerating by Degrees, became in Process of Time, much [275] more savage than those of their own Species in the Country from whence these two Originals came." Presumably these originals, forced into self-reliance, had degenerated because their feeble human reason had been overwhelmed by an irrational "nature," and more adequate guides had been forgotten.

The ambiguity of the Fourth Voyage lies not in the Yahoos, but in the positions of Gulliver and, especially, of the Houyhnhnms. The function of the Houyhnhnms may be to present an ideal of the true life of reason, to be admired even if unattainable, and to be contrasted with the Yahoos to chasten the pride of that lump of deformity, man, by showing him the vanity of his pretensions. But if Swift did intend the Houyhnhnms to stand as an ideal contrast, he has badly mismanaged the matter. The Houyhnhnms do not strike the reader as altogether admirable beings; indeed they are sometimes absurd, and even repellent, and we are disgusted by Gulliver's exaggerated devotion to them. The dispassionate arguments of the assembly, for instance, about the nature and future fate of Gulliver and the Yahoos, show the characteristic and unpleasant coldness of the Houyhnhnm race; while Gulliver's master displays their equally characteristic self-satisfaction, carried here to the point of absurdity, when he criticises Gulliver's physical qualities. Gulliver tells us how his master interrupted his account of the relations of the European Yahoos with their horses, to point out the inferiority for all practical purposes of the Yahoo shape—"the Flatness of my Face, the Prominence of my Nose, mine Eyes placed directly in Front, so that I could not look on either Side without turning my Head; that I was not able to feed myself without lifting one of my fore Feet to my Mouth; and therefore Nature had placed those Joints to answer that Necessity." Throughout the book there are obvious blunders which cannot be explained away by the inevitable lack of positive attraction in rational Utopias. One of Swift's most

---

[1] By T. O. Wedel, "On the Philosophical Background of *Gulliver's Travels*," *SP*, XXIII (October 1926), 434–450.

attractive characters, Don Pedro de Mendez, is placed in a position at the end of the book where comparison with the Houyhnhnms is inevitable, and our sympathies are alienated by the humourless arrogance both of the Houyhnhnms themselves, and of Gulliver when, absorbed in admiration of his former master, he avoids his own family to concentrate on "the neighing of [276] those two degenerate Houyhnhnms I keep in my Stable." Clumsiness of this kind is not usual with Swift, who is well aware, as a rule, of the way to enlist our sympathy for a character, and shews his awareness in the drawing of M. B. Drapier, and of Gulliver in the Voyage to Lilliput. The whole course of his work makes it unlikely that he could be unaware of the unpleasantness of such passages as these. Possibly, then, the effect is a deliberate one, and the Houyhnhnms, far from being a model of perfection, are intended to show the inadequacy of the life of reason. This would be in keeping with the usual method of Swift's satire, and with the negative quality which has been observed in it. The characteristic of Swift's satire is precisely his inability, or his refusal, to present us straightforwardly with a positive to aim at. It may be, at bottom, a psychological or a spiritual weakness; he turns it to satiric strength, and produces satire which is comfortless but is also disturbing and courageous. He will leave us with nothing more than a few scattered hints of what is desirable and attainable, or sometimes, when what is desirable is clearly not to be had, with a half-ironic acceptance of the best that is to hand. A full, clear, and wholly unambiguous account of a state of life to aim at would be unusual and unexpected in Swift. It is his habit to look sceptically, not only at the evils of the world, but at those, including himself, who criticise such evils, and at those who present schemes for the betterment of mankind. Gulliver is quaintly indignant and surprised at the evils which still exist six months after the publication of his travels, and in *A Tale of A Tub* the Digression on Madness ends with a confession which undermines the whole: "Even I myself, the Author of these Momentous Truths, am a person whose Imaginations are hardmouth'd, and exceedingly Disposed to run away with his Reason." In fact, there is not usually a "norm" in Swift's satire, positively and unequivocally stated. As far as any positive position can be discovered, it must be by piecing together the hints and implications and indirections typical of Swift's whole method; it is foreign to that method to embody in one person or one race a state of things of which he fully approves. It is, indeed, more than a matter of satiric method for a man "betwixt two Ages cast," who had little of [277] which he could approve wholeheartedly. The spirit of compromise and commonsense, the love of the middle way, affected him sufficiently to undermine any more rigorous standards, while failing to satisfy him as it satisfied his younger contemporaries; and his position was further complicated by a strong feeling for existing forms and a dislike of innovation, which, like Dryden, he regards as dangerous. Any suggestion of radical remedies is distrusted by him even as he presents it, and he will withdraw from it into irony, or fall back into compromise, as he does in the ambiguous *Argument against Abolishing Christianity.*

In *Gulliver's Travels,* this characteristic method re-appears. In the first two books, no one person or group of persons is put forward for our approval, and neither the Lilliputians, the Brobdingnagians, nor Gulliver himself, can be regarded as a consistent satiric norm against which the moral and political vagaries of eighteenth century England are to be precisely measured. Swift slips from one side to another according as his isolated satiric points require it, and we are at one moment to admire, at another to dislike, the creatures of his imagination. Even in Laputa, a set of serious political schemes, such as the visionary project of "persuading Monarchs to chuse Favourites upon the Score of their Wisdom, Capacity, and Virtue," appears among the absurdities of the projectors. Gulliver himself is now honest and kindly, now credulous or pompous, according to the momentary demands of the satire. During his adventures in Brobdingnag he is frequently ridiculous and on one occasion definitely unpleasant; his complacent attitude to warfare, in Chapter VI, horrifies the giant King. In none of the first three books are we left with a consistent standard embodied in any creature, and it would seem that if the Houyhnhnms are presented fairly and squarely for our approval a change is involved not only in Swift's normal method but in his whole attitude of mind. He would hardly present the radical primitivism and rationalism of Houyhnhnm-land as desirable, at least without the ironic and sceptical withdrawal which his uncertain temperament demanded.

One would expect to find that Swift uses the Houyhnhnms in the same indirect way as he does the peoples of the earlier [278] books, not as a complete statement of the right kind of man or society, attainable or not, but as a satiric contrast in which good and less good are mixed in a proportion which we must decide for ourselves, with the aid of such hints of the author's as we can piece together. And in fact Swift is just as ready to sacrifice the consistency of the Houyhnhnms to their satiric function of innocent comment on unknown humanity as he is any of his other creatures. The opinion of Gulliver's master on the "prodigious Abilities of Mind" of English lawyers, which should qualify them to instruct others in wisdom and knowledge, leads to a valid satiric point, but does not show the Houyhnhnm in a very good light when one considers the damning account he has just heard of their moral depravity and lack of intellectual integrity. No doubt one reason why the Houyhnhnms are a race of animals is for satiric distance; but of course Swift's insistence on the animal in Book IV has a significance beyond that of satiric effectiveness. Several of the Houyhnhnms' characteristics seem to be intended to show their remoteness, and their irrelevance to the ordinary life and standards of mankind. Primitivism is used for this effect; they have great difficulty in understanding such humanly simple matters as Gulliver's clothes, his ship, his writing, and the Houyhnhnm in his dealings with Gulliver in Chapter III is not only unattractive, but unattractive in a particular way. "He brought me into all Company," Gulliver says of him, "and made them treat me with Civility because as he told them privately, this would put me into good Humour and make me more diverting." This may be intended to lessen Gulliver's status and lower his pride, but Swift could hardly have missed its effect of displaying the lack of humanity and sympathy, the cold curiosity of the Houyhnhnms. There is, too, the solemn criticism of Gulliver's physical characteristics in Chapter IV, part of which has already been quoted. This passage stresses the fact that man is not well endowed, either physically or mentally, to live a "natural" life; but it also shows the Houyhnhnm's inability to grasp the human point of view, his self-righteousness, and his determination to belittle these creatures who in their own land claim to rule over the Houyhnhnm race. The Houyhnhnms are alien and unsympathetic creatures, [279] not man at his best, as Godwin suggested, or man as he might be, but a kind of life with which humanity has nothing to do. The word Houyhnhnm, we are told, means "Perfection of Nature." These are not human beings, but virtuous animals, perfect but limited natural creatures, of a "nature" not simply unattainable by man, but irrelevant to him, and incapable not only of the depths, but also of the heights, to which humanity can reach. The Houyhnhnms have no shame, no temptations, no conception of sin: they are totally unable to comprehend the purpose of lying or other common temptations of man. They can live by reason because they have been created passionless. In man, we know, the passions are apt to get astride of the reason, which is not strong enough to restrain them, and the result in its extremest form is seen in the Yahoos, but the Houyhnhnms have no passions to control: "As these noble Houyhnhnms are endowed by Nature with a general Disposition to all Virtues, and have no Conceptions or Ideas of what is evil in a rational Creature, so their grand Maxim is, to cultivate Reason, and to be wholly governed by it." The point of the description lies in "as" and "so." The Houyhnhnms can live harmlessly by reason because their nature is different from ours.

Swift makes much of the differing natures of the Houyhnhnms, the Yahoos, and Gulliver himself. In the Houyhnhnms, nature and reason are one and the same. They have no "natural affections" in our sense; Nature, they say, has taught them to be equally benevolent to everyone, and to make a distinction of persons only on the rational grounds of "a superior Degree of Virtue." Marriage is undertaken simply as "one of the necessary Actions in a reasonable Being." Nor have they any fear of death, which they greet with the same complete absence of emotion that they show towards every other event, great or small. These attitudes are not those which Nature teaches human beings, as Swift recognizes both in *Gulliver's Travels* and elsewhere; man has affections and passions, and Swift seems not to regard them as wholly bad. The painful and universal fear of death in mankind was a subject which particularly interested and affected him, and the curious episode of the immortal Struldbrugs in the Third Voyage is an attempt to [280] deal with it. Gulliver wished to take some of the Struldbrugs back with him to England, "to arm our People against the Fear of Death," that dread which Nature has implanted in us, but not in the Houyhnhnms. In the *Thoughts on Religion* reason is brought to bear on the problem: "It is impossible that anything so natural, so necessary, and so universal as death, should ever have been designed by providence as an evil to mankind." But reason is powerless against man's fear of death, and his clinging to life on any terms; and Swift puts forward the idea that although in general reason was intended by Providence to govern our passions, in this God intended our passions to prevail over reason. Man cannot in all respects govern his passions by reason, he suggests, because he has not been equipped by Providence to do so;

perhaps both love of life and the propagation of the species are passions exempted by Providence, for particular purposes, from the control of reason. The precise amount of irony in such statements is always difficult to gauge, though the *Thoughts on Religion* are not satirically intended; but at least the passage shows Swift's feeling that such deep-rooted passions as these are part of the nature of man, created by God, and cannot and perhaps should not be ruled by reason. The Houyhnhnms are rational even in those things in which the wisest man's passions inevitably and even perhaps rightly rule him, and the handling of them seems to suggest not only the remoteness but the inadequacy by human standards, of the life of Reason. They have only the negative virtue of blamelessness.

The Houyhnhnms refer repeatedly to Gulliver's fellow-humans in terms which press home the contrast between themselves and mankind. Men are creatures "pretending to Reason," the character of a rational creature was one which mankind "had no Pretence to challenge." Again the Houyhnhnms thought that "Nature and Reason were sufficient Guides for a reasonable Animal, as we pretended to be." Man has no right to lay claim to the life of Reason, for in him nature and reason are not, as in the Houyhnhnms, identical, and there is that in his nature which is outside reason's legitimate control. But this is not necessarily to say that man's nature is thoroughly evil, and his situation hopeless, as in the case of the degenerate [281] Yahoos, nor is man treated in these terms. Gulliver and the other humans of Book IV are clearly distinguished from the Yahoos as well as from the Houyhnhnms, and the difference in their mental and physical habits is strongly insisted upon. They stand apart from the two races of this animal world, separated from both by characteristics of which neither the naturally virtuous and rational animals, nor the vicious and irrational ones, have any knowledge—in fact by the characteristics proper to humanity. Man does indeed share the Yahoos' propensity to evil, but he has compensating qualities which the bestial Yahoos have not possessed since their first degeneration; and with these qualities he may surpass the cold rational virtue of the Houyhnhnms. The member of that race who is treated with most sympathy by Swift is the humble sorrel nag, one of the servant breeds who were "not born with equal Talents of Mind." Into the incompletely rational mind of the nag, some near-human warmth and devotion can creep, and he is the only creature in Houyhnhnmland to show any affection; Gulliver's last link with the country as he sails away is the voice of the "Sorrel Nag (who always loved me) crying out . . . Take Care of thyself, gentle Yahoo."

With this partial exception, there is no sign among the Houyhn-hnms of kindness, compassion, or self-sacrifice, yet elsewhere in *Gulliver's Travels* there is sympathetic treatment of love, pity, and a deliberate intervention of one man in the life of another, very different from the Houyhnhnm's equal benevolence, detachment, and rational respect for virtue. Even in Book I, where moral satire is not at its most serious, there is an insistence on the importance of gratitude among the Lilliputians, by whom, we are told in Chapter VI, ingratitude is regarded as a capital crime. Gratitude is shown in action in Gulliver's behaviour to the Lilliputian King, when despite the King's unjust sentence upon him he cannot bring himself to retaliate, for, he tells us, "Neither had I so soon learned the Grati-tude of Courtiers, to persuade myself that his Majesty's present Severities quitted me of all past Obligations." In Book II there is the forbearance of the Giant King and the affection between Gulliver and the protective Glumdalclitch, and in Book IV great prominence is given to the Captain and crew [282] of the ship which rescues Gulliver. Swift makes it plain that the Portuguese sailors are admir-able human beings, and emphasizes in them the very qualities which the Houyhnhnms neither possess nor would understand. It is Don Pedro who persuades Gulliver to abandon his design of living as a recluse, following as far as he can the life of a rational detached virtue which the Houyhnhnms have taught him to admire, and in-stead to commit himself once more to the human relationships proper to mankind. Gulliver's duty as Don Pedro sees it is to return to a life of humanity, tolerance, and affection among his own people, and Gulliver, finding he can do no better, reluctantly agrees. But his behaviour towards his own family, set in a place where it contrasts forcibly with the tolerant practical goodwill of Don Pedro, is ex-aggerated to the point of madness. Only with difficulty can he endure the sight of the wife and children for whom he had shown so charm-ing a fondness in the past. Gulliver, once a normal affectionate hu-man being, concerned with the well-being of his friends, is now a solitary misanthrope, absurd and yet terrible in his self-concentra-tion and his loathing of those he had once loved. He had been, he tells us, a great lover of mankind, and his conduct in the previous voyages shows that he was particularly affectionate to his own family. Now they "dare not presume to touch my Bread, or drink out of the same Cup." To this point Gulliver has been led by his pride in the unaided reason. He has become inhuman, losing the specifically human virtues in his attempt to achieve something for which humanity is not fitted. He is ruined as a human being, and the failure of his fellows to attain his own alien standards has made him hate them. We are reminded of Swift's letter (of the 26th November, 1725) to Pope: "I tell you after all, that I do not hate mankind: it is 'vous autres' who hate them, because you would have them reasonable animals, and are angry for being disappointed." Gulliver is one of 'vous autres,' for to set for humanity the irrelevant standards of absolute reason is to end as Gulliver ended, in hatred and defeat. Swift was well aware of the process of disillusionment which has been attributed to him, and he exemplifies it in Gulliver, the true misanthrope, who believes man should try to rule himself by "Reason alone." [283]

On this interpretation, neither the master Houyhnhnm nor the misanthropic Gulliver who once thought so highly of mankind is presented as an ideal of behaviour. Like all the peoples of the *Travels* the Houyhnhnms have some characteristics, such as honesty and truthfulness, which we might well try to follow, and they are used for particular satiric points, but as a whole they represent an inadequate and inhuman rationalism, and the negativeness of their blameless life is part of Swift's deliberate intention. For us, with our less perfect but also less limited nature, to try to live like them would be to do as the Stoics did, according to Swift's remark in his *Thoughts on Various Subjects:* "The Stoical Scheme of Supplying our Wants by lopping off our Desires, is like cutting off our Feet when we want Shoes." It would mean abandoning the purely human possibilities as well as the disadvantages of our own nature, The Houyhnhnms may indeed be compared with the passionless Stoics of the Sermon *Upon the Excellency of Christianity,* who are contrasted with the Christian ideal of positive charity. Gulliver, in his turn, shows the loss of hope, proportion, and even common humanity in a man who tries to limit the complex nature of man to "Reason alone." Something more than Houyhnhnm harmlessness is needed in a world of human beings, and in so far as there is any positive presentation of right living to be found in *Gulliver's Travels,* it is in the representatives of that humanity which Gulliver rejects. For it is not, after all, a purely destructive view of humanity that Swift shows us. "Reason and Nature," indeed are set up only to be shown as inadequate. Swift never doubted that man should make use of reason to control his bad instincts where he can, but to live by reason alone is neither possible nor desirable if we are to remain human beings. Yet we have the generous King of Brobdingnag, whose people are the "least corrupted" of Yahoos or humans, and of whom Swift says, with his habitual indirection, "it would be hard indeed, if so remote a Prince's Notions of Virtue and Vice were to be offered as a Standard for all Mankind." And there is Don Pedro de Mendez, who shows to what unselfish goodness man can attain. Don Pedro is guided by 'Honour and Conscience,' and for Swift, as we know from the sermons, conscience was not a natural sense of right and wrong, or [284] Shaftesbury's "aesthetic perception of the harmony of the universe," but a faculty which must itself be guided, by the divine laws which we can know only from a source outside ourselves, from revelation. "There is no solid, firm Foundation for Virtue," he tells us in the sermon On the Testimony of Conscience, "but on a Conscience which is guided by Religion." "There is no other Tie thro' which the Pride, or Lust, or Avarice, or Ambition of Mankind will not certainly break one time or other." For him, as for so many Churchmen concerned with the controversies of the period, Reason is an insufficient guide without Revelation. The sermons, with their systematic attack on the supposed sufficiency of the moral sense, the scheme of virtue without religion, are clearly relevant to the theme of the fourth Voyage of *Gulliver's Travels*, and here we find the positive aspect of Swift's intention more explicitly set out. The sermon *Upon the Excellency of Christianity* shows, in its account of the ideal Christian, a creature who is meek and lowly, "affable and courteous, gentle and kind, without any morose leaven of pride or vanity, which entered into the composition of most Heathen schemes." The description applies far more nearly to Don Pedro and the early Gulliver than to the Houyhnhnms, or to Gulliver the misanthrope, into whose composition pride certainly enters. While allowing a place to the passions and affections, and their possibility, under guidance, for good, Swift does not fall into the Tillotsonian position that human nature's "mild and merciful" inclinations and the maternal and other natural affections are more important than revealed religion. An implied disapproval of such a position is expressed in Swift's version of Anthony Collins' *Discourse of Freethinking*, in which Tillotson, naturally, is praised. Both affections and reason have their place in the well-regulated man, but they are to be subjected to the laws of God.

Reason and gratitude may both suggest to a man that he should obey his parents, but the surest and most lasting cause of obedience must be the consideration "that his Reason is the Gift of God; that God commanded him to be obedient to the Laws, and did moreover in a particular manner enjoin him to be Dutiful to his Parents" (*On the Testimony of Conscience*). Swift would no doubt have agreed with that passage from [285] Butler's sermon *Upon Compassion* (published in the same year as *Gulliver's Travels*) in which passions and affections, carefully guided, are treated as necessary in creatures who are imperfect and interdependent, "who naturally and, from the condition we are placed in, necessarily depend upon each other. With respect to such creatures, it would be found of as bad consequence to eradicate all natural affections, as to be entirely governed by them. This would almost sink us to the condition of brutes; and that would leave us without a sufficient principle of action." The passage forms a comment on the contrasting creatures of Houyhnhnm-land, for Swift is as well aware as Butler of the complex nature of man, the possessor not only of evil impulses but of passions and affections which under the guidance of conscience and religion (to which reason must be subject) can issue in virtuous action, especially that compassionate assistance to our fellow men, whether or not our reason judges them worthy of it, which "the Gentile philosophy" fails to produce. In *Gulliver's Travels* there is not only a traditional Christian pessimism; there may well be a positive Christian ideal suggested in the conduct of the good humans, though it is presented with Swift's habitual obliquity and restraint. [286]

from The Irony of Swift

F. R. LEAVIS

[Swift's irony in Section IX of the *Digression Concerning the Original, the Use, and Improvement of Madness in a Commonwealth*] may be critical, but "critical" turns out, in no very long run, to be indistinguishable from "negative." The positives disappear. Even when, as in the Houyhnhnms, they seem to be more substantially present, they disappear under our "curiosity." The Houyhnhnms, of course, stand for Reason, Truth and Nature, the Augustan positives, and it was in deadly earnest that Swift appealed to these; but how little at best they were anything solidly realized, comparison with Pope brings out. Swift did his best for the Houyhnhnms, and they may have all the reason, but the Yahoos have all the life. Gulliver's master "thought Nature and reason were sufficient guides for a reasonable animal," but nature and reason as Gulliver exhibits them are curiously negative, and the reasonable animals appear to have nothing in them to guide. "They have no fondness for their colts or foals, but the care they take in educating them proceeds entirely from the dictates of reason." This freedom from irrational feelings and impulses simplifies other matters too: "their language doth not abound in variety of words, because their wants and passions are fewer than among us." And so conversation, in this model society, is simplified: "nothing passed but what was useful, expressed in the fewest and most significant words. . . ." "Courtship, love, presents, jointures, settlements, have no place in their thoughts, or terms whereby to express them in their language. The young couple meet

From *The Common Pursuit* by F. R. Leavis (New York: George W. Stewart, 1952), pp. 84–87. By permission of Chatto and Windus, Ltd., London, and George W. Stewart, Publisher, Inc., South Norwalk, Connecticut.

and are joined, merely because it is the determination of their parents and friends: it is what they see done every day, and they look upon it as one of the necessary actions of a reasonable being." The injunction of "temperance, industry, exercise, and cleanliness . . . the lessons enjoined to the young ones of both sexes," seems unnecessary; except possibly for exercise, the usefulness of which would not, perhaps, be immediately apparent to the reasonable young.

The clean skin of the Houyhnhnms, in short, is stretched over a void; instincts, emotions and life, which complicate the problem [84] of cleanliness and decency, are left for the Yahoos with the dirt and the indecorum. Reason, Truth and Nature serve instead; the Houyhnhnms (who scorn metaphysics) find them adequate. Swift too scorned metaphysics, and never found anything better to contend for than a skin, a surface, an outward show. An outward show is, explicitly, all he contends for in the quite unironical *Project for the Advancement of Religion,* and the difference between the reality of religion and the show is, for the author of the *Tale of a Tub,* hardly substantial. Of Jack we are told, "nor could all the world persuade him, as the common phrase is, to eat his victuals like a Christian." It is characteristic of Swift that he should put in these terms, showing a complete incapacity even to guess what religious feeling might be, a genuine conviction that Jack should be made to kneel when receiving the Sacrament.

Of the intensity of this conviction there can be no doubt. The Church of England was the established "common form," and, moreover, was Swift's church: his insane egotism reinforced the savagery with which he fought to maintain this cover over the void, this decent surface. But what the savagery of the passage from the *Digression* shows mainly is Swift's sense of insecurity and of the undisguisable flimsiness of any surface that offered.

The case, of course, is more complex. In the passage examined the "surface" becomes, at the most savage moment, a human skin. Swift's negative horror, at its most disturbing, becomes one with his disgust-obsession: he cannot bear to be reminded that under the skin there is blood, mess and entrails; and the skin itself, as we know from *Gulliver,* must not be seen from too close. Hypertrophy of the sense of uncleanness, of the instinct of repulsion, is not uncommon; nor is its association with what accompanies it in Swift. What is uncommon is Swift's genius and the paradoxical vitality with which this self-defeat of life—life turned against itself—is manifested. In the *Tale of a Tub* the defeat is also a triumph; the genius delights in its mastery, in its power to destroy, and negation is felt as self-assertion. It is only when time has confirmed Swift in disappointment and brought him to more intimate contemplation of physical decay that we get the Yahoos and the Struldbrugs.

Here, well on this side of pathology, literary criticism stops. To attempt encroachments would be absurd, and, even if one were [85] qualified, unprofitable. No doubt psychopathology and medicine have an interesting commentary to offer, but their help is not necessary. Swift's genius belongs to literature, and its appreciation to literary criticism.

We have, then, in his writings probably the most remarkable expression of negative feelings and attitudes that literature can offer —the spectacle of creative powers (the paradoxical description seems right) exhibited consistently in negation and rejection. His verse demands an essay to itself, but fits in readily with what has been said. "In poetry," he reports of the Houyhnhnms, "they must be allowed to excel all other mortals; wherein the justness of their similes and the minuteness as well as exactness of their descriptions are, indeed, inimitable. Their verses abound very much in both of these. . . ." The actuality of presentment for which Swift is notable, in prose as well as verse, seems always to owe its convincing "justness" to, at his least actively malicious, a coldly intense scrutiny, a potentially hostile attention. "To his domesticks," says Johnson, "he was naturally rough; and a man of rigorous temper, with that vigilance of minute attention which his works discover, must have been a master that few could bear." *Instructions to Servants* and the *Polite Conversation* enforce obviously the critical bearing and felicity of Johnson's remark.

A great writer—yes; that account still imposes itself as fitting, though his greatness is no matter of moral grandeur or human centrality; our sense of it is merely a sense of great force. And this force, as we feel it, is conditioned by frustration and constriction; the channels of life have been blocked and perverted. That we should be so often invited to regard him as a moralist and an idealist would seem to be mainly a witness to the power of vanity, and the part that vanity can play in literary appreciation: *saeva indignatio* is an indulgence that solicits us all, and the use of literature by readers and critics for the projection of nobly suffering selves is familiar.

No doubt, too, it is pleasant to believe that unusual capacity for egotistic animus means unusual distinction of intellect; but, as we have seen, there is no reason to lay stress on intellect in Swift. His work does indeed exhibit an extraordinary play of mind; but it is not great intellectual force that is exhibited in his indifference to the problems raised—in, for instance, the *Voyage to the Houyhnhnms* —by his use of the concept, or the word, [86] "Nature." It is not merely that he had an Augustan contempt for metaphysics; he shared the shallowest complacencies of Augustan common sense: his irony might destroy these, but there is no conscious criticism.

He was, in various ways, curiously unaware—the reverse of clair-voyant. He is distinguished by the intensity of his feelings, not by insight into them, and he certainly does not impress us as a mind in possession of its experience.

We shall not find Swift remarkable for intelligence if we think of Blake. [87]

Swift's Yahoo and the Christian Symbols for Sin

ROLAND M. FRYE

I said in mine heart concerning the estate of the sons of men, that God might manifest them, and that they might see that they themselves are beasts.—ECCLESIASTES 3. 18.

I

Swift's treatment of the Yahoo in the fourth book of *Gulliver's Travels* has been the center of a prolonged critical controversy. Involving and epitomizing as it does the so-called "misanthropy" of Swift, this controversy has a significance which extends beyond the particular work in question, although that is significant enough in itself. Merrel D. Clubb. who has traced the history of the controversy, writes that "the longer one studies Swift, the more obvious it becomes that the interpretation and verdict to be placed on the 'Voyage to the Houyhnhnms' is, after all, the central problem of Swift criticism." [1]

The Yahoo was, of course, a controversial figure even in the eighteenth century, but Clubb significantly sees the principal deluge of anti-Yahooism as coming between the years 1800 and 1914. [2] For example, he quotes De Quincey as saying that Swift's "own *yahoo* is not a more abominable one-sided degradation of humanity, than is

Reprinted from the *Journal of the History of Ideas*, XV (April 1954), 201–217. By permission.

[1] Merrel D. Clubb, "The Criticism of Gulliver's 'Voyage to the Houyhnhnms,' 1726–1914," *Stanford Studies in Language and Literature* (1941), 206–7.

[2] *Ib.*, 219.

he himself." [3] Again, we have Thackeray's well-known lecture on Swift, in which the post-Romantic attitude is crystallized in its typical form:

As for the moral [of the fourth voyage], I think it horrible, shameful, unmanly, blasphemous. . . . It is Yahoo language: a monster gibbering shrieks, and gnashing imprecations against mankind,—tearing down all shreds of modesty, past all sense of manliness and shame; filthy in word, filthy in thought, furious, raging, obscene.[4]

To the post-Romantic mind, largely divorced as it was from the main stream of Christian realism, and in good part given over to the exaltation of man, Swift's Yahoo as a filthy monster might very well seem "blasphemous." [5] [201]

Much has been made of Swift's misanthropy. He has been accused of having a diseased mind and the Yahoo has been presumed to be a reflection of his mental disorder. It is undeniably true that Swift regarded man's nature as depraved, his unaided conscience as a blind guide, and his carnal reason as an imperfect instrument—witness his sermons "On the Testimony of Conscience" and "On the Trinity." If such views are sufficient to establish misanthropy, however, then some of the greatest figures of the Christian tradition will keep Dean Swift company on the anthropophile's Index Librorum Prohibitorum. As an effective satirist, Swift was of course writing with overemphasis and with unusual intensity, and this is perhaps one reason his position has seemed more extreme than that of other men of similar views whom we regard as moderate because their mode of expression allowed of moderation. The purpose of this paper, however, is not to add to the present long list another subjective reaction to Swift's view of man, but is rather to explore the relation between one of his imaginative creations, the Yahoo, and that traditional view of human nature which is known as Christian anthropology. By examining the terminology, the symbols, and the typical phraseology

[3] *The Collected Writings of Thomas De Quincey*, ed. David Masson (Edinburgh, 1890), XI, 14. Quoted in Clubb, 223.
[4] W. M. Thackeray, *English Humourists of the Eighteenth Century*, 1st ed. (New York, 1853), 37. Quoted in Clubb, 221.
[5] Thus, in his *Nature and Destiny of Man* (London, 1946), I, 100–1, Reinhold Niebuhr writes that "no cumulation of contradictory evidence seems to disturb modern man's good opinion of himself. He considers himself the victim of corrupting institutions which he is about to destroy or reconstruct, or of the confusions of ignorance which an adequate education is about to overcome. Yet he continues to regard himself as essentially harmless and virtuous."

of this tradition, as it is found both in the Bible and also in the homiletic and admonitory literature of Christianity, we will be better able to understand both Swift's intention and his rhetoric in creating the Yahoo as a filthy, depraved, and thoroughly repulsive figure.

Gulliver's Travels was published in a period of flux so far as theology and religious symbolism were concerned. In his valuable study, "On the Philosophical Background of *Gulliver's Travels*," T. O. Wedel summarizes the matter as follows: "In theological terms, what was happening of course was the avowed or tacit denial of the doctrine of original sin. Human nature was being absolved of corruption. The ancient Christian faith, in the words of Pascal, had rested on but two things, 'the corruption of nature and the redemption by Jesus Christ.' Half at least of Pascal's formula is seldom spoken of after 1700." [6] When Wedel says that original sin "is seldom spoken of after 1700," he is undoubtedly implying a comparison with the preceding century and a half of English Protestantism. That the doctrine was by no means an unfamiliar one is indicated by the following statement which appeared in *The Tribune* of Dublin in 1719:

The Corruption of Human Nature is a Text that has so long been preached upon, that one might justly conclude the Subject long since exhausted. Yet it continues still to be a darling Theme, not only among some loose and profligate Writers, with a View to dissolve the natural Obligations to [202] Virtue; but likewise by great Numbers of grave and orthodox Divines, who have held it forth as a doctrine of the utmost Importance in Religion, and the Belief of it, absolutely necessary to denominate a Man a good Christian.[7]

Although the conception of original sin was certainly not lost, its popularity had entered upon a decline even in Swift's day, a decline which was to be accelerated with the passage of time. Of equal importance is the fact that even when the idea of natural depravity was retained and emphasized, it gradually lost the symbols traditionally associated with it. In order to understand the Yahoo fully, it is necessary, as we shall see, to keep these symbols in mind.

As a professional clergyman, Swift may rightly be assumed to have had an intimate acquaintance with these symbolic vehicles of orthodox thought. Indeed, it would be illogical to expect him to approach the problem of human nature and human sin in terms of what we

---

[6] Wedel, *SP*, XXIII (1926), 441.
[7] *The Tribune*, no. 20 (Dublin, 1719). I am indebted to Mr. Louis Landa for this quotation and also for helpful suggestions and encouragement throughout.

currently think of as the lay mind. His training, as well as the daily field of his duties, required serious thinking upon these problems and upon their Biblical base, thinking which might not be encountered to the same degree among his purely literary confrères. That such a personal background, and sincere personal convictions, should have found expression in Swift's satire ought not to surprise us. Thus if we observe the reactions of those for whom these traditional symbols retained vividness and truth, we discover a sympathetic understanding of Swift's intentions in creating the Yahoo. Surely Deane Swift, the biographer of his cousin Jonathan, is well qualified to elucidate this matter, and he declares that the fourth book was conceived in Christian terms. Indeed, he says, the author was fulfilling his duties as "a preacher of righteousness" and "a watchman of the Christian faith" when he described the Yahoo:

And shall we condemn a preacher of righteousness, for exposing under the character of a nasty unteachable *Yahoo* the deformity, the blackness, the filthiness, and corruption of those hellish, abominable vices, which inflame the wrath of God against the children of disobedience. . . . ? [8]

John Hawkesworth, in his 1755 edition of *Gulliver*, points to the same interpretation:

Whoever is disgusted with this picture of a *yahoo*, would do well to reflect, that it becomes his own in exact proportion as he deviates from virtue, for [203] virtue is the perfection of reason: the appetites of those abandoned to vice are not less brutal and sordid than that of a *yahoo* for asses flesh, nor is their life a state of less abject servility. [9]

Furthermore, we find that John Wesley in his *Doctrine of Original Sin* (1757) quotes at great length from the "Voyage to the Houyhnhnms" in order to describe man's depravity. [10] In their interpretations, Deane Swift, Hawkesworth and Wesley place the fourth book within its intended frame of reference, having understood its traditional symbolism. My task here is to discover that symbolism, its sources and traditional applications as Jonathan Swift knew it, and to apply it to his picture of the Yahoo. The result of this study will surely not

---

[8] Deane Swift, *An Essay upon the Life, Writings, and Character of Dr. Jonathan Swift* (London, 1755), 219.

[9] John Hawkesworth, ed., *The Works of Jonathan Swift . . .* (London, 1755), I, 217.

[10] John Wesley, *Works* (New York, 1856), V, 510–12. I am indebted to Canon Wedel for this citation.

provide the only frame of reference for the fourth book, but I hope that it will indicate an important avenue of approach.

One point should be made at the outset. In a study such as this one, there can be no attempt to delineate the fully-rounded Christian view of man. It can scarcely be otherwise here, for I am following Swift's treatment of the Yahoo, where the primary concern is with sin and folly. Thus, the "image of God" motif is only incidentally touched upon. Furthermore, the vigorous castigations of the flesh by a number of the theologians whom I quote should not be allowed to stand without some comment, for otherwise an injustice would be done both to these writers and to the tradition of which they are a part. These men were not bigoted, ascetic, or prudish in their attitudes toward man. They were merely using the terms "flesh" and "body" as symbolic vehicles; they were not denying man access to the legitimate outlets for his normal physical drives.

II

Of *Gulliver's Travels*, T. O. Wedel says that when "Swift wrote his own treatise to vex the world, scepticism and the belief in the corruption of human nature, nature had given way to rationalism and an optimistic faith in man." [11] Mr. Louis Landa suggests that, although it cannot be proved, there is justification for thinking that Swift's sermon "On the Testimony of Conscience" is an oblique answer to Shaftesbury, or at least to some similarly flattering view of man's natural benevolence.[12] It would seem reasonable that some such [204] reaction against the growing faith in man's natural goodness lies behind the satiric picture of the Yahoo. Certainly, this is at least implied by Deane Swift when he refers to critics of the Yahoo as "these mighty softeners; these kind pretenders to benevolence; these hollow charity-mongers" (p. 220). That Swift regarded theories of natural benevolence as preliminary to moral anarchy, is evidenced by his sermon "On the Testimony of Conscience," as well as by other strains of his work. The result of these theories would be the overthrow of individual honesty and virtue. With this in mind, it would seem quite possible that Swift conceived the "Voyage to the Houyhnhnms" as Christian apologetics, among other things, and that he incorporated into it a sharp satiric attack upon a theologically dan-

---

[11] Wedel, 447.
[12] Louis Landa, ed., *Swift's Irish Tracts and Sermons* (Oxford, 1948), 114.

gerous doctrine—in this case, upon the conception of man as naturally inclined to goodness. That such an attack would be closely allied with Augustinian theology need not be emphasized. What should be pointed out is that Swift's treatment is thoroughly consistent with certain normative positions of Protestantism in general and of Anglicanism in particular.

Christian symbolism has traditionally used "the flesh" as representative of man's natural propensity towards evil. Bishop Gilbert Burnet, in his *Exposition of the Thirty-Nine Articles* (1699), writes in support of Article IX, "Of Original or Birth Sin," that "it is certain that in Scripture this general corruption of our nature is often mentioned." He then proceeds to quote nine typical passages which emphasize man's natural proclivity for evil, and concludes in this wise: "*The flesh is weak. The flesh lusteth against the spirit. The carnal mind is enmity to the law of God, and is not subject to the law of God, neither indeed can be: and they that are in the flesh cannot please God:* where by *flesh* is meant the natural state of mankind, according to those words, *That which is born of the flesh is flesh, and that which is born of the Spirit is spirit.*" [13] Such was the conventional division of man for admonitory purposes, with the spirit as the valuable, redeemable part, and the flesh representing all the natural inclinations to evil which warred against the higher powers.

The most definite and most complete identification of the Yahoo with Gulliver is in terms of the flesh or the body. This is clearly stated when Gulliver is first able to inspect "the beast" at close range. "My Horror and Astonishment are not to be described," he says, "when I observed, in this abominable Animal, a perfect human [205] Figure." [14] Later, Gulliver's master among the Houyhnhnms similarly observes that Gulliver "agreed in every Feature of [his] Body with other *Yahoos*" (pp. 243–44). This perfect correspondence between man and Yahoo in the body is even further emphasized by an elaboration of how they differ. Man differs in having the gift of speech and in having some faculty of reason, even though he does abuse it. There are other minor differences, but throughout the book the

[13] Gilbert Burnet, *An Exposition of the Thirty-Nine Articles* (London, 1850), 132. Scriptural quotations are from Matt. 26.41; Mark 14.38; Gal. 5.17; Rom. 8.7–8; and John 3.6.
[14] *Gulliver's Travels*, ed. Herbert Davis and Harold Williams (Oxford, 1941), 213–14. All references are to this edition.

reiterated identification is physical. After the episode at the river when he is the object of fleshly desire, Gulliver says "I could no longer deny, that I was a real *Yahoo*, in every Limb and Feature, since the Females had a natural Propensity to me as one of their own Species." [15] The consistent reference is to physical similarities—in short, only one correlation seems valid, that Yahoo is man in "the flesh."

We have seen Bishop Burnet's gloss of this term as indicative of the weakness and evil in man which wars upon the spiritual. Burnet is not alone in this interpretation. Mark Frank (1613–64), who died Master of Pembroke Hall, Cambridge, and chaplain to Archbishop Selden, glosses I Corinthians 9.27 (subjection of the body) in this way: "And by the 'body' here may be understood either the flesh itself, or the fleshliness of it; the body itself, or the sinful passions and affections rising in it." [16] The Rev. John Bradford, a Smithfield martyr of 1555, writes in his "Seventh Meditation" that the body "is to the soul nothing else but a prison, and that most strait, vile stinking, filthy." [17] Another important Smithfield martyr, John Hooper, Bishop of Gloucester and Worcester, writes in terms strikingly close to those of Swift. Hooper's description of man "as he is, a vile piece of earth with all his pride and pomp," [18] is similar in thought, though inferior in style, to Swift's "Lump of Deformity, and Diseases both in Body and Mind, smitten with *Pride*" (p. 280), a passage which Wesley quotes verbatim from Gulliver for use in his treatment of original sin. Again, when Bishop Hooper,[19] urging the need for [206] self-examination in the light of Scripture, says that whoever "*beholds himself well in that mirror and glass,* will find such a deformity and disgraced physiognomy, that he will abhor his own proportion so horribly disfigured," he is even more misanthropic than Gulliver, who made it a practice "*to behold my Figure often in a Glass,* and thus if

[15] *Gulliver's Travels,* 251. For other such physical identifications, see 219, 221, 222, 256, 262.

[16] Mark Frank, *Sermons* (Oxford, 1859), I, 402. See also 411.

[17] John Bradford, *Writings* (Philadelphia: British Reformers Series, n.d.), 412. See also Henry Bullinger, *The Decades* (Cambridge, 1849–51), IV, 386, and Archbishop Edwin Sandys, *Sermons* (Cambridge, 1841), 447.

[18] John Hooper, *Writings* (Philadelphia: British Reformers Series, n.d.), 78.

[19] A discussion such as this necessitates a topical treatment, and it has frequently been impossible for me to cite authorities in a strictly chronological order, as I should have wished to do. Thus we move from Hooper to Wesley and back to Hooper.

possible habituate myself by Time to tolerate the Sight of a human Creature." [20] Bradford speaks of the flesh in the conventional terms when he says: "What a charnel-house of stinking carrion is this body and life of wicked man. . . ." [21]

Jeremie Collier, writing in 1686, treats the same subject in detail. Knowledge, he says, is what sets us "at the greatest distance from the Brutes beneath us," but the mind is hindered in its pursuit of knowledge by "the present constitution of our Bodies." [22] Further, the body subjects us to passions which may prevent our examining "things with that deliberation and indifferency which is necessary to the finding out moral Truth" (p. 18). Like Burnet, Frank, Bradford, Hooper and Wesley, Collier makes much of the biblical pronouncements on the flesh, and in treating Romans 8.6 and 13, he writes: "For the Apostle assures us [that] if we live after the Flesh, and make Provision to fulfill the Lusts thereof, we shall die, for to be carnally or sensually minded is death, and that we cannot expect to live hereafter except we mortify the deeds of the Body" (p. 30). Collier is here speaking in soteriological terms, of course, but the use of the body as a symbol for evil is typical.

Collier points out that man debases himself to the level of the brute beasts if he surrenders to the flesh: ". . . to make the Soul a Slave to the Body; to employ the powers of Reason (the Image of the Glorious God) in providing for the gratification of the Animal Life; is a most degenerous and dangerous abuse of so great a privilege: And when God hath made us little lower than the Angels, ought we not to blush to make our selves less than the Beasts that perish?" (pp. 28–29). A glance through earlier theologians reveals the deep roots of this tradition. Writing to the same effect in 1633, Matthew Griffith expresses the human dichotomy in these terms: "Without this *body* man had bin an *Angell;* and without this *soule* but a [207] *Brute*." [23] Bullinger declares that through sin, men "that were like unto God made themselves brutish," while Hooker speaks to the same effect in his *Ecclesiastical Polity*, and Miles Coverdale

---

[20] Hooper, 76; *Gulliver's Travels*, 279; italics mine.

[21] Hooper, 257–8. See also John Calvin, *The Institute of the Christian Religion*, II, i, 8; Bishop Joseph Hall, *Devotions* (London, 1846), 452; and Richard Fiddes, *Practical Discourses* (London, 1713), I, 97.

[22] Jeremie Collier, *The Difference between the Present and Future State of Our Bodies* (London, 1686), 17.

[23] Matthew Griffith, *Bethel: or, a Frame for Families* (London, 1633), 202.

translates Erasmus' *Enchiridion* in these words: "If we incline to the flesh, it maketh us beasts."[24]

I suggest that these ideas form part of the intellectual background of the fourth book. The human body was traditionally understood to represent man's natural depravity; it is a logical representation of this tradition, therefore, that the Yahoo has "a perfect *human* figure." According to this view, the Yahoo would then represent those elements in his nature which man must distrust, and which, in Christian terms, he must seek to subdue. The Yahoo is that fleshly element in human nature which cannot be disavowed, which may in fact degrade man to the level of the brute beasts, and which vitiates any argument for the self-redemptive power of human reason and the final efficacy of natural benevolence. As Swift says in his September 29, 1725, letter to Pope: "I have got materials toward a treatise, proving the falsity of that definition *animal rationale,* and to show it would be only *rationis capax.*"

As Swift indicates, this capacity for reason is what distinguishes man from Yahoo. The Houyhnhnm assembly recognizes in Gulliver "some Rudiments of Reason," and Gulliver at last comes to regard his Portuguese rescuer, Don Pedro, as having "some little Portion of Reason." He is never graced with more than "some Glimmerings of Reason," "some Marks of Reason," and the like, but this is an incontrovertible mark of distinction. Yet even this small pittance is degraded by man. At one point Gulliver quotes the master Houyhnhnm as saying that men seem to make no other use of this "small Pittance of *Reason*" than "by its Assistance to aggravate our *natural* Corruptions, and to acquire new ones which Nature had not given us." In the same vein, Gulliver says that his countrymen make "no other Use of Reason, than to improve and multiply those Vices, whereof their Brethren in this Country had only the Share that Nature allotted them."[25]

Such a view of man's use of reason to corrupt himself and to increase even the ills to which his flesh is already heir can be paralleled in a sermon preached on "the scorner" by Richard Fiddes, whom [208] Swift befriended and whose sermons he possessed. The scorner "studies Vice as an Art," says Fiddes, "and his Thoughts are

[24] Bullinger, IV, 351; Richard Hooker, *Works,* ed. John Keble (New York and Phila., 1849), I, 297; Miles Coverdale, *Writings and Translations* (Cambridge, 1844), 505.
[25] *Gulliver's Travels,* 263, 271, 219, 222, 243, and 262. For similar references see 232, 240, 251–2, and 256.

taken up with enquiring how far the Improvement of it may be carry'd. He affects to be thought the Author of some new Discovery in the Theory of Sin, or to do some eminent Service towards promoting the Practice of it." [26] In a striking passage, also cited by Wesley, Gulliver says that although the master Houyhnhnm "hated the *Yahoos* of this Country, yet he no more blamed them for their odious Qualities, than he did a *Gnnayh* (a Bird of Prey) for its Cruelty, or a sharp Stone for cutting his Hoof. But, when a Creature pretending to Reason, could be capable of such Enormities, he dreaded lest the Corruption of that Faculty be worse than Brutality itself" (p. 232). Quite pertinent to this is another passage from Jeremie Collier's sermon. Having just said (as quoted above) that reason is the image of God in man, he proceeds:

And when God hath made us little lower than the Angels, ought we not to blush to make ourselves less than the Beasts that perish? Now that Sensuality does degrade us in this manner is apparent, it being unquestionably more scandalous and uncreditable to abuse the use of Reason, than to want it; for the one only argues natural incapacity; which because it could not be prevented, is no just reproach to any Being; but the other besides ingratitude to the Donor implies most egregious folly (p. 29).

Mark Frank, discussing the manner in which we, as "men of reason," debase ourselves, writes that "we must both needs confess that we have done brutishly and unreasonably, and cannot but be ashamed we have so unmanned ourselves, and betrayed the very essence and glory of our nature [*i.e.*, the image of God]: not done like men" (p. 429). The basic ideas in these passages are practically identical: The corruption of reason is far more culpable than the absence of it; by perverting his reason, man becomes far more contemptible than a brute beast. This is the ground-work of the whole satire of Part IV, according to Deane Swift, who elucidates the Yahoo by referring to

The reasoning of St. Peter throughout his whole second chapter of his second epistle; that creature man, that glorious creature man, is deservedly more contemptible than a brute beast, when he flies in the face of his Creator by enlisting under the banner of the enemy; and perverts that reason, which was designed to have been the glory of his nature, even the directing spirit of his life and demeanor, to the vilest, the most execrable, the most hellish purposes. *And this manifestly appears to be*

---

[26] Richard Fiddes, *Practical Discourses* (London, 1713), I, 93.

*the ground-work of the whole satyre contained in the voyage to the
Houyhnhnms* (p. 221, italics mine). [209]

He then observes that "Dr. Swift was not the first preacher, whose
writings import this kind of philosophy," a statement which he but-
tresses by citing biblical uses of bestial symbolism (II Esdras 8.29–
30; Isaiah 56.10–12; Philippians 3.2; I Corinthians 15.32; Matthew
3.7; Titus 1.12–13; Revelation 22.14–15; Matthew 7.15 and 10.16).

Thus we may say of the Yahoo that he represents "the flesh," or,
as Matthew Griffith, quoted above, says of man without a soul, that
"he is but a brute." Whole man, on the contrary, is flesh *plus* reason.
Both are joined together in him and interact the one upon the other;
such was the traditional conception. Man has a spirit, "the only seat
of our understanding and reason," as Bishop Peter Browne (c. 1661–
1735) describes it, which should govern the flesh, containing "those
bodily appetites which are common to us with brutes." [27] Actually,
however, the reverse is too frequently the case, so that the flesh
"often drags the spirit with it, to wallow in the mire." [28] Thus it is
that man's lower elements are responsible for corrupting his spiritual
and rational faculties. Between the two there can be nothing but
enmity until "the absolute conquest of the one or the other." [29] In
this conflict, the relevance of the Yahoo to the human dilemma becomes quite apparent.

III

The Yahoo may not only be related to Christian symbolism of the
flesh, but may also be seen as embodying many of those elements
of filth and deformity which are emblematic of sin throughout the
Scriptures, beginning with the Levitical pollutions and carrying on
far into the New Testament. Nor did Swift introduce the *literary*
employment of dung, deformity and corruption, as is evident if we
recall terms used in Milton's descriptions of Sin in *Paradise Lost*,
and in Spenser's stripping of Duessa in *The Faerie Queene*.[30] To
illustrate the vitality of this tradition in England, let me begin with
three examples from the pulpit. I submit that if Swift had been guilty
of any one of these statements, it would have been cited innumerable

---

[27] Peter Browne, *Sermons* (Dublin, 1749), II, 134, 133.
[28] *Ibid.*, II, 142.   [29] Browne, II, 139. See also Frank, I, 404.
[30] *Paradise Lost*, II, 650–66, 795–800; X, 629–37, and *The Faerie Queene*,
I, viii, 46–48.

times as proof of his diseased outlook. In one of his Lincoln's Inn sermons, John Donne describes man's condition in this way: "Between that excremental jelly that thy body is made of at first, and that jelly which thy body dissolves to at last; there is not so noisome, [210] so putrid a thing in nature." [31] Such, according to Donne, is man's mortal condition. Writing in 1667, B. Agas describes the godless who professed to be Christians: "As dross among Gold, or as scum upon a pot, such are these, a meer filth among the pure professors. They are the Gospels reproach and Religions shame, equally disgracing both the one and the other, as a dead blasted limb a living Body, or as a loathsome leperous scab a beautiful face." [32] In the same vein, Jeremie Taylor (1613–67) asks in his *Contemplation of the State of Man:* "What is man but a vessel of dung, a stink of corruption, and, by birth, a slave of the devil?" [33] Filth is employed in each of these three passages, in two of which terms for excrement are used. Two also employ a noisome or stinking smell as characteristic of evil, while a third adds the deformity of body and of face.

In Scripture, many passages can be found which reveal this type of terminology for sin. I quote only a few characteristic ones. In Psalms 14.3 we read that "they are all gone aside, they are altogether become filthy: there is none that doeth good, no, not one." Much of the same idea is found in Job 15.16: "How much more abominable and filthy is man, which drinketh iniquity like water?" In Ezekiel 24.13, the prophet carries this message to the sinful people of Jerusalem: "In thy filthiness is lewdness." As for the symbolism of deformity, Isaiah 1.6 describes the corrupt Israelites in these terms: "From the sole of the foot even unto the head there is no soundness in it; but wounds, and bruises, and putrefying sores: they have not been closed, neither bound up, neither mollified with ointment." The frequent New Testament admonitions to "cleanse ourselves from all filthiness" of sin need not be enumerated, as they are well enough known to come to the mind merely by suggestion.

These Biblical uses of filth and deformity indicate the importance of the concept. It is in these terms that Donne, Agas, and Taylor must be understood in the passages quoted above. Archbishop Tillotson (1630–94), in the first of a series of sermons entitled *The*

---

[31] John Donne, *Works* (London, 1839), IV, 231.
[32] B. Agas, *Gospel Conversation, with a short Directory Thereunto* (London, 1667), 47.
[33] Taylor, *The Whole Works* (London, 1880), I, 396.

Shamefulness of Sin, treats the theme in a somewhat similar fashion: "The natural Ruggedness and Deformity of Sin and Vice render it very shameful. . . . How strangely do we see Men concerned with all their Diligence and Skill, to cover and palliate any Defect or Deformity in their Bodies. . . . Now in regard of our Souls and better part, Sin hath all the monstrousness and deformity in it, which we [211] can imagine in the Body, and much more. . . ." [34] Although he does not use bodily deformity as a direct symbol for sin here, Tillotson does draw his parallel very close.

Writing in 1659 on Job 15.16 ("How much more abominable and filthy is man, which drinketh iniquity like water?"), Anthony Burgess glosses the text in such a way as to illustrate the employment of filth, stench, and the like as symbolic for sin: "The property is twofold, *abominable,* even as a carkass is abominable that hath lost the soul which did animate it, so is man being made carnal and natural, having lost the Spirit of God and his image; *Abhominable* [sic], that denoteth such loathsomeness that we cannot endure to behold or come near the object loathed, that we cannot endure the sight of it. . . ." The last clause is strikingly similar to the view of many readers who see the Yahoo as denoting "such loathsomeness that [they] cannot endure to behold or come near the object loathed, that [they] cannot endure the sight of it." This is surely one of the reactions which Swift wished to elicit—assuming that the reader would go on to make Burgess' connection of loathesomeness with sinfulness:

Thus man is abominable and loathsome in the eyes of God, and he ought to be so in his own eyes, to his own self, a natural man should not be able to bear or endure himself, because of that loathsome sinfulness that doth adhere to him: how much are *Pelagian*-Doctrines that cry up a purity in man's nature, contrary to this Text? . . . The second property attributed to man is *filthy:* The Hebrew word is only used here, and *Psal.* 14.3 and *Psal.* 53.3. Concerning the root of it, there is no certainty, only it is generally translated that which is *putrid rotten* and *stinking,* and because rotten and putrifying things are unuseful and unprofitable. [35]

William Beveridge (1637–1708), Bishop of St. Asaph, in his outline of a sermon on the admonition of II Corinthians 7.1 to "cleanse ourselves from all filthiness of the flesh and spirit," says that by filthi-

[34] John Tillotson, *Sermons* (London, 1700), VIII, 151–52.
[35] Anthony Burgess, *The Doctrine of Original Sin* (London, 1659), 439.

ness St. Paul meant sinfulness, and refers to James 1.21 and to II Peter 2.22 as examples of such symbolism. Again, he says the lust of the flesh brings vengeance upon "the body; witness the stinking breath, loathsome botches, inflamed blood, putrefied flesh. . . ." Further, uncleanness "razeth out the image of God, and stampeth the image of beasts upon us." [36] Matthew Griffith comes even closer to the Yahoo when he says: "Could I character or you but conceive a man in pure naturals, you would not take him for a man but for [212] some monster" (p. 153). It is in this sense, and not in Edward Young's, that Swift has made "a monster . . . of the human face divine."

Peter Browne, Bishop of Corke and Ross, follows the well-established symbolic system in a sermon on the cleansing blood of Christ. He carefully develops the idea that it is impossible for us to understand before the judgment how our *souls* have been polluted or how Christ will purify them, and so we resort to "a form of speaking," and he says that "the holiest person in the world is all over leprous, filthy and abominable in the sight of God, till he is washed in the blood of the lamb," thus expressing the intangible in terms of the concrete.[37] Again, he says that "vice and wickedness have a direct tendency, even in this life to wrest our lineaments." After the resurrection the wicked will be able to see this in themselves and "shall appear in their own eyes the most detestable and loathsome of all beings, terrified with their own deformity." [38]

In the third part of his sermon entitled "The Apples of Sodom," Jeremie Taylor describes the sin of concealing sin in terms of filth, ugliness and disease. Concealment and hypocrisy "are the covers of our shame, like menstrous rags upon a skin of leprosy: but so sometimes we see a decayed beauty besmeared with a lying fucus, and the chinks filled with ceruse." [39] Mark Frank writes that, in view of our sins, ". . . those lips, which we cry up for sweetness, would stink in our conceit with rottenness; the teeth that look white as ivory, we should behold black with calumny and slander, as the soot of the foulest chimneys; . . . the hands that look so white and delicate, would appear filthy, bloody, and unclean" (p. 135).

[36] William Beveridge, *Thesaurus Theologicus* (Oxford, 1816), II, 86, 198, and 198 resp.

[37] Browne, I, 19–20, and 12.   [38] Browne, II, 214.

[39] Taylor, I, 729. Other uses of the filthy rag symbol may be found in Thomas Becon, *Writings*, 375 and 380, and John Fox, *Writings*, 52 (both Philadelphia: British Reformers Series, n.d.). The Biblical source for the symbol is Isa. 64.6.

Another significant treatment of filth and defilement in terms of sin is found in an interesting book by the nonconformists Benjamin Keach and Thomas Delaune, entitled *A Key to Open Scripture Metaphors* (1682). In a section on the metaphorical use of filth we find the following passage:

Sin is compared to an unclean thing, and Man by reason of Sin is said to be defiled; who can bring a clean thing out of an unclean? . . . Some things are so unclean and filthy, that they defile every thing they touch. Sin is such an Uncleanness; who can touch it, meddle with it, and not be defiled by it? . . . Some Uncleanness is so loathsome, that it causes such things to stink, as come near it; Sin makes the Sinner stink, his Person stink, his Life [213] stink, and his Services and Prayers, and all his best Actions to stink in the Nostrils of God.[40]

In another section, Keach and Delaune write to somewhat the same effect: "By *Mud, Dirt,* and other *Filth* the Members and Apparrel of a man are polluted and contaminated; which contamination is brought frequently to denote the Filthy nature of sin, *Esa.* 64.6; 2 *Cor.* 7.1; *Eph.* 5.27; *Tit.* 1.15; 2 *Pet.* 2.10, 20 (with ver. 13.22); *Jud.* ver. 23; *Jam.* 1.21; *Rev.* 3.4." [41]

Scripturally, this employment of deformity or filth or both as symbols for sin seems to go back to the ceremonial pollutions which are proscribed in Leviticus. Discussing these in his essay "Of the Guilt and Defilement of Sin" (1740), Isaac Watts writes that God would not allow those to come into His presence

. . . whose Hearts or Lives are *defiled* (that is) under sinful Disorders. This was typified by the *Levitical* Pollutions of old, when some bodily Defilements excluded the *Israelites* from the Camp, and the Tabernacle where God dwelt . . . to shew that the *disorderly Nature* of Sin made Persons unfit to converse with God. Thus all the ceremonial Pollutions of the *Jews* typify'd one of these two, either the *Guilt* of Sin, or its *Disorder* and Vitiosity.[42]

In the same essay, Watts adds:

---

[40] Benjamin Keach and Thomas Delaune, *Tropologia: A Key to Open Scripture Metaphors* (London, 1682), Bk. IV, 355.

[41] Keach and Delaune, Bk. I, p. 131. For a similar treatment, see Andrew Symson, ed. of Thomas Wilson's *Complete Christian Dictionarie* (London, 1655), s.v. "filth," "filthy," "filthiness" and "to pollute." Also see Browne, II, 288.

[42] Isaac Watts, *The Ruin and Recovery of Mankind . . . Whereunto are subjoined Three Short Essays* (London, 1740), 422.

The *Defilement* therefore appears evidently to be nothing but a Figure of Speech borrowed from material things, whereby either the *Guilt* or the *Disorder* of Sin, the relative or real Evil of it are represented (pp. 426–7).

Frank elucidates the symbolism in the same way: "Wheresoever is deformity, or whatsoever is deformed, it is sin that caused it, or sin that is it." [43]

These examples of the use of filth and deformity to symbolize man's sin and imperfection could be multiplied. I have chosen only [214] a few typical ones for my purpose, and I wish now to turn to Swift's use of the same traditional material. First, however, it should be made clear that there is no question of establishing any of the foregoing as sources for any part of *Gulliver's Travels*. The tradition here illustrated, a tradition which employed filth and deformity as symbolic of sin, was part and parcel of the intellectual climate in and before Swift's time, and I suggest that it is within such a frame of reference that we should read Swift's description of the Yahoo.

It is not necessary to debate whether a discharge of excrement upon the head would be regarded as defilement in the Biblical sense. Such, at any rate, is Gulliver's first greeting from the Yahoos. But even before this incident, while he is still more or less unbiased in his outlook, Gulliver remarks that the Yahoo is an "ugly Monster," "singular, and deformed," for whom he immediately conceives a strong antipathy, "full of Contempt and Aversion." They are "detestable Creatures," and he has never seen "any sensitive Being so detestable on all Accounts." The chosen leader of the herd is "more *deformed* in Body and *mischievous*" than any of the rest. The Houyhnhnms describe all evil things in terms of "the Deformities or ill Qualities of the *Yahoos*," who are "the most filthy, noisome and deformed Animal which Nature ever produced." The use of deformity and monstrosity as exemplified in these quotations is spread throughout the book. So, also, is the use of filth. The Yahoo has a "strange Disposition to Nastiness and Dirt; whereas there appears to be a

[43] Frank, I, 422. In addition to the material already cited, see the following: Becon, 336–7; Hooper, 257–8, 342, 351, 407; Richard Baxter, *The Saints' Everlasting Rest* (New York: American Tract Society, n.d.), 45–6; and summary of attitude, with quotations from Archbishop Ussher and others whom I have not cited, in B. Rajan, *"Paradise Lost" and the Seventeenth Century Reader* (London, 1947), 81–2.

natural Love of Cleanliness in all other Animals." They are "those odious Animals," or "an odious Animal," or "odious Vermin," or "so vile an Animal" with "odious Qualities" and a "most *offensive Smell*." [44] It should not be necessary to expand the list, for it is about such passages as these that the furor of controversy has raged. The point is, that both implicitly and explicitly, such employment of deformity and filth by Swift the artist coincides with the symbolism of natural pravity and actual sin as employed by the theologians. The very words used by Swift in describing the Yahoo are through- out [215] strikingly like—and frequently identical with—those used by the theologians in treating "the flesh" and the sins to which it incites man. Compare with Swift's terms, as summarized above, these words already quoted from the theologians: deformity, brute, beast, animal, monster, excremental, dung, filth, stink, noisome, putrid, vile, loathsome, detestable. Such a close convergence can- not be explained away as fortuitous.

The correspondence, however, can be drawn even closer. The Yahoos may be seen, in almost every aspect of their being, in terms of the laws of pollution in the Old Testament. The food of the Ya- hoos, with certain exceptions (roots, berries, fish), is definitely pol- luting. Let us analyze their diet. They eat asses' flesh, battle for the possession of a dead cow, feed upon "the corrupted Flesh of Ani- mals" and other carrion, kill and devour cats and dogs, as well as "Weasels and *Luhimuhs* (a Sort of *wild* Rat)." [45] Each one of these delicacies is proscribed as polluting under the Levitical code. Leviti- cus 11.3 prohibits the eating of asses' flesh, and in the thirty-ninth and fortieth verses of the same chapter the consumption of any meat from a dead carcass, whether that of a clean or unclean animal, is forbidden. The twenty-seventh verse declares that cats and dogs are unclean. Finally, weasels and rodents are prohibited in the

[44] *Gulliver's Travels*, 207–8, 213, 214, 246, 259, 255, 247, 249, 221, 250, 231, 232, and 248. Although I do not maintain that this list is complete, attention is directed to the following passages on characteristic Yahoo traits: Descriptions in terms of filth, stench, odiousness and vileness (in addition to the thirteen references quoted above): 208, 214, 226, 244, 245, 247, 250, 256, 270, 272, 273, and 279; Descriptions in terms of monstrousness, brutishness, and animal- ity: 207, 208, 212, 213, 219, 221, 223, 225, 231, 243, 244, 245, 247, 249, 250, 251, 255, 257, 263, 273, and 280; Descriptions in terms of the deformed, de- testable, and contemptible: 207, 208, 213, 214, 220, 221, 222, 226, 227, 244, 245, 246, 255, and 273. Such passages give a coloration to the entire fourth book.

[45] *Gulliver's Travels*, 213, 214, 244, 245, 250, and 255.

twenty-ninth verse.[46] Thus we see that in diet the Yahoos are guilty of those defilements "whereby either the *Guilt* or the *Disorder* of Sin . . . are represented."

Of further relevance is the fact that the Yahoos are themselves described in such a way as to subject them by their very nature to the Levitical proscription. Leviticus 11.27 declares unclean "whatsoever goeth upon his paws, among all manner of beasts that go on all four, those are unclean to you: whosoever toucheth their carcass shall be unclean until the even." The connection is made much clearer by Bishop Simon Patrick's 1698 commentary on this text: "*Leviticus 11.27.* [*And whatsoever goeth upon his paws, etc.*] Hath feet with fingers like unto a hand; for so it is in the Hebrew, *Whatsoever goeth upon his hands:* Such as the Ape, the Lion, the Bear, Dogs and Cats, etc. whose forefeet resemble hands: These might neither be eaten, nor their carcases touched, without incurring uncleanness until Sunset." [47] Had the Yahoo been created earlier, he might have been included in the bishop's exegetical list. He certainly meets all the qualifications. [216]

IV

What are we to conclude on the basis of the evidence cited here? I certainly would not suggest that the system of symbols and metaphors which I have outlined above is the only frame of reference within which the Yahoo should be studied and interpreted. There are influential thinkers outside the main stream of Christian realism— for example, Montaigne and Charron in France, and Hobbes in England—whose views of the nature of man are in the climate of opinion which influenced Swift. The contributions of those men are well known, and need no development here. Without depreciating the importance of these and other considerations, however, I do suggest that for a full understanding of Swift's intent we must keep in mind the basic and striking similarities between the Yahoo as he is presented in *Gulliver* and the picture of human sin and corruption as painted by the theologians. The Yahoo in his physical resemblance to man suggests the original depravity of man's nature which is called "the flesh," which can degrade man to the level of the brute

---

[46] Simon Patrick, *Commentary upon Leviticus* (London, 1698), 160, 186, and 179, confirms the currency of these interpretations in the age of Swift.
[47] Patrick, 179.

beasts, and against which all must war. At the same time, the Yahoo suggests through his deformity and filth the breaking forth of that propensity towards sin into the commission of actual sins. I do not argue for exact correspondence so much as for artistic adaptation of theology to Swift's purposes.

Clearly, the correspondence between Swift's descriptions and these symbols of Protestant-Christian theology is too close to have been fortuitous. If Thackeray and others who have been sickened by Swift's imagination had carried their studies back into the expressions of well-known theologians of the sixteenth and seventeenth centuries, they would have avoided a needless misunderstanding both of the Yahoo and of Swift. Certainly, Hawkesworth, Deane Swift, and Wesley understood this important element of the Yahoo's meaning, as we have seen from their remarks on the subject. Indeed, Gulliver states the case when he says: "I had some Rudiments of Reason, added to the natural Pravity of those Animals." [48] What Swift has done is to appropriate ready-made symbols and a Christian rhetoric apt for his purposes, which he has embodied in a fantasy and elevated to the level of great art. [217]

[48] *Gulliver's Travels*, 263. The implications drawn here will also have relevance for other works of Swift, *e.g.*, the verse and some of the Brobdingnagian descriptions, which have not been discussed in this paper because of the necessity for concentration upon the Yahoos.

The Pride of Lemuel Gulliver

SAMUEL H. MONK

Gulliver's Travels is a complex book. It is, of course, a satire on four aspects of man: the physical, the political, the intellectual, and the moral. The last three are inseparable, and when Swift writes of one he always has in view the others. It is also a brilliant parody of travel literature; and it is at once science fiction and a witty parody of science fiction. It expresses savage indignation at the follies, vices, and stupidities of men, and everywhere implicit in the book as a whole is an awareness of man's tragic insufficiency. But at the same time it is a great comic masterpiece, a fact that solemn and too-sensitive readers often miss.

A friend once wrote me of having shocked an associate by remarking that he had laughed often on rereading *Gulliver's Travels*. "What should I have done?" he asked me. "Blown out my brains?" I am sure that Swift would have approved my friend's laughter. To conclude that *Gulliver's Travels* expresses despair or that its import is nihilistic is radically to misread the book. All of Swift's satire was written in anger, contempt, or disgust, but it was written to promote self-knowledge in the faith that self-knowledge will lead to right action. Nothing would have bewildered him more than to learn that

Reprinted from *The Sewanee Review*, LXIII (Winter 1955), 48–71. Copyright © 1955 by The University of the South. By permission. Samuel H. Monk's original footnote reads: "A public lecture delivered at the University of Minnesota, 1952. Students of Swift will recognize my very great indebtedness to the work of other critics and scholars. It would be pedantic to acknowledge borrowings so numerous and so self-evident. I hope that it is sufficient here to acknowledge this general indebtedness and to express my gratitude to those who over a period of twenty-five years, have helped me better to understand Jonathan Swift."

he had led a reader to the desperate remedy of blowing out his brains. But the book is so often called morbid, so frequently have readers concluded that it is the work of an incipient madman, that I think it worth while to emphasize the gayety and comedy of the voyages [48] as an indication of their author's essential intellectual and spiritual health. True, seventeen years after finishing *Gulliver's Travels*, Swift was officially declared *non compos mentis*. But his masterpiece was written at the height of his powers, and the comic animation of the book as a whole rules out the suspicion of morbidity and mental illness.

We laugh and were meant to laugh at the toy kingdom of the Lilliputians; at the acrobatic skill of the politicians and courtiers; at the absurd jealousy of the diminutive minister who suspects an adulterous relationship between his wife and the giant Gulliver. We laugh at the plight of Gulliver in Brobdingnag: one of the lords of creation, frightened by a puppy, rendered ludicrous by the tricks of a mischievous monkey, in awe of a dwarf; embarrassed by the lascivious antics of the maids of honor; and at last content to be tended like a baby by his girl-nurse. We laugh at the abstractness of the philosophers of Laputa, at the mad experimenters of Balnibarbi. And I am sure that we are right in at least smiling at the preposterous horses, the Houyhnhnms, limited and so positive in their knowledge and opinions, so skilled in such improbable tasks as threading needles or carrying trays, so complacent in their assurance that they are "the Perfection of Nature." Much of the delight that we take in *Gulliver's Travels* is due to this gay, comic, fanciful inventiveness. Swift might well say in the words of Hamlet: "Lay not that flattering unction to your soul/That not your trespass but my madness speaks." Swift did not wish us to blow out our brains; he did wish us to laugh. But beyond the mirth and liveliness are gravity, anger, anxiety, frustration—and he meant us to experience them fully.

For there is an abyss below this fantastic world—the dizzying abyss of corrupt human nature. Swift is the great master of shock. With perfect control of tone and pace, with perfect timing, he startles us into an awareness of this abyss and its implications. We are forced to gaze into the stupid, evil, brutal [49] heart of humanity, and when we do, the laughter that Swift has evoked is abruptly silenced. The surface of the book is comic, but at its center is tragedy, transformed through style and tone into icy irony. Soft minds have found Swift's irony unnerving and depressing and, in self-protection, have dismissed him as a repellent misanthrope. Stronger minds that prefer unpalatable truths to euphoric illusions have found this irony bracing and healthful.

Before I discuss the book itself it is necessary to speak of certain ideas and tendencies that were current in Swift's world. *Gulliver's Travels* was written at the height of that phase of European civilization which we know as the Enlightenment, and the Enlightenment was the first clearly defined manifestation of modernity—the modernity of which our age may be the catastrophic conclusion. Swift wrote always in opposition to the Enlightenment and as an enemy of "modernism." He detected with uncanny prescience the implications of such characteristic ideas as the following: (1) Rationalism, especially Cartesianism, with its radical tendency to abstract truth into purely intellectual concepts, and its bold rejection of the experience and wisdom of the past. Swift doubted the capacity of human reason to attain metaphysical and theological truth. A safer guide in this life seemed to him to be what he called "common forms," the *consensus gentium,* the time-approved wisdom of the race. (2) Experimental and theoretical science, fathered by Bacon and Galileo, vindicated by Newton, and propagandized and nourished by the Royal Society. The science of Swift's day was predominantly concerned with physics and astronomy. Swift, I think, could not imaginatively relate to the moral—*i.e.,* the totally human —life of man the efforts of an astronomer to plot the trajectory of a comet or of a physicist to comprehend a universe that is "really" no more than abstract mass, extension, and motion. Moreover science gave sanction to the idea of progress, deluding men with the promise of an ever expanding and improving [50] future, which to Swift seemed necessarily chimerical, man being limited as he is. And finally science unwittingly fostered the secularization of society and of human values, promising men mastery of nature and the abolition of all mysteries, and, by implication at least, of religion. Swift was a religious man. (3) The new conception of man, which was the result of both rationalism and science. It taught the essential goodness of human nature in a sentimental and optimistic tone of voice that irritated Swift and compelled him to reply with all his powers in *Gulliver's Travels.* (4) The new moneyed wealth of England, based upon trade and speculation and bolstering up the national importance of the middle class. Swift regarded this wealth and its owners as irresponsible and dangerous to the state. Divorced from land and the responsibilities implied in the ownership of land, it seemed to him abstract and at the same time frighteningly ambitious; and he had to look only to London and the Court to be assured that this new, vulgar, wealthy class was corrupting both the individual and the social and political institutions of England. (5) The increasing power of centralized government—in Swift's day a few ministers, the Crown, and the court. To Swift, such power seemed necessarily evil since it was divorced from concrete human needs.

Why was Swift inimical to these tendencies—all of which are familiar aspects of our world today? Very simply, I think, because he was a Christian and a humanist. As a Christian he believed that man's fallen nature could never transcend its own limitations and so fulfil the hopes of that optimistic age; as a humanist he was concerned for the preservation of those moral and spiritual qualities which distinguish men from beasts and for the health and continuity of fruitful tradition in church, state, and the sphere of the mind. As both Christian and humanist, he knew that men must be better than they are and that, though our institutions can never be perfect, they need not be corrupt. The "savage [51] indignation" which motivates all of Swift's satires arises from his anger at the difference between what men are and what they might be if they only would rise to the full height of their humanity. If he indulged no Utopian hopes, he also never gave way to cheap cynicism.

Two famous letters, written in the fall of 1725, the year before *Gulliver's Travels* was published, tell us much about Swift's state of mind at this time. In the first, to Pope, he writes:

. . . . when you think of the world, give it one lash the more at my Request. I have ever hated all Nations, Professions, and Communities; and all my love is towards Individuals; for Instance, I hate the Tribe of Lawyers, Physicians . . . . Soldiers, English, Scotch, French, and the rest. But principally I hate and detest that animal called Man, although I heartily love John, Peter, Thomas, and so forth. This is the system upon which I have governed myself many Years . . . . and so I shall go on until I have done with them. I have got Materials toward a Treatise, proving the falsity of that Definition, *Animal rationale* and to show that it should be only *rationis capax*. Upon this great foundation of Misanthropy (although not in Timon's Manner) the whole building of my travels is erected; and I will never have Peace of Mind until all honest Men are of my Opinion. . . .

This letter makes three important points.

(1) Swift's life and letters support his assertion that he could

and did love individuals. His hatred was directed against abstract man, against men existing and acting within semi-human or de-humanized racial or professional groups. Apparently he felt that when men submerge their individual judgments and moral beings in such groups, they necessarily further corrupt their already corrupted natures. When for example an individual thinks or acts or feels not as a free moral agent responsible to God, but as a politician, a lawyer, a bishop, he abrogates to some [52] degree his humanity. He becomes the instrument of a force that is larger than himself, but not so large as the moral law: and in so doing he becomes at least potentially evil. We hear a great deal today of group dynamics, group psychology, and mass communication. Swift would oppose these forces on the ground that they abridge the freedom which is necessary to the completely moral and responsible life.

(2) Swift dissociates his "misanthropy" from that of Plutarch's Timon of Athens, the hero of Shakespeare's play, who withdrew in bitter disillusionment merely to rail in solitude against mankind. Swift knew how sterile such an attitude is. His own satire is seldom merely invective. It is not paradoxical to say that it arises from philanthropy, not misanthropy, from idealism as to what man might be, not from despair at what he is.

(3) Swift rejects the definition of man as *animal rationale* in favor of the definition *animal capax rationis*. I think that he has Descartes in mind here, Descartes, who apparently had forgotten that God made man a little lower than the angels (pure intelligences) and consequently capable of only enough reason to order his world here and to find his way, with God's grace, to the next. The second letter, to Pope and Bolingbroke, amplifies this point.

I tell you after all I do not hate Mankind, it is *vous autres* who hate them, because you would have them reasonable Animals, and are angry at being disappointed: I have always rejected that Definition, and made another of my own. I am no more angry with ——— than I was with the Kite that last Week flew away with one of my Chickens; and yet I was pleased when one of my servants shot him two days after.

Swift argues that the man really in danger of becoming a misanthrope is he who holds an unrealistic view of the potentialities of human nature and who expects that men can somehow transcend their limitations and become, shall we say, angels. In the [53] phrase *vous autres*, Swift includes all the secular, scientific, deistic, optimistic—in a word, liberal—thinkers of the Enlightenment; and he turns in anger from them. The philanthropist will not be angry when he has to recognize the corruptions and limitations of human nature; he will settle for a creature who is *capable* of reason and will do the best he can with him. The word *capable* is a positive concept, not a negative one. It imposes a sort of moral imperative on man to exploit his capability to its fullest. As Swift makes plain in *Gulliver's Travels*, this task is large enough to occupy the whole attention of man. It is fallacious and stupid to attribute to our race qualities that it can never possess. To do so is pride, the besetting sin of men and angels, the sin that disrupts the natural and supernatural order of God's creation. The theme of pride looms large in *Gulliver's Travels*.

Seven years after the publication of *Gulliver's Travels*, Pope published his well-known comment on the tragic duality of man:

> Placed on this isthmus of a middle state,
> A being darkly wise, and rudely great:
> With too much knowledge for the Sceptic side,
> With too much weakness for the Stoic's pride,
> He hangs between; in doubt to act, or rest;
> In doubt to deem himself a God, or Beast;
> In doubt his Mind or Body to prefer;
> Born but to die, and reas'ning but to err;
> Alike in ignorance, his reason such,
> Whether he thinks too little, or too much:
> Chaos of Thought and Passion, all confused:
> Still by himself abused, or disabused;
> Created half to rise, and half to fall;
> Great lord of all things, yet a prey to all;
> Sole judge of Truth, in endless Error hurl'd:
> The glory, jest, and riddle of the world!

The idea that man occupies an anomalous, a middle, state in creation was a familiar one in Swift's day. The whole of living [54] creation was conceived to be carefully ordered and subtly graded in one vast "chain of being," descending from God, through an almost infinite number of pure intelligences, to man, and thence through the lower animals to microscopic forms of life, which finally end in nothing. Man occupies the most uncomfortable position in this chain, since to a limited degree he shares the intelligence of higher creatures, and to an unlimited degree the sensuality of animals. He is the middle link because he is the transitional point between the purely intelligent and the purely sensual. With Pope, with

Addison, and a number of other writers this image, for reasons which we shall not inquire into, became one of the chief supports of the optimism of the Enlightenment—optimism concerning God, nature, and man. To Pascal, in his moving 72nd *Pensée*, it suggested tragic thoughts about the disproportion of man. Swift used it as an instrument of comedy, of irony, and of satire. In three of the four voyages, it plays an important role.

So much for background. Let us turn to the book. The first character to demand our attention is Gulliver himself. He is the narrator, the principal actor. We see through his eyes, feel his feelings, share his thoughts. We are in his company from first to last, and it is important that we come to know him as quickly as possible. What is he like and what is his role in the book? He is first of all a bit of a bore, for his mind is irritatingly circumstantial and unimaginative: observe the numerous insignificant biographical details which he gives us in the first pages of the book. Gradually, however, we come to like him and to enjoy his company. In all respects he is an average good man. He has had some university education both at Cambridge and at Leyden, where he studied medicine. He is observant (and we eventually come to be grateful for his gift of close observation and circumstantial reporting, once he has something worth observing and reporting), reasonably intelligent, thoroughly capable in an emergency, and both brave and hopeful. If he lacks [55] imagination and inventiveness, so much the better; for we can be sure that what he tells us, no matter how strange, is true. He is simple, direct, uncomplicated. At the outset he is full of naive good will, and, though he grows less naive and more critical as a result of his voyaging among remote nations, he retains his benevolence throughout the first three voyages. It is a pity that so fine an example of the bluff, good-natured, honest Englishman should at last grow sick and morbid and should be driven mad—but that, I am afraid, is what befalls him.

All of this Gulliver is; but let us notice carefully what he is NOT. He is NOT Jonathan Swift. The meaning of the book is wholly distorted if we identify the Gulliver of the last voyage with his creator, and lay Gulliver's misanthropy at Swift's door. He is a fully rendered, objective, dramatic character, no more to be identified with Swift than Shylock is to be identified with Shakespeare. This character acts and is acted upon; he changes, he grows in the course of his adventures. Like King Lear, he begins in simplicity, grows into sophistication, and ends in madness. Unlike King Lear he is never cured.

The four voyages "into several remote nations of the world," are so arranged as to attain a climactic intensification of tone as we travel through increasing darkness into the black heart of humanity. But the forward movement is interrupted by the third voyage, a macabre scherzo on science, politics, economics as they are practiced by madmen—Swift's term for those who misuse and abuse human reason. Observe that the tone of each voyage is established by the nature of the event that brings about the adventure: in the first voyage (the most benign and the gayest) accident, or at worst, the carelessness of the lookout, accounts for the shipwreck; in the second, much more savage in tone, Gulliver is left alone in a strange land, through the cowardice of his shipmates; in the third, he is captured and later abandoned by pirates (evil in action); in the fourth, his crew of cutthroats mutinies, seizes the ship, and leaves him to starve on [56] a near-by island. Gulliver thus describes this crew to his Houyhnhnm master:

I said they were Fellows of desperate Fortunes, forced to fly from the Places of their Birth, on Account of their Poverty and their Crimes. Some were undone by Lawsuits; others spent all they had in Drinking, Whoring, and gaming; others fled for Treason; many for Murder, Theft, Poisoning, Robbery, Perjury, Forgery, Coining false Money; for committing Rapes and Sodomy; for flying from their Colours, or deserting to the Enemy; and most of them had broken Prison. . . .

The good ship *Adventure* was a little world which housed the whole of unregenerate human nature.

It is best to consider the first two voyages together and to notice how effectively Swift uses the idea of the great chain of being. Pascal, writing of man's disproportion, had asked: "For in fact, what is man in nature: A nothing in comparison with the Infinite, an All in comparison with the Nothing, a mean between nothing and everything." Swift transposes this theme into another key, and makes it the major instrument of his satire. In the first two voyages, Gulliver is made aware of his disproportion; placed on this isthmus of a middle state, in the voyage to Lilliput he looks down the chain of being and knows himself an awkward, if kindly, giant in that delicate kingdom; in the voyage to Brobdingnag he looks up the chain and discovers a race of "superior beings," among whom his pride shrivels

through the humiliating knowledge of his own physical insignifi-
cance. The emphasis here is upon size, the physical; but it is none the
less notable that Lilliputia calls into operation Gulliver's engaging
kindliness and gentleness, and that Brobdingnag brings out his moral
and physical courage. Though comically and tragically disproportioned, man has moral virtues which he can and does exercise. [57]

But Swift's satire is a two-edged sword. What of the inhabitants
of these strange lands? They too are disproportioned. From the start
the Lilliputians win our interest and liking: these pigmies ingeniously
capture the Hercules whom chance has cast on their shore; they
humanely solve the problem of feeding him; their pretty land and
their fascinating little city take our fancy. But in the end what do
they prove to be? prideful, envious, rapacious, treacherous, cruel,
vengeful, jealous, and hypocritical. Their primitive social and political systems have been corrupted; they are governed by an Emperor
who is ambitious totally to destroy the neighboring kingdom, and by
courtiers and ministers who are chosen not for their fitness for office,
but for their skill in walking the tightrope, leaping over sticks or
creeping under them. "Climbing," Swift once remarked, "is performed in the same Posture with Creeping." These little people, like
Gulliver himself, are an instance of the disproportion of man. Their
vices, their appetites, their ambitions, their passions are not com-
mensurate with their tiny stature. They appear to Gulliver as he
and his kind must appear to the higher orders of beings—as ven-
omous and contemptibly petty.

In Brobdingnag we meet creatures ten times the size of Europeans,
and we share Gulliver's anxiety lest their moral natures be as brutish
as their bodies. But the reverse is true; and through a violent and
effective shift of symbol, tone, and point of view, Gulliver, who
seemed lovable and humane among the Lilliputians, appears an
ignominious and morally insensitive being in contrast to the enlightened and benevolent Brobdingnagians. Since Gulliver is we,
his shame, insufficiency, and ludicrousness are ours.

When the peasants discover him, they feel both curiosity and
repulsion: the farmer picks him up "with the Caution of one who
endeavours to lay hold on a small dangerous Animal in such a Manner that it shall not be able either to scratch or to bite him, ..."
Gulliver fears that his captor may dash him to the [58] ground,
"as we usually do any little hateful Animal which we have a Mind
to destroy." The change in tone and intent is obvious.

Gulliver is submitted to one humiliation after another, but he is still capable of a fatuous blindness to the defects of European society, and when the King questions him about England he describes with uncritical enthusiasm its class system, its constitution, its laws, its military glory, and its history. In the questions which the king asks and which Gulliver meets with only an embarrassed silence, the voice of morality is heard condemning the institutions of the modern world. And the verdict of a moral being on European man is given in words as icy as controlled contempt can make them: "But, by what I have gathered from your own Relation, and the Answers I have with much Pains wringed and extorted from you; I cannot but conclude the Bulk of your Natives to be the most pernicious Race of little odious Vermin that Nature ever suffered to crawl upon the Surface of the Earth."

Such a conclusion is inevitable, for the King is high-minded, benevolent, and, in Swift's sense of the word, rational: *i.e.*, he and his people think practically, not theoretically; concretely, not metaphysically; simply, not intricately. Brobdingnag is a Swiftian Utopia of common good sense and morality; and Gulliver, conditioned by the corrupt society from which he comes, appears naive, blind, and insensitive to moral values. His account of the history of England in the seventeenth century evokes the King's crushing retort:

. . . . it was only an Heap of Conspiracies, Rebellions, Murders, Massacres, Revolutions, Banishments; the very worst Effects that Avarice, Faction, Hypocracy, Perfidiousness, Cruelty, Rage, Madness, Hatred, Envy, Lust, Malice, and Ambition could produce.

Notice the carefully arranged disorder of that list, the calculated [59] avoidance of climax. This is a favorite device of Swift: the irrational, the appetitive, the evil nature of man *is* disorder.

The King is horrified when Gulliver offers him a way to complete dominion over his subjects by teaching him to make gunpowder. And Gulliver, speaking as a European, feels contemptuous surprise: "A strange Effect of *narrow Principles* and *short Views!*" The King is baffled by the concept of political *science*—how can the *art* of government be reduced to a science:

He confined the knowledge of governing within very *narrow Bounds*; to common Sense and Reason, to Justice and Lenity, to the Speedy Determination of Civil and criminal Causes; with some other obvious Topicks which are not worth considering. And he gave it for his Opinion; that whoever could make two Ears of Corn, or two Blades of Grass to grow upon a Spot of Ground where only one grew before would deserve better of Mankind, and do more essential Service to his Country, than the whole Race of Politicians put together.

The learning of the Brobdingnagians is simple and practical, "consisting only in Morality, History, Poetry, and Mathematicks." Observe that Swift omits metaphysics, theoretical science, and theology from the category of useful knowledge.

Swift's attack on pride in the first two voyages is made more powerful because of his brilliant use of the chain of being. In so far as we recognize ourselves in the Lilliputians or in Gulliver in Brobdingnag, we become aware of our pettiness—of the disproportion of our race and of the shocking difference between what we profess and what we are. But Swift uses the good giants to strike an unexpected blow at human vanity and to introduce a motif which he employed with deadly effect in the last voyage. That motif is disgust, of which, as T. S. Eliot has remarked, he is the great master. Philosophers of the century were never tired of admiring the beautiful perfection of the human body, its intricateness, its perfect articulation, its happy appropriateness to [60] the particular place that men occupy in the scheme of things. But how does this glorious body appear to lesser creatures—say to an insect: Swift forces us to answer by making us share Gulliver's disgust at the cancerous breasts and lousy bodies of the beggars; at the blotched color, the huge pores, the coarse hairs, and the nauseous odors of the maids of honor. Such is the skin, presumably, that the Brobdingnagians love to touch. Our beauty is only apparent; our disproportion is real.

The third voyage has always been considered the least successful; that may well be, but it is none the less interesting. Structurally it is loosely episodic, lacking unity of action and tone. Into it Swift seems to have put all the material that he could not work into the other three voyages. It is a fantasia on two themes which Swift treats under a single metaphor: the metaphor is science, the themes are politics and the abuse of reason. In short, the voyage is a digression on madness, on the divorce of man and good sense in the modern world.

At this point, I fear, it is necessary to defend Swift, since he will seem merely stupid and prejudiced to a generation that enjoys the blessings of chlorophyll, television, the common cold, and the hydrogen bomb. Moreover, to liberals he will appear an unenlightened political reactionary. I have said earlier that in my opinion Swift distrusted science because it seemed irrelevant to the moral life of man. Though no scientist, he was not an ignoramus. He had read contemporary science—Descartes, Newton, and the yearly *Transactions of the Royal Society*. The Flying Island is conceived on sound scientific principles; some of the mad experiments of the scientists of Balnibarbi are grotesque distortions of ideas actually advanced by members of the Royal Society. The philosophers of the Flying Island are lost in the abstractions of mathematics, music, and astronomy to the great neglect of all practical reality, including their wives. The very tailors measure Gulliver for clothes by abstruse mathematical processes and contrive a suit which fits him not at all. Swift [61] lived before the age of applied science, but I do not think that he would be surprised to learn that modern citizens of his Flying Island contrived the most significant event of the twentieth century—Hiroshima.

It is also necessary to apologize for Swift's political views. He was a Tory, a conservative—opprobrious terms today. In economics he was an agrarian; in politics a royalist; in religion a high churchman. He disapproved the founding of the National Bank; could make no sense of a national debt, a gadget invented in his time; he distrusted the new moneyed wealth, the ancestor of modern capitalism, which increased the power and importance of trade, and he found his distrust justified in 1720 by the disastrous collapse of South Sea stocks. Innovation and experimentation in politics he detested and fought. He would have hated the improvisations of the New Deal; he would have deplored the vast powers of our Federal Government; he would have loathed the whole program of the Labor Party in Britain. And were he alive, he would fight the abstract state of this century with every weapon within reach.

Too many liberals are unaware of the fact that a man may be a non-liberal without being illiberal; that he may distrust the abstract power of government, the theoretical formulae of economists, politicians, and social scientists and the like without ceasing to be actively and effectively concerned for human welfare. Swift was a Tory who fought valiantly and at times successfully for the oppressed. Living in Ireland, contemptuous of the Irish, detesting their Catholicism, he none the less became their champion against the oppression and exploitation of his adopted country by the English Court and Parliament. He is one of the heroes of modern Ireland because he first gave effective expression to Irish nationalism. He earned the right to the last sentence of the epitaph which he composed for his own tombstone: *Abi Viator/ et imitare, si poteris/ Strenuum pro virili/ Libertatis Vindicatorem.* [62]

The Flying Island is not only a trope for science; it is also a mordant image of the concentration of political power in the hands of a clique remote from human needs, motivated by pure theory, and given to experiment and improvisation. Laputa (perhaps, as has been suggested, Spanish *La Puta*, "the whore") is a symbol of such government: it is controlled by madmen who govern scientifically, not morally; it is a *flying* island, and hence out of touch with subject territories, which it exploits and tyrannizes over by means of what we call today air power; it can withhold sun and rain as a punitive device, or can harass through bombing raids, or even tyrannously crush all opposition by settling its great weight upon the land below. One contrasts this form of government with that of the wise and good King of Brobdingnag.

When Gulliver visits the subject land of Balnibarbi, which is of course England, he sees the result of eighteenth-century statism.

The People in the Streets walked fast, looked wild, their Eyes fixed, and were generally in Rags. We passed through one of the Town Gates, and went about three Miles into the Country, where I saw many Labourers working with several Sorts of Tools in the Ground, but was not able to conjecture what they were about; neither did I observe any Expectation either of Corn or Grass, although the Soil appeared to be excellent.

This is what comes of experimentation in government and of financial speculation. It strongly suggests the memories that some of us have of the great depression. A modern Tory has used it effectively as the basis of an attack on the late Labor Government.

But there are other ills consequent to the abstract state. Too great a concentration of power leads to tyranny; tyranny breeds fear; fear breeds the obnoxious race of spies and informers. The abstract state becomes the police state. [63]

I told him that in the Kingdom of *Tribnia*, by the Natives called *Langden*, where I had sojourned some time in my Travels, the Bulk of the People consist in a manner wholly of Discoverers, Witnesses, Informers, Accusers, Prosecutors, Evidences, Swearers; together with their several subservient and subaltern Instruments; all under Deputies. The Plots in that Kingdom are usually the Workmanship of those Persons who desire to raise their own Character of profound Politicians; to restore new Vigour to a crazy Administration; to stifle or divert general Discontents; to fill their Pockets with Forfeitures; and raise or sink the Opinion of publick Credit, as either shall best answer their private Advantage. It is first agreed and settled among them, what suspected Persons shall be accused of a Plot: then, effectual Care is taken to secure all their Letters and Papers, and put the Criminals in Chains. These Papers are delivered to a Set of Artists, very dexterous in finding out the mysterious Meanings of Words, Syllables, and Letters. For Instance, they can decypher a Close-stool to signify a Privy-Council; a Flock of Geese, a Senate; a lame Dog, an Invader; a Codshead, a [King]; the Plague, a Standing Army; a Buzzard, a Prime Minister; the Gout, a High Priest; a Gibbet, a Secretary of State; a Chamber pot, a Committee of Grandees; a Sieve, a Court Lady; a Broom, a Revolution; a Mouse-trap, an Employment; a bottomless Pit, The Treasury; a Sink, the C[our]t; a Cap and Bells, a Favourite; a broken Reed, a Court of Justice; an empty Tun, a General; a running Sore, the Administration.

One cannot read that passage without thinking of certain testimony given in late years in Washington.

Such are the fruits of madness—of that pride which impels us to trust our reason beyond its proper scope and which suggests that we can build a heavenly city on earth on principles divorced from humanity and morality.

The climactic fourth voyage is the great section of *Gulliver's Travels*. It has provoked violent attacks on Swift and his book, entirely, I think, because it has been misunderstood. It has [64] offended the unreflective and pious Christian, the sentimentalist, and the optimist. Thackeray, lecturing to the ladies in London in 1851, the year in which the Great Exhibition seemed to give the lie to every opinion that Swift held, may serve as an example, by no means unique, of the capacity of this voyage to shock. He advised his ladies not to read the last voyage, and to hoot the Dean. And the meaning that he found in it was "that man is utterly wicked, desperate, and imbecile, and his passions are monstrous, and his boasted power mean, that he is and deserves to be the shame of brutes, and ignorance is better than his vaunted reason." "It is Yahoo language," he continues, "a monster gibbering shrieks and gnashing imprecations against mankind . . . filthy in word, filthy in thought, furious, raging, obscene."

The legend of Swift as a savage, mad, embittered misanthrope largely rests upon this wrong-headed, sensational reading of the last voyage. In my opinion the work is that of a Christian-humanist and a moralist who no more blasphemes against the dignity of human nature than do St. Paul and some of the angrier prophets of the Old Testament. Swift has been misunderstood for several reasons.

1. The sheer intensity and violent rhetoric of the voyage are overwhelming and may well numb the critical sense of certain readers.

2. Gulliver in the frenzy of his mad misanthropy has been too facilely identified with Swift. Gulliver speaks for Gulliver and not for his creator in the final pages of the book, and careful reading should reveal the plain fact that he becomes the victim of Swift's irony as he grows to hate the human race. The final pages of the book are grimly comic.

3. The primary symbols of the voyage have been totally misunderstood. The Houyhnhnms have been regarded as Swift's ideal for man, and the Yahoos have been identified as his representation of what men are. Neither of these opinions, I believe, is correct. [65]

Let us begin with the Houyhnhnms and the Yahoos. In the first two voyages Gulliver is shown uncomfortably situated on the isthmus of a middle state between the very large and the very small. In this voyage he also stands on an isthmus, but now it is between the purely rational and the purely sensual—between Houyhnhnm and Yahoo. Neither of these symbols can stand for man, since Gulliver himself is the symbol of humanity. Unfortunately for poor Gulliver, he shares somehow in the nature of both extremes. Swift simply isolates the two elements that combine in the duality of man, the middle link, in order to allow Gulliver to contemplate each in its essence.

Does Swift recommend that Gulliver (who, remember, is we) should strive to become a Houyhnhnm? We discover that in every sense Houyhnhnmland is a rationalistic Utopia. The Houyhnhnms are the embodiment of pure reason. They know neither love nor grief nor lust nor ambition. They cannot lie; indeed they have no word for lying and are hard put to it to understand the meaning of opinion. Their society is an aristocracy, resting upon the slave labor of the Yahoos and the work of an especially-bred servant class. With icy, stoical calm they face the processes of life—marriage, childbirth, accident, death. Their society is a planned society that has achieved the mild anarchy that many Utopian dreamers have aspired to. They practice eugenics, and since they know no lust, they control the size of their population; children are educated by the state; their agrarian economy is supervised by a democratic council;

government is entirely conducted by periodic assemblies. The Houyhnhnms feel natural human affection for each other, but they love every one equally. It is all very admirable, but it is remote from the possibilities of human life.

Does Swift intend us to accept this as his ideal way of life? He who loved and hated and fought and bled internally through *saeva indignatio?* I think not. The Houyhnhnms are obviously Cartesians and as obviously stoics. "Neither is *Reason* among [66] them a Point problematical as with us," reports Gulliver, "where Men can argue with Plausibility on both Sides of a Question; but strikes you with immediate Conviction; . . . ." This is the Houyhnhnm version of Descartes' rational intuition of clear and distinct ideas. Now Swift was anti-Cartesian from his first published satire, for the simple reason that he held that Descartes was self-deluded and that man's reason was incapable of the feats that Descartes attributed to it. The Houyhnhnms are stoics, and Swift recorded his view of stoicism in *Thoughts on Various Subjects:* "The Stoical Scheme of supplying our Wants, by lopping off our Desires, is like cutting off our Feet when we want Shoes." It is Gulliver, not Swift, who is dazzled by the Houyhnhnms and who aspires to rise above the human condition and to become pure intelligence as these horses and the angels are.

The most powerful single symbol in all Swift is the Yahoos. They do not represent Swift's view of man, but rather of the bestial element in man—the unenlightened, unregenerate, irrational element in human nature—the id or the libido, if you will. Hence the Houyhnhnms classify Gulliver with them; hence the female Yahoo wishes to couple with him; hence despite his instinctive recoiling from them, Gulliver has to admit with shame and horror that he is more like them than he is like the Houyhnhnms. This I think is clear. Because of his neglect or misuse of human reason, European man has sunk nearer to the Yahoo pole of his nature than he has risen toward the Houyhnhnm pole. The seeds of human society and of human depravity, as they exist in Europe, are clearly discerned in the society and conduct of the Yahoos. Gulliver looks into the obscene abyss of human nature unlighted by the frail light of reason and of morality, and the sight drives him mad.

Repelled by what he sees, he, not Swift, identifies the Yahoos with man; and he, not Swift, turns misanthrope. Since he will not be a Yahoo, he seeks to become, as nearly as possible, a Houyhnhnm. But he can do so only by denying his place in and [67] responsibility to the human condition, by aspiring above the middle link, which is man, to the next higher link, that of the purely rational. The wise Houyhnhnm, to whom he gives his terrifying account of European man and society, concludes that "the corruption of reason" is worse than brutality itself, and that man is more dangerous than the Yahoo. This is profoundly true. But its effect on Gulliver is to awaken loathing of all that is human.

Lear, gazing on the naked, shivering Edgar, disguised as a Tom o' Bedlam, cries: "Thou art the thing itself; unaccommodated man is no more but such a poor, bare, forked animal as thou art." And in that intense moment, he goes mad. Something of the same thing befalls Gulliver. He thinks he has seen the thing itself. Though the Houyhnhnms never acknowledge that he is more than an unusually gifted Yahoo, he aspires to their rationality, stoicism, and simple wisdom; and persuaded that he has attained them, he feeds his growing misanthropy on pride, which alienates him not only from his remote kinsmen, the Yahoos, but eventually from his brothers, the human race. Looking back with nostalgia on his lost happiness in Houyhnhnmland, he recalls:

I enjoyed perfect Health of Body, and Tranquility of Mind; I did not feel the Treachery or Inconstancy of a Friend, nor the Injuries of a secret or open Enemy. I had no Occasion of bribing, flattering, or pimping, to procure the Favour of any great Man, or of his Minion. I wanted no Fence against Fraud or Oppression: Here was neither physician to destroy my Body, nor Lawyer to ruin my Fortune: No Informer to Watch my Words and Actions, or forge Accusations against me for Hire: Here were no Gibers, Censurers, Backbiters, Pickpockets, Highwaymen, Housebreakers, Attorneys, Bawds, Buffoons, Gamesters, Politicians, Wits, Spleneticks, tedious Talkers, Controvertists, Ravishers, Murderers, Robbers, Virtuoso's; no Leaders or Followers of Party and Faction; no Encouragers to Vice, by [68] Seducement or Examples: no Dungeon, Axes, Gibbets, Whippingposts, or Pillories; No cheating Shopkeepers or Mechanicks; No Pride, Vanity or Affection: No Fops, Bullies, Drunkards, strolling Whores, or Poxes: No ranting, lewd, expensive Wives: No stupid, proud Pedants: No importunate, over-bearing, quarrelsome, noisy, roaring, empty, conceited, swearing Companions: No Scoundrels raised from the Dust upon the Merit of their Vices; or Nobility thrown into it on account of their Virtues: No Lords, Fiddlers, Judges or Dancingmasters.

From the moment that the banished Gulliver despairingly sets sail from Houyhnhnmland, his pride, his misanthropy, his madness are apparent. Deluded by his worship of pure reason, he commits the error of the Houyhnhnms in equating human beings with the Yahoos. Captured by a Portuguese crew and forced to return from sullen solitude to humanity, he trembles between fear and hatred. The captain of the ship, Don Pedro de Mendez, like Gulliver himself, shares the nature of the Houyhnhnm and the Yahoo; and like the Gulliver of the first voyage he is tolerant, sympathetic, kindly, patient, and charitable; but Gulliver can no longer recognize these traits in a human being. With the myopic vision of the Houyhnhnms, he perceives only the Yahoo and is repelled by Don Pedro's clothes, food, and odor. Gradually, however, he is nursed back to partial health, and is forced to admit in the very accent of his admired horses, that his benefactor has a "very good *human* Understanding." But the Gulliver who writes this book is still under the control of his *idée fixe,* and when we last see him he prefers the smell and conversation of his two horses to the company of his wife and children. This is misanthropy in Timon's manner, not Swift's. In the brilliant and intricately ironic coda with which the book ends, Swift directs his savage, comic gaze straight at Gulliver and his insane pretensions.

My Reconcilement to the *Yahoo*-kind in general might not [69] be so difficult, if they would be content with those Vices and Follies only which Nature hath entitled them to. I am not in the least provoked at the Sight of a Lawyer, a Pickpocket, a Colonel, a Fool, a Lord, a Gamester, a Politician, a Whoremunger, a Physician, an Evidence, a Suborner, an Attorney, a Traytor, or the like: This is all according to the due Course of Things: But when I behold a Lump of Deformity, and Diseases both of Body and Mind, smitten with *Pride,* it immediately breaks all the Measures of my Patience; neither shall I ever be able to comprehend how such an Animal and such a Vice could tally together.

The grim joke is that Gulliver himself is the supreme instance of a creature smitten with pride. His education has somehow failed. He has voyaged into several remote nations of the world, but the journeys were not long, because of course he has never moved outside the bounds of human nature. The countries he visited, like the Kingdom of Heaven, are all within us. The ultimate danger of these travels was precisely the one that destroyed Gulliver's humanity— the danger that in his explorations he would discover something that he was not strong enough to face. This befell him, and he took refuge in a sick and morbid pride that alienated him from his species and taught him the gratitude of the Pharisee—"Lord, I thank Thee that I am not as other men."

Swift himself, in his personal conduct, displayed an arrogant pride. But he was never guilty of the angelic, dehumanizing pride of Gulliver, who writes in a letter to his Cousin Sympson:

I must freely confess, that since my last Return, some corruptions of my *Yahoo* Nature have revived in me by Conversing with a few of your Species, and particularly those of my own Family, by an unavoidable Necessity; else I should never have attempted so absurd a Project as that of reforming the *Yahoo* Race in this Kingdom; but, I have now done with all such visionary Schemes for ever. [70]

Jonathan Swift was stronger and healthier than Lemuel Gulliver. He hated the stupidity and the sinfulness and the folly of mankind. He could not accept the optimistic view of human nature that the philosophers of the Enlightenment proposed. And so he could exclaim to his contemporaries: "O wicked and perverse generation!" But, until he entered upon the darkness of his last years, he did not abandon his fellow man as hopeless or cease to announce, however indirectly, the dignity and worth of human kind. [71]

from *The Personality of Jonathan Swift*

IRVIN EHRENPREIS

For Houyhnhnmland (the third part of *Gulliver* in order of composition) my reasoning depends on two related assumptions. The first is that although the houyhnhnms embody traits which Swift admired, they do not represent his moral ideal for mankind. The other is that the houyhnhnms combine deistic and stoic views of human nature —views against which, as a devout Anglican, he fought. By "deistic" I mean the vague tradition in which men like Swift tended to lump free thinkers, deists, Socinians, and some Latitudinarians. The term "deist" was seldom used with any precision in the eighteenth century. Bolingbroke would not have admitted to the title, although his works were normally received as subversive of Christianity. Avowed deists were extremely rare, but Swift threw the label about with great freedom. By "stoic" I mean the doctrine of disinterested virtue, with its emphasis on man's self-sufficiency, its advocacy of a life without passion, its impossible and un-Christian goal of indifference to grief, death, and other misfortunes. But I shall not attempt to distinguish between these traditions because they are intimately blended in the reasoning of both their adherents and their opponents.[1]

Reprinted by permission of the publishers from Irvin Ehrenpreis, *The Personality of Jonathan Swift* (Cambridge, Mass.: Harvard University Press, Copyright, 1958, by Irvin Ehrenpreis), pp. 99–109. Also by permission of Methuen and Co., Ltd., London. The footnotes have been renumbered for this reprinting.
[1] See Louis Landa's "Introduction to the Sermons," in *Prose Works*, ed. Herbert Davis (Oxford, 1939–   ), IX, 108–14. (Cited below as Davis.)

Even a hasty reader might notice signs which support my [99] assumptions. A rather light hint is the houyhnhnms' ignorance of bodily shame: Gulliver says he asked his houyhnhnm master's forgiveness

if I did not expose those parts, that nature taught us to conceal. He said . . . he could not understand why nature should teach us to conceal what nature had given.[2]

Here, Gulliver's error resides in his logic rather than his modesty. It was not nature that taught us to conceal our genitalia; it was a supernatural moral law.

A more serious clue is a saying of Gulliver's master, that "*Reason* alone is sufficient to govern a *rational* creature." [3] This maxim runs contrary to the spirit of Christianity: except by removing men from the category of "rational creatures," no sincere Anglican could agree with the wise houyhnhnm. Swift devotes two of his extant sermons to annihilating such doctrines, and these sermons are the best of all commentaries on Houyhnhnmland. He excludes the possibility of virtue without Christianity except through rare "personal merit," as in Socrates and Cato, who happened to be blessed with a disposition (not reason) naturally good. "There is no solid, firm foundation of virtue, but in a conscience directed by the principles of religion." [4]

Deistic philosophers run in another direction. William Wollaston, one of Swift's detestations, writes,

To act according to right reason, and to act according to truth are in effect the same thing . . . . To be governed by reason is the general law imposed by the author of nature upon them, whose uppermost faculty is reason.[5] [100]

Similarly, the inexhaustible benevolence of the houyhnhnms sounds, even *prima facie*, like a parody of such antecedents of deism as the Earl of Shaftesbury, who says,

To deserve the name of good or virtuous, a creature must have all his inclinations and affections, his dispositions of mind and temper, suitable, and agreeing with the good of his kind . . . this affection of a creature

---

[2] *Gulliver's Travels*, ed. Sir Harold Williams (London, 1926), p. 333. (Cited below as *Gulliver*.)
[3] *Gulliver*, p. 367.
[4] "On the Testimony of Conscience" and "Upon the Excellency of Christianity." See Davis, IX, 249, 154.
[5] *The Religion of Nature Delineated* (London, 1722), p. 36.

toward the good of the species or common nature is . . . proper and natural to him.[6]

Shaftesbury is at pains to show that the Christian doctrine of rewards and punishments can be inconsistent with virtue. It is also suggestive that William Godwin, one of the fullest flowers of the deistic tradition, should have been infatuated with the houyhnhnms, calling them a description of "men in their highest improvement," and finding in Swift's exposition of their government "a more profound insight into the true principles of political justice, than [in] any preceding or contemporary author."[7]

Swift, for more than fifty years, was a priest in the Church of England. There is no doubt that he took his responsibilities as a pastor more seriously than most of his clerical colleagues took theirs. He reformed the worship in his cathedral to make it more regular and fuller than it had been for many years. He prayed in secret, went to church early so as not to be seen, wrote for his dearest friend some prayers which are models of intense but traditional religious expression. He gave a third of his income to charity and saved half the remainder to leave a fortune to charity. His sermons, the [101] remarks of his intimates, his own private papers, all confirm Swift's devotion to his faith and his calling. Nevertheless, he had suffered so many accusations of impiety—from misinterpreters of *A Tale of a Tub* and other works—that he would not bring religion openly into a satire like *Gulliver*.

In providing the houyhnhnms with good qualities, he was therefore duplicating the method of More's *Utopia;* and, to only this extent, R. W. Chambers is correct in writing,

Just as More scored a point against the wickedness of Christian Europe, by making his philosophers heathen, so Jonathan Swift scored a point against the wickedness of mankind by representing *his* philosophers, the Houyhnhnms, as having the bodies of horses.[8]

So, in his sermon "On the Excellency of Christianity," Swift argues that although there were "great examples of wisdom and virtue

---

[6] *Characteristicks*, ed. J. M. Robertson (London, 1900), I, 280. Of course, Shaftesbury, in spite of his influence, was a sound Christian.

[7] *The Inquirer* (London, 1797), p. 134; *Political Justice*, ed. F. E. L. Priestley (Toronto, 1946), II, 209n. For detailed evidence, see James Preu, "Swift's Influence on Godwin's Doctrine of Anarchism," *Journal of the History of Ideas*, XV (1954), 371–83.

[8] *Sir Thomas More* (London, 1935), p. 128.

among the heathen wise men," nevertheless, "Christian philosophy is in all things preferable to heathen wisdom." [9] As admirable creatures, the houyhnhnms represent beings (neither horses nor men) capable of pursuing the natural virtues summed up in reason and given us by nature as one remove from God; in their way—which is not the human way—they are perfect, and do not want religion. As absurd creatures, they represent the deistic presumption that mankind has no need of the specifically Christian virtues. Gulliver is misled as, in *Joseph Andrews*, "Mr. Wilson" is ruined by a club of "philosophers" who "governed themselves only by the infallible guide of human reason," but who reveal their immorality when one of them withdraws, "taking with him the wife of one of his most intimate friends," and another refuses to pay back a loan which "Mr. Wilson" [102] had made to him. While under the spell, the victim says,

I began now to esteem myself a being of a higher order than I had ever before conceived; and was more charmed with this rule of right, as I really found in my own nature nothing repugnant to it. I held in utter contempt all persons who wanted any other inducement to virtue besides her intrinsic beauty and excellence.[10]

Gulliver is not defrauded by the houyhnhnms, for they are not human (or equine); but the rule of nothing-but-reason leads him to repudiate all human obligations and to detest his wife. Swift wished men to be as rational as possible; he believed that religion helps them to become so, and that reason leads them toward revelation. But the deistic effort to build a rational system of morals outside revelation, he regarded as evil and absurd.

In the fourth voyage, Swift was probably aiming at a particular exponent of deistic thought, a correspondent with whom he had arguments about such doctrines while he was writing *Gulliver's Travels*. To identify the person, I shall limit myself at first to the most striking attributes of the houyhnhnms: their emotionless serenity, their benevolence, and their reliance on reason.

Of the houyhnhnms' indifference to such feelings as fear of death or filial love, one needs no reminding; this superiority to human pas-

[9] Davis, IX, 243.

[10] Fielding's *Works*, ed. W. E. Henley (London, 1903), I, 240–1 (Book III, Chapter 3).

sions appears throughout the fourth voyage. In Chapter VIII Gulliver surveys some of their other felicities. *"Friendship* and *benevolence,"* he says, [103]

are the two principal virtues among the houyhnhnms; and these not confined to particular objects, but universal to the whole race. For, a stranger from the remotest part, is equally treated with the nearest neighbour, and where-ever he goes, looks upon himself as at home . . . . They will have it that *nature* teaches them to love the whole species, and it is *reason* only that maketh a distinction of persons, where there is a superior degree of virtue.[11]

In 1719 Swift re-opened a correspondence with Bolingbroke which had been suspended for more than two years. In his answer Bolingbroke has a long passage on friendship, to which Swift replied in detail. After another exchange, the correspondence once more lapsed. When Swift wrote again, Bolingbroke sent him a very long letter which included further and extended reflections on friendship, such as,

Believe me, there is more pleasure, and more merit too, in cultivating friendship, than in taking care of the state . . . none but men of sense and virtue are capable of [it].[12]

It was Bolingbroke who wrote a whole treatise to prove that compassion, or kindness to strangers, depends on reason and nothing else; and in it he made such remarks as, "An habit of making good use of our reason, and such an education as trains up the mind in true morality, will never fail to inspire us with sentiments of benevolence for all mankind." In another essay he has declarations like, "Sociability is the great instinct, and benevolence the great law, of human nature." [13]

In Bolingbroke's next letter, he placed Swift on the opposite side of a quarrel about the Christian religion and [104] ancient morality. He harps on the theme that "a man of sense and virtue may be unfortunate, but can never be unhappy." Almost two years later (August 1723), Swift received a double letter from Pope and Boling-

---

[11] *Gulliver,* pp. 379–80.
[12] See Swift's *Correspondence,* ed. F. E. Ball (London, 1910–14), III, 24–30, 89. (Cited below as Ball.)
[13] *Reflections concerning Innate Moral Principles* (London, 1752), p. 55; *Philosophical Works* (London, 1754), IV, 256.

broke, both dilating on friendship; Pope's has so many maxims relating to this subject that it is more an essay than a letter. The two
men emphasize their contentment, their indifference to ordinary vicis-
situdes, their philosophical serenity. They preach a cool moderation
remote from the ordeals of Swift's preceding year. "Reflection and
habit," wrote Bolingbroke,

have rendered the world so indifferent to me, that I am neither afflicted
nor rejoiced, angry nor pleased, at what happens in it . . . . Perfect
tranquility is the general tenor of my life.[14]

While Swift may have envied such complacency, he could not imitate
it. He sent a sarcastic riposte ridiculing their pretensions to detached
and philosophic calm. "Your notions of friendship are new to me,"
Swift says; "I believe every man is born with his *quantum,* and he
cannot give to one without robbing another." As for their noncha-
lance, he told Pope, "I who am sunk under the prejudices of another
education . . . can never arrive at the serenity of mind you possess." It was their sort of vapidity that Swift meant to deride, two
years later, when he jeered at how Bolingbroke in 1723 had been "full
of philosophy, and talked *de contemptu mundi.*"[15]

The next development of the correspondence seems related to
Gulliver's most often-quoted comment on the houyhnhnms, his praise
of their devotion to reason (i.e., to reason alone): [105]

As these noble houyhnhnms are endowed by nature with a general disposition to all virtues, and have no conceptions . . . of what is evil in a
rational creature, so their grand maxim is, to cultivate *reason,* and to be
wholly governed by it. Neither is *reason* among them a point problematical as with us, where men can argue with plausibility on both sides of
the question; but strikes you with immediate conviction; as it must needs
do where it is not mingled, obscured, or discoloured by passion and
interest.[16]

In the autumn of 1724, the undercurrent of Swift's quarrel with his
friend becomes traceable; and it flows about this very problem of
what reason unaided can do. Bolingbroke sent a long defence of
deistic thought and an attack on Christianity (by implication), to
rebut a letter that is now lost, from Swift. The dean had directly

[14] Ball, III, 111, 172.   [15] Ball, III, 175, 291.   [16] *Gulliver,* pp. 378-9.

accused him of being an *esprit fort,* or free thinker.[17] In a tremendous harangue, Bolingbroke first takes the word to mean atheist, and repudiates that title; then he says, among similar remarks,

If indeed by *esprit fort,* or free-thinker, you only mean a man who makes a free use of his reason, who searches after truth without passion or prejudice, and adheres inviolably to it, you mean a wise and honest man, and such a one as I labour to be. The faculty of distinguishing between right and wrong, true and false, which we call reason or common sense, which is given to every man by our bountiful creator, and which most men lose by neglect, is the light of the mind, and ought to guide all the operations of it. To abandon this rule, and to guide our thoughts by any other [Bolingbroke means Christian revelation], is full as absurd as it would be, if you should put out your eyes, and borrow even the best staff . . . when you set out upon one of your dirty journeys . . . . The peace and happiness of mankind is the great aim of these free-thinkers.[18] [106]

In Bolingbroke's philosophical works there are many other similarities to the teachings of houyhnhnms. In fact, Gulliver's list of the subjects which generally come up in their conversations could serve almost as well for those works: friendship and benevolence, order and "oeconomy," the visible operations of nature, ancient traditions, the bounds and limits of virtue, the unerring rules of reason, etc.[19] Of course, however, Swift omits the purpose of Bolingbroke philosophizing, which (according to his eighteenth-century critics) was the destruction of Christianity. Swift believed that a good Christian is a rational person, that reason leads one to Christian faith, that these two gifts are in harmony, and that man must strive to enlarge them both.

One final touch is that Bolingbroke's editor calls his philosophical writings for the most part "nothing more than repetitions of conversations often interrupted, [and] often renewed."[20] For I have assumed that the letters from Bolingbroke had the effect of reminding Swift of topics more freely canvassed when the two men had talked together.[21]

[17] *The Letters of Jonathan Swift to Charles Ford,* ed. D. Nichol Smith (Oxford, 1935), pp. 100–1.
[18] Ball, III, 208–9. That Bolingbroke means Christian revelation is clear from his parallel with Locke's *Essay concerning Human Understanding,* IV, xix, 4, 8.
[19] *Gulliver,* p. 393.   [20] *Philosophical Works,* III, 334.
[21] D. G. James saw the connection between the houyhnhnms and Bolingbroke, but he quite misunderstood it; see his *Life of Reason* (London, 1949),

Although my observations pause here, there is a humorous post-script to the houyhnhnms. Viscount Bolingbroke was no horse, and it would have been convenient to discover one which was not only a deistic thinker but also a master of human beings. By a helpful chance, it happens that Swift once described such an animal, in a letter. The episode may be no more than an odd coincidence, but it seems worth reporting. For on this occasion Swift's horse behaved more [107] rationally than his servant, and the master treated the man like an animal.

At Christmas time, 1714, the dean rode out of Dublin, planning to collect his groom and his valet on the way. When he met them, they were incapably drunk; and he found that the groom could not travel. Swift nevertheless rode on, but noticed that Tom, the valet, who usually rode behind him, failed to keep up. He waited, and Tom galloped to him. Swift scolded him, and Tom answered foolishly. "He was as drunk as a dog," Swift wrote,

tottered on his horse, could not keep the way, sometimes into the sea, then back to me; swore he was not drunk. I bid him keep on, lashed him as well as I could; then he vowed he was drunk, fell a crying, came back every moment to me. I bid him keep on.

At last, from the galloping and turning backwards and forwards, Tom's horse "grew mad" and threw the valet down. Then Swift came up and called a boy and man to get the horse from him; but

he resisted us all three, was stark mad with drink. At last we got the bridle from him, the boy mounted and away we rode, Tom following after us. What became of him I know not.[22]

The episode has a peculiar interest, not only because the horse was English and the servants Irish, but because the name of the horse which "grew mad" and threw Tom down was Bolingbroke. The editor of Swift's correspondence says that the horse Bolingbroke was a gift, and that Swift named him; but we do not know who the donor was. In June 1713, Vanessa asked Swift, "How does Bolingbroke perform?" Swift, en route to Ireland, said the horse fell under him; [108] and in the end it was shipped over to its new country. Swift mentions Bolingbroke several times again, but after three years

pp. 256–61. I am indebted to Miss Kathleen Williams for this reference. Miss Williams, whose book on Swift will soon be ready, has come to conclusions like my own as to the meaning of the fourth voyage.

[22] Ball, II, 263.

he exchanged him for another horse. We never heard of him again, unless perhaps in *Gulliver's Travels*.[23]

But the refutation of Bolingbroke is merely a component of this Voyage, throwing a less interesting light upon its meaning than on the history of its composition. Swift's implications go further, in Part IV, than anywhere else in *Gulliver*. If the houyhnhnms are a false ideal for humanity, the yahoos are a false debasement of our nature. The representation of men as apes suggests Calvinist doctrines. In depicting our case as hopeless, and denying our power in any way to move toward salvation except through the arbitrary action of unmerited, unpredictable grace, the Puritans sink us to the category of mindless beasts. As the truly Christian alternative to both deistic and Dissenting errors, Swift provides Captain Pedro de Mendez, "the finest of all the European characters" in *Gulliver*.[24] It is in this image of humility, compassion, and charity (disdained by the infatuated Gulliver) that he would like us to rest. "Connaissons donc notre portée; nous sommes quelque chose, et ne sommes pas tout."[25]
[109]

[23] Ball, II, 44 & n, 45 & n, 242, 280–1, 305–6.
[24] Arthur E. Case, *Four Essays on Gulliver's Travels* (Princeton, 1945), p. 121.
[25] Blaise Pascal, *Pensées*, ed. Victor Giraud (Paris, 1938), p. 39.

Note on Irvin Ehrenpreis's "The Origins of *Gulliver's Travels*"

RICARDO QUINTANA

This article I have found interesting from beginning to end. If I
say I scarcely believe a word of it, I do so in all good humor. Swift-
ians everywhere respect Ehrenpreis's work, and they owe it to him
and to themselves to weigh his observations with care. In the present
instance I think many of his conclusions concerning *G.T.* are unsound, and I shall try, as best I can within very limited space, to
show why I do. But I would not want to seem to dogmatize. My
attitude is that of one who is delighted to debate the questions
raised here and who looks forward to a continuing discussion.

A theory informs E.'s investigation of *G.T.* It is this: Swift's imagination worked essentially in terms of people, of the people he had
known in the course of his career; we must accordingly approach
G.T. through the people Swift somehow had in mind while he was
composing. "I suggest," writes E., "that the common approach to
Swift's satire, with an emphasis on manipulation of ideas, or else
in terms of the technique of fiction, usually misleads one." (I am
unable in this brief critique to consider the validity of such an approach to *G.T.* I take issue with E. here, and again in his next to
final paragraph where he refuses to allow a whole structural pattern

Reprinted from *Philological Quarterly*, XXXVII (July 1958), 354–355. By
permission. Irvin Ehrenpreis's article, "The Origins of *Gulliver's Travels*," first
appeared in *PMLA*, LXXII (1957), 880–899, and then in 1958 was reprinted
in his book, *The Personality of Jonathan Swift*, as Chapter V, part of which
is reprinted in this book (pp. 246–254).

or intention to *G.T.* I believe, as I have set forth elsewhere, that *G.T.* does in fact possess a kind of unity through thematic unfolding and by way of comic disclosures and climax.)

In response to his theory, E. goes in search of the people who triggered Swift's imagination. The findings for the four Parts of *G.T.* may be summarized as follows. Part I: Case's theory concerning the political allegory is accepted in general, but refined upon: in several minor episodes Bolingbroke seems to have been more clearly in Swift's mind than Case perceived. E's discussion of the *Voyage to Lilliput*, reinforcing as it does the now-accepted interpretation of the political allegory, raises no crucial issues. Part II: Looking for a real person behind the King of the Brobdingnags, E. is satisfied that he has found one—namely, Sir W. Temple. Perhaps. But one feels that Temple's presence here, even had it been conclusively established—and that is scarcely the case—does not throw new light. Part III: The person pointed to here, E. believes, is Swift's friend and fellow-cleric, Thomas Sheridan: "Sheridan possessed to an extreme degree the characteristic on which Gulliver builds his portrait of the Laputans . . ." Again, one's comment can only be, Perhaps. Surely the weakness here, as in the case of Sir W. T., is that any methodical search through the list of people Swift knew is bound to suggest possible parallels in *G.T.* Part IV: The most important and most controversial part of [354] E.'s article (sections IV and V) concerns the Houyhnhnms. We are told that "although the Houyhnhnms embody traits which Swift admired, they do not represent his moral ideal for mankind." They are, in fact, deistic, and their belief that reason alone is sufficient to govern a rational creature is a deistic formula; they were devised with the deist Bolingbroke in mind; and Swift was saying "in the fourth voyage, that anyone who believes in the adequacy of reason without Christianity must see himself as a Houyhnhnm and the rest of mankind as Yahoos." E.'s reasoning in support of this position strikes me as quite faulty at two levels: at the level of the history of ideas; and in respect of what may be called Swift's satiric logic.

Where the ideas of Swift's era are in question, especially such ideas as appear in theological-philosophic discussion, it is fatal to disregard context. It is here that E. seems to have fallen into serious error. The Houyhnhnms' maxim that "*Reason* alone is sufficient to govern a rational creature" is, E. contends, contrary to the spirit of Christianity and contrary to Anglicanism; and to the annihilation of such a doctrine Swift devoted two of his sermons ("Upon the Ex-

cellency of Christianity" and "On the Testimony of Conscience"),
"and these sermons are the best of all commentaries on Houyhnhnm-
land." I submit that they are no such commentaries at all. "On the
Testimony of Conscience" is directed against old dissenters and
present non-conformists who would plead the dictates of conscience
for their behavior. The context has almost nothing in common with
the satirical situation established in *G.T.*, Part IV. As for "Upon the
Excellency of Christianity," it is a traditionally Anglican exposition
of the grounds of Christianity: Revelation bestows upon Christianity
a certitude for lack of which the best of the pagans floundered. It
is concerned with the grounds of belief, not with the rationale of
ethical conduct. For Swift and the Anglicans generally, principles
of ethics and morals were taken up in a substantially different context, in which it was characteristically held, as Swift himself did in
the *Letter to a Young Clergyman,* that the heathen philosophers,
though deprived of Revelation and therefore falling short of Christian truth, nevertheless afforded a sound comment "upon the moral
Part of the Gospel." Now, what *is* the context within which rationalism is being attributed to the Houyhnhnms? Surely the statement
that "reason alone is sufficient to govern a rational creature" and
Gulliver's observation that "their grand maxim is to cultivate reason
and to be wholly governed by it" occur in connection exclusively
with moral doctrine—they have been called forth by the repulsively
irrational behavior of the Yahoos. It has taken us a long time to see
(as we now do, thanks greatly to Maynard Mack) that the *Essay
on Man* is not a deistic manifesto. It would be a pity, I think, were
we now to let ourselves in for a period of confusion regarding the
Houyhnhnms. In Part IV Swift was not expounding the grounds of
Christian belief; he was writing a great satire, the chief theme of
which is the moral dualism of man, a being not *rationale,* only
rationis capax.

I must put in a word about Swift's satiric logic. Are we really to
take it that the comic-satiric import of the *Voyage to the Houyhnhnms* resides in a grave message to the effect, as E. would have it,
"that anyone who believes in the adequacy of reason without Christianity must see himself as a Houyhnhnm and the rest of mankind
as Yahoos"? When Gulliver faints at the smell of humanity, are we
to understand that his error lies in his forgetting to add Christianity
to reason? Part IV, I submit, is not this sort or any sort of tract on
the grounds of Christian belief. It is a magnificently imaginative and
comic symbolization of man's perennial moral dilemma. [355]

Errors Concerning the Houyhnhnms

GEORGE SHERBURN

Heretofore I have always regarded the work of Professor Ehrenpreis on Swift as both sound and brilliant. I am therefore unhappy to find him expounding views on *Gulliver's Travels* that seem to me quite mistaken. Since he has announced that I do not accept his interpretations,[1] it is in some sense a duty to expose my own views, which I do not imagine to be very original.

Surely it is arguable whether one should regard Swift's satire as triggered by personalities rather than by "manipulation of ideas." Any decision in the matter is sheer opinion—did the egg come before the hen or not? Many will surely feel that Brobdingnag was portrayed in order to present some of Swift's ideas rather than to magnify Sir William Temple. Swift probably learned much from Sir William, but many of the commonplaces found in the character of the King of Brobdingnag might come from different sources. If we grant that, having started to expound ideas as to reason in affairs of government, Swift drew upon the teachings of Temple, one may still doubt whether even a vague identification of the King of Brobdingnag with Sir William is notably illuminating. Swift—to contradict flatly—

Reprinted from *Modern Philology*, LVI (November 1958), 92–97. By permission of The University of Chicago Press. Copyright 1958 by the University of Chicago.

[1] "The Origins of *Gulliver's Travels*," *PMLA*, LXII (1957), 880–99. References to the article will hereafter be to page only. References to *Gulliver's Travels* and one or two other works by Swift will be to the edition edited by Herbert Davis.

did have "a set of values to defend or objects to attack," and he clothed his views in the best thinking he could find, even if on rare occasions he had to borrow it.

My main objection, however, is to Ehrenpreis' interpretation of the Houyhnhnms. One may doubt whether there will ever be unanimous agreement as to what Swift was doing in parts of A Tale of a Tub or in Gulliver's fourth voyage. But we may attempt agreement on what he was not doing. Ehrenpreis is not alone in misunderstanding the Houyhnhnms, but I think he is the first to suggest the impossible notion that, in the Houyhnhnms, Swift is satirizing deism. To Ehrenpreis deists apparently are simply people who glorify reason. He cites from Wollaston a passage that Swift, he assumes, would detest. It reads: "To act according to right reason, and to act according to truth are in effect the same thing. . . . To be governed by reason is the general law imposed by the author of nature upon them, whose uppermost faculty is reason" (p. 890). This certainly sounds like Gulliver. We know what Swift thought of Wollaston, but we do not know what he would have thought of this quoted passage. It is merely assumed that he would have disapproved. One notes that the very first among Swift's "Thoughts on Religion" concerns the place of reason in religion. It says: "I am in all opinions to believe according to my own impartial reason; which I am bound to inform and improve, as far as my capacity and opportunities will permit" (IX, 261). In what respects this passage differs in doctrine from the quotation from Wollaston it would be difficult to demonstrate.

It thus becomes an assumption requiring more than remarks about reason to establish that the fourth voyage of Gulliver concerns religion. In a letter to Pope [92] (September 20, 1723) Swift, glancing at Pope's Catholicism, remarks: "You have no more to do with the constitution of Church and State, than a Christian at Constantinople." He evidently felt that Gulliver was similarly comfortable in all his various "remote" voyages. State intrudes, but church is irrelevant in these strange regions. We need further study of the curious abstractionist art of most imaginary voyages, whereby the writer reduces the mind of his fictitious author to an essential state ("right reason") and obliterates "accidental" aspects, not to be treated. This abstractionism is perhaps best seen in the letters written by foreign travelers or spies, whether Persian (Montesquieu) or Chinese (Goldsmith). What these writers seek is to picture right reason shining out undiffracted by any local or accidental prejudices. The attempt embodies a well-known dream (or fiction) of the century. Various aspects of life and manners are, by this unbiased reason, eclectically chosen for presentation, and other aspects disappear. So there is no clear glimmer of religion in Gulliver's fourth voyage that would indicate any attitude toward revealed Christianity, whether favorable or unfavorable. Having made his Houyhnhnms horses, Swift could hardly make them Anglicans—though at least one writer has reproached him for not having done so. By the fundamental metaphor, religion is excluded. There seems to be no point in having made them horses if they are to satirize deists; but, in creating beings definitely extra-human and superhuman, Swift might naturally turn to his favorite animal—which, however, he treats with unrealistic playfulness. The threading of needles, the weaving of mats, and the riding about drawn by Yahoos are simply examples of Swift's having a playful time of it; but the control, composure, affection, and intelligence of the animal were qualities that Swift obviously admired and here consistently portrayed.

In assuming that the reason of the Houyhnhnms is obnoxious to Swift, Ehrenpreis possibly is not alone, though he takes an extreme position. Professor John F. Ross ("The Final Comedy of Lemuel Gulliver," *University of California Publications in English* [1941], p. 189) recognized in passing the Houyhnhnm claim to be "perfection of nature," but he felt that in such case their "intellectual limitations and arrogance" should not admit of equine tastes. He writes:

> In every point wherein man and horse differ, the [Houyhnhnm] automatically and even absurdly assumes that the advantage lies obviously with the horse; for example, that four legs are better than two, or that the human anatomy is defective since Gulliver cannot eat without lifting one of his "fore feet" to his mouth. While, Swift, in pursuit of his purpose, is chary of making the horses absurd, there are enough comic touches to guard the attentive reader from assuming that Swift accepts Gulliver's worshipful attitude toward the horses.

Ehrenpreis has a similar objection to the Houyhnhnm notion that genitalia need not be concealed. The only answer to such comment is that the Houyhnhnms—some of the time—are horses, and as such, when depicted by Swift, would hardly prefer human traits to equine. Such comments recall the reverse observation of the eighteenth-century Frenchman who remarked that in Houyhnhnmland horses had the reasoning powers of men. If that had been true, Gulliver would never have known them. Swift was trying, impossibly, to make his creatures both horse and "perfection of nature."

But in assuming that Houyhnhnm reason would be obnoxious to Swift, one neglects this remark about "perfection [93] of nature." A further playful statement by Swift—outside *Gulliver*—may here well be cited. In a letter to Charles Ford (ed. D. Nichol Smith, p. 100) he says: "I would have you know that I hate Yahoos of both Sexes, and that Stella and Madame de Villette [Bolingbroke's wife] are onely tolerable at best, for want of Houyhnhnms." There can, then, obviously be no doubt that, for Swift as well as for Gulliver, the Houyhnhnms were a *ne plus ultra*. In chapter viii Gulliver tells us that "these noble Houyhnhnms are endowed by nature with a general disposition to all virtues"—a statement which, whether "worshipful" or not, indicates high praise, and there is no evidence that Swift, though at times playful, did not share Gulliver's opinion.

In view of the evidence presented, the Houyhnhnms cannot be regarded as objects of satire. In view of phrases that Ehrenpreis wrongly interprets, they might be so regarded. Like others before him, Ehrenpreis mistakenly thinks Swift gives the Houyhnhnms only one quality of consciousness: reason. He speaks (p. 891) of their "rule of nothing-but-reason" and of their "devotion to reason (i.e., to reason alone)" (p. 893). But this is neither Swift nor Gulliver. More than once Gulliver remarks, and Ehrenpreis quotes (and misinterprets) him as saying, "Reason alone is sufficient to govern a *rational* creature" (pp. 890, 893). The proper word to emphasize here is *govern*, and, thus clarified (with reason the governor and the other aspects of consciousness subject to it), the idea is a commonplace accepted by Anglicans and deists and even by atheists from ancient times on down. Ehrenpreis errs grossly in saying that this maxim "runs contrary to the spirit of Christianity" and to that of sincere Anglicans. It simply places reason in a hierarchy above the emotions or "inferior mind" and gives, by implication, reason something other than itself to govern. It is not "alone" in the mind. In *Gulliver* this governing function of reason is repeatedly emphasized (pp. 243, 251, 252, 261, 264). The opposite principle, as Gulliver continues to say in chapter viii, is to be governed ("discoloured") by passion and interest. At stake here are moral and psychological concepts: there is no hint of an interest in the Christian revelation, as Ehrenpreis seems to assume.

We must not too readily assert a total lack of emotion among the Houyhnhnms. We must weigh words in reading what Swift makes Gulliver say. Consider, for example, the word *fondness* when it is remarked (chap. viii): "They have no fondness for their colts or foles; but the care that they take in educating them proceedeth entirely from the dictates of reason. And I observed my master to show the same affection to his neighbour's issue that he had for his own." Swift knew, what the Freudians now teach, that fondness and fondling are educationally bad. Care and affection are emotional traits, and, to recur to our commonplace ("Reason the card, and passion is the gale"), we may note that *care* implies something that reason must govern. To enforce the disparaging connotation of *fondness,* one may quote Dr. Johnson's magnificently concise disparagement of Otway's tavern companions: "Their fondness was without benevolence and their familiarity without friendship" (*Lives of the Poets,* ed. Hill, I, 243).

The Houyhnhnm reason has less to govern than does the human or the anarchic Yahoo brain. The Houyhnhnms do not live, as Ehrenpreis asserts, in "emotionless serenity" but rather in controlled serenity. Swift was no Stoic extirpating the passions, and to him it would seem irrational to try to conceive creatures [94] that were "devoted to reason alone"—as Ehrenpreis makes him say (p. 893). The Houyhnhnms have emotions: they hate and abhor the Yahoos and include English Yahoos (as reported by Gulliver) in their horror. So far as appetites go, Swift (or Gulliver) tells us, "their wants and passions are fewer than among us" (chap. iv). But he nowhere denies them wants and passions. Goldsmith's story of Asem the Man-Hater tries to depict "pure" reason, and the picture, most unlike Swift's, has to obliterate friendship and benevolence (Houyhnhnm traits) as not exclusively rational. Gulliver's exposé of his own dear country causes his Houyhnhnm master to "lift his eyes with amazement and indignation" (chap. iv). That may seem to be as far as rationally controlled emotion can go, but the sorel nag (who, to be sure, did not have top "horse sense") was much moved—as were more conservative Houyhnhnms—at Gulliver's departure: "My master and his friends continued on the shore till I was almost out of sight; and I often heard the sorel nag (who always loved me) crying out . . . Take care of thy self gentle Yahoo" (chap. xi).

This is not emotionless.

If one starts with the assumption that Swift got initial stimulus from persons and not from ideas, one may also assume that this fourth voyage concerns the erroneous thinking of Bolingbroke. Years ago Professor Edith Rickert proved to her own satisfaction that in *Midsummer Night's Dream* Bottom was a caricature of King James I. There can be no conclusive argument against such equation of persons. Even if we could go to Glubbdubdrib and call Swift's ghost from the vasty deep and even if it denied, when asked, that in writing *Gulliver* it had had any thought of Temple, Sheridan, or Bolingbroke, Ehrenpreis could rightly, in our century, still retort to the ghost, "In your *subconscious* you did have them in mind." But for the rest of us there is a burden of awaited proof involved.

Personally I should agree with the ghost if it asserted that Bolingbroke (doubtless present in the first voyage) had no part in the fourth—just as I believe that religion has no part and that Swift's sermons throw little or no light on the voyage. The letter of Bolingbroke to Swift (September 12, 1724), since Ehrenpreis quotes it, does require comment. It is a confused and confusing letter. In various other *loci* Bolingbroke at times wrote as a deist or as an atheist or as a rationalist believer in the historical revelation of Christianity, even while detesting metaphysical theology. Swift himself was no great lover of metaphysics, and he is dogmatic rather than argumentative about the mysteries of religion. What he tells us of the Trinity or even of the creation of Eve out of Adam's rib is simply: we are to believe.

In this particular letter Bolingbroke is differentiating two types of *esprit fort*—a term that Swift apparently has applied to him. One type of freethinker, Bolingbroke says, "is so set upon pulling down your house [the Established Church] about your ears, that if he was let alone, he would destroy the other [natural religion] for being so near it, and mingle both in one common mine. I therefore not only disown, but detest this character." Then follows the passage that Ehrenpreis quotes and which he mistakenly explains as meaning that if we abandon "the light of the mind" (common sense) and use the Christian revelation as guide, we shall blind ourselves to the truth. What follows in the letter proves that this explanation cannot possibly be what Bolingbroke means. The two types of freethinkers are (1) those who undermine religion by syllogistic metaphysical pomposity and (2) [95] those who follow the light of the mind, common sense. Bolingbroke at times equates these logic-choppers, whom he detests, with Christian theologians; but not here, since he goes on to say of *his* (2) type of *esprit fort:*

Such free-thinkers as these, I am sure you cannot, even in your apostolical capacity disapprove, for since the truth of the divine revelation of Christianity is as evident, as matters of fact, on the belief of which so much depends, ought to be, agreeably to all our ideas of justice, these free-thinkers must needs be Christians on the best foundation, on that which St. Paul himself established—I think it was St. Paul—*omnia probate, quod bonum est tenete.*[2]

After this bow toward historical Christianity, Bolingbroke continues: "The peace and happiness of mankind is the great aim of these [my type of] free-thinkers"; and at this rate Swift, who knew when to let (friendly) sleeping dogs lie, was not likely to pick a "quarrel" (Ehrenpreis' word) with his confused friend. Swift, like Bolingbroke, detested logic-choppers, and the contrast between followers of the light of reason and the metaphysicians is a commonplace of the time. Among his "Thoughts on Religion" (*Works*, IX, 261) Swift peaceably says: "Every man, as a member of the commonwealth, ought to be content with the possession of his own opinion in private, without perplexing his neighbour or disturbing the public." There were plenty of things Swift would quarrel about, but quarrels over religious doctrine tended to bore or infuriate him. And so religion is left out in all four voyages of *Gulliver*.[3]

The Houyhnhnms represent Swift's clearly imperfect concept of "perfection of nature." He did perhaps as well as could be expected. The Yahoos represent an opposite, and in between is poor fallible Gulliver, who at times speaks for Swift and at times only for himself. It is not strange that the portrayal of the Yahoos is far more powerful than is that of the "perfect" Houyhnhnms. Depictions of hell have been in all ages more vivid and more numerous than pictures of heaven. It is logically impossible, of course, to depict perfection.

---

[2] Swift's *Correspondence*, ed. Ball, III, 209. The text as printed by Ball is not well punctuated. The original is in the British Museum Add. MSS 4805, fols. 97–101. The subject of *ought* is *matters of fact.*

[3] Gordon McKenzie in "Swift: Reason and Some of Its Consequences," *University of California Publications: Five Studies in Literature* (1940), p. 103, shrewdly remarks: "The complete omission of religion seems at first glance very curious; yet on closer inspection it becomes clear that the very rightness of the society makes religion unnecessary. . . . Undoubtedly in Swift's mind the Houyhnhnms lived the truly religious life."

Spinoza, almost a contemporary of Swift, in connection with the attributes of the Deity, made the keen assertion, "Determinatio est negatio." To make an affirmation about Perfection is to qualify, limit, and debase it by excluding other perfect attributes. Swift was a man obsessed by the imperfections of man and society, and possibly he was the last type of man who should attempt to portray anything supernatural, but such a man may be psychologically compelled to make the attempt. Although the life of the Houyhnhnms is, to say the least, austere, one drops from it to a lower level when considering the known imperfections of human society in any age.

Gulliver at times, suspended as he is between what man in this life can never be and what man in this life is all too prone to become, certainly speaks for Swift in the passages satirical of political, social, and moral corruption in England. One notes that it is only through conversations with his critical Houyhnhnm master that Gulliver comes to see in part the baseness of life in what had been his own dear country. His judgment in these matters is excellent from Swift's point of view: are we then prepared suddenly to imagine [96] him a fool, praising highly "rational" creatures who are obnoxious to Swift?

But, one is asked, why, if the Houyhnhnms are so perfect, did Gulliver's contact with them so completely unfit him for life in human society? The easy and obvious answer is that Swift was driving to a misanthropic conclusion. The Houyhnhnm state was too high; Gulliver could not attain unto it. He was merely a man, and in this life could never come near to achieving "perfection of nature." We have on record very few cases of direct contact between a man and Perfection. The most celebrated case is that of St. Paul, who was struck blind by the light of heaven and remained so for three days. Paul, however, was under explicit divine commands for action; Gulliver had seen no sudden light, but he had seen an ideal way of life and yet had no explicit commands to follow thereafter. As a character in a static narrative, Gulliver was the victim of a misanthropic author. The folklore of human contacts with divinity follows a pattern somewhat like that of Paul. Such contacts are likely to be fatal, if too intimate. Aeneas could "see" his divine mother Venus only when she was concealed in a cloud. Imprudent Semele demanded an undraped, undisguised sight of her lover Jupiter—and all the world knows what happened to *her*. Mythology doubtless offers other cases, and one must conclude that too close a contact between imperfect man and the perfection that man in this life cannot attain is traditionally likely to be most unhappy. Gulliver's final state is not surprising, for Swift had low views of man's potentialities. One may faintly suppose that he thought the socially dislocating effect of Houyhnhnm ideals on Gulliver (Everyman?) no more extreme than would be the dislocating effects of a complete, rigid (and quite unknown) obedience to Christian ideals in an eighteenth-century world. But such an idea seems hardly in Swift's character. Certainly, however, one aspect of the despair in Swift's mind grew from his ardent perception of highest values and his further perception that such values were far, far out of man's reach. [97]

from Note on Irvin Ehrenpreis's
The Personality of Jonathan Swift

LOUIS A. LANDA

What may be striking to some readers of this book, though not to one who knows the zest with which the author has carried on his research, is the boundless accumulation of facts, the sheer weight of detail, the minutiae which buttress the judgments. Any Swift scholar, disheartened by the misconceptions and distortions of the past, is likely to feel a desperate urge merely to set down the simple, hard, unvarnished facts. Such feelings undoubtedly inspired the essay on Swift's old age, so frequently treated with melodramatic lack of restraint and embodied in Johnson's line: "Swift expires a driv'ler and a show." There was no melodrama, though perhaps even more wretchedness than the myth suggests, with friends dead or falling away and a great genius sinking into physical and mental lethargy —and aware of it. This study is a model of its kind (though not so substantial as the one on "History"), a cool marshalling of the known facts, with more cogency and pathos (and artistry) than in the customary inflamed accounts. A companion study is the one on Swift's madness, with its chastisement of the rumor mongers from Johnson through Thackeray to Middleton Murry, who have transformed Swift's infirmities into raging insanity or downright imbecility. The better modern medical studies of Swift have tried to avoid the confusion inherent in the term "insanity," especially since they stress the physiological or non-cerebral aspects of his illnesses; and Mr.

Reprinted from *Philological Quarterly*, XXXVIII (July 1959), 351–352. By permission.

Ehrenpreis, following this trend, relies particularly on Sir Walter Russell Brain, the distinguished English neurologist, who has explained Swift's final years in terms of the ravages of old age, senility, Ménière's syndrome, and orbital cellulitis, with a consequent stroke in 1742. This emphasis on deteriorative organic factors does not, however, rule [351] out mental and emotional factors interwoven with or intensified by the neurological aspects, nor does it ignore the existence in Swift of strong and long-continued obsessional qualities. Mr. Ehrenpreis, in the excellent study on "Obscenity," treats very sensibly the most widely discussed of these obsessions.

In the essay on "Gulliver" the interpretation of Swift's masterpiece is carried into new ground. Mr. Ehrenpreis's basic notion is that "Swift's imagination worked in terms of people." Thus if we want the real origin and model of the King of the Brobdingnags, we must turn to Sir William Temple. Similarly, the King of Laputa is modelled on Thomas Sheridan, and in Part I Gulliver is a sublimation of Bolingbroke. A considerable body of evidence is presented to show that Swift was writing or thinking about these men in the years immediately preceding and during the composition of *Gulliver's Travels*. In the instances of Bolingbroke and Sheridan the contact was intimate, through correspondence or actual intercourse. Temple, though long dead, was kept vividly alive in Swift's recollection, Mr. Ehrenpreis maintains, by virtue of certain historical, political, or personal parallels linking him to Bolingbroke and by Swift's retention of ideas gleaned from Temple and now appropriate for *Gulliver's Travels*. Mr. Ehrenpreis does not argue for a precise correspondence between the historical personages named and the figures in the book. He recognizes the differences, but he wishes to stress the striking associations and similarities. The difficulty is not in accepting some of the similarities but in the inference drawn, that these men were somehow the starting point for Swift's fictional characters, that Swift "did not invent a set of values to defend, or objects to attack; he started from human embodiments of those values or vices, and he addressed himself to people whom he wished to encourage, refute, or annihilate." Surely this theory of origins is beyond demonstration and can be at best only suggestive.

It leads to what is the most glaring interpretation in the book (and one which I hope Mr. Ehrenpreis will either modify or retract). We are told that the Houyhnhnms are, in part, a representation of deism, that Swift created them in this extreme rationalistic guise to expose them, and that in so doing he was aiming at Bolingbroke, with whom he corresponded on the subject of free-thinking and deism while *Gulliver's Travels* was being written. I should like to state two objections, all too baldly because of limitations of space. In the first place I believe that Mr. Ehrenpreis, like many others, has fallen into a semantic trap: he identifies the *language* of rationalism with the *substance* of deism. In the eighteenth century Locke and Tillotson were charged with being deists (or were used by them) because their rationalistic language was at times ambivalent and could plausibly be wrenched into unintended meanings. Swift is similarly vulnerable. True, much of the phraseology in which he has enveloped the Houyhnhnms has the strongest rationalistic implications, but it is not accurate to identify the general abstract concepts which are the essence of Houyhnhnm character as the sole property of the deists. These were, in the widely diffused rationalism of the period, normative concepts for everyone, ideals by definition, beyond criticism—and universally used to measure the deficiencies of man and society by rationalists *and* antirationalists (almost everyone was both at times). Such concepts as right reason and universal benevolence might be called decorative ideas, inoperative in human behavior in any very practical sense, but present to be reverenced, and merely as stated carrying the strongest rhetorical persuasiveness and demanding assent. Similarly with other rationalistic ideals observable in the Houyhnhnms. In the second place, I should not, in interpreting the Houyhnhnms, apply the logic and conclusions of the sermons as Mr. Ehrenpreis does, though I agee with him that in some respects the sermons can throw light on *Gulliver's Travels.* The particular sermons used make their points in the light of complex doctrinal and ethical traditions and in the context of a divine scheme of things. But in Part IV of *Gulliver* we have a different order of ideas or level of reality, with more limited issues, in which man is considered in terms of his private and public virtues, an appraisal of him as a mundane domestic, political, and social creature. The two orders cannot be fused so neatly without subtly transforming Swift's intention. [352]

Except for this one essay, my reservations are rare and minor. This is a valuable book by a well informed scholar, and a prerequisite for those who wish a better understanding of Swift. [353]

Conversion on the Road
to Houyhnhnmland

CALHOUN WINTON

Critics considering *Gulliver's Travels* may meditate by night on the bitter struggle among the Lilliputians described in the First Voyage. One faction of little men, it will be remembered, contended that eggs should be broken at the larger end before they are eaten; the rival party preferred breaking the smaller end. Six rebellions have been raised, Gulliver tells us, and "Many hundred large Volumes have been published upon this Controversy," though the great prophet of the country, Lustrog, had long ago written "That all true Believers shall break their Eggs at the convenient End. . . ." [1] Heeding the words of Lustrog, we Lilliputian critics of the twentieth century may, must approach Swift's masterpiece from the convenient end, recognizing that it is many different things at once. It is, or at least the voyages to Lilliput and Brobdingnag are, a fable for children. It is also a mature political satire, simultaneously local and timeless; it is a satiric parody of travel books; it is a proto-fictional narrative; it is, finally, a prose comedy of great verve. Profoundly amusing though Swift's work may be, however, his end, he asserted, "in all my labours is to vex the world rather than divert it. . . ." [2]

Reprinted from *The Sewanee Review*, LXVIII (Winter 1960), 20–33. Copyright © 1960 by The University of the South. By permission.
[1] *Gulliver's Travels*, ed. Herbert Davis (Oxford, 1941), pp. 33–34. All references are to this edition. I have attempted to restrict documentation to specific matters; my general indebtedness to students of Swift is, I trust, apparent.
[2] Letter to Pope in *The Correspondence of Jonathan Swift, D.D.*, ed. F. Elrington Ball (London, 1910–14), III, 276.

Swift's grave should be quiet. Casual readers are repelled by the immortal but senile Struldbruggs, by the solemn horses and filthy Yahoos of Houyhnhnmland; critics struggle to encompass Swift's labors in one gigantic schema, and criticism swells to the proportions of the Lilliputian controversy's "many hundred large [20] Volumes." A vexed world eyes the critics of the *Travels* with justifiable suspicion.

Nevertheless, eggs must be broken. It is the purpose, then, of this essay to lighten portions of *Gulliver's Travels* perhaps now dark; to propose a reading of the book which while admittedly not complete is germane to the total significance of Swift's great work. To put the matter directly, *Gulliver's Travels* is a satiric presentation of what Swift regarded as the new, "enlightened" religion (often referred to loosely then and now as "deism") and a defense, couched in Swiftian irony, of Augustinian Christianity. Gulliver becomes, in this reading, a pilgrim symbolic in the way Bunyan's traveler is symbolic (and I think the parallel with *A Pilgrim's Progress* is intentional, though I cannot prove it), a sort of eighteenth-century English Everyman whose pilgrimage from a position of complete religious ignorance culminates with "conversion," in the full sense of the word, to the faith of the Houyhnhnms, the reasonable faith of the hyper-reasonable horses, in Houyhnhnmland's new Eden.

Two matters are assumed as proved. First, that Swift was a practicing believer in institutional Christianity; second, that Gulliver is not Swift. Doubters are referred in the first case to the work of Mr. Louis Landa and to Swift's own writings, especially his sermons and his "Thoughts on Religion." [3] A man's religion is in a final sense unknowable of course, but from all visible evidence we gather that Swift was as faithful to his calling of Anglican priest as to that of Tory pamphleteer or Irish patriot, indeed much more faithful. The notoriously unsympathetic first biographer John Boyle, Earl of Cork and Orrery, wrote after Swift's death: "[He] performed the duties of the church with great punctuality and a decent degree of devotion," adding that "although he hath been often accused of irreligion, nothing of [21] that kind appeared in his conversation or behaviour." [4] One familiar with the clerical career of, say, Sterne, will

[3] See especially Louis Landa, *Swift and the Church of Ireland* (Oxford, 1954); and his "Introduction" to Swift, *Irish Tracts and Sermons*, ed. Herbert Davis (Oxford, 1948), pp. 97–137. The latter hereafter referred to as *Irish Tracts*.

[4] *Remarks on the Life and Writings of Dr. Jonathan Swift, Dean of St. Patrick's, Dublin, in a series of Letters From John Earl of Orrery, to his son, the Honourable Hamilton Boyle* (Dublin, 1752), p. 5.

recognize this as being no faint praise in eighteenth-century England. The second proposition, that Gulliver does not equal Swift, has been demonstrated in recent years by Mr. John Bullitt, Mr. W. B. Ewald, and Mr. Martin Price.[5] Swift, like many other writers of his time, almost always used a *persona*, a fictive spokesman. Thus the narrator, the *persona*, of *A Tale of a Tub* is a scribbler, a pedant, a minute philosopher, a sober rationalist who is more than a little mad; he is of course not Swift. Readers of the last century and indeed some of Swift's day were baffled by his complex ironic spokesmen, and the tendency to equate the artist with the artifact is not dead, as those who teach literature to undergraduates will know. Let it be admitted that the subject of Swift's masks is a difficult one; still, recent criticism has reduced the problem to intelligibility if not simplicity.

The question to be addressed, then, if these two assumptions are granted, is, by what means, in what way, does the Christian Swift operate as the creator of *Gulliver's Travels?* That he was a keen observer of the temporal state of religion is apparent from *A Tale of a Tub*, in which he dramatizes in the story of Peter, Martin, and Jack the troubles of European Christianity in the seventeenth century: sectarian dispute, sordid struggles for wealth, specious theologizing. It is interesting to note, however, that a few years later in *An Argument Against Abolishing Christianity* (1708) his major concern is no longer sectarian controversy but religious apathy. The narrator argues against abolishing nominal Christianity, "the other [*i.e.* real Christianity] having been for some Time wholly laid aside by general Consent, as utterly inconsistent with all our present Schemes of Wealth and [22] Power." Nominal Christianity, he argues, "some scattered Notions about a superior Power," is of use for keeping "Children quiet when they grow peevish. . . ." The English people generally, he looks upon (with approval, of course—he is the *persona* of an "enlightened" man) "to be as Free-Thinkers, that is to say, as stanch Unbelievers, as any of the highest Rank." [6] One of the people, the "stanch Unbelievers," is, as we shall see, Lemuel Gulliver.

From posterity's high ground we recognize that the increasing apathy of certain intellectual leaders toward organized religion was

[5] In, respectively, *Jonathan Swift and the Anatomy of Satire* (Cambridge, Mass., 1953); *The Masks of Jonathan Swift* (Oxford, 1954); and *Swift's Rhetorical Art* (New Haven, 1953).

[6] *Miscellanies in Prose and Verse* (London, 1727), I, 144, 157–158.

bound up with a changing view of the nature of man which in turn was associated with the impact of the new scientific movement on Western thought. To an artist of the early eighteenth century, even an artist-priest like Swift, the causes of this nominal Christianity remained obscure though certain effects became increasingly clear. Benevolism, for example, the view that man is essentially good, or at least not inherently disposed to evil, began to find skillful proponents in increasing numbers during the seventeenth and early eighteenth centuries, though its roots in the Christian tradition were at least as old as the Pelagian heresy of the fourth century. So-called deists and free-thinkers like Toland and Wollaston, latitudinarian preachers within the Establishment, the Cambridge Platonists of Emmanuel College—Lemuel Gulliver's alma mater—all tended to emphasize the reasonable, the virtuous qualities of mankind and to avoid that line of the Christian tradition generally called Augustinian which reminded one of his ultimate ancestor old Adam, the man of clay. One of the most effective spokesmen for the enlightened view of man, if we may judge by his total influence in England and Europe generally, was the third Earl of Shaftesbury, who in his *Characteristicks* (1711) described man as essentially virtuous and the universe harmonious. Man's benevolence is sacramental, so to speak: it is an outward and visible sign of his graceful harmony [23] with society. To this tendency Swift, in his sermons as well as in his writings generally, was unalterably opposed. "By nature," cry those who view the Dean as a brooding pessimist. Perhaps, but it should be reiterated that his opposition to the new view of man was firmly rooted in orthodox Christian doctrine, as his sermons testify.

Gulliver himself, as we see him in the first three voyages, is no Christian. Indeed, his world is a world without religion. "Scattered Notions about a superior Power" simply never enter his mind. He is an educated man, a surgeon of Queen Anne's England, perhaps a Dissenter (so his father's sending him to Emmanuel College may indicate), a contemporary of that other celebrated English traveler Robinson Crusoe. But in a crisis the two men react very differently and the difference is significant. Crusoe, storm-beset in an open boat, approaches almost certain death on the rocks with his companions. "However," Crusoe qualifies in his ingratiating way, "we committed our souls to God in the most earnest manner. . . ." Gulliver, snatched up in his box by a Brobdingnagian eagle, then dropped in the sea, bestows no such gifts on Divinity. His reaction is simply that of a caged animal: he is trapped and drowning; he wishes he were not.

> I was not able to lift up the Roof of my Closet, which otherwise I certainly should have done, and sat on the Top of it, where I might at least preserve myself from being shut up, as I may call it, in the Hold. Or, if I escaped these Dangers for a Day or two, what could I expect but a miserable Death of Cold and Hunger! I was four Hours under these Circumstances, expecting and indeed wishing every Moment to be my last.

But Gulliver is not only an *anima naturaliter pagana* by temperament; his eyes literally do not see the outward manifestations of religion. Crusoe busies himself with Friday's creed and Friday's [24] God, but there is no need in Gulliver's world for the latter hypothesis. The countries he visits, Lilliput, partially Utopian Brobdingnag, and the others, apparently have few or no churches or churchmen. The fact does not seem to Gulliver odd. His own religion the Lilliputians deduce from his watch, which, the investigating committee reports, "we conjecture . . . is either some unknown Animal, or the God that he worships: But we are more inclined to the latter Opinion, because he assured us . . . that he seldom did any Thing without consulting it." Exactly, for Gulliver of the first three books is kin to Swift's earlier narrators in *A Tale of a Tub* and *An Argument*: a worshiper of time (recall the *Tale's* "Dedication to Prince Posterity"), of the contemporary, curious, given to "scientific" computations, proud of modern England and generally self-satisfied. He is symbolically Swift's modern man, ignorant of tradition, both literary and religious, but hopeful and confident, benevolent and reasonable, naturally generous, naturally unreflective, "a Person," as Gulliver is characterized (Part III, ch. iv) "of much Curiosity and easy Belief. . . ." A potential Shaftesburian, in harmony with the universe.

The universe is at first cooperative. In Lilliput Gulliver can observe the follies of the little people without taking thought of his own or those of his England. The King of Brobdingnag, however, reveals some of the realities of human nature and European civilization to the traveller, who is staggered but unconvinced. "Yet thus much I may be allowed to say in my own Vindication," Gulliver comments after his memorable interview with the King; "that I artfully eluded many of his Questions; and gave to every Point a more favourable turn by many Degrees than the strictness of Truth would allow. . . . I would hide the Frailties and Deformities of my Political Mother, and place her Virtues and Beauties in the most advantageous Light."

In the Third Voyage Gulliver sees many of his specific, personal ideals shattered: the mathematical Laputians are so [25] entwined in their calculations that they are blind to their wives' infidelities; the Academy of Projectors in Lagado performs experiments curiously like those of the Royal Society in Gulliver's England. "The only Inconvenience is, that none of these Projects are yet brought to Perfection; and in the mean time, the whole Country lies miserably waste, the Houses in Ruins, and the People without Food or Cloaths." This is especially discouraging for the explorer, who admits "I had my self been a Sort of Projector in my younger Days." Most disheartening of all, perhaps, are the Struldbruggs of Luggnugg, who have found immortality but not happiness. Gulliver, whose watch was his oracle, had assumed that unlimited time guaranteed unlimited happiness. But the Struldbruggs—

They were the most mortifying Sight I ever beheld; and the Women more horrible than the Men. Besides the usual Deformities in extreme old Age, they acquired an additional Ghastliness in Proportion to their Number of Years, which is not to be described. . . . The Reader will easily believe, that from what I had heard and seen, my keen Appetite for Perpetuity of Life was much abated.

By the end of the Third Voyage, then, Gulliver's self-assurance has received stern treatment. The mathematician so proud of his computations in Lilliput has seen pure mathematics in action, in Laputa; the experimental scientist eager to dissect a Brobdingnagian louse has watched the Academy of Projectors at work; the worshiper of time has looked on the Struldbruggs, possessors of an infinite amount.[7] It was enough to shake the confidence of the stablest new man.

Moreover, the civilized European (as Professor Case has reminded us) appears increasingly hostile. Abandoned by cowardly shipmates in Brobdingnag, set adrift by pirates to Laputa, [26] Gulliver is at the beginning of the Fourth Voyage betrayed and put ashore by his own crew, mutineers. Despite his optimism and innate generosity, Gulliver has been compelled to scrutinize human nature and the products of human ingenuity.

But life, or Swift, has a final irony reserved for the benevolent

[7] For a more detailed discussion of the unity of the Third Voyage, see John H. Sutherland, "A Reconsideration of Gulliver's Third Voyage," *Studies in Philology*, LIV (1957), 45–52.

Gulliver. The land in which he finds himself is, he discovers, inhabited by beasts of singularly disgusting mien. "Upon the whole, I never beheld in all my Travels so disagreeable an Animal, or one against which I naturally conceived so strong an Antipathy." Later, among the Houyhnhnms, the rational horses who rule the land, he learns that the odious creatures he has seen are called Yahoos, and, worst blow of all to the pride of the increasingly disillusioned Gulliver, that the horses regard him as a Yahoo, citing like characteristics: similar physique, similar coloring, even (he finds when a female Yahoo embraces him) similar appetites.

Had Gulliver attended church, whether Dissenting or Anglican, in England he might have been better prepared for the animality of the Yahoos, as Mr. Roland Frye has pointed out. The very imagery Swift uses to describe the appearance of the beasts is drawn from, or at least paralleled by that of, seventeenth and eighteenth-century sermons, in which the preachers describe sinful man. Anthony Burgess, Dissenting minister and Fellow of Emmanuel College, had written in *The Doctrine of Original Sin* (1659):

Thus man is abominable and loathsome in the eyes of God, and he ought to be so in his own eyes, to his own self, a natural man should not be able to bear or endure himself, because of that loathsome sinfulness that doth adhere to him: how much are *Pelagian*-Doctrines that cry up a purity in mans nature, contrary to this Text?

Peter Browne, Bishop of Cork and Ross while Swift was Dean of St. Patrick's, and sometime Provost of Trinity College, Dublin, [27] averred that "the holiest person in the world is all over leprous, filthy and abominable in the sight of God, till he is washed in the blood of the lamb. . . ." [8]

What staggers Gulliver, then, and what he is unable ultimately to accept is simply the concept of man as beast, as *animal capax rationis*. He has been unwilling in Lilliput to associate the pettiness of the little people with his own pettiness; unwilling to adduce from the irrational activities of the projectors or the mathematical absurdities of the Laputians a criticism of projecting, mathematical England. In Houyhnhnmland he is forced to acknowledge as true what has been a nagging suspicion: that man, for all his pride of knowledge and

---

[8] Burgess, p. 439; Browne, as quoted in Roland M. Frye, "Swift's Yahoo and the Christian Symbols for Sin," *Journal of the History of Ideas*, XV (1954), 213. I am much indebted to Mr. Frye's penetrating article.

conquest, is, in some aspects, very like an animal. This commonplace, or platitude, of Western thought between the time of the Psalmist and the seventeenth century has somehow eluded Gulliver's attention. He is unable to face the paradox of man's duality; he attempts to escape it. The horses offer what is apparently a solution. Their conduct is regulated by reason, they are mildly benevolent and moderately friendly but otherwise without emotions. Marriage is a convenience for continuing the race, death involves losing a companion for whom while alive one didn't have overmuch affection. "[T]he married Pair pass their Lives with the same Friendship, and mutual Benevolence that they bear to all others of the same Species, who come in their Way. . . ." *Eros* and *agape* are replaced in Houyhnhnmland by a vague *philia*.

Here Gulliver finds what he has subconsciously sought: the veritable Garden of Eden of a new, an enlightened religion. Here is a country without the superstitions of the sects, with a universal standard of benevolence, a country governed by reason. The horses live for the most part by the principles of Shaftesbury, or, as Mr. Irvin Ehrenpreis has recently suggested, perhaps those of Swift's deist friend Viscount Bolingbroke, with whom [28] Swift was corresponding during the probable period of the *Travels'* composition.[9] Shaftesbury, who was of course vastly better known as a philosopher than Bolingbroke, had held in *An Inquiry concerning Virtue:*

We have found, that to deserve the name of *good* or *virtuous*, a Creature must have all his Inclinations and Affections, his Dispositions of Mind and Temper, sutable, and agreeing with the Good of his *Kind*, or of that *System* in which he is included. . . . To stand thus well affected, and to have one's Affections *right* and *intire*, not only in respect of one's self, but of Society and the Publick: This is *Rectitude, Integrity*, or *Virtue*.

"Must have all his Inclinations and Affections." This surely describes the Houyhnhnms, exemplars of what Swift might call deist rectitude in a deist Garden of Eden.[10] The Eden image is specifically reinforced by Swift in the account of the Yahoos' coming. "He took

[9] Irvin Ehrenpreis, "The Origins of *Gulliver's Travels*," *Publications of the Modern Language Association of America*, LXXII (1957.), 880–899.

[10] Treatise IV of the *Characteristicks*. Version quoted in 1727 ed., II, 77. It would of course be imprecise for us to label Shaftesbury a deist. See A. O. Aldridge, *Shaftesbury and the Deist Manifesto* (Philadelphia, 1951). But Swift used the terms "deist" and "free-thinker" rather loosely, and there are indications that he had Shaftesbury in mind when he did so; see L. A. Landa, "Introduction to the Sermons," in *Irish Tracts*, pp. 114–115.

Notice of a general Tradition, that *Yahoos* had not been always in their Country: But, that many Ages ago, two of these Brutes appeared together upon a Mountain; whether produced by the Heat of the Sun upon corrupted Mud and Slime, or from the Ooze and Froth of the Sea, was never known." The reminiscence is, of course, not only of the Judeao-Christian account but also of a classical creation myth, the Deucalion and Pyrrha story.

The horses had fenced in and controlled the Yahoos, so the presence of the new Yahoo Gulliver at large in their garden is as surprising to them as the loquacious serpent was to Eve; [29] moreover they find his human dualism menacing, unbearable. Gulliver's master is in fact suspected of un-Houyhnhnm activities:

In the last general Assembly, when the Affair of the *Yahoos* was entered upon, the Representatives had taken Offence at his keeping a *Yahoo* (meaning my self) in his Family more like a *Houyhnhnm* than a Brute Animal. That, he was known frequently to converse with me, as if he could receive some Advantage or Pleasure in my Company: That, such a Practice was not agreeable to Reason or Nature, or a thing ever heard of before among them. The Assembly did therefore *exhort* him, either to employ me like the rest of my Species, or command me to swim back to the Place from whence I came.

Gulliver is thus exiled from his happy rural seat. As he departs, the new convert to the reasonable religion takes leave of his master in a ludicrously comic parody of the Catholic Christian kissing the ring of a bishop or pope.

I took a second Leave of my Master: But as I was going to prostrate myself to kiss his Hoof, he did me the Honour to raise it gently to my Mouth. I am not ignorant how much I have been censured for mentioning this last Particular. Detractors are pleased to think it improbable, that so illustrious a Person should descend to give so great a Mark of Distinction to a Creature so inferior as I.

Gulliver is a convert and he returns to the world with the marks of his conversion: a desire to impart his new-found religion to others, a disgust for those who fail to accept his faith as gospel and, indeed, for those who savor in any respect of Yahooness. The class is large: it includes the human race.

The friendly Portuguese who rescues Gulliver, Pedro de Mendez, exercises Christian charity which Gulliver is almost incapable of recognizing, so thoroughly is his mind saturated with the image of the good horse. "In Gratitude to the Captain," he [30] relates, "I sometimes sate with him at his earnest Request, and strove to conceal my Antipathy against human Kind, although it often broke out; which he suffered to pass without Observation." So, too, the sight of his family fills Gulliver "with Hatred, Disgust and Contempt . . ." but they also return good for evil and at last win his grudging acceptance. "I BEGAN last week to permit my Wife to sit at Dinner with me, at the farthest End of a long Table; and to answer (but with the utmost Brevity) the few Questions I asked her. Yet the Smell of a *Yahoo* continuing very offensive, I always keep my Nose well stopt with Rue, Lavender, or Tobacco-Leaves." Gulliver is still unable to bear the mortal stench; he reacts violently to those manifestations of pride which he had once accepted without objection: "[W]hen I behold a Lump of Deformity, and Diseases both in Body and Mind, smitten with *Pride*, it immediately breaks all the Measures of my Patience. . . ." This is what the gullible Gulliver did not learn in Emmanuel College, the paradox familiar to the Psalmist who found man "a little lower than the angels" yet, in the sight of God, "altogether become filthy; there is none that doeth good, no, not one."

Gulliver is not content with merely practicing his new-found faith; he must convert others. Swift wryly observed in his sermon "On the Testimony of Conscience" that "it is certain, that Men who profess to have no Religion, are full as zealous to bring over Proselytes as any Papist or Fanatick can be." [11] Gulliver finds the task more difficult than he had anticipated, "for," as he remarks in a letter to his "publisher," "instead of seeing a full Stop put to all Abuses and Corruptions [note the use of terms commonly applied in the eighteenth century to religion], at least in this Little Island, as I had Reason to expect: Behold, after above six Months Warning, I cannot learn that my Book hath produced one single Effect according to mine Intentions. . . ." Gulliver has, of course, fallen victim himself, like others shot through [31] with Yahooness, to the very sin of pride which he reprehends so severely in his fellow humans. His religion, the religion of the Deists, which was so effective and desirable in Houyhnhnmland where the Yahoos were fenced in will simply not work in this naughty world. It is, Swift ironically implies, an in-human faith. As

[11] *Irish Tracts*, p. 157.

if to strengthen the point, Swift puts in the mouth of the previously unliterary Gulliver a quotation from the *Aeneid*. He imposed on himself, Gulliver writes in the final chapter, "as a Maxim, never to be swerved from, that I would *strictly adhere to Truth*. . . ."

> —Nec si miserum Fortuna Sinonem
> Finxit, vanum etiam, mendacemque improba finget.

"Nor, if Fortune has made Sinon unhappy, would wicked Fortune make me also false and deceitful." The words, of course, are Sinon's to the Trojans; the plea of literature's most famous liar, fashioned to place within the walls of Troy, the horse.

The quotation is in a sense a final symbol. A symbol of Gulliver's pride, the pride of a modern man condescending to quote or misquote from the ancient writers who meant so little to him. Of the gullibility of Gulliver and of his readers. And of the perilous new religion, Swift implies, the religion of reason and nature, so tempting to rational and rationalistic moderns but so deficient, Swift must have felt, as an analysis of the human condition. Skillfully constructed, beguiling; hollow, false. A Trojan horse—the Houyhnhnm. "*Reason*," Swift once said in a sermon,

> itself is true and just, but the *Reason* of every particular Man is weak and wavering, perpetually swayed and turned by his Interests, his Passions, and his Vices. Let any Man but consider, when he hath a Controversy with another, although his Cause be ever so unjust, although the World be against him, how blinded he is by the Love of himself, [32] to believe that Right is Wrong, and Wrong is Right, when it maketh for his own Advantage. Where is then the right Use of his Reason, which he so much boasteth of, and which he would blasphemously set up to controul the Commands of the Almighty? [12]

I am far from asserting that this essay does more than suggest another way, though I believe a legitimate one, of viewing Swift's protagonist; *Gulliver's Travels* is after all a chef d'oeuvre whose margin fades as we move. Yet respect for one's readers demands some answer to at least one question: Why did Swift not make all this clear? It was permissible for him to allow the horses to deceive Gulliver, but why should he hoodwink us? Why did he not raise signposts as Bunyan did? Many possible answers suggest themselves: the matter of literary tact, Swift's ingrained love for a hoax, his

---

[12] "On the Trinity," in *Irish Tracts*, p. 166.

changing literary audience (*i.e.*, one in which Swift's religious views were decreasingly acceptable). But perhaps the best answer for the present is that, better than many of his time, Swift realized the potency of art. "I have been better entertained," he wrote in *A Letter to a Young Gentleman, Lately entered into Holy Orders,* "and more informed by a Chapter in the *Pilgrim's Progress,* than by a long Discourse upon the *Will* and the *Intellect,* and *simple* or *complex Ideas.*" Lemuel Gulliver, eighteenth-century pilgrim, has alway entertained. His creator intended that he likewise inform. [33]

Swift and the Passions

CHARLES PEAKE

The general ideas or assumptions about mankind which underlie a satirist's criticisms of human behaviour are easily misunderstood. It is in the nature of satire to concern itself with the abuses, defects and excesses of the human faculties and passions rather than with their more acceptable manifestations, and the most remarkable and memorable passages in a satire tend to be those in which faults are most vigorously and uncompromisingly attacked. But these characteristics of the form are often mistaken for characteristics of the author's mind; because the satirist may say nothing good of some aspect of human nature or behaviour, the reader is apt to assume he has nothing good to say of it. This tendency to attribute to the satirist extreme or exaggerated views is reinforced by the predisposition of many readers to think of satirists as extremists or eccentrics—a predisposition which helps to make the personal applications of the satire more tolerable and more easily ignored.

Most English satirists have suffered in some degree from this kind of treatment, but perhaps none more than Swift, on whom a great variety of extreme opinions and psychological disorders have been foisted with little or no warrant. No one doubts that Swift was an extraordinary man, but it does not follow that all his opinions were extraordinary or eccentric. On the contrary, there is surprisingly little in the view of mankind presented in his writings which can justly be labelled eccentric. Such eccentricity as there is resides for the most part in the peculiar force and violence with which he presents his ideas rather than in the ideas themselves.

Reprinted from *Modern Language Review*, LV (April 1960), 169–180. By permission. Footnotes have been renumbered for this reprinting.

Here I am concerned with only one of the many extravagancies attributed to Swift—his supposed hatred of the human passions. I shall refer to the exposition of this idea in Professor Ricardo Quintana's *The Mind and Art of Jonathan Swift,** because his book remains the most widely-read general work on Swift, and therefore has played and continues to play an important part in the propagation of a misconception which distorts Swift's views about mankind and leads to serious misinterpretation of his most important satirical work.

Professor Quintana says that Swift was influenced by the neo-stoical beliefs that

the passions are utterly reprehensible; reason must and can govern; the life which is proper to man is a life of unimpassioned reason.

(I hope to show that of these three statements only the middle one would have been acceptable to Swift, and even that is vitiated by the implication it derives from its context—that the reason's government consists of the suppression and final elimination of the passions which it is supposed to govern.) Swift, it is said, carried these ideas, with a harshness peculiar to himself, to the point where he thought that

passions could only be evil, virtue only the conquest of the lower self through rational restraint.

Professor Quintana admits as an exception to the general rule that in *Thoughts on* [169] *Religion* Swift allowed the right of the passions to prevail over reason in two important respects—the propagation of the species and the love of life.

If it be true that Swift had a peculiarly extreme hatred of the passions, then this hatred must be taken into account in interpreting Gulliver's fourth voyage; but it must first be asked whether the whole theory is not primarily based on a misunderstanding of that voyage. Perhaps the best and simplest way to test the theory is to compare it with Swift's many explicit observations about the nature and function of the human passions.

That Swift's way of thinking about life was to some extent influenced by neo-stoicism is very likely; it is equally likely that he was influenced by the neo-Epicureans. Both labels were invented because they seemed to characterise roughly two important currents of ideas

* Oxford, 1936, pp. 59 ff. (reprinted London, 1953).

of the seventeenth century. All educated men would have been influenced by them in some way. But in neither case would Swift have acknowledged his indebtedness willingly. His criticisms of Epicurus and his seventeenth-century followers are beside the point here; but it is interesting to notice his opinion of that view of the passions which he is supposed to have held with peculiar harshness:

The Stoical Scheme of supplying our Wants, by lopping off our Desires; is like cutting off our Feet when we want Shoes.[1]

It is the nature of Swift's criticism of the Stoics which is particularly significant; many years later in A Sermon upon the Excellency of Christianity, in Opposition to Heathen Philosophy he attacked them on similar grounds.[2] In his opinion the Stoics did not face the facts of human nature. Passions, and such special forms of the passions as desires, were fundamental to mankind, and to suppose that men could lop them off and live 'a life of unimpassioned reason' was absurd.

Even if he had thought it possible, it is very unlikely that Swift would have regarded the elimination of the human passions as desirable (though he would have seen little point in discussions of the desirability of the impossible). He believed that passions were implanted in man for a divine purpose; they supplied the motive power of all human action, and consequently, although they might be perverted into evil courses, their proper function was to lead man to piety and virtue.

Like Pope, Swift believed that all the human passions could be seen as 'Modes of Self-love',[3] and that it was impossible to call self-love good or bad since all good came from the proper control of this great passion by reason and all bad from an improper relationship between them.

The motives of the best actions will not bear too strict an enquiry. It is allowed, that the cause of most actions, good or bad, may be resolved into the love of ourselves; but the self-love of some men, inclines them to please others; and the self-love of others is wholly employed in pleasing themselves. This makes the great distinction between virtue and vice. Religion is the best motive of all actions, yet religion is allowed to be the highest instance of self-love.[4]

[1] Prose Writings of Jonathan Swift, ed. Herbert Davis (1939 ff.), I, 244. For writings not yet included in this edition, references are to The Prose Works of Jonathan Swift, ed. Temple Scott (1897–1908).
[2] Prose Writings, IX, 244.   [3] Essay on Man, II, 93; and see ll. 53 ff.
[4] Prose Works, I, 278.

The significance of the last sentence is made clear in the sermon referred to above. One of the chief defects of the old philosophies, Swift said, was that they offered [170] no reward for virtue which would appeal to the better part of man. Human nature was such as never to pursue heartily any course, without hope of reward, and no reward could be a greater inducement to virtue than the incorruptible crown offered by Christianity. Those philosophers who said virtue was its own reward were advancing an idea too 'abstracted' to be 'an universal influencing principle'.[5]

It is perhaps already clear that the suggestion that Swift regarded the passions as 'utterly reprehensible' or 'evil' is very wide of the mark. To adapt Swift's own image, one might as well pass moral judgements on one's feet. The passions were what carried a man through life: whether they carried him along the straight and narrow path or into the mire of sin depended on his control and direction of them.

The control and direction of the passions was the duty of the reason, and virtue was the result of the proper performance of that duty (not 'the conquest of the lower self').[6] Evil passions were not passions intrinsically bad, but passions which were not properly controlled and directed. The poem *To Stella Who Collected and Transcribed his Poems* illustrates the whole conception:

> Yet when I find your Passions rise,
> And Anger sparkling in your Eyes,
> I grieve those Spirits should be spent,
> For nobler Ends by Nature meant.
> One Passion, with a diff'rent Turn,
> Makes Wit inflame, or Anger burn;
> So the Sun's Heat, with different Powers,
> Ripens the Grape, the Liquor sours.[7]

So far was Swift from thinking that the passions were necessarily evil, that he says they are designed for noble ends; but such ends were attained only when the passions were moderated and guided by the reason.

---

[5] *Prose Writings*, ix, 244.

[6] Cf. 'Fear and Hope are the two greatest natural Motives of all Men's Actions: But, neither of these Passions will ever put us in the Way of Virtue, unless they be directed by Conscience' (*Prose Writings*, ix, 155). Fear and hope are two obvious subdivisions of self-love, and to Swift conscience was self-knowledge, a function of the reason. See the rest of the sermon quoted in this note ('On the Testimony of Conscience'), *Prose Writings*, ix, 150 ff.

[7] *The Poems of Jonathan Swift*, ed. Harold Williams (Oxford, 1937), ii, 731.

As Professor Quintana has observed, Swift appears to make two exceptions to this rule of reason:

Although reason were intended by providence to govern our passions, yet it seems that, in two points of the greatest moment to the being and continuance of the world, God hath intended our passions to prevail over reason. The first is, the propagation of our species, since no wise man ever married from the dictates of reason. The other is, the love of life, which, from the dictates of reason, every man would despise, and wish it at an end, or that it never had a beginning.[8]

It seems unlikely that Swift intended this passage to present seriously his view of the providential relationship between passions and reason. The supposition concerning God's plan seems primarily an ironic device to emphasize the universality of two kinds of human folly. That Swift was not in fact admitting exceptions to the government of reason is confirmed by the *Letter to a Very Young Lady,* where he congratulates the lady on having made

a Match of Prudence, and common Good-liking, without any Mixture of that ridiculous Passion which hath no Being, but in Play-Books and Romances.[9] [171]

Although sexual love and love of life were two of the chief threats to the rule of reason, Swift did not believe that they need overcome the reason or that it was part of God's plan that they should do so. The exceptions are merely apparent, not real.

But although it was the prime function of the reason 'to govern our passions', every man's mind was fallible and swayed by the passions which it was its duty to control. The Houyhnhnms, whose reason was 'not mingled, obscured, or discoloured by Passion and Interest', might assert that '*Reason* alone is sufficient to govern a *Rational* Creature', but theirs was not the condition of humanity.[10] Man was not a rational creature, but only *rationis capax,* and his reason could never be an infallible guide:

Reason itself is true and just, but the *Reason* of every particular Man is weak and wavering, perpetually swayed and turned by his Interests, his Passions, and his Vices.[11]

I do not wish to digress into a discussion of Swift's views concerning the infallibility of abstract Reason (within its proper limits) and

[8] *Prose Writings,* IX, 263.   [9] Ibid. IX, 89.
[10] *Prose Writings,* XI, 251 and 243.   [11] Ibid. IX, 166.

the fallibility of the reason 'of every particular man', but it is important to notice the distinction, because, whatever might be true of the Houyhnhnms, Swift did not believe that a man's unaided reason was alone sufficient to govern his passions. This is made quite clear in a passage in *The Publick Spirit of the Whigs,* where Swift is commenting on some of Steele's general observations:

In the Fourth, he affirms, That *Men's Beings are degraded when their Passions are no longer governed by the Dictates of their own Mind;* directly contrary to the Lessons of all Moralists and Legislators; who agree unanimously, that the Passions of Men must be under the Government of Reason and Law; neither are Laws of any other Use than to correct the Irregularity of our Affections.[12]

A man's passions had to be controlled not only by his own reason, which was influenced by the forces it should govern, but also by the common consent of the Reason of all mankind, by the human laws which expressed that general Reason, and by the laws laid down by divine wisdom in the Scriptures.

Swift sometimes seems to emphasize the reason's duty to moderate the passions rather than its duty to direct them, but the distinction is not practically important; violent passions could not easily be directed into virtuous courses, and, on the other hand, passions not given their proper outlet were likely to burst out in uncontrolled pursuit of some easy satisfaction. To say of a man that he was in 'Judgment weak, and Passion strong' [13] was almost equivalent to saying that he was moved by evil passions; the same association of strong passions and evil ends may explain why Swift thought it natural to mankind 'to be more *violent in an ill Cause* than a good one'.[14]

Among the perversions of the passions which were particularly liable to get out of hand, Swift mentions avarice, lust and ambition, which most frequently run to wild extremes; political prejudice, which casts a blindness over the understanding; and romantic love, which 'darkens Reason's light'.[15] I have already quoted from Swift's attack on this last 'ridiculous Passion' in the *Letter to a Very Young Lady,* but it is important to notice that he was warning the young lady not against [172] the passion of love, but against the affectations

---

[12] Ibid. viii, 46–7.   [13] *Poems,* iii, 800.   [14] *Prose Writings,* vi, 78.
[15] Ibid. iii, 80–1, and iii, 35; and *Poems,* ii, 402. (The verse is of doubtful authority, but the general idea is common enough in Swift's writings.)

of 'romantic love'—which in his opinion was not a genuine passion at
all but the invention of the authors of 'Play-Books and Romances':

Conceal your Esteem and Love in your own Breast, and reserve your
kind Looks and Language for private Hours; which are so many in the
Four and Twenty, that they will afford Time to employ a Passion as exalted
as any that was ever described in a *French* Romance.[16]

It was not the exalted passion of love but the public display of that
passion which Swift was condemning.

He was always especially critical of such displays of passion or
emotion. There may well have been some psychological reason for
this; but Swift could have argued that the unrestrained expression
of passion in public meant either that the passion had broken free
from the restraints of reason or that the expression of it was exaggerated and insincere. He was very ready to suspect the latter. When
Lady Ashburnham died, he wrote to Stella,

She was my greatest favourite, and I am in excessive concern for her loss.

But just over a week later, when her mother and sister, who were
meeting for the first time since her death, cried together, Swift was
impatient:

There is something of farce in all these mournings, let them be ever so
serious. People will pretend to grieve more than they really do, and that
takes off from their true grief.[17]

This is a harsh comment, but the harshness is directed against the
public (and perhaps affected) expression of grief, not against the
grief itself, which Swift shared. He did not ask for complete impassivity, but for restraint such as was displayed by the Duke of
Ormonde, the dead lady's father:

He bore up as well as he could, but something falling accidentally in
discourse, the tears were just falling out of his eyes, and I looked off to
give him an opportunity (which he took) of wiping them with his handkerchief. I never saw any thing so moving, nor such a mixture of greatness
of mind, and tenderness, and discretion.[18]

Similar restraint and discretion were required by Swift of the
writer or speaker in their appeals to the emotions of their audiences.
The lengthy warning to the young clergyman against 'the Art of
wetting the Handkerchiefs of a whole Congregation' [19] has sometimes

---

[16] *Prose Writings*, ix, 86.
[17] *Prose Works*, ii, 409–10 and 415.
[18] Ibid. ii, 411.
[19] *Prose Writings*, ix, 68 ff.

been taken as evidence of Swift's disapproval of all such appeals, but this is to ignore the specific purpose of Swift's letter of advice. In the first place, he is concerned only with the preaching of sermons; and, in the second, he is not writing an *Art of Preaching* but a commonsense guide for the ordinary clergyman who has no special gift for addressing public audiences.

Unlike the great orators of the past who had to sway an audience into reaching an immediate decision, the preacher had merely to direct 'Christian Men in the Conduct of their Lives', and his sermons would have a more lasting influence if they were directed at the reason rather than the passions. Much the same point is made in the sermon *Upon Sleeping in Church:*

Nor, lastly, are Preachers justly blamed for neglecting human Oratory to move the Passions, which is not the Business of a Christian Orator, whose Office it is only to work upon Faith and Reason. All other Eloquence hath been a perfect Cheat, to stir up [173] Men's Passions against Truth and Justice, for the Service of a Faction, to put false Colours upon Things, and by an Amusement of agreeable Words, make the worse Reason appear to be the better. This is certainly not to be allowed in Christian Eloquence.[20]

An earlier passage in the same sermon shows that Swift was not intending to assert that there were no proper uses for eloquence, but merely that its power had been abused, and that it could not be regarded as a necessary part of the clergyman's equipment:

Wit and Eloquence are shining Qualities, that God hath imparted, in great Degrees, to very few, nor any more to be expected, in the Generality of any Rank among Men, than Riches and Honour.[21]

This leads to the second point, mentioned above, about the *Letter to a Young Clergyman*—that it was designed, not to make clergymen into great preachers, but to preserve them from making fools of themselves, to warn them 'against some Mistakes, which are obvious

---

[20] *Prose Writings*, IX, 214. Locke has a very similar passage: 'All the art of rhetoric, besides order and clearness, all the artificial and figurative application of words eloquence hath invented, are for nothing else but to insinuate wrong ideas, move the passions, and thereby mislead the judgment, and so, indeed, are perfect cheats; and, therefore, however laudable or allowable oratory may render them in harangues and popular addresses, they are certainly, in all discourses that pretend to inform or instruct, wholly to be avoided' (*Essay Concerning Human Understanding*, Bk. III, ch. 10, xxxiv). The idea is, of course, a commonplace in the seventeenth-century discussions of pulpit oratory.

[21] *Prose Writings*, IX, 213.

to the Generality of Mankind'. Swift says that his chief objection to the 'moving Manner of Preaching, is the frequent Disappointment it meets with', and adds,

Nor is it a Wonder that this Expedient should so often miscarry, which requires so much Art and Genius to arrive at any Perfection in it.

That Swift should warn the novice against immoderate or ill-judged attempts to rouse the congregation is only what one might expect; every tutor gives the same advice. A reasoned sermon might at the worst be dull and unconvincing, but a rhetorical sermon might stir up irrational and therefore dangerous passions, or, if ineffective, might expose the clergyman, his office, and even Christian doctrine to ridicule.

Yet Swift recognized that there was a proper place for 'moving' oratory in the sermon, provided that the clergyman had the gift and employed it 'as seldom and with as much Caution' as possible. The section of the *Letter* dealing with this aspect of preaching concludes with a paragraph where Swift, as though conscious that his condemnation of inept and ill-considered attempts to move the passions of the congregation might be mistaken for an attack on all impassioned speech, makes his true position clear:

If your Arguments be strong, in God's Name offer them in as moving a Manner as the Nature of the Subject will properly admit; wherein Reason, and good Advice will be your safest Guides: But beware of letting the pathetick Part swallow up the rational: For, I suppose, *Philosophers* have long agreed, that Passion should never prevail over Reason.

In *Thoughts on Various Subjects,* where Swift is not specifically referring to preaching, the usefulness of restrained appeals to the passions is similarly recognized:

In a *Glass-House,* the Workmen often fling in a small Quantity of fresh Coals, which seems to disturb the Fire, but very much enlivens it. This may allude to a gentle stirring of the Passions, that the Mind may not languish.[22] [174]

Obviously the passions which might most profitably be stirred by the writer or orator were those forms of self-love which were the source of all virtuous action; and Swift strongly disapproved of any attempts to undermine their influence on man. The love of fame, for instance, had no rational basis, but Swift not only appealed to it

[22] Ibid. i, 242.

frequently, but also defended it against shortsighted rational criticism:

The humour of exploding many things under the name of trifles, fopperies, and only imaginary goods, is a very false proof either of wisdom or magnanimity, and a great check to virtuous actions. For instance, with regard to fame: there is in most people a reluctance and unwillingness to be forgotten. We observe even among the vulgar, how fond they are to have an inscription over their grave. It requires but little philosophy to discover and observe that there is no intrinsic value in all this: however, if it be founded in our nature, as an incitement to virtue, it ought not to be ridiculed.[23]

The implications of this passage are alone sufficient to refute the suggestion that Swift aspired to a life of unimpassioned reason. Love of fame was a human passion to which writers and orators had always appealed, and in doing so, it is implied here, they were not addressing themselves to man's lower self but to an instinct providentially designed as 'an incitement to virtue'. To ridicule the irrationality of such a passion was to run counter to the divine plan, and to employ the reason in matters beyond its scope.

Swift's belief that appeals to the passions could be justified only if they fulfilled two conditions—that they should be proper to the form and subject of discourse and that they should be supplementary to the appeal to reason—was by no means peculiar to him. It is often expressed in seventeenth-century discussions of preaching as well as in more general critical contexts, and seems to have been a commonplace in literary circles. For instance, in *The Tatler*, no. 66 (which has been attributed to Swift) the preaching of a certain Dean is praised on the grounds that 'he never attempts your passions till he has convinced your reason'; [24] and, in a letter to Swift, Bolingbroke criticized Seneca for his

impudent manner of talking to the passions, before he has gone about to convince the judgement, which Erasmus, if I remember right, objects to him.[25]

[23] *Prose Works*, I, 278. Cf. Delany's *Observations upon Lord Orrery's Remarks on the Life and Writings of Dr Jonathan Swift* (1754), p. 16: 'Swift well knew . . . that the love of praise is one of the noblest instincts, with which God has endowed the human heart: as being one great incitement to every valuable excellence.'
[24] *The Tatler*, ed. G. A. Aitken (1898), II, 120.
[25] *The Correspondence of Jonathan Swift*, ed. F. Elrington Ball (1910–14), III, 111.

Swift's general views about the nature and function of the passions were as much part of the common stock of his time as were his views concerning appeals to the passions. In *The Christian Hero* Steele had argued that Christianity, unlike Stoicism, required 'not an utter Extirpation, but the Direction only of our Passions', since the passions, especially the desire for fame or reputation, urged men on to virtuous behaviour; [26] and the second epistle of the *Essay on Man* contains a more coherent statement of the same theory of the passions which I have tried to build up piecemeal from Swift's writings.[27] This theory can be called 'stoic' only in the least technical sense of the term. Certainly Swift believed that a wise man would not be too easily moved and would, in any case, restrain the expression of [175] his emotions. Thus, in a letter to Pope describing the wretchedness of the Irish people, Swift apologized 'for being more moved than perhaps becomes a clergyman, and a piece of a philosopher'; [28] and he advised the young clergyman that study of the heathen philosophers would lessen his admiration and increase his fortitude.[29] He distinguished between true philosophic control of the emotions and mere impassivity or insensitivity: referring to the impeachment of Ormonde, he wrote,

Upon this Occasion, although I am sensible it is an old Precept of Wisdom to admire at nothing in human Life, yet I consider at the same Time how easily some Men arrive to the Practice of this Maxim by the Help of plain Stupidity or Ill nature, without any Strain of Philosophy, and although the uncertainty of human Things be one of the most obvious Reflections in Morality; yet, such unexpected, sudden, and signall Instances of it as have lately happened among us are so much out of the usuall Form, that a wise Man may perhaps be allowed to start and look aside as at a sudden and violent Clap of Thunder, which is much more frequent and more naturall.[30]

Although in these passages Swift recommends what are loosely called the stoic virtues and often, especially in his correspondence, uses variants of the term 'philosophy' to refer to the practice of them, he maintains in his sermon *Upon the Excellency of Christianity* that fortitude, temperance and patience were Christian rather than stoic virtues.[31] There is certainly no justification for believing that he was

[26] *Tracts and Pamphlets by Richard Steele*, ed. Rae Blanchard (Baltimore, 1944), p. 52.
[27] *Essay on Man*, II, 53 ff.   [28] *Correspondence*, IV, 90.
[29] *Prose Writings*, IX, 74.   [30] Ibid. VIII, 133–4.   [31] Ibid. IX, 249.

influenced to any special or peculiar extent by stoic doctrines, or that his supposed hatred of the passions can be attributed to the influence of neo-stoicism. It would be strange if one of the most passionate of writers and one of the most adept at rousing the passions of his readers should have conceived of the passions as 'utterly reprehensible' and of all appeals to them as addressed to man's lower self.

And yet, that this is a not uncommon view of Swift's position is shown by some of the suggested readings of Gulliver's fourth voyage. The interpretation of that voyage is complicated by the difficulty of distinguishing between Swift's conception of human nature and his criticism of human behaviour, between his opinions and his methods of expressing them in satire, and between the variety of satirical methods which he employs. The relationship of the imaginary races of Houyhnhnms and Yahoos to the human race is the critical crux.

If, like many critics in the past, we follow Gulliver in identifying the Yahoos with mankind, then they cease to be an imaginary species at all, and become instead men, in their raw state, as seen through the eyes of a mentally-deranged misanthrope. But this interpretation, as several critics have pointed out, conflicts with some of the most obvious facts of the narrative. The Houyhnhnms recognize the differences between Gulliver, an ordinary man, and the Yahoos; he is teachable, civil, and clean, and, above all, he has 'some Rudiments of Reason'.[32] Although Gulliver, on his return, confuses mankind, even his own family, with the Yahoos, yet he never from the beginning confused himself with them, and the contrast between the Yahoos and the magnanimous Portuguese sea-captain (whom Gulliver at first treats as a Yahoo) is too striking to be accidental. Gulliver's confusion of Yahoos and men must be taken as part of Swift's satirical technique: on the one hand it is part of the apparatus of verisimilitude—Gulliver had very similar difficulties in adjusting himself to his fellow-men and his family on his return from [176] Brobdingnag; and on the other hand it is a means of shocking the reader into attention and of presenting human vices as physically disgusting.

That the Houyhnhnms and Yahoos are allegorical creatures is now generally accepted, but remarkably diverse interpretations of their significance are offered.

The Houyhnhnms, it is agreed, represent reason or the life of reason, and until recently no one doubted that they were intended as

[32] Ibid. XI, 240.

Swift's picture of an ideal society, an ideal way of life. Working on this assumption, some critics praised the nobility of the conception, while others condemned Swift for advocating an existence so bloodless and antipathetic. Here, it is argued, is the life of unimpassioned reason exhibited in its purest form (the Houyhnhnms do not display even the universal passions of sexual love and love of life) and no one in his right mind could consider it a desirable condition for humanity.

But there seems to be no justification at all for supposing that the Houyhnhnms are Swift's picture of an ideal human society. The difference between Houyhnhnms and men is not merely a matter of behaviour; it is a fundamental difference of nature. The Houyhnhnms and the Yahoos stand on either side of the human psyche as Brobdingnagians and Lilliputians stand on either side of his physique. Gulliver was twelve times as big as the Lilliputians and the Brobdingnagians were twelve times as big as he. Swift carefully placed Gulliver in a similarly central position between the Houyhnhnms and the Yahoos: Gulliver's master reports to the Assembly,

That he observed in me all the Qualities of a *Yahoo*, only a little more civilized by some Tincture of Reason; which however was in a Degree as far inferior to the *Houyhnhnm* Race, as the *Yahoos* of their Country were to me.[33]

Swift did not condemn men for not behaving like Houyhnhnms any more than he condemned them for not being as big as the Brobdingnagians. The Houyhnhnm way of life is not offered as a model for human imitation: like the social system of Erewhon, it represents imaginatively a point of view from which human behaviour and human society can be profitably examined.

The counter-theories put forward by some recent defenders of Swift—that the description of the Houyhnhnms is intended as an ironical illustration of the deficiencies of the life of pure reason, or that the close of the book tries to show the foolishness and wretchedness of men who, like Gulliver, attempt to submit their lives wholly to the rule of reason—seem to me misguidedly ingenious and much less plausible than the theories they are designed to replace. Swift was far too good and conscientious a satirist to bury a vital part of his message so deep that over two hundred years should pass before it was disinterred. No common reader doubts that the Houyhnhnms

[33] *Prose Writings*, xi, 256.

are presented for his admiration as noble though inhuman creatures worthily called 'the Perfection of Nature'; [34] that the account of Gulliver's happiness among them is intended as a picture of the blessings of a simple and rational life; or that Gulliver, despite disappointments and difficulties of adjustment, is supposed by the author to have become a wiser and better man as a result of the teaching and example of the Houyhnhnms. And Swift's satire was directed to the ordinary man, the common reader, not to learned and ingenious critics. Whatever significance we may attach to the allegorical races, it must not run counter to the whole tenor of the voyage. The satirical function of the two races [177] has never been a source of difficulty for the ordinary reader; he understands that Swift is contrasting the life of civilized man with the life of a nobler order of beings and showing striking similarities between human behaviour and that of disgusting brutes, in order to present a terrible indictment of the way men live.

Apart from minor inconsistencies, to be found in all four voyages, difficulties arise only when critics attempt to define the precise significance of the allegorical creatures in order to relate them to Swift's fundamental assumptions and beliefs about human nature. The problem is to find definitions which emphasize those characteristics of the two races which are emphasized in the story, and which do not conflict irreconcilably with what Swift has written elsewhere.

Thus it is not enough to say that the Houyhnhnms represent the life of reason; the word 'reason' requires qualification because the reason of the Houyhnhnms is not like that of men. The reason of the Houyhnhnms is infallible, and so free from doubt that they have no word for opinion and cannot understand 'how a Point could be disputable'; [35] but 'the *Reason* of every particular Man is weak and wavering', not merely subject to doubts but even the cause of them.[36] The absence of passions and the infallibility of their reason distinguish the Houyhnhnms more surely from any conceivable human creatures than do any physical differences. Their way of life is not a representation of an ideal which might be attainable if men submitted to the rule of reason, but an attempt to translate into terms of behaviour the great abstraction, Ideal Reason, by its very nature 'true and just'. The Houyhnhnms do not exhibit even the desirable forms of the passions, because passions of any kind are incompatible with

[34] Ibid. xi, 219.   [35] *Prose Writings*, xi, 251.
[36] See 'Thoughts on Religion' (*Prose Writings*, ix, 262).

the abstraction they represent. Instead of the human motive power of the passions the Houyhnhnms 'are endowed by Nature with a general Disposition to all Virtues'.[37] Their life is, in fact, not so much a matter of unimpassioned reason, which suggests the presence of subdued and controlled passions, as a life of Reason in which passions never enter because they are excluded from the Houyhnhnms' allegorical constitution. It is absurd to complain of the absence of such qualities as love, or parental affection, or grief for the dead; and even more absurd to argue that the absence of these qualities indicates Swift's disapproval or hatred of them. If an author presents an allegorical figure of Justice, it cannot properly be objected that the personification does not exhibit Mercy—nor can it be maintained that the absence of mercy indicates that the author disapproved of that quality. The passionless life of the Houyhnhnms does not imply Swift's advocacy of a life of unimpassioned reason for men; though Gulliver's happiness amongst them may be intended to suggest how much richer and more satisfying human life could be in a society based on the principles of universal reason.

The passionless Houyhnhnms are contrasted with the bestial Yahoos, moved only by lust, greed, envy, fear, and the other perversions of the passions they share with humanity. The stock distinction between the reason and the passions suggests that, if the Houyhnhnms represent the life of Ideal Reason, the Yahoos probably represent the life of unadulterated passion. Then it can be argued that the vileness of the representation reflects Swift's hatred of the passions. But besides conflicting with what Swift says elsewhere of the passions, this interpretation ignores the fact [178] that the characteristic of the Yahoos most repeatedly emphasized is not that they have passions but that they have no reason. The Yahoo is not *rationis capax*, and therefore, as the Houyhnhnm points out, cannot be blamed for his 'odious Qualities'; he is the incarnation of Ideal Absence of Reason as the Houyhnhnm is the incarnation of Ideal Reason. To Swift the passions were morally neutral; no moral judgement could be passed on the behaviour of the Yahoos because they were devoid of reason. Mankind is condemned not for having passions, but for failing to use the capacity for reason to direct the passions, or rather for employing the reason to invent unnatural perversions of the passions.[38]

This interpretation of the fourth voyage is fully consistent with

[37] *Prose Writings*, XI, 251.   [38] *Prose Writings*, XI, 232.

Swift's views concerning human nature expressed elsewhere, with his claim that

> His Satyr points at no Defect,
> But what all Mortals may correct,[39]

and with the general purpose of *Gulliver's Travels*, which was, to borrow Hawkesworth's phrase, 'to mortify pride'.[40] The comparison with the Houyhnhnms humbles man's pride in his rationality by presenting a genuine *animal rationale;* the comparison with the Yahoos destroys man's pride in the use he has made of his capacity for reason. The target for Swift's satire is man's corrupted and corrupting reason, not his passions.

It might still perhaps be argued that the violence of Swift's attack on the perversions of the passions indicates that, whatever his theoretical opinions may have been, at a deeper level he had an intense aversion for the passions themselves. There may be an element of justice in this argument—an element expressed by Professor Sherburn in his suggestion that Swift's recognition of the turbulence of his own emotions was partly responsible for his insistence on the need for their restraint.[41] But there is no real discrepancy between Swift's acceptance of the stock theory of the nature and function of the passions and the violence of his attacks on certain manifestations of them. His belief that the passions were the force behind all human actions necessarily led him to find the cause of all vice and folly in perverted or misdirected passions; but it is the evil of the perversion, not of the passion itself, which occasions the violence of Swift's attacks.

Passions, emotions, affections, desires, spirits, instincts—Swift used all these terms to refer to the inner forces which moved mankind. (Generally he called the more powerful or the dominant forces in a man's nature 'passions', but, as the passage from the poem to Stella illustrates, the term is not confined to that meaning.) He believed that these forces were the ultimate source of all that was good and

[39] Poems, II, 571.

[40] *The Works of Jonathan Swift* (1768), note at end of volume II.

[41] 'Methods in Books about Swift' (*S.P.* xxxv (1938), 653–4). In this important article Professor Sherburn suggested that 'a thorough examination of all his casual utterances would probably reconcile Swift to the commonplace position that the passions are essential as stimuli to action—certainly self-love is regarded by him as such'; and added, 'On the other hand, he habitually abuses the emotional aspects of the mind, possibly in part because he knew himself their victim'.

all that was bad in human behaviour. Restraint was necessary, because when a man abandoned himself to his passions he was throwing away the specifically human faculty of the reason which was
designed to guide the passions to the noble ends for which God had
implanted them in man. But to suggest that Swift had an abnormal
hatred of the passions, considered them 'utterly reprehensible' or
[179] necessarily evil, or believed that 'the life which is proper to
man is a life of unimpassioned reason', is to ignore the greater part
of his observations on human nature and to impose a distorting and
unjustifiable interpretation upon his major satirical work.

N O T E

Since this article was accepted for publication several important discussions of some of the points raised in it have appeared. In particular, Kathleen Williams in her *Jonathan Swift and the Age of Compromise* (1958) has examined Swift's views on the passions, discussed
some of the same passages, and reached conclusions hardly different from mine. It would not have been possible to remove these
passages without disrupting my argument and as there are important
differences of emphasis and direction in the two discussions it seemed
to me that some overlapping on a matter so crucial to a proper understanding of Swift could do no harm. Moreover, in her interpretation of Gulliver's fourth voyage, Kathleen Williams argues on the
same lines as Irvin Ehrenpreis in *The Personality of Swift* (1958)
that the Houyhnhnms are to be seen ironically and that their depend-
ence on reason was connected by Swift with the Deists. For all the
ingenuity with which both critics maintain this interpretation, I
cannot help feeling that it credits Swift with excessive subtlety at
the expense of presenting him as a less effective satirist. Swift wrote
'to the Vulgar, more than to the Learned' and there needs to be very
good reasons for supposing that he concealed his satirical point not
only from the Vulgar but also from the Learned for more than two
centuries. For a refutation of Ehrenpreis's case see George Sherburn,
'Errors Concerning the Houyhnhnms' (*M.P.* LVI (1958), 92–7). [180]

APPENDICES

Summary of Parts I, II, and III of *Gulliver's Travels*

PART I: A VOYAGE TO LILLIPUT

Gulliver's Travels records the amazing adventures in unknown parts of the world that were experienced by a middle-class Englishman of the eighteenth century. Lemuel Gulliver of Nottinghamshire was sent by his father to Cambridge University for three years, but when the expense became too great, the boy became an apprentice to a well-known London surgeon for four years. During this time Gulliver used his allowance money to study in his free time the lore of the sea, for he yearned to become a traveller. Later he went to Leyden to study medicine and as soon as he was qualified took a position as a ship's surgeon. On his return from his first voyage he married and tried to settle down as a London physician, but he failed financially. He again tried his luck as a sea-going doctor, but his life remained unsuccessful and uneventful until he accepted a post on the *Antelope*, a ship heading for the South Seas.

The ship was wrecked in a violent storm near Van Diemen's land, and all on board perished except Gulliver, who swam to the shore of an uncharted island and then fell into a deep sleep from exhaustion. Upon waking, he discovered that someone had tied his arms, legs, body, and hair to the ground so that he could not move. His captors turned out to be little people under six inches tall. When he tried to pull himself loose, they stung him with hundreds of tiny poisoned arrows. He therefore gave up resisting and allowed the little people to carry him by means of a cart especially constructed for the purpose to their chief city. Here he was chained and guarded in an abandoned temple, into which he could barely crawl. He was visited by the Emperor of Lilliput, as the country was called, who very graciously gave orders that Gulliver should be well fed, clothed, and taught the language of the country.

Gulliver was fascinated to see that all objects and animals in the land were exactly proportioned to suit the diminutive size of the Lilliputians, and they were amazed at the immense size and strangeness of objects he carried with him, such as his snuffbox, comb, pistol, and watch. When the Lilliputians understood that they could trust Gulliver, he was given his freedom. He used his time by carefully studying the customs and ideas of the Lilliputians. He admired some of their laws, although he noted that they were not always carried out. One law was directed against those who falsely accuse someone else of a crime; if the accused one is found to be innocent, the accuser is put to an ignominious death. Their laws were more stringent against those who were guilty of fraud than those who steal, for the Lilliputians said that a person can usually protect his property, but an honest person is helpless against superior cunning. According to another law, good conduct was rewarded; anyone who could prove that he had not committed a crime for seventy-three moons was given a sum of money and a special title of honor.

The Lilliputians, however, usually proved to be as petty in behavior and thinking as they were in size. They competed for high positions in government by dancing on a tight rope, and they tried to win colored ribbons from their Emperor by jumping over or crawling under a stick he held out. They divided themselves into political parties, known as High Heels and Low Heels, on the basis of the height of the heels on their shoes. They bickered so violently over whether eggs should be broken on the big end or the little end that the defeated faction, the Big-Endians, were driven by the Little-Endians into exile on the neighboring island of Blefuscu.

When war broke out with the people of Blefuscu, Gulliver won the victory for the Lilliputians by swimming to Blefuscu and capturing the entire enemy fleet, but again the Lilliputians demonstrated their pettiness by demanding that the Blefuscudians be enslaved. When Gulliver refused to allow this, the Lilliputians, who were already tired of the great expense of supplying Gulliver's needs, turned against him and planned to blind him and cut off his food supply. The treasurer of the nation was one of Gulliver's worst enemies at court, not only because Gulliver was so expensive, but because the treasurer unjustly, and illogically, suspected Gulliver of having a romance with his six-inch high wife.

In disgust Gulliver left Lilliput for Blefuscu, where he was well received. Soon he found a boat that had been washed ashore, fixed it up, set sail, and was picked up at sea by a ship returning to England. After being home with his wife and children only two months, he felt the urge to travel again. Leaving his wife a good sum of money that he had inherited from an uncle, he went on board the *Adventure*, a merchant ship bound for Surat.

PART II: A VOYAGE TO BROBDINGNAG

During its voyage the *Adventure* was blown off course far to the east of the Molucca Islands. The captain sent Gulliver and a party of men ashore at an unknown land that they sighted to replenish the ship's water supply. Gulliver became separated from the others and then was startled to see them rowing frantically out to sea being chased by a giant. Gulliver hid in a farmer's field, in which the grain was at least forty feet high. He was caught by a farmer, who like all the adults of Brobdingnag was a giant about sixty feet tall, and taken home to the farmer's family. Here he had narrow escapes with the house cat and the baby of the family, who picked Gulliver up and put his head in his mouth.

The farmer's nine-year-old daughter, whom Gulliver called Glumdalclitch, took charge of Gulliver, protected him, and taught him the language of the Brobdingnagians. The farmer made much money exhibiting Gulliver as a freak throughout the country, but he was so eager to increase his fortune that he neglected Gulliver's health. When Gulliver appeared to be too frail to be useful to him any longer, the farmer sold him to the Queen of Brobdingnag, who wanted him as a pet. The Queen had Gulliver supplied with a box just the right size for his living quarters and completely outfitted with furnishings his size.

Although the Queen and Glumdalclitch, who stayed on to serve as Gulliver's nurse after he was sold, treated Gulliver with much kindness, he had many hardships and dangers at court. Flies, wasps, a dog, rats, a frog, and a monkey—all giant size—attacked him on different occasions. The Queen's dwarf, who had been picked on by others larger than he all his life, got even with the world by tormenting Gulliver in various ways, such as dropping him into a bowl of cream or wedging his legs into a marrow bone at the Queen's table.

The behavior of the farmer and the dwarf illustrates the grossness in personality of these physically gross Brobdingnagians. Gulliver experienced this grossness in other ways too. Because the Brobdingnagians were so much larger than he, he saw them as though he were looking through a microscope. He saw hideous sores and cancers on Brobdingnagians in a town square, as well as lice crawling over their bodies. He was horrified to witness a beheading of a criminal, for to him the spouting of blood was greatly magnified. The Queen's Maids of Honor teased him by undressing before him, but the coarseness of their skin, their enlarged blemishes, and their loose behavior only revolted him.

The King of Brobdingnag held discussions with Gulliver, during which Gulliver proudly described in detail the society, politics, religion, legal system, and international relations of England. But instead of being favorably impressed as Gulliver hoped he would be, the King pointed out many evils that had horrified him in Gulliver's account and concluded that Gulliver's people must be "the most pernicious race of little odious vermin that nature ever suffered to crawl upon the surface of the earth." Later Gulliver tried to please the King by offering to teach his people how to make gunpowder, but again the King reacted with revulsion.

While Gulliver was sitting in his portable box near the sea one day, a huge bird flew down and picked it up and dropped it far out in the water. Luckily, a passing ship spied the floating box, and Gulliver was saved and taken back to England. Back home he had difficulty at first getting used to normal-sized people. Instead of speaking in an ordinary voice, he yelled as he had been forced to do to make the Brobdingnagians hear him. He had trouble getting used to buildings and people being so small; he felt as he did when he was the giant in Lilliput. He angered people he passed on the road by telling them to get out of his way so that he would not trample them. When he finally began acting reasonably once more, his wife begged him not to go to sea again.

PART III: A VOYAGE TO LAPUTA, BALNIBARBI, GLUBBDUBDRIB, LUGGNAGG, AND JAPAN

In spite of his wife's protests, Gulliver allowed himself to be persuaded by the captain of the *Hope-well* to serve as ship's surgeon

on that vessel's voyage to the Far East. In the vicinity of Japan, the
ship was taken by pirates, and Gulliver was set adrift alone in a
canoe. Eventually he landed on the Island of Balnibarbi. He was
surprised to see another island about four miles and a half in diameter
and crowded with people flying over him. Responding to his pleas
to be allowed to come aboard, the people of the flying island of
Laputa let down a chair on a chain and drew him up.

He found most of the people of Laputa to be theoretical mathe-
maticians and musicians. The chief male citizens were so absorbed
in their speculations at all times that they hired servants to stay near
them with bladders full of pebbles on the ends of sticks with which
they struck the mouths and ears of the men when it was their turn
to speak or listen. These scientists despised practicality to such an
extent that their houses were misshapen from poor planning, and
everyone was clumsy. They had no imagination or inventiveness, and
they believed in astrology.

Their island flew by means of a large magnet suspended in the
center of the island; it was turned to repel the earth when the
Laputans desired to go up, and it was turned to attract the earth
when they wished to descend. The Laputans caused the island to
hover over cities on the island below to pick up taxes and supplies
by means of packthreads. When a city below was rebellious, the
King of Laputa had the flying island hover for a long time over that
city, shutting off the benefits of the sun and the rain.

Gulliver asked for and received permission to visit the city of
Lagado on the island below. In Lagado he found an Academy of
Projectors, where scientists experimented endlessly with new schemes
for improving conditions in the country. The country had formerly
been well kept up and productive, but now the land was fallow, and
the people, under the direction of the Projectors, were busily but
ineffectively trying to grow things. So far all the new ideas of the
Projectors had failed. When he visited the Academy, Gulliver saw
one scientist trying to extract sunbeams out of cucumbers, another
trying to reduce human excrement to its original food, another trying to use spiders for the production of silk, and another who was
trying to teach mathematics to students by having them swallow
wafers with solutions to problems written on them.

Gulliver then visited another island known as Glubbdubdrib, a
land peopled entirely by magicians. The Governor entertained Gulliver by calling up whatever spirits from the dead that Gulliver
wished to meet. The visiting ghosts included Alexander the Great,

Hannibal, Caesar, Pompey, Brutus, Homer, and Aristotle. Gulliver found these men admirable and then compared them with modern leaders and writers, finding the moderns much inferior to the ancients.

The land of Luggnagg was next on Gulliver's itinerary. He was chiefly interested here to see the Struldbruggs, who live forever. He imagined how wonderful it would be to have eternity in which to procure riches, study the arts, sciences, and history, and then use his unusual wisdom to educate the young. He was greatly disenchanted when he discovered that the Struldbruggs did not become rich, educated, and wise; they just became senile, peevish, morose, and dead to all natural affection. They found no joy in life, but simply vegetated. All other Luggnaggians despised them and thanked heaven that they were not condemned to hideous immortality. Gulliver's encounter with them reconciled him to the idea of death.

After this, Gulliver journeyed to Japan, stayed there briefly, took passage on a ship to Holland, then crossed to England where he rejoined his family.

Bibliography

The following list includes the works reprinted in this book and many other works that may be used for research papers on Part IV of *Gulliver's Travels*. Those writings that are most directly concerned with this subject are marked with an asterisk. The student should make a strong effort to consult those that are marked but not reprinted in this book.

BIBLIOGRAPHICAL

The works listed in this first section will guide the student to other works by and about Swift in addition to those found in this bibliography.

Cambridge Bibliography of English Literature, ed. F. W. Bateson, II, 581–596 (Cambridge, England: Cambridge University Press, 1940).

Cambridge Bibliography of English Literature, ed. George Watson, V (Supplement), 456–460 (Cambridge, England: Cambridge University Press, 1957).

*Clubb, Merrel D. "The Criticism of Gulliver's 'Voyage to the Houyhnhnms,' 1726–1914," *Stanford Studies in Language and Literature* (Stanford University, California, 1941), pp. 203–232.

Davis, Herbert. "Recent Studies of Swift: A Survey," *University of Toronto Quarterly*, VII (1938), 273–288.

Landa, Louis A. and Others. *English Literature, 1660–1800: A Bibliography of Modern Studies, 1926–1938*, Vol. I (Princeton, N.J.: Princeton University Press, 1950).

————. *English Literature, 1660–1800: A Bibliography of Modern Studies, 1939–1950*, Vol. II (Princeton, N.J.: Princeton University Press, 1952).

————. "English Literature, 1660–1800: A Current Bibliography," *Philological Quarterly*, Vols. XXX– (1951–). Each July issue continues the bibliography compiled in the two previously listed bibliographies by Landa and others.

Landa, Louis A. and J. E. Tobin. *Jonathan Swift: A List of Critical Studies Published from 1895 to 1945* (New York: Cosmopolitan Science and Art Service Co., 1945).

Teerink, H. *A Bibliography of the Writings in Prose and Verse of Jonathan Swift, D. D.* (The Hague: Martinus Nijhoff, 1937).

Tobin, J. E. *Eighteenth Century English Literature and Its Cultural Background: A Bibliography* (New York: Fordham University Press, 1939), pp. 161–167.

PRIMARY SOURCES (WORKS BY JONATHAN SWIFT)

The Collected Poems of Jonathan Swift, ed. Joseph Horrell (London: Routledge and Kegan Paul, Ltd., 1958).

The Correspondence of Jonathan Swift, D. D., ed. F. Elrington Ball. 6 vols. (London: G. Bell and Sons, Ltd., 1910–1914).

Gulliver's Travels, ed. Henry Morley (London: G. Routledge and Sons, 1890).

Gulliver's Travels: The Text of the First Edition, ed. Harold Williams (London: W. Clowes and Sons, 1927).

Gulliver's Travels, 1726, ed. Herbert Davis, introd. Harold Williams. *The Prose Works of Jonathan Swift,* Vol. XI (Oxford: Basil Blackwell and Mott, Ltd., 1941).

*Gulliver's Travels, introd. Jacques Barzun (New York: Crown Publishers, Inc., 1947).

*Gulliver's Travels, introd. Robert B. Heilman (New York: Modern Library, 1950).

Gulliver's Travels, introd. Peter Quennell (London: William Collins and Sons, Ltd., 1952).

Gulliver's Travels, introd. John F. Ross (New York: Rinehart and Company, Inc., 1953).

Gulliver's Travels, ed. and introd. Ricardo Quintana (New York: Modern Library College Editions, 1958).

Journal to Stella, ed. Harold Williams. 2 vols. (Oxford: Clarendon Press, 1948).

The Letters of Jonathan Swift to Charles Ford, ed. D. Nichol Smith (Oxford: Clarendon Press, 1935).

The Poems of Jonathan Swift, ed. Harold Williams. 3 vols. (Oxford: Clarendon Press, 1958. Second Edition).

The Prose Works of Jonathan Swift, ed. Herbert Davis (Oxford: Basil Blackwell and Mott, Ltd., 1939–   ).

The Prose Works of Jonathan Swift, ed. Temple Scott. 12 vols. (London: Bell, 1897–1908). ("Bibliography of the Writings of Jonathan Swift" found in XII, 113–196.)

Satires and Personal Writings, ed. W. A. Eddy (New York: Oxford University Press, 1932).

Swift On His Age: Selected Prose and Verse, ed. Colin J. Horne (New York: Barnes and Noble, Inc., 1953).

Vanessa and Her Correspondence with Jonathan Swift, ed. A. M. Freeman (London: Selwyn and Blount, 1921).

SECONDARY SOURCES

Articles

Ashley Montagu, M. F. "Tyson's *Orang-Outang Sive Homo Sylvestris* and *Gulliver's Travels,*" *PMLA,* LIX (1944), 84–89.

Baughan, D. E. "Swift's Source of Houyhnhnms Reconsidered," *ELH,* V (1938), 207–210.

Block, Edward A. "Lemuel Gulliver: Middle-Class Englishman," *Modern Language Notes,* LXVIII (1953), 474–477.

Bracher, Frederick. "The Maps in *Gulliver's Travels,*" *Huntington Library Quarterly,* VII (1944), 59–74.

————. "The Name Lemuel Gulliver," *Huntington Library Quarterly,* XII (1949), 409–413.

Brown, A. C. L. "*Gulliver's Travels* and an Irish Folk Tale," *Modern Language Notes,* XIX (1904), 45–46.

Brown, James. "Swift as Moralist," *Philological Quarterly,* XXXIII (1954), 368–387.

Colie, Rosalie L. "Gulliver, the Locke-Stillingfleet Controversy, and the Nature of Man," *History of Ideas Newsletter,* II (1956), 58–62.

Dargan, H. M. "The Nature of Allegory as Used by Swift," *Studies in Philology,* XIII (July 1916), 159–179.

Darnall, F. M. "Old Wine in New Bottles," *South Atlantic Quarterly,* XLI (1942), 53–63.

————. "Swift's Religion," *Journal of English and Germanic Philology,* XXX (1931), 379–382.

Duff, I. F. Grant. "A One-Sided Sketch of Swift," *Psychoanalytic Quarterly,* VI (1937), 238–259.

*Dyson, A. E. "Swift: The Metamorphosis of Irony," *Essays and Studies,* N.S., XI (1958), 53–67.

Eddy, William A. "Cyrano de Bergerac's *Histoire comique du soleil,* a Source for *Gulliver's Travels,*" *Modern Language Notes,* XXXVIII (1923), 344–345.

————. "D'Ablancourt's Sequel to Lucian's *True History*—A Source of *Gulliver's Travels,*" *Modern Language Notes,* XXXVI (1921), 419–422.

————. "Rabelais—A Source for *Gulliver's Travels,*" *Modern Language Notes,* XXXVII (1922), 416–418.

*Ehrenpreis, Irvin. "The Origins of *Gulliver's Travels*," *PMLA*, LXXII (Dec. 1957), 880–899. (Reprinted in his *The Personality of Jonathan Swift*.)

———. "Swift and Satire," *College English*, XIII (1952), 309–312.

———. "Swift's Voyages," *Modern Language Notes*, LXV (1950), 256–257.

*Elder, Lucius W. "The Pride of the Yahoo," *Modern Language Notes*, XXXV (1920), 206–211.

Elliott, R. C. "Gulliver as Literary Artist," *ELH*, XIX (1952), 49–63.

Fink, Z. S. "Political Theory in *Gulliver's Travels*," *ELH*, XIV (1947), 151–161.

Frantz, R. W. [Note on D. E. Baughan's article in *ELH*, V, 207–210], *ELH*, VI (1939), 82.

*———. "Swift's Yahoos and the Voyagers," *Modern Philology*, XXIX (1931), 49–57.

*Frye, Roland M. "Swift's Yahoo and Christian Symbols for Sin," *Journal of the History of Ideas*, XV (Apr. 1954), 201–217.

Gove, Philip B. "Gildon's 'Fortunate Shipwreck' as Background for *Gulliver's Travels*," *Review of English Studies*, XVIII (1942), 470–478.

Greenberg, Robert A. "Swift's *Gulliver's Travels*, Part IV, Chapter III," *Explicator*, XVI (1957), item 2.

*Horrell, Joseph. "What Gulliver Knew," *Sewanee Review*, LI (Autumn 1943), 476–504.

*Jarrett, James L. "A Yahoo *versus* Jonathan Swift," *Western Humanities Review*, VIII (1954), 195–200.

*Jeffery, Francis. "Scott's Edition of Swift," *Edinburgh Review*, XXVII (Sept. 1816), 1–58.

Jourdan, G. V. "The Religion of Dean Swift," *Church Quarterly Review*, CXXVI (1938), 269–286.

*Karpman, Ben. "Neurotic Traits of Jonathan Swift, as Revealed by *Gulliver's Travels*," *Psychoanalytic Review*, XXIX (1942), 26–45, 165–184.

Kelling, Harold D. "*Gulliver's Travels*: A Comedy of Humours," *University of Toronto Quarterly*, XXI (1952), 362–375.

Kermode, J. F. "Yahoos and Houyhnhnms," *Notes and Queries*, CXCV (July 22, 1950), 317–318.

*Kliger, Samuel. "The Unity of *Gulliver's Travels*," *Modern Language Quarterly*, VI (Dec. 1945), 401–415.

*Landa, Louis A. "Jonathan Swift," *English Institute Essays, 1946* (New York: Columbia University Press, 1947), pp. 20–40.

*———. Note on Irvin Ehrenpreis's *The Personality of Jonathan Swift* in "English Literature, 1660–1800: A Current Bibliography," *Philological Quarterly*, XXXVIII (July 1959), 351–353.

*———. "Swift, the Mysteries, and Deism," *Studies in English, Depart-*

ment of English, University of Texas, 1944 (Austin, Tex.: University of Texas Press, 1945), pp. 239–256.

McCracken, George. "Homerica in Gulliver's Travels," Classical Journal, XXIX (1934), 535–538.

*McKenzie, G. "Swift: Reason and Some of its Consequences," University of California Publications in English, VIII (1940), 101–129.

"The Melancholy of Swift: Society and Solitude," Times Literary Supplement, Oct. 20, 1945, p. 498.

*Monk, Samuel H. "The Pride of Lemuel Gulliver," Sewanee Review, LXIII (Winter 1955), 48–71. Reprinted in James Clifford (ed.), Eighteenth Century English Literature (New York: Oxford University Press, 1959), pp. 112–129.

*Moore, John B. "The Role of Gulliver," Modern Philology, XXV (May 1928), 469–480.

Moore, John R. "The Geography of Gulliver's Travels," Journal of English and Germanic Philology, XL (1941), 214–228.

———. "A New Source for Gulliver's Travels," Studies in Philology, XXVIII (1941), 66–80.

———. "The Yahoos of the African Travellers," Notes and Queries, CXCV (Apr. 29, 1950), 314–317.

*Nock, S. A. "Gulliver and Yahoos," Saturday Review of Literature, Sept. 17, 1932, p. 113.

*———. "Not a Yahoo," Saturday Review of Literature, July 16, 1932, p. 846.

Papajewski, Helmut. "Swift and Berkeley," Anglia, LXXVII (1959), 29–53.

*Peake, Charles. "Swift and the Passions," Modern Language Review, LV (Apr. 1960), 169–180.

*Preu, James. "Swift's Influence on Godwin's Doctrine of Anarchism," Journal of the History of Ideas, XV (1954), 371–383.

*Quintana, Ricardo. [Note on Irvin Ehrenpreis's "The Origins of Gulliver's Travels," PMLA, LXXII (1957), 880–899 in] "English Literature, 1660–1800: A Current Bibliography," Philological Quarterly, XXXVII (July 1958), 354–355.

———. "Recent Discussions of Swift," College English, II (1940), 11–18.

Raymond, John. "The Excremental Vision," New Statesman, June 7, 1958, pp. 735–736.

Redinger, Ruby V. "Jonathan Swift, the Disenchanter," American Scholar, XV (1946), 221–226.

Reiss, Edmund. "The Importance of Swift's Glubbdubdrib Episode," Journal of English and Germanic Philology, LIX (Apr. 1960), 223–228.

Rockwell, F. S. "A Probable Source for Gulliver's Travels," Notes and Queries, CLXIX (Aug. 24, 1935), 131–133.

Rogers, Katharine M. "My Female Friends: The Mysogyny of Jonathan Swift," *Texas Studies in Literature and Language*, I (Autumn 1959), 366–379.

*Ross, John F. "The Final Comedy of Lemuel Gulliver," *Studies in the Comic, University of California Publications in English*, VII (1941), 175–196.

*Ruoff, James E. "Swift's *Gulliver's Travels*, Part IV, Chapter III," *Explicator*, XV (1956), item 20.

Sams, Henry W. "Swift's Satire of the Second Person," *ELH*, XXVI (1959), 36–44.

Secord, A. W. "Gulliver and Dampier," *Modern Language Notes*, LI (1936), 159.

————. [Review of W. A. Eddy's *Gulliver's Travels; a Critical Study*], *Journal of English and Germanic Philology*, XXIII (1924), 460–472.

*Sherburn, George. "Errors Concerning the Houyhnhnms," *Modern Philology*, LVI (1958), 92–97.

————. "Methods in Books about Swift," *Studies in Philology*, XXXV (1938), 635–656.

*Smith, D. Nichol. "Jonathan Swift: Some Observations," *Essays by Divers Hands, Being the Transactions of the Royal Society of Literature of the United Kingdom*, XIV (1935), 29–48.

*Stone, Edward. "Swift and the Horses: Misanthropy or Comedy?" *Modern Language Quarterly*, X (Sept. 1949), 367–376.

* "Swift," *North British Review*, CII (Jan. 1870), 169–188.

*Tallman, Warren. "Swift's Fool: A Comment upon Satire in *Gulliver's Travels*," *Dalhousie Review*, XXXIX (1961), 470–478.

"Thackeray's Lectures—Swift," *Blackwood's Magazine*, LXXIV (Oct. 1853), 494–518.

Tilton, John W. "*Gulliver's Travels* as a Work of Art," *Bucknell Review*, VIII (Dec. 1959), 246–259.

*Tuveson, Ernest. [Note in] "English Literature, 1660–1800: A Current Bibliography," *Philological Quarterly*, XXXVIII (July 1959), 355–358.

————. "Swift: The Dean as Satirist," *University of Toronto Quarterly*, XXII (1953), 368–375.

Ussher, Arland. "Swift and Mankind," *Dublin Magazine*, XXII (1947), 7–11.

*Wasiolek, Edward. "Relativity in *Gulliver's Travels*," *Philological Quarterly*, XXXVII (1958), 110–116.

*Webster, Clarence M. "Notes on the Yahoos," *Modern Language Notes*, XLVII (1932), 451–454.

*————. "The Yahoo's Overthrow," *Times Literary Supplement*, May 14, 1931, p. 390.

*Wedel, T. O. "On the Philosophical Background of *Gulliver's Travels*," *Studies in Philology*, XXIII (Oct. 1926), 434–450.

Whibley, Charles. *"Gulliver's Travels," Blackwood's Magazine,* CCXX (Oct. 1926), 549–560.

White, H. O. "The Art of Swift," *Hermathena,* LXIX (1947), 1–8.

*Williams, Kathleen M. "'Animal Rationis Capax': A Study of Certain Aspects of Swift's Imagery," *ELH,* XXI (1954), 193–207.

*———. "Gulliver's Voyage to the Houyhnhnms," *ELH,* XVIII (Dec. 1951), 275–286.

*Wilson, James R. "Swift's Alazon," *Studia Neophilologica,* XXX (1958), 153–164.

*———. "Swift, the Psalmist, and the Horse," *Tennessee Studies in Literature,* III (1958), 17–23.

*Winton, Calhoun. "Conversion on the Road to Houyhnhnmland," *Sewanee Review,* LXVIII (Winter 1060), 20–33.

Books

Acworth, Bernard. *Swift* (London: Eyre and Spottiswoode, 1947).

*Adams, Robert M. "Swift and Kafka." In *Strains of Discord: Studies in Literary Openness* (Ithaca, N. Y.: Cornell University Press, 1958), pp. 146–179.

Beattie, James. *Dissertations, Moral and Critical* (Dublin, 1783), I, 245–247.

Berkeley, George-Monck. *Literary Relics* (London, 1789).

Berwick, Donald M. *The Reputation of Jonathan Swift, 1781–1882* (Philadelphia, 1941).

Berwick, Edward. *A Defence of Dr. Jonathan Swift, Dean of St. Patrick's, Dublin; in Answer to Certain Observations Passed on his Life and Writings, in the Fifty-third Number of the Edinburgh Review* (London, 1819).

Boas, George. *The Happy Beast* (Baltimore, Md.: Johns Hopkins Press, 1933).

*Bullitt, John M. *Jonathan Swift and the Anatomy of Satire* (Cambridge, Mass.: Harvard University Press, 1953).

*Case, Arthur E. *Four Essays on Gulliver's Travels* (Princeton, N.J.: Princeton University Press, 1945).

Collins, John Churton. *Jonathan Swift, a Biographical and Critical Study* (London: Chatto and Windus [1893], 1902, New Edition).

Craik, Henry. *The Life of Jonathan Swift,* 2nd ed. (London: Macmillan & Co., Ltd., 1894).

*Davis, Herbert. *The Satire of Jonathan Swift* (New York: The Macmillan Company, 1947).

*Delany, Patrick. *Observations upon Lord Orrery's Remarks on the Life and Writings of Dr. Jonathan Swift* (London, 1754).

Dilworth, W. H. *The Life of Jonathan Swift* (London, 1758).

Drake, Nathan. *Essays, Biographical, Critical, and Historical Illustrative of the Tatler, Spectator, and Guardian,* 2nd ed. (London, 1814).

*Eddy, William A. *A Critical Study of Gulliver's Travels* (Princeton, N.J.: Princeton University Press, 1923).

*Ehrenpreis, Irvin. *The Personality of Jonathan Swift* (Cambridge, Mass.: Harvard University Press, 1958).

*Ewald, William B., Jr. *The Masks of Jonathan Swift* (Cambridge, Mass.: Harvard University Press, 1954).

Forster, John. *Life of Jonathan Swift* (London: J. Murray, 1875).

Frye, Prosser Hall. "Jonathan Swift." In *Literary Reviews and Criticisms* (New York: G. P. Putnam's Sons, 1908).

*Godwin, William. *The Enquirer* (London, 1797).

*Gosse, Edmund. *A History of Eighteenth Century Literature* (New York: The Macmillan Company, 1889).

Gove, Philip B. *The Imaginary Voyage in English Prose Fiction* (New York: Columbia University Press, 1941).

*Greenacre, Phyllis. *Swift and Carroll: A Psychoanalytic Study of Two Lives* (New York: International Universities Press, 1955).

Gwynn, Stephen. *The Life and Friendships of Dean Swift* (New York: Henry Holt, 1933).

Hardy, Evelyn. *The Conjured Spirit—Swift* (London: Hogarth Press, 1949).

Harrison, G. B. "Jonathan Swift." In *The Social and Political Ideas of Some English Thinkers of the Augustan Age, A.D. 1650–1750,* ed. F. J. C. Hearnshaw (London: G. G. Harrap and Co., 1928).

*Hawkesworth, John. "An Account of the Life of the Rev. Jonathan Swift, D. D., Dean of St. Patrick's, Dublin." In *The Works of Jonathan Swift,* Vol. I (London, 1755).

Hayward, John. "Jonathan Swift." In *From Anne to Victoria,* ed. B. Dobree (London: Cassell and Co., 1937).

Hubbard, Lucius L. *Notes on the Adventures and Surprizing Deliverances of James Dubourdieu and his Wife, A Source for Gulliver's Travels. Also the Adventures of Alexander Vendchurch London, 1719* (Ann Arbor, Mich.: Ann Arbor Press, 1927).

Jackson, Robert W. *Jonathan Swift, Dean and Pastor* (New York: The Macmillan Company, 1939).

———. *Swift and His Circle* (Dublin: The Talbot Press, 1945).

Johnson, M. *The Sin of Wit: Jonathan Swift as a Poet* (Syracuse, N.Y.: Syracuse University Press, 1950).

*Johnson, Samuel. *Lives of the English Poets,* ed. G. B. Hill, Vol. III (Oxford: Clarendon Press, 1905).

Knight, G. Wilson. "Swift and the Symbolism of Irony." In *The Burning Oracle* (London: Oxford University Press, 1939).

*Leavis, F. R. "The Irony of Swift." In *The Common Pursuit* (London: Chatto and Windus, 1953), pp. 73–87.

*Leyburn, Ellen D. *Satiric Allegory: Mirror of Man* (New Haven, Conn.: Yale University Press, 1956).

Mason, William Monck. *History and Antiquities of the Collegiate and Cathedral Church of St. Patrick* (Dublin, 1820), pp. 225–244.

Masson, David. *Essays Biographical and Critical: Chiefly on English Poets* (Cambridge: Macmillan & Co., Ltd., 1856).

*Mitford, John. "Life of Swift." In *The Poetical Works of Jonathan Swift* (Boston: Houghton Mifflin Company, 1880), I, ix–cviii.

More, Paul Elmer. *Shelburne Essays, Tenth Series* (Boston: Houghton Mifflin Company, 1919).

*Murry, John Middleton. *Jonathan Swift: A Critical Biography* (New York: Noonday Press, 1955).

Newman, Bertram. *Swift* (London: George Allen and Unwin, 1937).

*Orrery, John Boyle, fifth Earl of. *Remarks on the Life and Writings of Dr. Jonathan Swift* (London: A. Millar, 1752).

*Orwell, George. "Politics vs. Literature: An Examination of *Gulliver's Travels.*" In *Shooting an Elephant and Other Essays* (New York: Harcourt, Brace and Company, 1945), pp. 53–76.

Poll, Max. *The Sources of Gulliver's Travels* (Cincinnati, O.: University of Cincinnati Press, 1903).

*Price, Martin. *Swift's Rhetorical Art* (New Haven, Conn.: Yale University Press, 1953).

*Quintana, Ricardo. *The Mind and Art of Jonathan Swift* (New York: Oxford University Press, 1936).

*————. *Swift: An Introduction* (London: Oxford University Press, 1955).

Read, Herbert. *The Sense of Glory* (Cambridge, England: Cambridge University Press, 1929).

Roscoe, Thomas. "Life and Works of Jonathan Swift, D.D." In *Works of Jonathan Swift, D.D.* (New York: Derby and Jackson, 1860), I, 17–193.

*Rossi, M. M. and Joseph M. Hone. *Swift, or the Egotist* (London: Victor Gollancz, Ltd., 1934).

Ross, John F. *Swift and Defoe: A Study in Relationship* (Berkeley and Los Angeles, Calif.: University of California Press, 1941).

*Scott, Walter. "Introduction." In *The Works of Jonathan Swift* (London: Bickers and Son, 1883), XI, 3–13.

*Sheridan, Thomas. *The Life of the Rev. Dr. Jonathan Swift, Dean of St. Patrick's, Dublin*, 2nd ed. (London, 1787).

*Stephen, Leslie. *Swift* (London: Macmillan & Co., Ltd., 1882).

*Swift, Deane. *An Essay upon the Life, Writings, and Character of Dr. Jonathan Swift* (London, 1755).

Taylor, William D. *"Gulliver's Travels."* In *Jonathan Swift: A Critical Essay* (London: Peter Davies, Ltd., 1933), pp. 228–233.

*Thackeray, William M. *English Humourists of the Eighteenth Century* (New York: Harper and Brothers, 1853).

Van Doren, Carl. *Swift* (New York: Viking Press, 1930).

Warton, Joseph. *Essay on the Genius and Writings of Pope*, Vol. II (London, 1782).

*Watkins, W. B. C. *Perilous Balance* (Princeton, N.J.: Princeton University Press, 1939).

Whibley, Charles. *Jonathan Swift* (Cambridge, England: Cambridge University Press, 1917).

Williams, Harold. *"Swift's Early Biographers."* In *Pope and His Contemporaries: Essays Presented to George Sherburn*, ed. James L. Clifford and Louis A. Landa (Oxford: Clarendon Press, 1949).

Williams, Harold. *The Text of Gulliver's Travels* (Cambridge, England: Cambridge University Press, 1952).

*Williams, Kathleen M. *Jonathan Swift and the Age of Compromise* (Lawrence, Kan.: University of Kansas Press, 1958).

Exercises

These topics are for papers approximately 600 words in length that will introduce the student to research techniques and prepare him for longer papers to be written later. These short papers can be based entirely on writings in this casebook, but additional materials found in the library may also be used.

1. Write a summary of the reactions of some eighteenth-century critics to Part IV of *Gulliver's Travels*.
2. Write a summary of the reactions of some nineteenth-century critics to Part IV of *Gulliver's Travels*.
3. What are some of the theories as to why Swift chose horses as his chief characters in Part IV?
4. Discuss the appropriateness of the Yahoos as symbols in Part IV.
5. How is class and racial prejudice involved in Part IV?
6. What have some twentieth-century critics said about Swift's misanthropy in Part IV?
7. How does Swift use the mirror image in Part IV?
8. What attitude toward government is expressed in Part IV, and how is it expressed?
9. How is eighteenth-century anti-intellectualism illustrated in Part IV?
10. Write an essay on Yahoo customs and their significance.
11. What attitude toward the legal profession is expressed in Part IV, and how is it expressed?
12. How does Swift satirize the medical profession in Part IV?
13. Write a character sketch of Gulliver's Houyhnhnm master.
14. Analyze the role of Captain Pedro de Mendez in Part IV.
15. Describe Houyhnhnm family life and explain its significance.

MEDIUM-LENGTH RESEARCH PAPERS

These topics are for papers of approximately 600–1500 words. The papers can be based mainly on materials in this book, but students should be

317

encouraged to extend their investigation with the resources of the
library.

1. Write a summary of the reactions of several twentieth-century critics
   to Part IV of *Gulliver's Travels*.
2. To what degree is Part IV the work of a misanthrope?
3. What are the basic issues in the argument between Ehrenpreis and
   Sherburn? Which one is more convincing and why?
4. How do Monk and Quintana differ in interpreting Part IV? Which
   one is more convincing and why?
5. What are the basic points of agreement in the writings by Wedel,
   Ross, Stone, Monk, Williams, and Winton?
6. What are the basic points of agreement in the writings by Davis,
   Landa, Moore, Quintana, and Sherburn?
7. Defend or attack the idea that the country of the Houyhnhnms is a
   utopia.
8. Analyze the elements of satire Swift uses in "A Voyage to the
   Country of the Houyhnhnms."
9. How do Moore and Ross differ in interpreting the role of Gulliver
   in Part IV? Which one is more convincing and why?
10. Attack or defend Kathleen Williams's idea that the Houyhnhnms have
    many faults. Use other critics to help support your point of view.
11. How does Gulliver in Part IV differ from Gulliver in Parts I and II?
12. What are some of the explanations by critics of the role of Gulliver
    in Part IV? Which explanation do you accept, if any, and why?
13. How is the eighteenth-century ideal of moderation illustrated in
    Part IV?
14. How is the eighteenth-century ideal of simplicity illustrated in Part
    IV?
15. How is the eighteenth-century ideal of order illustrated in Part IV?
16. What experiences in Swift's life might have motivated him to write
    "A Voyage to the Country of the Houyhnhnms"?
17. What are the theories concerning Swift's attitude toward sex, and
    what support for these theories can you find in Part IV?
18. What relationships can you point out between Swift's profession as
    a clergyman and his "A Voyage to the Country of the Houyhnhnms"?
19. What is the significance of Gulliver's behavior after he leaves the
    land of the Houyhnhnms?
20. Analyze Swift's use of humor in Part IV.
21. What institutions of human society are satirized in Part IV, and how
    are they satirized?
22. Analyze and evaluate the structure of Part IV.
23. What understanding of and attitude toward the passions does Swift
    reveal in Part IV?

24. Write a critical essay on the universality of Part IV.
25. What are the arguments for and against identifying Gulliver in Part IV with Swift?
26. What have biographers and critics said about Swift's scatology? How is this illustrated in Part IV?
27. Evaluate Swift's use of irony in Part IV.
28. Defend or attack the idea that the Houyhnhnms have a totalitarian state.
29. Contrast twentieth-century evaluations of Part IV with eighteenth- and nineteenth-century evaluations of it.

LONG RESEARCH PAPERS

These topics are for papers of more than 1500 words. The papers should be based on documents in this casebook and other materials found by means of extensive library work.

1. Find out everything you can about Swift's relationship with the deists and show how this is reflected in "A Voyage to the Country of the Houyhnhnms."
2. Analyze and evaluate various interpretations of the allegorical significance of the Yahoos, Houyhnhnms, and Gulliver.
3. How does Swift use characterization, incidents, and imagery to develop the idea of man's need for self-knowledge in "A Voyage to the Country of the Houyhnhnms"?
4. Relate Swift's use of the word "nature" in Part IV to other eighteenth-century concepts of nature.
5. Relate Swift's use of the word "reason" in Part IV to other eighteenth-century concepts of reason.
6. Compare and contrast Swift's view of human nature as revealed in Part IV with the view of human nature of one other major eighteenth-century writer as revealed in one of his works.
7. Compare and contrast "A Voyage to the Country of the Houyhnhnms" with some other satirical works that use animal characters written in other periods.
8. Relate Swift's attitude toward the sin of pride as revealed in Part IV to writings on this subject by other great writers of any period.